Blotter

Blotter

The Untold Story of an Acid Medium

ERIK DAVIS

THE MIT PRESS
CAMBRIDGE, MASSACHUSETTS
LONDON, ENGLAND

The MIT Press would like to thank the anonymous peer reviewers who provided comments on drafts of this book. The generous work of academic experts is essential for establishing the authority and quality of our publications. We acknowledge with gratitude the contributions of these otherwise uncredited readers.

This book was set in Warnock Pro and Gopher by the MIT Press.
Printed and bound in the United States of America.

Library of Congress Cataloging-in-Publication Data

Names: Davis, Erik, author.
Title: Blotter : the untold story of an acid medium / Erik Davis.
Description: Cambridge, Massachusetts : The MIT Press, [2023] | Includes bibliographical references.
Identifiers: LCCN 2022057210 | ISBN 9780262048507 (paperback)
Subjects: LCSH: LSD blotter art—Themes, motives. | McCloud, Mark, 1954—Art collections. | Art—Private collections—California—San Francisco. | Art and society—History—20th century. | Appropriation (Art)
Classification: LCC NC1883.4 .D38 2023 | DDC 744.7—dc23/eng/20230609
LC record available at https://lccn.loc.gov/2022057210

10 9 8 7 6 5 4 3 2

"I don't believe that pudding ever was cooked! In fact, I don't believe that pudding ever will be cooked! And yet it was a very clever pudding to invent."

"What did you mean it to be made of?" Alice asked, hoping to cheer him up, for the poor Knight seemed quite low-spirited about it.

"It began with blotting paper," the Knight answered with a groan.

"That wouldn't be very nice, I'm afraid—"

"Not very nice alone," he interrupted, quite eagerly: "but you've no idea what a difference it makes mixing it with other things— . . ."

—Lewis Carroll, *Through the Looking Glass*

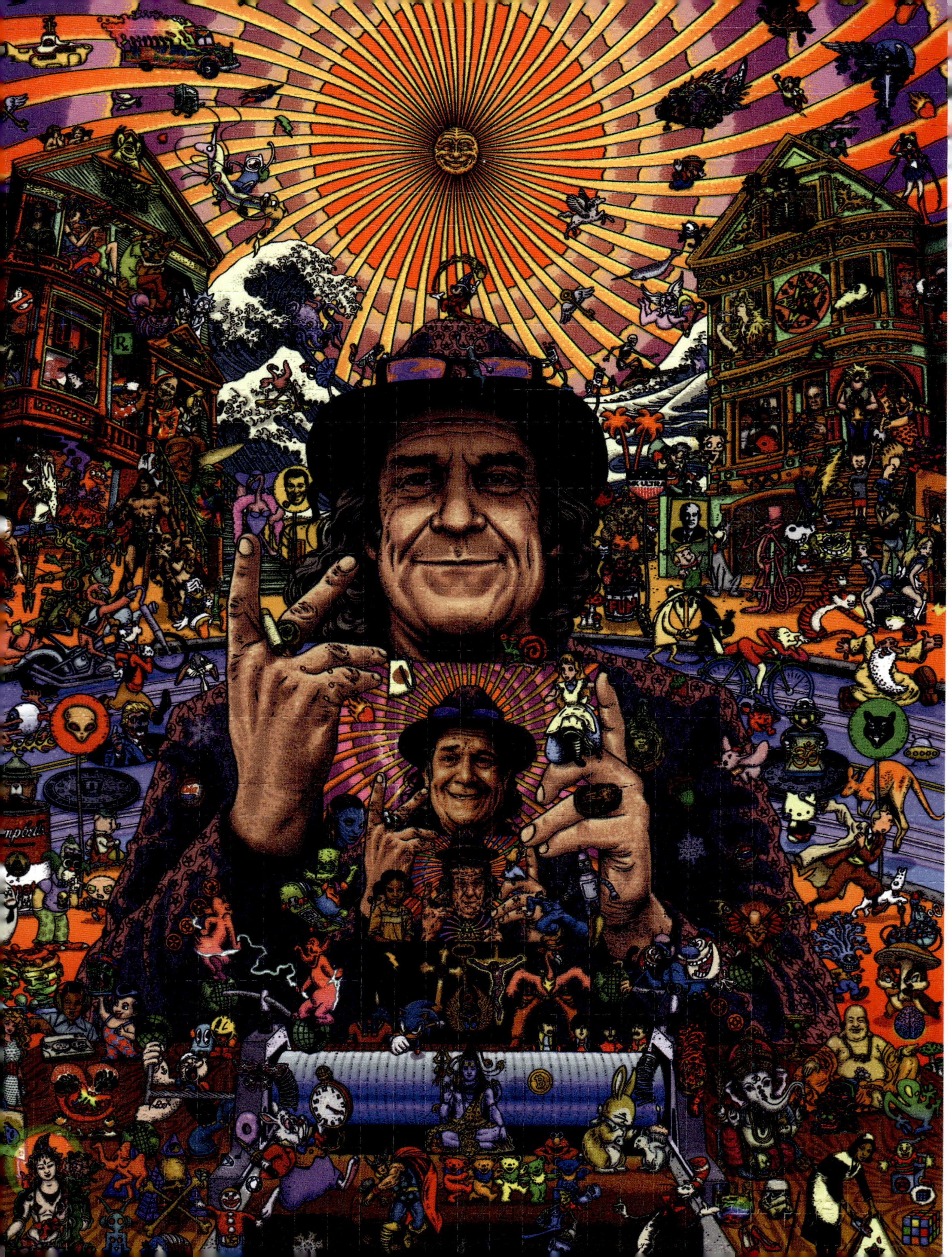

The Institute of Illegal Images (III) is housed in a somewhat dilapidated shotgun Victorian in San Francisco's Mission District, which also happens to be the home of a gentleman named Mark McCloud. The shades are always drawn; the stairs are rotting; the door is peppered with stickers declaring various subcultural affiliations: "Acid Baby Jesus," "Haight Street Art Center," "I'm Still Voting for Zappa." As in many buildings from that era, at least in this city, the first-floor parlor has high ceilings, whose walls are packed salon-style with the core holdings of the institute: a few hundred mounted and framed examples of LSD blotter.

The III maintains the largest and most extensive collection of such paper products in the world, along with thousands of pieces of the materials—illustration boards, photostats, perforation boards—used to create them. Gazing at these crowded walls, the visitor is confronted with a riot of icons and designs, many drawn from art history, pop media, and the countercultural unconscious, here crammed together according to the *horror vacui* that drives so much psychedelic art. There are flying saucers, clowns, gryphons, superheroes, cartoon characters, Escher prints, landscapes, op-art swirls, magic sigils, Japanese crests, and wallpaper patterns, often in multiple color variations.

The Passion of Mark McCloud, Nicolás Rosenfeld, Argentina. Blotter sheet, 7½ × 10 in.

Balancing this carnivalesque excess, at least to some degree, is a modernist sense of order. This announces itself principally through two core features of the blotter form: repetition and the grid. Many frames house full "sheets" of blotter: square or rectangular pieces of cardstock, printed and often perforated according to an abstract rectilinear grid demanded by the exigencies of blotter production. These grids are made up of individual hits or tabs, generally a quarter-inch square or so and numbering anywhere from 100 to 400 to 900 units per sheet, depending on block size and design. While some sheets are illustrated with a single image that cloaks the entire grid, many assign the exact same figure to each hit, resulting in sheets that loosely resemble Andy Warhol's canvases of Campbell's soup cans. Other framed exhibits contain mere fragments from larger designs, sometimes nothing more than a single, hairy hit, perhaps the last extant example of a run from the 1980s that has otherwise been literally swallowed up.

How to refer to all this paper? Users have called the stuff "blotter" or "tickets," while police have used terms like "paper doses." These days such pieces are often known as "blotter art," a term that in many ways reflects the III's own efforts to reframe this illicit ephemera into aesthetic objects (which is why I will stick to the more neutral "blotter"). There is another factor: over the last few decades, the blotter format has become a genre of popular art and a perfectly legal collectable. Though formally resembling their illegal forebears, editions of so-called "vanity blotters," undipped in LSD and frequently signed, are produced for collectors and casual fans rather than drug traffickers—who nonetheless can and do dose such wares when they need or want to. Though ignored by the larger art world, the vanity blotter market keeps on trucking, despite (or because of) the low cost of entry and a lack of critical valuation or collector apparatus.

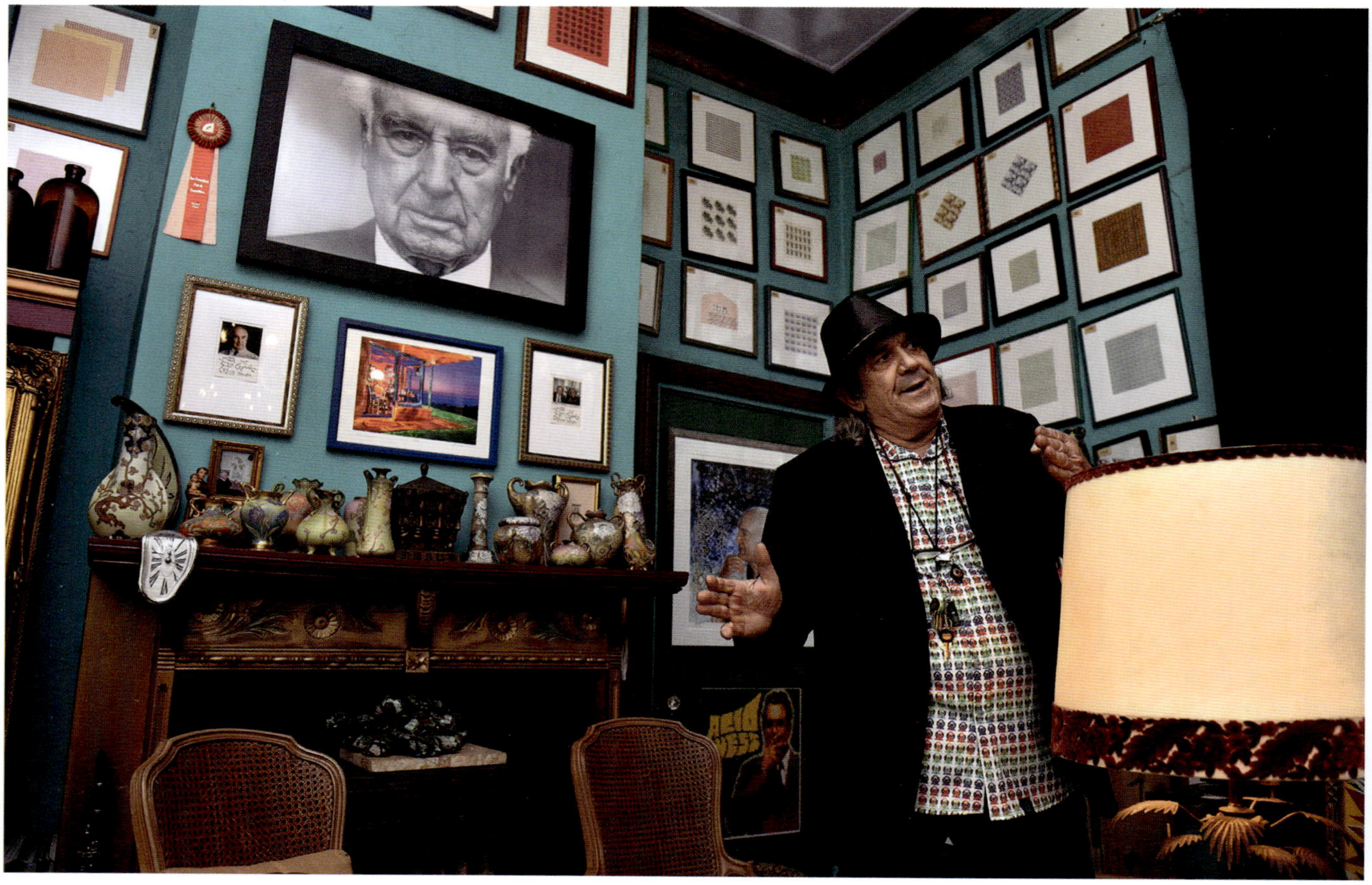

The Institute of Illegal Images, San Francisco. Photo by Charles Russo.

The institute's holdings, which comprise hundreds of thousands of sheets of paper, include an extensive collection of vanity blotter. But the exhibits that pack those tall parlor walls represent the cream of an earlier and more furtive era, when printed blotters played a central role in the black-market distribution of a demonized and intensely powerful psychoactive substance. While I will cover the story of vanity blotter later on, this essay focuses on the historical development of "vintage" street blotters, as well as the printed, screened, or hand-stamped designs and images that decorate those papers. Behind these concrete stories, I am also interested in meditating on blotter not just as art, or as an historical artifact, but as a kind of media, even a "meta-medium."

I add the "meta-" here in part because, phenomenologically speaking, LSD is known to stage fantastic visual performances that, for all their

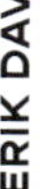

novelties, recirculate images and motifs drawn from the history of art, the modes of fashion, the icons and architectures of religious myth and esoteric tradition, and the advertisements, comic books, design styles, and signage of commercial modernity. Here, for example, is part of an experience report included in R. E. L. Masters and Jean Houston's *The Varieties of Psychedelic Experience* (1968). S, a forty-year-old editor and former medical student, took two 125 microgram doses, staggered one hour apart. Later,

> S is told to look at the flowered fabric on the couch on which he is sitting and to relate what he sees there. He perceives a great number of faces and scenes, each of them belonging to a different environment and to a variety of times: some to the American Gay Nineties, some to the nineteen twenties, some later. There are Toulouse Lautrec café figures, Berlin nightlife scenes and German art from the late twenties and mid-thirties. Here and there, a "Black Art" appears and he recognizes the world of Félicien Rops and drawings like those of the artist who has illustrated Michelet's *Satanism and Witchcraft*. There are various Modigliani figures, a woman carrying a harpoon, and persons such as appear in the classical Spanish art of the seventeenth century. Most interesting to him are "paintings" like those of Hieronymus Bosch. . . .
>
> Closing his eyes, S images mind in terms of a great domed interior supported by the steel frames of a giant Erector Set. He thinks about "a mind with a screw loose" and images an exquisitely jeweled screw that has come loose and is banging around inside the interior. "It is all presented like a television commercial, but in very vivid colors." . . . Following this "low level cartoon production," S reports a "magnificent, staggeringly beautiful" sequence of images. He is seeing immense zodiacal figures laid out in jeweled definition with blue and gold stones against the heavens that glow with a black interior light. . . .
>
> 1:00 p.m.: S images a number of additional cartoon sequences including a rather lengthy one set in Harlem that has to do with "a Negro making a cartoon about how a Negro would make a cartoon about a Negro making a cartoon about Negroes."[1]

Here LSD is already a kind of media machine, a "reality studio" or animation shop cranking out video mixes that sample from visionary art, bohemian styles, and astrological symbolism. While we can't know what significance a Black artist in Harlem held for S, we need to note the crucial and deeply psychedelic element of recursion that characterizes his final vision here, a self-reference across scale that not only recalls the fractals or paisley designs that mark acid perception but embeds the framing and production of imagery into the imagery itself—imagery that, for perhaps significant reasons, not infrequently resembles cartoons.

LSD's particular and peculiar relationship to technical mediation is, unsurprisingly, historically situated. First synthesized in 1938 but not tasted until 1943, acid is essentially a creature of the postwar era. As such, it enters the human world alongside an explosion in consumer advertising, the rapid development of electronic and digital media, new polymers, and a host of increasingly cybernetic approaches to the social challenges of control and communication. For many of its early enthusiasts, acid was like a cosmic transistor radio. As Lars Bang Larsen writes, "Hallucinogenic drugs were often understood as new media in the counterculture: only machinic and cybernetic concepts seemed sufficient to address vibrations, intensities, micro-speeds and other challenges to human perception that occur on the trip."[2] To paraphrase Timothy Leary, LSD seemed to "tune" the dials of perception, altering the ratios of the senses, "turning on" their associational pathways and gradients of intensity. These vibrating modulations in turn catalyzed transpersonal peaks that bloomed as insights, revelations, satoris, "groks." The actor and author Peter Coyote, who was a member of the visionary Diggers collective in the Haight during the 1960s, wrote that ingesting LSD "changed everything, dissolved the boundaries of self, and placed you at some unlocatable point in the midst of a new world, vast beyond imagining, stripped of language, where new skills of communication were required . . . [because] everything communicated in its own way."[3] Similarly, Marshall McLuhan, the pop media prophet of the era, told *Playboy* that LSD mimes the "all-at-onceness and all-at-oneness" of the new electronic media environment. All this set the stage for a kind of technical mysticism that recalls the media theorist Alexander Galloway's notion of "iridescent" mediation: "communication as luminous immediacy."[4] Alan Watts, commenting on the question of how often to take LSD, also turned to media metaphors, arguing that when you get the message, you hang up the phone.[5]

But what if the medium *is* the message?

In other words, what if the self-referentiality of acid consciousness—which can nest chains of Harlem cartoonists like Russian dolls, or loop the act of seeing back into the seer—also absorbs the material medium that delivers the LSD to your nervous system in the first place? Of course, the primary medium of this consciousness is the LSD molecule itself. But unlike macroscopic drugs like cannabis, LSD is so small and so powerful that its consumption almost always includes an inert housing—the water, tablets, sugar cubes, bits of string, or pieces of paper that transport the drug from manufacturer to tripper. In the law, this vehicle is described as the "carrier medium," an object impregnated with drugs, one that can be sold, seized, presented as evidence, and dissolved into the hearts, minds, and guts of consumers.

When you print images *onto* a paper carrier medium, you are adding another layer of mediation to an already loopy transmission. Hence, a meta-medium, a liminal genre of print culture that dissolves the boundaries between a postage stamp, a ticket, a bubble-gum card, and the communion host. This makes blotter a central if barely recognized artifact of psychedelic print culture, alongside rock posters and underground newspapers and comix, but with the extra ouroboric weirdness that it is designed to be ingested, to *disappear*. Blotter is the most ephemeral of all psychedelic ephemera. It is produced to be eaten, to blur the divide between object and subject, dissolving material signs and molecules into a phenomenological upsurge of sensory, poetic, and cognitive immediacy.

This book is also something of a blur, and necessarily so. Researching a criminal underground presents special challenges, including codes of silence, an embedded ethos of subterfuge and misdirection, the vagaries of bohemian oral history, and the intentionally obfuscated production and distribution of LSD itself. As such, *Blotter* cannot claim to be anything like a definitive history of LSD media or even of paper doses, whose widespread production, here and abroad, will not receive the depth of attention it deserves. Nor will this essay spend much time on the chemical manufacture of LSD, nor with the families associated with its production and high-level distribution. In many ways, *Blotter* is just the untold story, untold once again.

My focus instead is on the artifacts themselves, and on some of the people who made them. But there is something vital to establish first about the overall LSD trade, and we might as well hear it from one of that industry's most important students, the Drug Enforcement Agency. In a report entitled *LSD in the United States*, which came out of the San Francisco Field Office in 1995 and is available on the internet, the authors make the following crucial observation:

> In contrast to the trafficking of other drugs, in which profit is the sole motivating factor, LSD trafficking has assumed an ideological or crusading aspect. The influence of—and probable distribution by—certain psychedelic generation gurus has created a secretiveness and marketing mystique unique to LSD, particularly at the higher echelons of the traffic. Their belief in the beneficent properties of LSD has been, over the years, as strong a motivating factor in the production and distribution of the drug as the profits to be made from its sale.[6]

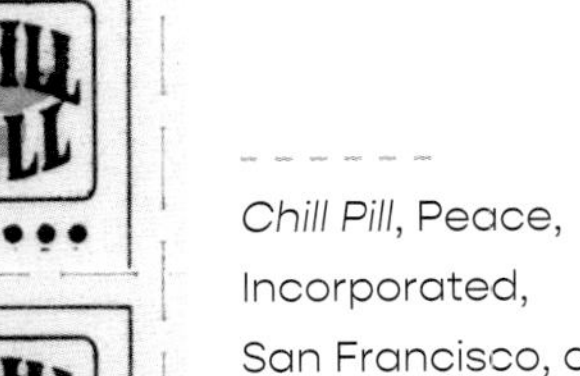

Chill Pill, Peace, Incorporated, San Francisco, ca. 1985. 1⅞ × 2½ in.

Bear in mind, this wasn't written by some bangled Haight Street nostalgist but by the DEA, and in the 1990s to boot, decades after the era of hippie idealism was put on ice. The message is clear: as a criminal enterprise, acid is its own kettle of fish, its fluids dosed with more than market forces. Similarly, while blotter takes shape in response to illegal commerce and the pragmatics of smuggling, it can never be *reduced* to the business of trafficking or "branding" because the acid trade was and is about more than money. Full stop.

The countercultural drive to the turn on the world is perhaps best captured by historian Christian Greer's notion of "psychedelic militancy." With this term, Greer reminds us that many psychedelicists were not lazy hippies but conscious combatants in the emerging culture war; as such, their desire to propagate LSD was as idealistic and even messianic as it was wild and hedonistic. As Greer's own work shows, while psychedelia's most forceful days lay back in the 1960s, the current of psychedelic militancy continued to animate the subcultural milieu at least into the 1980s, which is basically the same era that blotter became the dominant carrier medium for LSD. Such idealism does not cancel out the profit motive, but nor does it entirely dissipate into it. After all, the intensity and commitment required for cultural militancy are also useful values in criminal enterprises. In fact, by continuing to function as a dangerous outlaw zone while other facets of the counterculture were "co-opted," the LSD trade paradoxically helped keep such higher motives alive. Whether they were ignited by gnostic revelations, a partisan belief in cognitive liberty, or a mischief maker's desire to keep the infinite game going, the individuals and networks who kept and keep LSD circulating throughout the world were and are not just selling things but also dreaming dreams. Blotter reflects this imaginal and communicational excess, its images and designs marked by the same magic the drug provokes in so many of its celebrants. You can call such enchanted trafficking a "crusade" if you want, but to judge from its icons, it is a curiously undogmatic one, at once low-brow and sublime, beautiful and satiric, pragmatic and metaphysically aware.

For the following account, I have relied on a number of oral histories and interviews, along with underground print and online sources marked by varying degrees of dodginess. (Uncited quotations are drawn from personal interviews; pseudonymous sources and players are indicated with quotation marks around the first mention of their names.) Special mention must also be made of my extraordinarily fortunate access to a nearly complete run of *Microgram* through the mid-1990s. *Microgram* is an internal publication of the DEA's Forensic Sciences division that collates information from state and local crime labs across the United States, and occasionally from the globe; debuting in 1967, the publication's title explicitly references LSD. Indeed, the magazine's explanation of that name, offered in their twenty-fifth anniversary issue, reminds us of the peculiar way that LSD represents a "meta-media" characterized as much by information flow as by hallucinogenic pleasure:

> The name Microgram was suggested by our public information officer after we had brainstormed a number of ideas. The name is a play on the high potency of LSD—the newsletter would be small and provide potent information. It would also be brief and concise, like a telegram, thus micro+gram = Microgram. Microgram. Powerful stuff, words on a page.

While the bulk of the newsletter is devoted to technical pharmacology, its opening news section provides a monthly snapshot of novel street drugs. Though access to the newsletter is restricted, the first few decades of the publication's run have recently been made public by the dedicated drug librarians at the Erowid Center, who initially received the scans of a few issues from the legendary chemist Alexander Shulgin. Later, in 2003, Erowid scanned and published a special *Microgram* publication crucial for blotter historians—the 1987 *LSD Blotter Index*, compiled by Edward Franzosa, a brilliant Senior Forensic Chemist at the DEA.

NUMBER	LSD BLOTTER	NAME	WHERE SEEN
15235		DOT AND CIRCLE LSD at 42 mcg/du 1978 154%	NY, England
16814		MR. NATURAL #2 LSD at 47 mcg/du 1978 154%	MO, England
16929		MR. NATURAL #3 LSD at * mcg/du 1978 154%	IN
16963		PURPLE FLOWER LSD at 64 mcg/du 1978 154%	CA

102

[Franzosa ES, Harper CW, Crockett JH. "LSD Blotter Index". Microgram. DEA. 20(7), July 1987]

Page from *The LSD Blotter Index*, Dr. Edward Sykes Franzosa et al., 1987.

Erowid carefully gathered the remainder of their *Microgram* collection through research library requests, fellow librarians, and the occasional pal in the DEA.

Earlier issues of *Microgram*, as well as the *Blotter Index*, provide a concrete if necessarily incomplete record of the emergence and proliferation of blotter prints and designs on a nitty gritty level that supplements the accounts of underground players, whose memories can be frazzled and whose tendencies to self-mythologize can run high. But the central source for this essay remains one of those players, who also happens to have a phenomenal memory and only a modest drive for self-aggrandizement: Mark McCloud, the aforementioned curator, director, and in-house historian of the Institute of Illegal Images.

A photographer, sculptor, and former art professor, as well as a deep and crusty bohemian with subcultural affiliations from freak to punk, McCloud began collecting acid blotter around 1980, and mounted the first gallery show of the stuff, at the San Francisco Art Institute, in 1987. The aim of that show, he says now, was to demonstrate "the beautiful lesson that comes with eating art that changes your mind." McCloud's fanaticism and informed curation later helped develop the market for signature and vanity blotter. But his collecting mania also gave him access to the secretive acid underground, where McCloud himself would eventually set up shop, designing, printing, and perforating new blotter sheets used for the illegal distribution of LSD.

By producing printed artifacts in the gray margins of a black market, McCloud opened himself up to two frightening arrests and one major jury trial, which resulted in an acquittal based in no small measure on the designation of his holdings as "art." But his blotter making also gave him unparalleled access to other blotter makers, which enabled him to significantly expand his collection, and to understand it and those makers more thoroughly. Today the Institute of Illegal Images, which has no actual institutional support, and is in many ways indistinguishable from a hoard, stands as one of the most singular and extraordinary countercultural archives in existence—a ramshackle hall of paper mirrors that mediate and superimpose cosmos and commodity, consciousness and crime.

The Godfather

Mark McCloud was born in Buenos Aires, the son of a Californian industrial magnate who moved to Argentina to run a Kaiser production plant. Though he was raised with wealth and privilege, McCloud's life in 1950s

Argentina was hardly pampered. His neighborhood of Boulogne-sur-Mer was affluent but still plenty rough, and he spent his adolescence in gangs and tangling with cops. The political situation was also precarious. Attempts were made on his father's life, and a fellow classmate was kidnapped. Before he entered eighth grade, his parents shipped him off to the Webb School of California, a prep school in Claremont devoted to the production of "gentlemen."

Two weeks after McCloud arrived in Southern California, Frank Zappa's band The Mothers of Invention—who were also hunkered down in the Pomona Valley—released *Freak Out!*, an admonition that McCloud took very much to heart. He and his schoolmates tuned into the new freak culture, boned up on Aldous Huxley's drug writings, and started taking mescaline, LSD, and cannabis in the mountains surrounding Webb, whose drug policies were surprisingly liberal. But after graduation, McCloud still enrolled as a pre-med at the University of Santa Clara.

In December 1971, alone in his dorm room, McCloud swallowed his first tab of Orange Sunshine. Though McCloud was already an experienced tripper, this legendary acid product upended his reality. He believes to this day that he fell from a balcony to his death. He heard his bones crunch, and woke up thousands of feet below the surface of the earth. He wrangled with the Devil in Hell, dissolved into an infinite neon guitar string resonating through eternity, encountered the Blessed Trinity, tasted the rapturous unity of all things, and finally, through an "alternate hallway reality," managed to rewind time and get back to his body just before he slipped off the balcony.

McCloud emerged from his harrowing death-and-rebirth trip a very different young man. He abandoned pre-med and started taking art classes. His family disinherited him—temporarily, it would turn out—and he dropped out of school, spending the next few years in and out of an omen-peppered non-ordinary reality that he compares to the synchronistic tapestry that ties together Virginia Woolf's *Mrs. Dalloway*. Though the world sometimes appeared terrifying, it also revealed a mystical dimension that turned McCloud into an evangelist for LSD, which he came to see as the only antidote humans possess for the poison of death. "I really believe in tripping," he says. "It's not criminal. It's a healthy spiritual emancipating act."

After spending a few years in Paris, where he avoided the draft while shooting photography and studying at L'École du Louvre, McCloud returned to California. He earned an MFA from UC Davis, where he switched to sculpture, and went on to teach art at St. Mary's College and the University of Santa Clara. These years were also the bloom time for San Francisco's avant-garde punk culture, and McCloud dove into the scene, helping his friend V. Vale lay out the classic punk zine *Search & Destroy*. Around 1979, the Texan Nick West moved into McCloud's Mission studio. Back in Austin, West had started publishing a tabloid-sized photocopied punk zine called *Sluggo!* With the acquisition of a Multilith 1250 offset press, the zine then grew into a legendary multicolored mutant that helped constellate the fringe cultural obsessions that came to define the 1980s American underground. In addition to music, *Sluggo!* covered

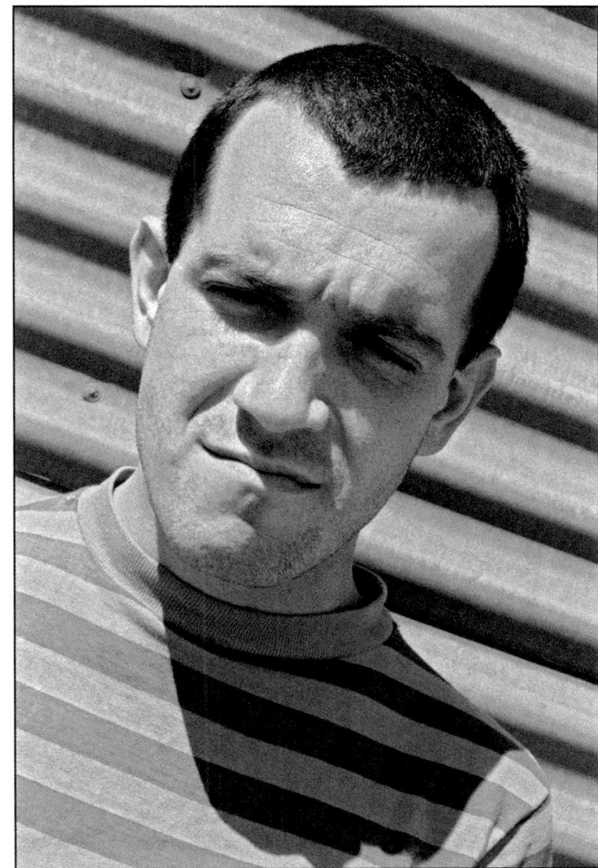

Mark McCloud, ca. 1980. Photo by Ruby Ray.

cattle mutilations, CIA mind control, Hopi prophecies, and, of course, the Church of the SubGenius—the Texas-bred parody religion whose deity, the this-is-not-a-pipe-smoking J. R. "Bob" Dobbs, would soon appear on his own sheet of acid.

Only a few issues of *Sluggo!* were printed in San Francisco before the magazine folded, but for one them, West added a printed tab of acid to the paste-up for one of the spreads, which relied heavily on collage. As McCloud tells it, this was his *a-ha* moment. He had already been casually stashing acid blotter for years, but suddenly saw just how potent the images and artifacts were in themselves. The blotters hitting the scene weren't just drugs—they were media art, material manifestations of a visionary and irascible subculture whose potent iconography demanded to be preserved. Despite blotter's ephemeral and snackable nature, McCloud committed to storing more of it in his freezer, and redoubled his efforts not to eat up the stash.

The Bay Area was also the heartland of the Grateful Dead, a band who played an outsize role in the lore and ethos of acid culture, and whose live shows, particularly in the 1980s and early '90s, formed the most important venue for the LSD trade in America. But in the late 1970s and early 1980s, which were also the years when blotter rose to dominance as a distribution medium, McCloud made his cultural home in San Francisco's hippie-mocking punk milieu. In other words, blotter became big at a time when—the Dead aside—psychedelia was no longer a visible part of popular culture. But here's the secret: *acid never disappeared.* Though

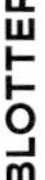

no longer a countercultural icon, LSD became a subcultural fuel by the end of the 1970s, having melted into a variety of often highly regional scenes of weirdness and exuberant transgression, including disco, funk, and the freakier edges of punk and post-punk. LSD deeply scrambled the DNA of groups like Devo, Black Flag, and the Butthole Surfers, whose first 45 cover was printed on Nick West's machine in San Francisco. In other words, even as psychedelia faded, acid just went further underground, and many blotters from the golden age of the 1980s carried the new weirdo iconography: demented clowns, J. R. "Bob" Dobbs, Zippy the Pinhead.

McCloud thrived in this zone of snarky mischief, but he continued to play the fine art game as well. In 1983, he won the second of his two NEA grants and purchased the building that currently houses the Institute of Illegal Images. When he moved in, he decided to more emphatically preserve his growing blotter collection by encasing the LSD papers in picture frames. "That changed everything," he says. "Within the frames, they became more than the sum of their parts. They glowed together." The frames also helped him keep his hand out of the cookie jar.

McCloud lived across the street from the artist David Ireland, who helped the sculptor land a spot on the artist board at the San Francisco Art Institute (SFAI). In 1987, with the twenty-year anniversary of the Summer of Love coming up, McCloud suggested that SFAI mount a show drawn from his blotter collection. The board agreed. There were fifty pieces or so in the show, which was called "The Holy Transfers of the Rebel Replevin"—a replevin being a legal maneuver to restore illegitimately seized property. In later years, McCloud began to amass full sheets of undipped street blotter, but the Holy Transfer exhibits mostly consisted of single hits and four-ways (large perforated units meant to be torn or cut into four smaller hits): pyramids, stars, flying saucers, soccer balls, and the like. Any LSD in the material had been intentionally burned away through exposure to light and air, which deconstructs the magic molecules. Magnifying glasses were provided to appreciate the detail.

The Holy Transfers of the Rebel Replevin, catalog cover, San Francisco Art Institute, 1987. 12 × 12 in.

In an essay that appeared in the show's fanciful catalog, the New York art critic Carlo McCormick, who covered the cultural fringes of downtown and beyond, underscores the kaleidoscopic quality of these objects. What acid blotter "is" depends on what lens you are bringing to the table, or the gallery. From a sociological perspective, McCormick saw McCloud's show as an "illicit history" of subversive images—the sort of icons that magnetize subcultural identities, like hippie buttons or biker insignia. He also underscored the economic logic of printed blotter, a rare example of a commercial art form aimed entirely at a black market. Since the quality of acid is rarely known by the purchaser beforehand, McCormick suggested, the presence of tiny labyrinths or golden dolphins on the hits reflects the same "fine art of persuasion" that applies vibrant swirly waves to detergent boxes. Plenty of LSD was (and is) distributed on blank white cardstock, but the pictures brashly announce that *this is no ordinary piece of paper*, even if, as always, the advertising was sometimes false. At the same time, it is not quite accurate to think of blotter images as brands or trademarks—the relationship between these signs and the psychoactive signified is more playful and open ended than in the case of, say, M&Ms

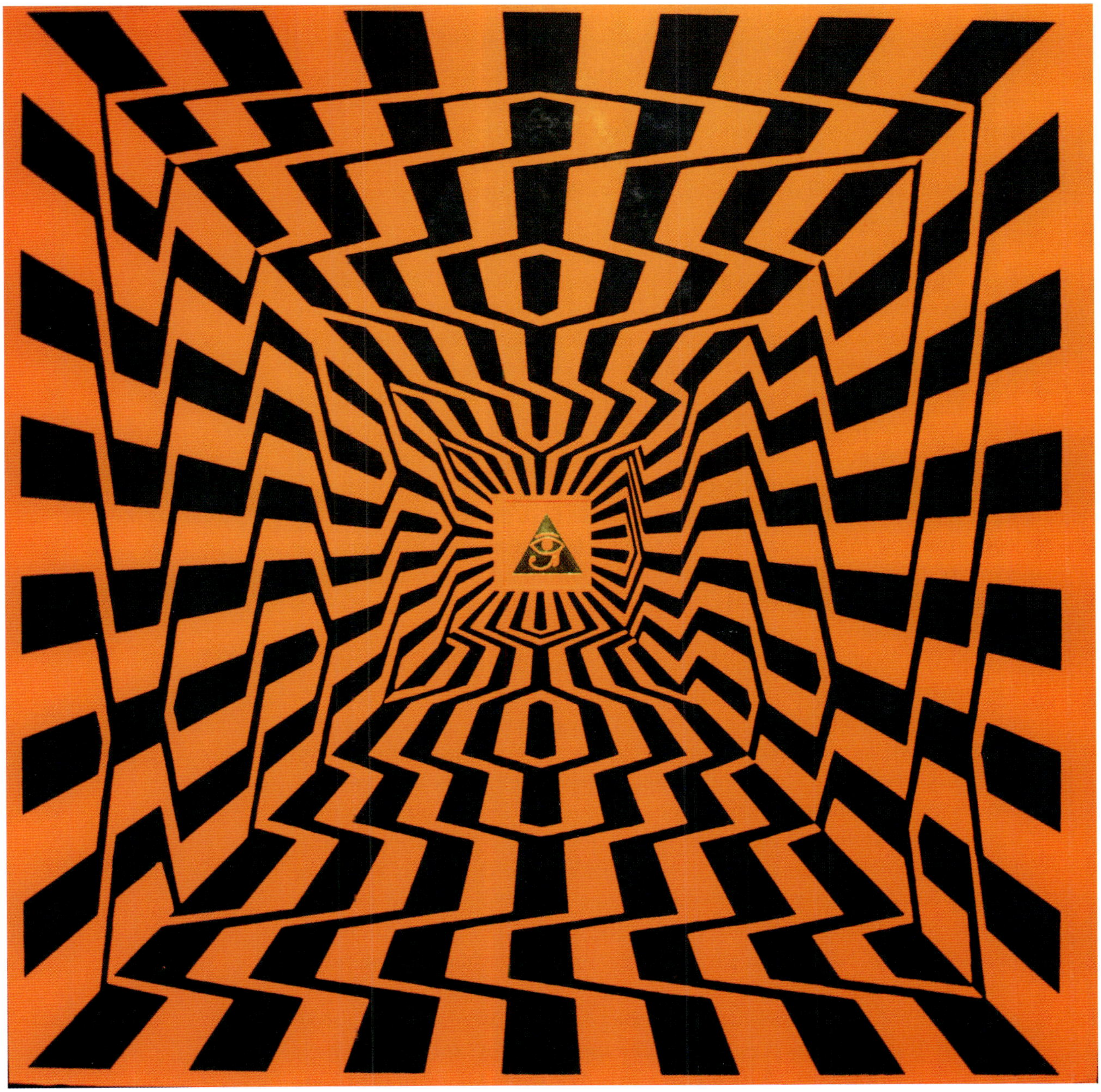

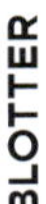

or Advil. Along with announcing the presence of goods, the images also function as a kind of insider promise, a knowing wink or a Masonic grip. McCloud calls them "symbols of a secret society."

McCormick also offers up the notion of blotter as a folk art. There are good reasons for this designation. As with other aspects of the youth movement, psychedelic commerce possessed an organic, collective, and DIY quality that reproduces and sometimes explicitly mimics aspects of more traditional folk cultures. That said, the anonymous craftspeople behind blotter art were, like most LSD users, white, college-educated, and drawn from the middle or upper class. Like McCloud, they were often refugees or defectors from privilege, and their work reflects an elite or at least educated understanding of art traditions, media politics, and social critique. These were not the sort of structurally marginalized populations, of color or not, who are usually associated with outsider or folk art. But acid has a way of scrambling categories, a point McCormick makes in his conclusion: "Those unable to acknowledge the LSD prints as 'art,' but willing to credit them as 'craft,' or 'folk art,' would benefit greatly if they all re-examined such a cultural hierarchy after taking some LSD themselves."[7]

"The Holy Transfers" show upset hierarchies in other ways as well. By bringing contraband into the gallery, McCloud blurred the boundaries between art and illicit commerce, and forced viewers to wrestle with the artifactual meaning of drugs. As McCormick put it, "The knowledge that the paper is dosed cannot but effect how one looks at the picture."[8] Indeed, though the forbidden chemistry on the blotters had been neutralized, the show was not without its risks. At a time when the DEA continued to hammer away at the LSD trade, and without the cover of today's mainstream enthusiasm for psychedelics, McCloud made himself vulnerable: an acid freak protected by a shield no thicker than a gallery wall text. On opening night, McCloud even identified a few members of law enforcement mingling with the art punks and Haight Street poster artists. One asked McCloud if he minded photographs. "Mind? Not at all. It's more a show for you guys than anyone."

McCloud was only half kidding. As an acid evangelist willing to put his love on the line, his motivations for throwing the show were as political as they were aesthetic. By lending his "illegal images" the imprimatur of gallery art, he wanted to honor designers and printers whose ephemeral work—unlike underground comix or psychedelic rock posters—was otherwise completely ignored, if not demonized. But he was also making a subtler argument about the motivations of the LSD underground. By showing off the care, subtlety, and wit of blotter artists, McCloud was equally demonstrating that, whatever crime was involved, acid folk like him actively pursued values beyond profit, including but not limited to values like "art." After all, if the production of blotter had been simply a criminal enterprise, the aesthetic labor involved in many of these designs, not to mention their sometimes elaborate packaging, would be a pointless waste of time and resources. The visible *superfluity* of blotter art, which exceeded the pragmatic demands of a brand or street token, in turn communicated the more intangible and spiritual ideals that animated the trade and the ongoing psychedelic current in the West.

The following January, in 1988, a stripped-down version of "The Holy Transfers" entitled "Cure of Souls" appeared at Jacaeber Kastor's Psychedelic Solution, a radical art gallery cloaked as a New York City headshop. Driven by Kastor's own voluminous collecting, Psychedelic Solution helped kickstart the serious trade in San Francisco's psychedelic rock poster art, which has since become a mature and well-organized collector market with top items trading in multiple tens of thousands of dollars. By appearing at Psychedelic Solution, McCloud's new gospel of acid art spread to a broader and more influential crowd, though not yet a collecting one. Christiane Amanpour covered the show, where McCloud mixed with older visionary artists like Peter Max and newer ones like Alex Grey. The criminalized underground made an appearance as well. During opening night, one fellow was caught trying to steal a framed sample of a blotter sometimes known as *The Valley of Lost Paradise*. Confronted by Kastor and McCloud, the guy explained that he had served time in Attica for dealing the very same edition. They gave him the piece and wished him well.

The most significant underground encounter that resulted from McCloud's blotter art campaign took place back in San Francisco earlier that fall. McCloud had put out a guestbook for the SFAI show; perusing it later, he noticed a business card featuring the R. Crumb comic-book character Mr. Natural, pointing his finger at the sky and declaring "Quest into the Unknown!" On the back of the card, its owner had scrawled, "If you want to meet most of the artists that make up your collection." McCloud was ecstatic. As a hunter of artifacts and stories alike, he had long been searching for entree into this hermetic community, and couldn't believe his good fortune.

But before we follow Mark McCloud into Wonderland, and meet some of the mad hatters and rainbow queens he discovered there, we need to take a step back. Like Alice and her self-referential "DRINK ME" bottle, we need to spend some time considering the curious relationship between drugs and carrier media—a relationship that grows especially curious with blotter, a medium that not only shoulders psychedelic molecules, but communicates messages all on its own, the principal one being something like "EAT ME."

Father of LSD, San Francisco, ca. 1984. 1 × 1½ in. This is one of the first pieces that McCloud decided to commit to a frame.

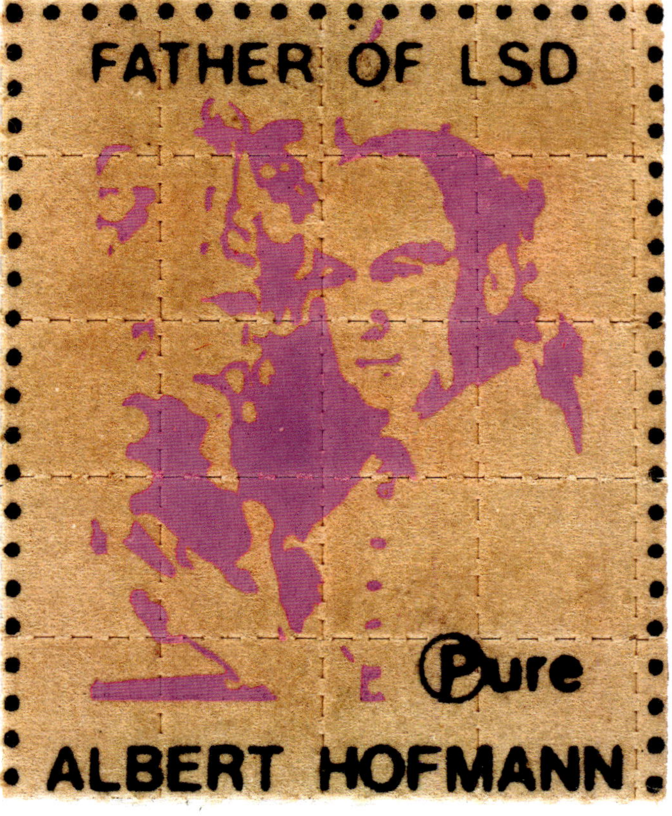

Acid Media

In 1938, as the now familiar story goes, the Swiss chemist Albert Hofmann was working for the Sandoz corporation, experimenting with various modifications of lysergic acid. This was the precursor molecule for a number of naturally occurring alkaloids of the ergot fungus, some of which had already proved quite profitable for his employer. LSD-25 was only the twenty-fifth in a series of molecules he crafted, and nothing much came of the effort. Five years later, and following what he later described as a "peculiar presentiment," Hofmann decided to resynthesize that unique material. As he neared the end of the process, he felt funny and went home, and enjoyed a stream of closed-eye visuals.

Returning to work the following Monday, April 19, Hofmann decided to intentionally test the LSD-25 on himself to root out the weirdness of the previous week.

Knowing the potential toxicity of ergot-related compounds, he showed great caution in restricting his initial dose to 250 micrograms—750 μg shy of a single milligram. Hofmann knew that the vast majority of drugs and toxins are active at a much higher number of milligrams per kilogram of body weight. For example, the standard dose of MDMA, at least according to Anne and Sasha Shulgin and their therapist friends, is around 125 mg; over-the-counter ibuprofen pills start at 100 mg; and potassium cyanide gets lethal around 100 mg, which is 400 times greater than the dose of LSD Hofmann took. But even that smidgin was enough to send the good doctor on a famously bizarre bicycle ride as he headed home early with an assistant, an event now commemorated every April 19 as Bicycle Day.

Acid's capacity to punch above its molecular weight would have a significant impact on the material history of the compound as well as the carrier media that shuttled it around the world and into the bodies of human beings. Because of its almost homeopathic potency, LSD has been distributed on and in an unusually diverse and creative range of media, including the tiny paper doses that are known as blotter even though they are rarely made of actual blotting paper. This is an uncommon carrier medium for drugs, to say the least. A single square of typically sized blotter provides far too little surface area to absorb the amount of material required for most drugs to sufficiently tweak the nervous system. In this sense, acid shapes its own unique media.

The material manifestations of LSD's carrier media are hardly incidental to the drug's meaning and import. Even when it's destined to dissolve and effectively disappear into human bodies, LSD, like all psychoactive drugs, is shaped and inflected by the forms it takes in the world before it is ingested. A bud of cannabis is not a block of hashish is not a chunk of shatter is not an Otterspace Watermelon Delta 8 gummy with "8 mg" of "THC." These differences go beyond methods of ingestion and metabolic dynamics; they speak as well to the sorts of meanings and performances that stage and frame the act of consuming things in the first place. In other words, the tangible materiality of psychoactive drugs—as economic, cultural, and physical objects—is inevitably compounded with the effects themselves. The bodies of drugs *matter*.

Roland Barthes makes a similar point about food. While we can subdivide and analyze the things we eat in chemical or nutritional terms, food "is also, and at the same time, a system of communication, a body of images, a protocol of usages, situations, and behavior." Food—this actual cannelloni, or paratha, or burrito—is inextricably embedded in matrixes of class, ecology, history, cultural identity, and social life—and, in the modern world, of advertising and lifestyle as well. As Barthes puts it, "Food sums up and transmits a situation; it constitutes an information; it signifies."[9] Psychoactive drugs, a cousin of food, are no different here. Their forms and histories inform, transmit, and signify even before you take them.

Like nearly all psychedelic drugs, LSD-25 was inspired by and ultimately derived from an organic material, in this case, one of a group of fungi species known as ergot. *Claviceps purpurea* is a parasite that attacks rye, and has been interacting with human populations, with often

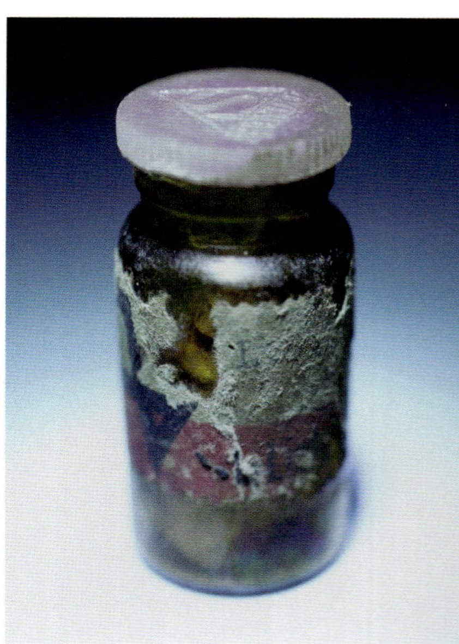

Bottle of Sandoz Delysid 25 μg pills. Photo by Jon Hanna.

devastating ferocity, for millennia. Besides horribly poisoning and often killing its unwitting consumers, some of whom go into psychotic convulsions, ergot also provided alkaloids used in folk remedies, which is why the pharmaceutical engineers at the Sandoz corporation were interested in the fungus in the first place.

Preparations of ergot derived from *C. purpurea* or a related *Claviceps* species may have been used traditionally for their psychoactive effects—a thesis Hofmann later believed could help explain the *kykeon* consumed during the Eleusinian Mysteries in ancient Greece. But that possibility remains largely speculative. As far as we know, LSD-25's visionary prowess first emerges in human history as a product of industrial semi-synthesis—an extractive capitalist apparatus that, depending on your characterization of modern science, suggests at the very least a colonialist exploitation of the organic world as much as a crafted continuity with it. This is important: if LSD represents a sort of magic, it is a magic of the modern West, in all its horror and promethean glory. Whatever its alchemical resonance, LSD sprouts from the brow of industrial chemistry, an industry founded on artificial dies and petroleum products, and it enlists shrinks and spies as some of its earliest shamans.

Acid's technical genesis as a purified and extraordinarily potent compound, as well as its lack of taste, color, and odor, powerfully shaped the molecule's material manifestations. LSD is essentially too potent to consume in the "raw" or unmixed form of a crystal powder (though plenty of folks have done so over the decades—some quite willingly). When Sandoz began marketing LSD to psychiatrists under the trade name Delysid, they distributed the molecule in two primary forms: jars of sugar-coated tablets that contained 25 μg each, and 1 milliliter ampoules of distilled water containing 100 μg each, which could be swallowed or injected. Sandoz also distributed amber glass containers that held 25 mg (25,000 μg) of pure powder, though these were not, of course, intended for direct consumption. Later industrial sources for LSD, including Eli Lilly in America and Spofa in Czechoslovakia, produced similar formats.

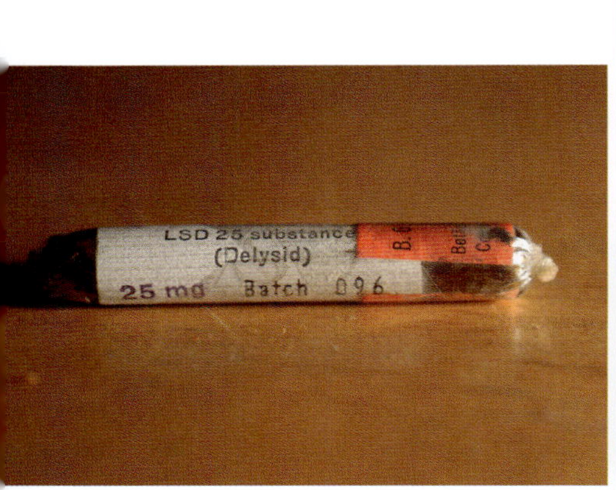

Left: Sandoz Delysid ampoule, 25 mg crystalline powder. Photo by Erowid.

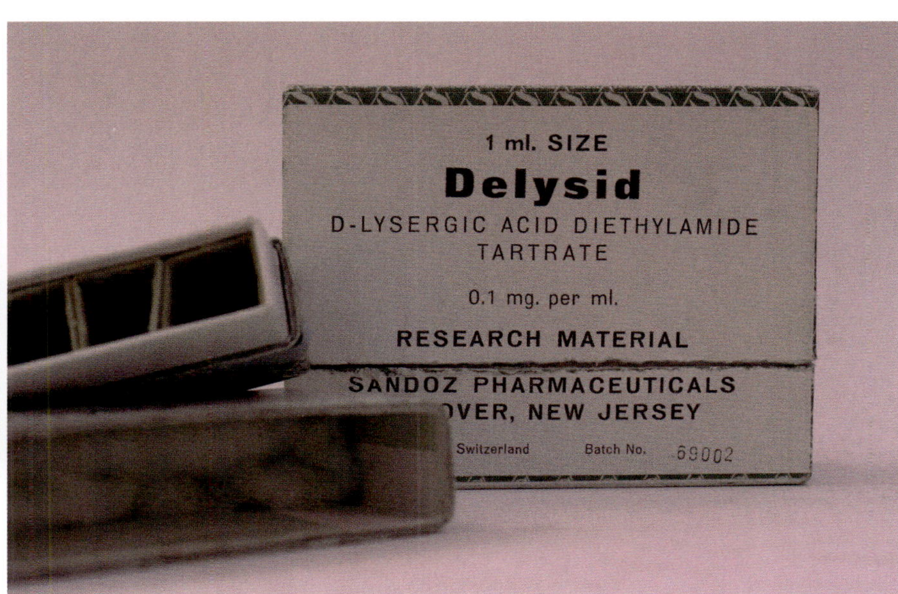

Right: Sandoz Delysid ampoule packaging. Photo by Jon Hanna.

The primary solution to the problems posed by LSD powder, as you might imagine, is water. A massive amount of LSD has been circulated over the decades in liquid form, by pharmaceutical companies, major underground producers, and low-level dealers and consumers, who might purchase a few hundred low-concentration drops in a small opaque vial or "Slim Jim." Things get more interesting when that liquid in turn impregnates a further carrier medium, whose plastic possibilities began to flower even before the molecule was rendered illicit. In 1960, Michael Hollingshead—who called himself, with some reason, the "man who turned on the world"—got his hands on a gram of Sandoz powder. He mixed it with distilled water and confectioners' sugar into a gelatinous paste he then transferred to a mayonnaise jar—the same container that served up Timothy Leary's first harrowing dose. A few years later, when Leary and crew returned to the United States from Zihuatanejo, a stash of liquid LSD spilled in Richard Alpert's suitcase, which meant that some of the pioneering psychonauts at the legendary Millbrook estate in upstate New York got high by sucking on Alpert's underwear.[10]

The most signature vernacular carrier for LSD liquid in the first years of the acid boom was the sugar cube. In his autobiography *Road of Excess*, the British wild man and Leary crony Brian Barritt describes dosing Tate & Lyle sugar cubes with an eye dropper full of the acid he had purchased from the legendary junkie writer Alexander Trocchi. "I didn't know that it could be absorbed through my pores until Mr. Cube began jiggling about and acting just like he was stoned out of his mind."[11] Mr. Cube was the Tate & Lyle logo, a cartoon sugar cube with hands and feet whose visionary dance through Barritt's sensorium reminds us that LSD not only unveiled modes of consciousness beyond quotidian modernity but could animate that banal commercial landscape into something mutant and goofy.

The first well-known "brands" of underground acid were produced by the brilliant and eccentric Augustus Owsley Stanley III, the scion of an illustrious Kentucky family who moved to the Bay Area following a stint in the Air Force. In late 1964, after figuring out how to make methamphetamine, Owsley started working on LSD with Melissa Cargill, a UC Berkeley chemistry whiz who may well have been responsible for their breakthrough methodology. We don't know much about Cargill because Owsley played the impresario, earning a reputation for his finicky obsession with chemical purity. Indeed, Owsley's crystal was reputed to be cleaner than Sandoz. Not only did it appear blue-white under fluorescent bulbs, but it shot out flashes of light when shaken—a piezoluminescent effect some LSD has that is rarely found in the natural world.

Owsley started distributing his acid, often for free, in the spring of 1965. He sifted his powder into gelatin capsules or passed it on as "Mother's Milk," a liquid that was tinted blue so that distributors could track which sugar cubes they had dosed. These methods were imprecise, and with a material as potent as LSD, careful dosage was key. Exposure to light, which degrades the molecule, was also an issue, as was the ease of counterfeiting capsules. While living in Los Angeles with Tim Scully and the Grateful Dead, Owsley pursued greater quality control, and to

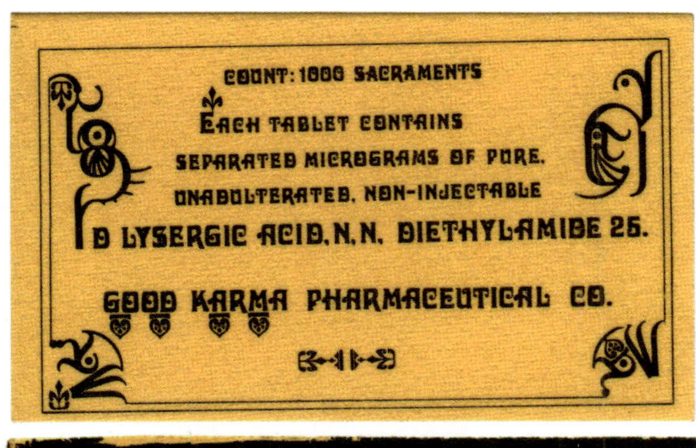

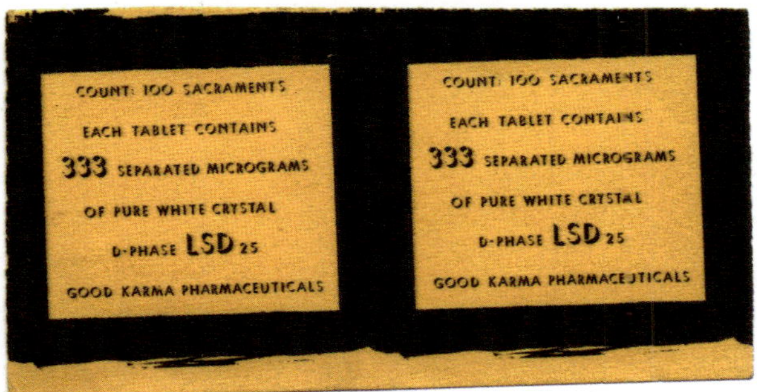

Good Karma Pharmaceutical Co. labels, early 1970s.

that end fashioned 4,000 or so of the first LSD tablets. Using a simple machine to triturate the material, thoroughly mixing it with binders, he then made a paste and spread it on Bakelite sheets to press evenly into tablets. Owsley decided to dye his tabs a purplish blue in order to confuse the drug tests then used by the police, which turned material purple if LSD was present. These notoriously powerful tabs, whose 250 micrograms were chosen in honor of Hofmann's initial dose, were often sold as Blue Cheer, which also happened to be the name of a popular detergent at the time—making Blue Cheer the first example of an underground LSD preparation that took shape in a parodic funhouse mirror held up to mainstream commodity culture. It would not be the last.

Owsley and Cargill soon returned to the Bay Area. Though by no means the sole freelance supplier of LSD, which was still legal at the time, Owsley was already the most celebrated. As Martin Lee and Bruce Shalin explain, Owsley "cultivated an image as a wizard-alchemist whose intentions with LSD were priestly and magical."[12] In some sense, Owsley himself became the brand, so much so that later street tabs were sometimes sold under the name "Owsley." But we would be wrong to see this image as image alone. While Owsley was happy to play the game and make money, he sincerely held magical and specifically alchemical views about LSD. He was convinced that, regardless of chemical purity, acid could only be truly great if the cooks in the lab had their hearts and minds in the right place. During the final stages of synthesis and crystallization, Owsley would reportedly pray over the batch, or at least curate the right soundtrack, blasting Quicksilver Messenger Service or calling up a local radio station to request the perfect cut. Despite the modern industrial protocols required, LSD manufacture also demanded cosmic intent—vibes that, through the strange loops of mystic materialism, would in turn enchant the final street product.

Working with Scully in Point Richmond at the end of 1966, Owsley whipped up a new batch of LSD that was destined for the Human Be-In, the game-changing "Gathering of the Tribes" held in Golden Gate Park in January the following year. Using a one-punch compression tablet machine he had purchased, Wile E. Coyote–like, from the Acme Manufacturing Company, Owsley's crew pressed the powder he had cooked up into 300,000 tablets. But what to call it? According to Owsley, he got the name from a well-known poster that the San Francisco illustrator Rick Griffin had designed for the event. Griffin's image featured a guitar-slinging Native American mounted on a horse, and, in a blend of the heavy and humorous characteristic of his marvelous work, a cartoon bird claw reaching down from heaven clutching two twelve-pointed lightning bolts. Owsley had the name of his next dynamite tab: White Lightning, a term that already lurked in American psychoactive history as a moniker for moonshine.

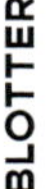

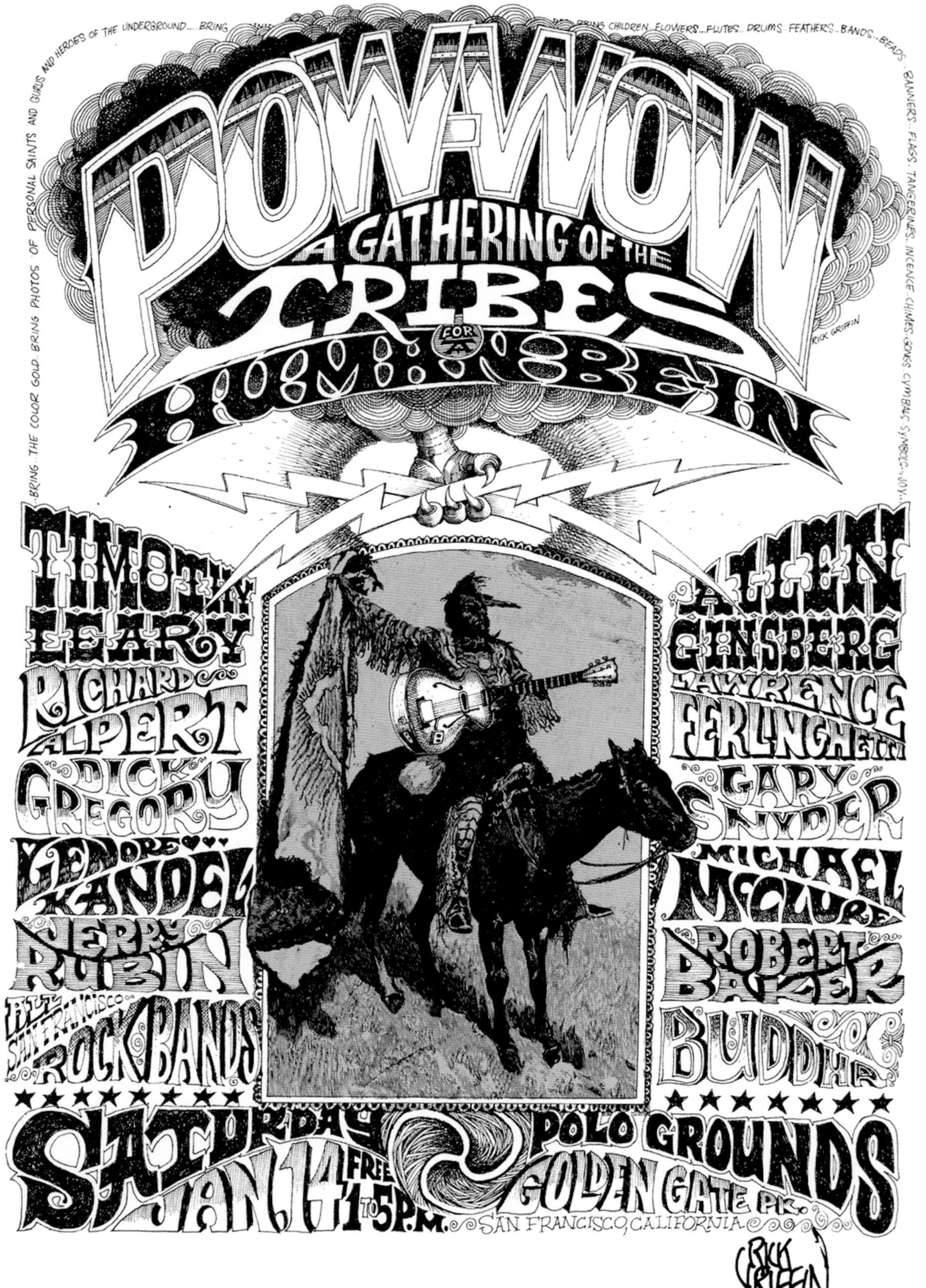

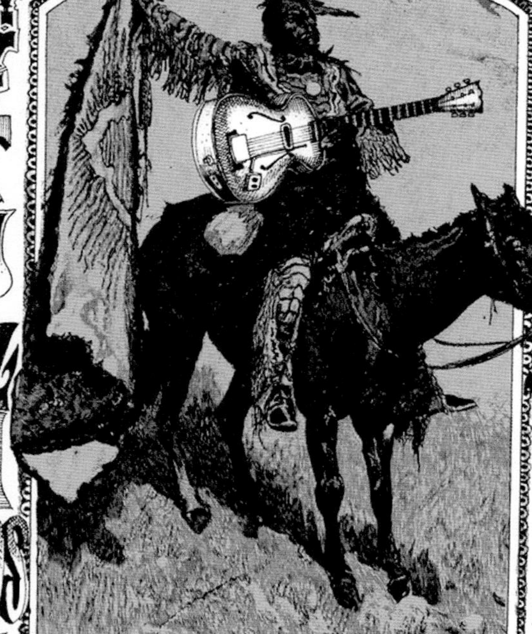
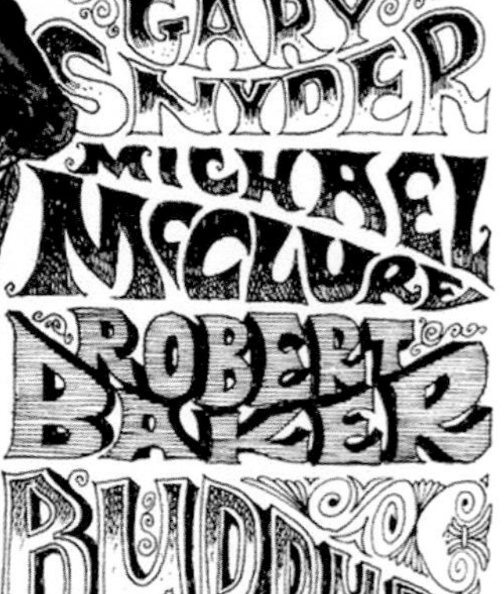
..BRING.. THE COLOR GOLD.. BRING PHOTOS OF PERSONAL SAINTS AND GURUS AND HEROES OF THE UNDERGROUND.... BRING CHILDREN.. FLOWERS...FLUTES.. DRUMS.. FEATHERS.. BANDS..BEADS.. BANNERS.. FLAGS.. TANGERINES.. INCENCE.CHIMES.GONGS.CYMBALS.SYMBOLS..JOY..
POW-WOW
A GATHERING OF THE
TRIBES
FOR A
HUMAN BE-IN
RICK GRIFFIN
TIMOTHY LEARY
RICHARD ALPERT
DICK GREGORY
LENORE KANDEL
JERRY RUBIN
ALL SAN FRANCISCO ROCK BANDS
ALLEN GINSBERG
LAWRENCE FERLINGHETTI
GARY SNYDER
MICHAEL MCCLURE
ROBERT BAKER
BUDDHA
SATURDAY JAN. 14 FREE 1 TO 5 P.M.
POLO GROUNDS
GOLDEN GATE PK.
SAN FRANCISCO, CALIFORNIA
RICK GRIFFIN

Perhaps Owsley's most insightful contribution to the history of LSD's material packaging, however, was a little unintentional experiment in social psychology he performed earlier in 1966. Along with Scully and Cargill, Owsley whipped up a 10-gram batch of pure crystalline LSD and divided it into five equal piles, which were then dyed different colors before being buffed with lactose and calcium phosphate to make the powder suitable for tableting. Once the tabs hit the street, where they were often called "barrels," the colors began to take on different phenomenological associations, despite the fact that the LSD was all demonstrably the same material. The red ones were, against type, supposed to be mellow, the greens speedy, and the blues a good blend of the two.[13] According to Scully, one of the colors was even supposed to be particularly "spiritual."

It's impossible to know if the freaks on the street truly experienced this range of reactions, but given what we know about LSD, not to mention the psychology of brands and placebos, it certainly stands to reason. According to a well-known fMRI study performed at Houston's Baylor College of Medicine in 2004, the brains of participants given a squirt of anonymous cola showed activity in different regions (particularly the hippocampus and dorsolateral prefrontal cortex) when the brand name for the sugar water was announced; however, this shift registered with Coke but not Pepsi, suggesting a clear neural correlation to brand power.[14] Things grow even more curious with placebos. Numerous studies have shown that the relative effectiveness of placebo pills varies depending on their color and shape, factors that are of course taken into account in the design and marketing of pharmaceutical preparations.[15]

Acid cranks these priming factors up to eleven. In the words of Stan Grof, who oversaw more LSD sessions than any other psychiatrist, LSD is, in contrast to typical drugs, a "nonspecific amplifier" rather than a mechanistic agent. And what generally gets amplified, according to Grof, is the psyche, which is highly sensitive to expectations, cultural narratives, and external suggestions. This sensitivity undergirds the well-known psychedelic principle of "set and setting," which, as drug historian Ido Hartogsohn explains, divides the nonpharmacological agents of drug experience into "set (personality, preparation, expectation, and intention of the person having the experience) and setting (the physical, social, and cultural environment in which the experience takes place)."[16] Even before Timothy Leary made this phrase a psychedelic mantra, psychedelic researchers recognized that the mindset of the tripper, coupled with specific features and qualities of the trip room, played an often significant role in the experience.

Pow Wow—A Gathering of the Tribes for a Human Be-In, Rick Griffin, 1967. Poster, 14 × 22½ in.

The important point here is that blotter, like all carrier media, directly contributes to the set and setting. Given the psyche's sensitivity to material and symbolic conditions, the physical packaging of LSD will impress itself to some degree upon the roiling incorporeal slipstream of the trip. Fat blue LSD tablets or plain sugar cubes or orange-colored blotters are not "the same" drug, even if their dosages are identical. The printed images of blotter add a whole other dimension of priming through their sometimes potent signs. With acid, again, the medium really is the message.

Once LSD became a Schedule I substance, the message from the mainstream news media changed considerably. Bohemian experiments and psychiatric hopes for cures gave way to a newly illicit "setting" that discursively reframed LSD as a deranged psychological dice-roll and its users as hedonistic criminals. Hartogsohn suggests that this new setting can be blamed in part for the noticeable increase in reports of paranoid trips and other bummers by the end of the 1960s. Prohibition also altered the dynamics of LSD's carrier media, since subterfuge and camouflage now became aspects of design. Previously, the relationship between underground LSD and its material mount—liquid in eye droppers, sugar cubes, blotting paper—was informal and reasonably transparent. In being criminalized, that relationship became scrambled, the sign decoupled from the signifier. By the end of the decade, LSD had surreptitiously invaded the bric-a-brac of the quotidian, having been trafficked in or on bubble gum, sponges, Pez candies, toothpicks, matchbooks, cookies, crackers, ion-exchange resin beads, powdered tea, finely ground rose hips, and even dried mushrooms.

Amid this chaos of carrier media, colorfully named tablets continued to proliferate. According to a 1970 *Microgram*, street freaks around the country were able to purchase Purple Haze, Grape Parfait, Yellow Dimples, Window Glass, Contact Lens, Domes, Flats, Chocolate Chips, Squirrels, Wedges, Owsleys, Peace, Strawberry Field, Smears, and other acid varieties.[17] Tablets often featured unusual colors—lavender, charcoal gray, raspberry, purple, blue—and curious shapes, including pyramids, pentagons, or tiny little dots. One poorly made pink tablet bore a peace symbol as a monogram, with equal claim to being a trademark and a badge of tribal affiliation.

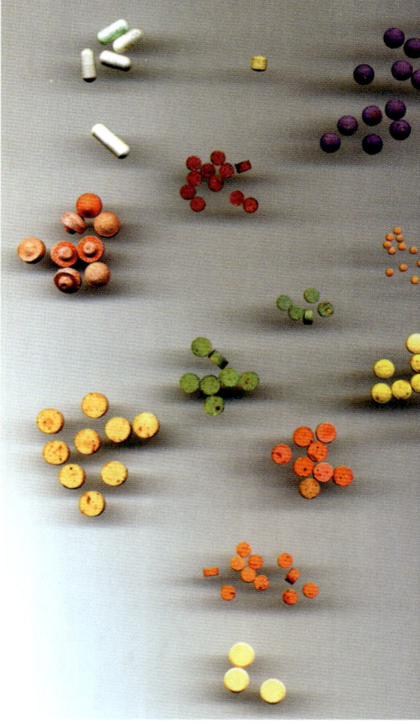

Pressed LSD pills from the late 1960s and 1970s, including White Lightning, Barrel, Blue Cheer/Purple Haze. Photo by Mark McCloud.

In 1968, a glut of LSD supply led to a corresponding drop in price. Facing this saturated market, a triumvirate out of San Francisco's North Beach decided to go after exceptional quality. They developed Clear Light, a powerful, extremely pure, and reliably dosed LSD that was infused into a novel package: machine-cut squares of clear hard gelatin a tenth of an inch per side. The name Clear Light was a promise about the mind-state the material itself produced: as a famously "clean" form of LSD, its effects were described as limpid even at high doses. In later decades, the first branded packaging of LSD microdoses (5 μg) were also named Clear Light.

The brand name also carried a mythopoetic echo. According to *The Tibetan Book of the Dead*, which Timothy Leary and company had psychedelicized in their widely influential 1964 book *The Psychedelic Experience*, the Clear Light names the overwhelming colorless blaze of the Absolute glimpsed by the newly dead as they first enter the bardo realms. On the street, Clear Light was also dubbed "windowpane" in honor of the translucent gelatin squares that held the acid. Unlike Clear Light, which was a particular formulation, "windowpane" came to be considered a genre of carrier media; some examples sold under the name were even made of cellophane or other plastic polymers. Other LSD gels were produced in a lenticular format, the lens shape further playing with LSD's optical theme—a cluster of luminous associations whose ultimate source may lie in the William Blake verse that furnished Aldous Huxley

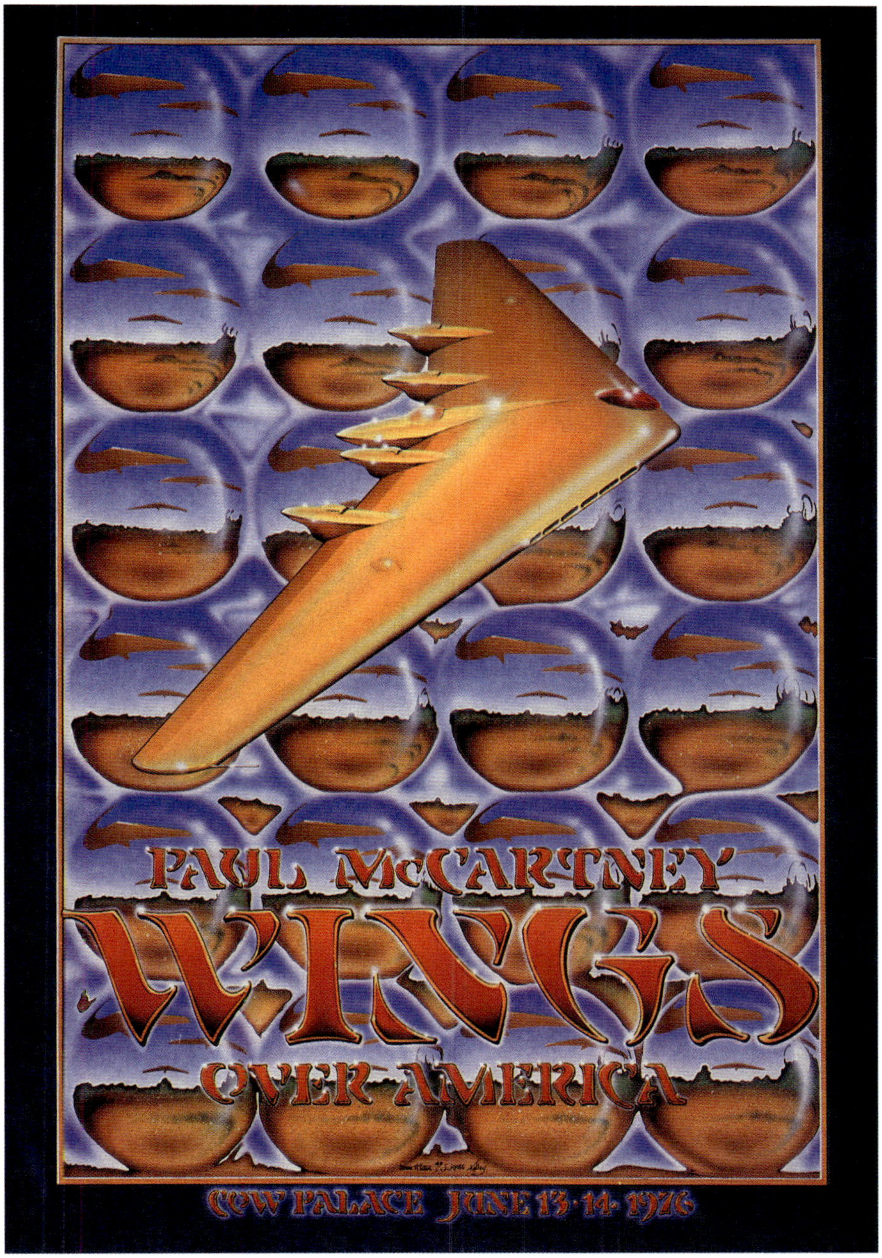

Wings Over America, Alton Kelley, Stanley Mouse, and Randy Tuten (COW760613-PO), 1976. Poster, 19 × 28 in.

the title of his mescaline book: "If the doors of perception were cleansed every thing would appear to man as it is, Infinite."[18] Some gels were even sold under the name "Contact Lens."

As with the name Clear Light itself, this sort of "medium is the message" recursion was common in LSD art and marketing. One subtle example here is the rock poster that Alton Kelley, Stanley Mouse, and Randy Tuten made for the Wings show at San Francisco's Cow Palace during the band's first North American tour in 1976. A golden flying wing jet, similar to the YB-35 built by Northrop right after World War II, soars in front of a curious array of translucent lenses offering distorted and slightly variant perspectives on that same airplane in flight over a landscape. Tuten later admitted that the image was based on the particular way that lenticular LSD gels bend light—another example of printed psychedelic media (the

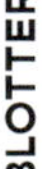

poster) mediating the way that an LSD carrier medium (the gel) incarnates the particular perceptual tunings that LSD itself affords.

The late 1960s also saw the appearance of another lambent LSD format, perhaps the most charismatic LSD brand of all time: Orange Sunshine. Working out of a lab in Windsor, California, the nerdy Owsley protege Tim Scully, partnering with a chutzpah-fueled New Yorker named Nick Sand, manufactured over a kilogram of crystalline LSD that was mixed with food coloring (and possibly tribasic calcium phosphate). The two cooks then used a powered triturate machine to add in lactose as a binder, and, using another industrial machine, Sand then pressed the resulting paste into small, flattened, orange barrels. Originally designed to melt under your tongue, these barrels possessed a notoriously crumbly texture, but they were clean and, at 300 μg, very powerful. Though other chemists at other laboratories would later take over production of the underlying acid, Orange Sunshine maintained its global identity for decades.

Sand wanted the Hells Angels to distribute Orange Sunshine, but Scully went instead with the Brotherhood of Eternal Love, a notorious "hippie mafia" that emerged from the sleepy canyons of Laguna Beach, California. The new acid was named by the Brotherhood's leader, a former thug from Anaheim named John Griggs, who converted to full-force psychedelic mysticism after taking LSD and reading *The Psychedelic Experience*. Griggs named the barrels after the diaphanous sparkle of sunlight reflecting off pond water in the mountains near Idlewild, where the Brotherhood owned a ranch. Following the chromatic template laid down by Owsley brands like White Lightning and Blue Cheer, Orange Sunshine served as a radiant but recognizable tag, suggesting a kind of holy California bubblegum.

Like Owsley, the Brotherhood combined canny marketing and drug-dealing savvy with psychedelic militancy. Griggs and his friends didn't just want to turn on the world, they *insisted* on it, and so gave away tens of thousands of Orange Sunshine tablets for free. The Brotherhood could afford such largesse because of their audacious global smuggling operation, which brought tons of Afghani hashish into the United States, often tucked inside surfboards or VW buses shipped from Pakistan. The Brotherhood's enormous profits, later generated as well by the cultivation of excellent Hawaiian cannabis, helped supplement their acid evangelism. By the early 1970s, Orange Sunshine had found its way to all fifty states and various freak scenes around the globe. Leary, close friends with the Brotherhood and a guru of sorts to Griggs, helped the cause, name-dropping the pills in his public lectures.

One Brotherhood member, John Gale, was particularly good at pumping the brand. He handed out fistfuls of tabs for free at a Who concert in Anaheim in the summer of 1968, his vest emblazoned with the phrase "Orange Sunshine Express"; at Grateful Dead shows, Gale was often seen in a go-to orange jumpsuit.[19] For a large Christmas happening held at Laguna Beach at the end of 1970, the Brotherhood sent out invitations bearing Orange Sunshine pills, and then tossed the remainder to the gathered crowds from an airplane. The cards, stamped with the Hallmark-meets-hippie slogan "Let Sunshine Do," showed a rainbow breaking through

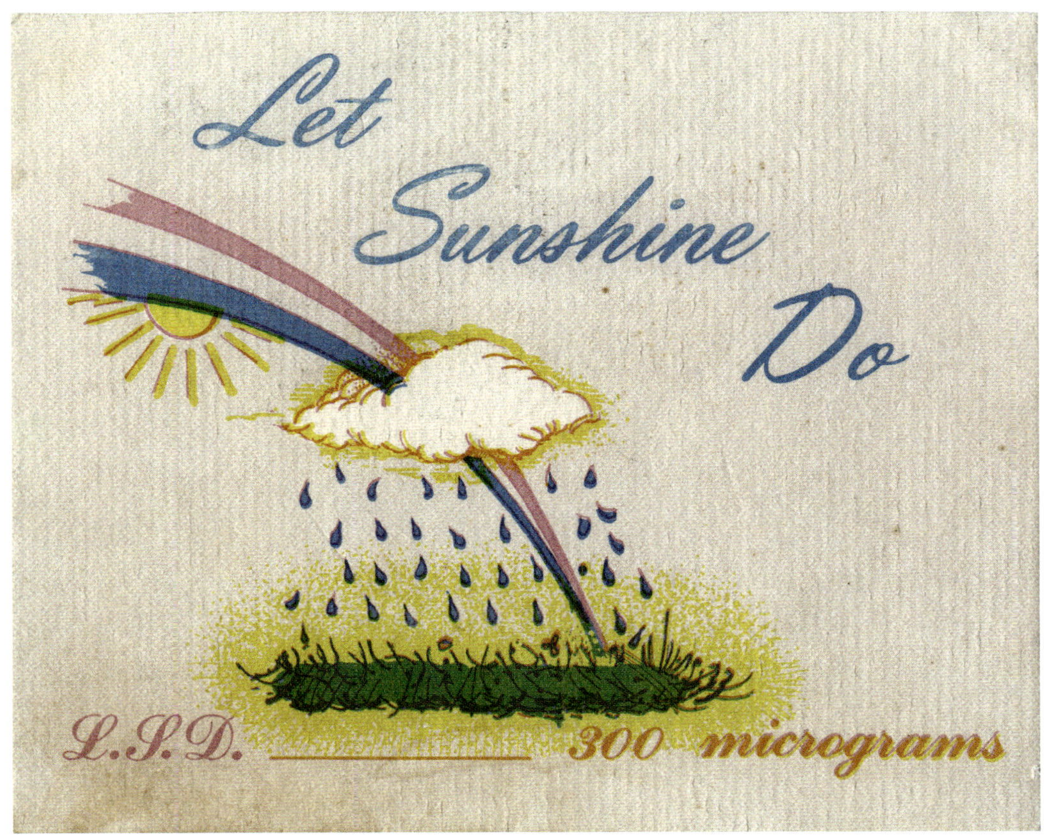

Let Sunshine Do, Bill Ogden, Laguna Beach, 1969. Brotherhood of Eternal Love promotional card, 4 × 5 in.

a cloud; at the end of the rainbow, a gummed red star held together a cellophane wrapper containing one tab of 300 μg LSD.

Though stamped out mechanically from synthetic ingredients cooked up on an industrial scale, Orange Sunshine was more than a mere commodity—and not just because the barrels were sometimes given away for free. The crumbly tablets came precharged with aura, energies that chemists like Scully, Sand, and Owsley all believed could be infused into LSD molecules at the time of manufacture. Whether or not you are satisfied to reduce such theurgic empowerment to the narrow notion of "branding," Orange Sunshine carried a powerful charisma that was transmitted to distributors, and in turn to consumers. "There have got to be cosmic influences connected with Sunshine," one lower-level dealer told some LSD historians. "There is a fantastic karma to this LSD. If you get on a dealing trip and do not abuse it—trying to make outlandish profits—you realize you have a lot of power on your hands with a tremendous responsibility for a lot of heads. You realize that you are not just selling drugs, but are selling to people a great and important part of their existence."[20]

While aspects of Orange Sunshine's aura anticipate the cheesy "lifestyle brands" of contemporary wellness capitalism and its multilevel marketing schemes, here the enchanted product has moral force: a sense of social duty and a wariness about the profit motive that nonetheless oils successful distribution. This attitude reflects the values that Grateful Dead guitarist Jerry Garcia characterized in the 1960s as the "hip economy," an arrangement in which money-makers like musicians and drug dealers flourish within and in service to a self-consciously marginal community's needs, including its revolutionary and spiritual aspirations and its pursuit of fun. Acid was always part of this economy, and even as '60s idealism declined and the underground foundered or went mainstream, the trade in charismatic acid like Orange Sunshine, Windowpane, and microdots—tiny pellet-sized tabs that emerged from the UK in the early 1970s—retained a trace of spiritual grace amid the piratical thrills, and sometimes considerable rewards, of clandestine commerce.

That said, the history of LSD has often been framed within the underground as a kind of Edenic narrative. Sandoz or Owsley crystal represent almost divine substances, praised for their *purity*, which then becomes debased by bad chemistry, venal commodification, and the wayward drift of druggy hedonism—a story that itself stands in for the dissipation of the revolutionary energies of the 1960s into the compromises of the 1970s and beyond. In their book *Acid Dreams*, Martin Lee and Bruce Shlain give us this view, outlining a decline they claim was already well under way by the late 1960s:

> So many people were getting high that the identification of drug use with the sharper forms of cultural and political deviance weakened considerably. Instead of being weapons in a generational war, marijuana and LSD often served as pleasure props, accoutrements of the good life that included water beds, tape decks, golden roach clips, and a host of leisure items. High school kids were popping tabs of acid every weekend as if they were gum-drops. And much of the LSD *was* like candy—full of additives and impurities. The physical contamination of street acid symbolized what was happening throughout the culture.

The authors go on to quote the cultural observer Michael Rossman: "The pill was no longer a sacrament, but a commercial token, stripped of its essential husk of love, ritual and supportive searching community."[21]

This narrative arc is crucial to keep in mind as we unfold the story of blotter. As mentioned earlier, though LSD was sometimes passed around in the 1960s on actual blotting paper, sheets of perforated and printed LSD paper do not come to dominate the acid trade until the late 1970s, reaching a long golden age in the 1980s and '90s. As such, the rise of blotter mirrors, and comes to mediate and challenge, the mythopoetic story of LSD's spiritual decline. For even as LSD lost the millennialist charge of the 1960s, it continued to foster spiritual discovery, social critique, tribal bonds, and aesthetic enrichment. During the blotter age, the quality of the molecule also improved significantly, its white sculptured crystals sometimes reaching and maybe surpassing the purity levels of yore. Many of the people who produced and sold this material remained idealists, or at least pragmatic idealists, with a taste for beautiful craft and an outlaw humor reflected in the design of many blotters, which sometimes poked fun at the scene and ironically riffed on the fact that the paper sacraments also served as "commercial tokens."

In these later years, many older LSD users continued to see blotter as a debased medium that bruised and degraded the holy molecule. Sand preferred pills; Owsley thought paper doses were an atrocious idea and let everyone know it. The truth is that, properly cared for and kept from light and air, humble blotters can hold their punch for quite some time. This persistent potency also gives us a symbolic key for understanding the medium. Blotter hits are signs not of decline but of canny transformation, as idealism gives way to subversion, militancy to mutation, counterculture to subculture. Mediating the profane as much as the sacred, blotter became the central vehicle of LSD's own weird drift through the post-hippie era.

A Kinky Caper

The village of East Hagbourne lies not far from Oxford, England, and it is here, according to the town website at least, that proprietors of a local paper mill first discovered blotting paper. Stories and dates vary, but it seems that sometime in the closing years of the eighteenth century, an improperly sized batch of paper—or possibly an accidental spill of sulfuric acid—resulted in a highly absorbent product. William Russell Slade, one of the clan who ran the mill, soon recognized the utility of such material in an era when ink—and its inevitable spills and seepings—was king. By the early nineteenth century, blotting paper was found on writing desks around the world.

Given its ubiquity, low cost, and significant absorption rate, blotting paper presents an obvious distribution medium for a highly dose-sensitive liquid drug. In *Albion Dreaming*, his wonderful history of the British LSD scene—which is every bit as significant and interesting as the more well-known US story—Andy Roberts reports that UK jazz musicians were consuming small blotting papers dosed with LSD as early as the late 1950s. By the mid-1960s, amidst the usual sugar cubes, the method had become well established. Evidence for this is provided by none other than the comedian Dudley Moore, who, performing as Whispering Jim Narg, "fresh from two years with the Ahuru Guru in the Himalayas," contributed the following verse to "Psychedelic Baby," a fruity pop song released on a *Private Eye* flexidisc in 1966:

> Psychedelic baby, won't you take a trip with me
> Dip your lump of sugar in the LSD
> If you want a kinky caper
> Then suck the blotting paper, psychedelic baby, with me.

A year later, just back from London, Bay Area music promoter and scene maker Chet Helms confirmed to the *Berkeley Barb* that blotter paper was the favored method of LSD distribution in the UK.[22]

One advantage to storing LSD on blotting paper is how easy and safe it becomes to transport, which is how the molecule made its way to the Amazon in 1966. As part of his research into healing and drugs, the Chilean psychiatrist and esotericist Claudio Naranjo, who had already cut his psychedelic teeth in California, traveled to the Putumayo region of Columbia to research plant medicines. According to Peter Stafford, Naranjo brought along some blotter paper impregnated with drops of LSD, which he passed on to a few members of the Cofán tribe. The Cofán enjoyed the colonialist *medicino*, and in turn provided Naranjo with local plant preparations, including the ingredients for ayahuasca. Besides initiating a beautiful encounter between novel Old World psychedelics and classic New World ones, Naranjo made another breakthrough: in order to indicate the strength and location of the invisible drops, Naranjo drew images of stars, moons, and suns on his blotter, producing the first illustrated acid blotter on record.

Coupon for LSD tablet, Bay Area, n.d. 2½ × 2½ in.

No doubt other LSD users had already been doodling on their paper for similar reasons, especially among the creatives in swinging London. But though blotting paper was widespread in the UK, it took the United States to subject the process to the sort of mechanical reproduction required to level up to a properly commercial scale. This is important: unlike capsules or tablets, which belong to the pharmaceutical mainstream, the invention of blotter as a standardized drug delivery device takes place entirely within the freak underground. The innovator here was Eric Ghost—a.k.a. Eric Brown—a New Yorker who, after a peripatetic life of military service, armed robbery, and prison, took LSD for the first time in the Lower East Side around 1965. He swallowed nearly 4,000 μg of Sandoz, smeared across a sugar cube, and the thermonuclear revelation occasioned by this enormous dose convinced him to cofound the Psychedelicatessen, a legendary if short-lived head shop that opened on 164 Avenue A in 1966. Like most acid manufacturers at the time, Ghost was messianic about the molecule and its potential to improve people and the world. "LSD is not about escape," he explained in a 1995 interview. "It's about reality!"[23]

Ghost started cooking LSD, and around 1968, he began distributing it as a cleverly packaged paper product. At the time, liquid LSD was usually transferred to materials like blotting paper or sugar cubes using a pipette or eye-dropper to dispense a single drop at a time. Ghost and a colleague accelerated this process by designing and building the Mark I: a device that allowed 100 pins to be dipped simultaneously into a pan of LSD in solution, and then moved as a single unit and impressed all at once onto an absorbent piece of paper. (LSD was and is sometimes dissolved in purified water, though alcohol or other solvents are more frequently used.) The pins, and the dosed paper that resulted, followed a compact pattern, which took the form of five tight rows of twenty columns each, packed onto a rectangular sheet roughly the size of a business card. Ghost had invented the core formal feature of acid blotter: the grid.

Each one of the Ghost's drops contained a hefty 1,000 μg of LSD, which were left to the distributor or client to manually slice into four smaller hits, each packing a still solid 250 μg punch. This arrangement—the "four-way"—would recur throughout the history of blotter, though it would appear much less frequently in the later, lower-dose years. Not coincidentally, the amount of LSD on a single one of these sheets amounted to an even gram, which makes for happy producers, who prefer the easy math, in part because their work almost invariably got them high as kites. Though later blotter producers would rarely dose a single sheet with an entire gram of material, the gram would continue to maintain its role as the commanding unit for bulk packaging and distribution.

Ghost's innovation of the grid form, and his mechanical hack for rapidly dosing the paper, brought blotter one step closer toward a properly "mass" medium. Ghost's quest for streamlined efficiency ensured that he would remain one of the steadiest sources for street acid over the next decade, but it also reflects a scalar effect that is arguably inherent in the drug itself. Simply put, it is extremely hard to make a small amount of LSD. Even the most boutique chemical batches produce tens of thousands of hits, which need, or want, to go somewhere. This quantitative excess fundamentally marks the acid trade, which, leaving aside the drive to turn on the world, is focused on volume and rapid dissemination rather than per-unit markup. Even the most "prestige" forms of the molecule, like Clear Light windowpane, were distributed at scale.

Over the decades, blotter makers would continually experiment with Ghost's grid, rendering the format explicit in dots and lines, altering the number and ratio of rows and columns, and messing with the size, number, and strength of the individual hits. While some of these variations were driven by technical or market considerations, others were forms of play and stylistic innovation. Even Ghost's lattice of spots resonated aesthetically, calling to mind the early abstractions of Piet Mondrian, or the constructions of Aleksandr Rodchenko, or the delicate weaves of Agnes Martin. Though acid distributors turned to the grid for reasons of economy and exigency, blotter's development into an aesthetic craft and ultimately a collectable art object demands that we see it as a kind of modernist outlier—a topic we will explore in a later section.

Ghost did not start out with actual blotting paper, however, opting instead for red litmus paper. The LSD molecule is basic enough to turn red litmus paper blue, which gave Ghost's acid the street name Blue Dot alongside the moniker 5 × 20. Initially, Ghost packaged his single gram sheets in a package that combined stealth and wit: an imitation box of Kodachrome film. "For brilliant color," the package read, in a slight variation from the official Kodak product. "100 Exposures." Each dosed sheet was in turn wrapped inside mylar, which not only protected the acid from damaging UV light, but also discouraged suspicious parties from opening the containers on a whim, potentially destroying unexposed film. If you did unwrap the mylar, you discovered, along with the sheet, a helpful text about "LSD (Lysergische Säure Diethylamide)," including sections like "Physiologic Effect," "Mode and Site of Action," and other data drawn from the psychedelic research of the day. "Psychologic effects are heavily dependent on set and setting," the writing proclaims; "it is important to flow with the drug and not to resist its effects."

Ghost's packaging establishes two recurrent thematic features of LSD on paper: a twinkly-eyed riff on the material's status as contraband; and a self-referential meditation on LSD as a medium of perception that, like other "technological" media, filters, transforms, and amplifies nondrug phenomena. But Ghost's meta-media prank, at once parody and homage, did not last long. He realized that, while his Kodachrome package

LSD (LYSERGISCHE SÄURE DIETHYLAMIDE)

HISTORIC FACTORS—Lysergic acid diethylamide tartrate (LSD-25) was synthesized in 1938 by a Swiss scientist named Hofmann, who was studying root alkaloids for their value as migraine headache cures. He recognized its perception-altering properties in 1943 when he ingested 250 micrograms in a self-experiment at Sandoz Lab. in Basel, Switzerland.

Lysergic acid, the precursor of LSD, is a constituent of ergot, a fungus that grows on rye and other grains. The drug is related to psilocybin, the active alkaloid of the Mexican mushroom, and to mescaline, which is found in the peyote cactus buttons, except that it is many times stronger than these hallucinogens. Morning glory seeds also contain LSD-like compounds, although in milder form.

PHYSIOLOGIC EFFECT—Physiologically, LSD has few effects. It is readily absorbed from the intestinal tract; thus there is little advantage to injection. In excessive dosages, some of the following side effects are sometimes experienced: nausea, dizziness, headache and palpitations. Periods of shivering alternate with heat flushes. Pupils are dilated; heart rate and blood pressure rise moderately, as does blood sugar. A fine tremor of the fingers and hands may be present. Tolerance to LSD develops rapidly, with cross tolerance to mescaline and psilocybin. No lethal dosage known to humans.

PSYCHOLOGIC EFFECT—Psychological effects are heavily dependent on set and setting. Set is the mental attitude and emotional condition of the user at the time of ingestion. Setting is the surrounding in which the drug is taken. It is wise to make first-time use of LSD under the guidance of an experienced user in supportive and familiar surroundings. It is important to flow with the drug and not to resist its effects.

MODE AND SITE OF ACTION—Neither the mode nor the site of action of LSD is definitely known. It is even unknown whether the various perceptual distortions—"hallucinations" and the like—can be attributed to a primary action of LSD or whether these different effects involve different mechanisms and sites of action. LSD is a serotonin inhibitor.

RESEARCH—LSD has been used highly successfully in alcoholics therapy and on terminal cancer patients to alleviate pain and help them die a more peaceful death. It has been used as a psychotherapeutic aid in general to increase insight and lift repressions, and with autistic children to increase socialization. It has been cited as a specific cure for frigidity, impotence and homosexuality.

ACUTE SIDE EFFECTS—Chlorpromazine (Thorazine®) is the most effective antagonist to LSD's effects. Reserpine may enhance the effects of LSD.

DOSAGE—75 to 225 micrograms is considered average.

MORE INFORMATION. If you have questions about this film, write to Department 841 at the address below. See the many Kodak books on sale at your photo dealer.

Consumer Markets Division 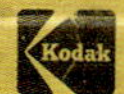 **Rochester, New York 14650**

KP 53193g 2-72 Printed in U.S.A.

Read This Notice: This product will be replaced if defective in manufacture, labeling, or packaging, or if damaged or lost by us or any subsidiary company. Except for such replacement, the sale, processing, or other handling of this product is without warranty or liability even though defect, damage or loss is caused by negligence or other fault. Since color dyes may in time change, this product will not be replaced for, or otherwise warranted against, any change in color.

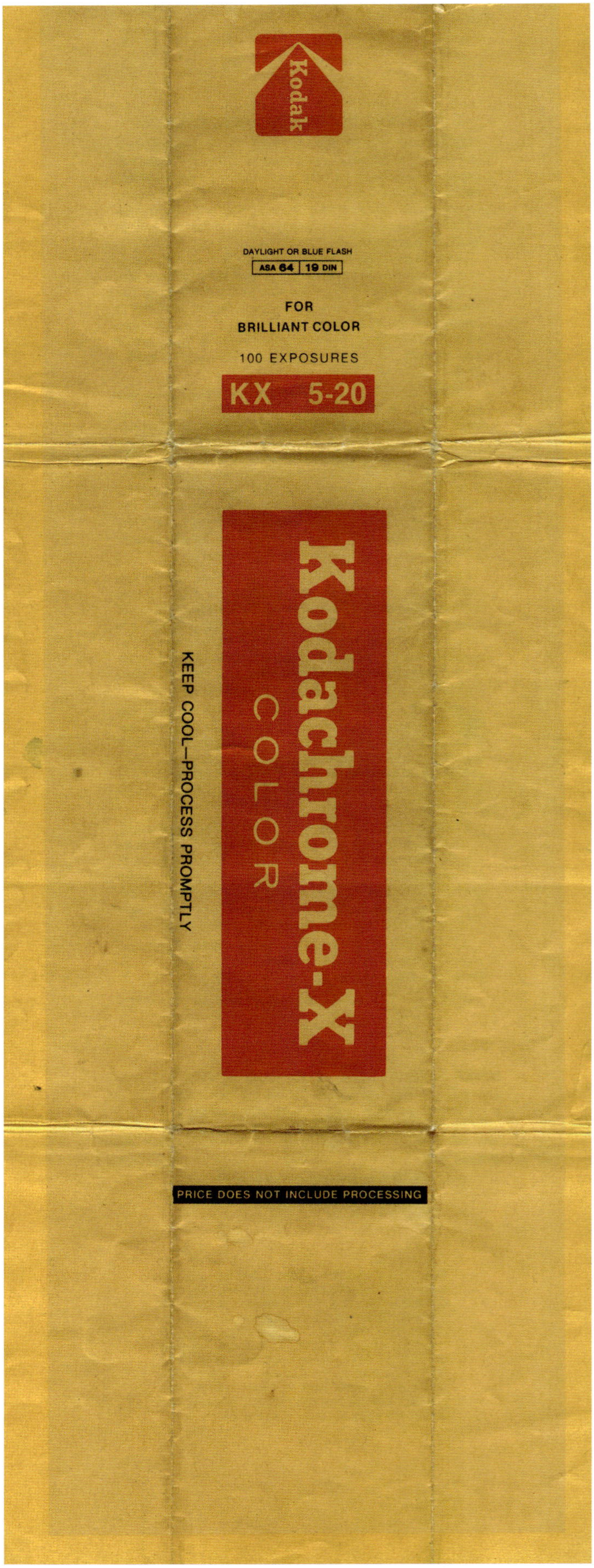

Kodak

DAYLIGHT OR BLUE FLASH

ASA 64 | 19 DIN

FOR
BRILLIANT COLOR

100 EXPOSURES

KX 5-20

KEEP COOL—PROCESS PROMPTLY

Kodachrome-X
COLOR

PRICE DOES NOT INCLUDE PROCESSING

disguised the LSD, his anomalous procurement of large orders of litmus paper left a potentially damning trace. He soon dropped the clever packaging and switched to common woodchip paper.

By 1970, "blotter acid" was an established street term; a year later Hunter S. Thompson included five sheets of the stuff in the psychoactive arsenal he and the good Dr. Gonzo brought to Las Vegas for their legendary debauch. Despite the name, however, actual blotting paper was rarely used. Blotter producers quickly realized that LSD is such a friendly molecule that it does not require highly absorbent paper; some early examples from the 1970s reportedly included thin-gauge cardboard. A much more important factor than absorbency was the purity of the paper, since the chlorine and other bleaching agents added to a good deal of paper stock tended to neutralize the magic chemistry.

Kodachrome-X, original packaging for Eric Ghost's 5 × 20 blotter strips, ca. 1968. 5 × 13½ in.

Influenced at times by Owsley's blotter pessimism, some psychedelic users remained skeptical of the format in its early years. They had their reasons. Because of LSD's sensitivity to light and oxygen, blotters were liable to degrade if not handled or stored properly, which is what the *Los Angeles Free Press* warned heads about in their street drug review column—a common feature of underground newspapers—in 1972.[24] At the same time, blotter also developed a reputation for purity, as it appeared to lack the adulterants and toxic by-products that marred many of the pressed pills then in circulation. (Zombie-like in its persistence, the rumor that LSD was sometimes cut with or contained strychnine is—almost—a total myth.) Nonetheless, street blotter continued to play second fiddle to tablets, gels, and microdots.

Ghost's decision to turn away from litmus paper led to the disappearance of the signifying blue dot. At the same time, his blotters did retain a visible trace of the pin drop; over time, and depending on exposure to air and light, the colorless spot of acid would darken. Perhaps due to their resemblance to punched computer cards, these later grids were sometimes known on the street as "computer acid."[25] Leaving aside such stains, the blotters in circulation at the dawn of the 1970s were essentially blank canvases, often categorized by the various hues of the cardstock ("orange blotters," etc.), which was generally preferred for its sturdiness and quality. These blank sheets were also highly tempting surfaces for inscription, especially given the *horror vacui* that seized the souls of so many psychedelic artists. Blotters started circulating that were decorated with doodles and hand-drawn images. Indeed, the first blotter acid mentioned in *Microgram*—pieces of coarse tan paper seized in the Northwest—featured drop spots individually encircled with hand-scrawled peace symbols.

Rubber-stamped blotters also appeared in these early years, by 1970 at the latest. A humble tool of hippie handicraft, as well as a crucial implement of early mail art, handstamps were usually made out of a wooden block covered with a layer of rubber. Many of the rubber-stamp images available on the market were almost designed to appeal to the aspiring blotter maker: wizards, smiling suns, Tantric mandalas, skulls. Providing an easy and informal way to block-print an image onto dosed paper, these handstamps were sometimes glued together for faster production speed, and could be pressed into ink pads featuring a rainbow array of colors.

Original images were sometimes hand carved, while at least one blotter maker took advantage of an offer from Cheerios: send in a box top, a few bucks, and a photograph, and the breakfast cereal giant would send you a custom rubber stamp.

Because of their scale and ease, handstamps were generally employed by small operations run by lower-level dealers, who might be dipping their own paper or decorating dosed "blanks" they had already purchased. Here it is important to recall that in most cases, the LSD supply trickled down from a small number of centralized labs, mostly in California. While some of these wellsprings dosed their own blotter or pressed pills high up the chain, a lot of LSD was distributed in crystal or liquid form through layers of intermediaries. This often left smaller-scale clients and street dealers in charge of loading the acid into its final carrier medium. The wide base of this distribution pyramid helps explain the great variety of blotter seen on the street, as well as the persistence over time of boutique practices like rubber stamps or doodles.

Handstamp impressions used for blotter, 1970s. 8½ × 11 in.

The Institute of Illegal Images contains many examples of rubber-stamp images that found their way onto blotters, including a Sufi flying heart, dragons, igloos, crescent moons, and that famous Flammarion engraving of a mystic traveler poking his head through the mundane sphere of the world. One of McCloud's favorites is dubbed *Indian Design #2* in the DEA's *Blotter Index*: a circle of worshipers holding hands before a mandalic mountain sunrise. Other stamp impressions were snatched from non-hippie cultural zones, like the perfectly ordinary Kosher stamp that decorated some hits, its Hebrew letters at once promising quality and poking fun at the promise. But rubber stamps could be deceptive as well. In the late 1970s, a major Santa Cruz LSD producer used an offset printer to produce blotter on a large scale, but disguised the size and professionalism of his operation by mimicking the smudgy, erratic application of rubber stamps wielded by hand.

In 1972, the drug column in the *St. Louis Outlaw* declared that "Captain Guts (blotter)" was "really good."[26] If this blotter is, as seems possible, the early *Captain L* sheet, then the drug review represents one of the first appearances of a new and far more significant technique for printing LSD paper: screen printing.[27] Also called silk screening, the method involves attaching a stencil onto a screen and manually pressing ink through the screen's negative space onto another surface. Screen printing was first used to decorate fabrics in Asia over a millennium ago, and the method was adopted in the eighteenth century by French textile artists, who began to stretch the stencil mesh over a wooden frame. In the early twentieth century, photo-imaged stencils radically increased the efficiency of the method, as did the addition of the humble squeegee. At the time, both fine artists and advertisers began to appreciate screen prints for their bright colors, variability, and ease of production, but the method really exploded in the 1960s. Pop artists were particularly drawn to it, with Andy Warhol praising the method as "simple—quick, and chancy."[28]

Warhol no doubt enjoyed screen printing's link to the advertising industry, which was in turn absorbing some of the sass and irony of pop art. Underground makers, on the other hand, appreciated the low overhead of

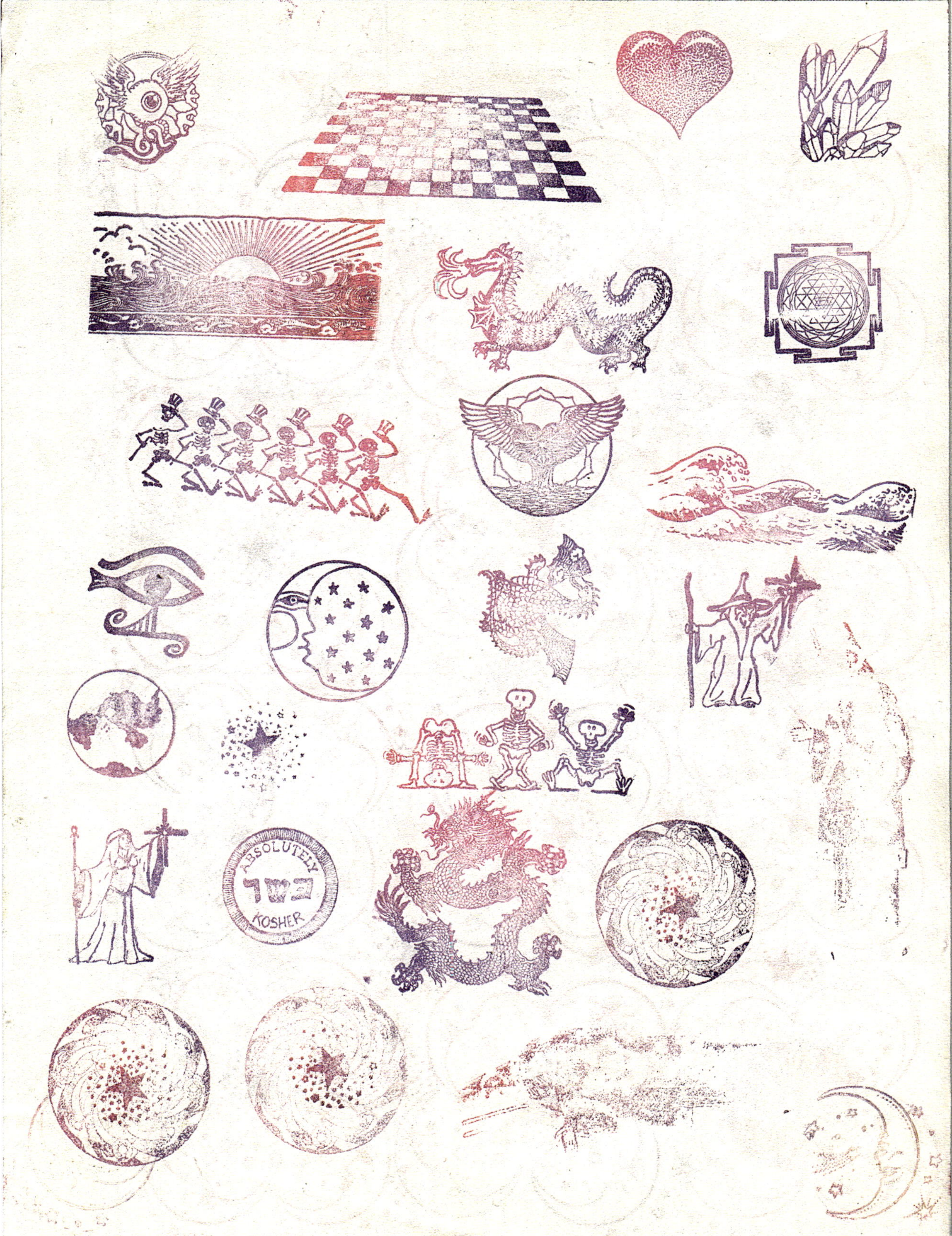
ABSOLUTELY
KOSHER

the method, as well as its embodiment of the crunchy, homegrown style of tool use celebrated in the *Whole Earth Catalog*. In this sense, screen printing joined do-it-yourself typography, IBM Selectric typewriters, and the Gestetner duplicating machine as technical practices "that gave agency to the authors, designers, artists, illustrators, editors, and publishers who were focused primarily on the urgency of their communication."[29] Freaks, revolutionaries, and gentle hippies alike embraced the method, which allowed for the easy propagation of text and images through movement media like posters, signs, and T-shirts. Blotter makers in particular appreciated the fact that, unlike a pill press, there was nothing suspicious about owning the tools of production.

Blotter makers also had recourse to another planographic method alongside screen printing: offset lithography, a photomechanical form of reproduction that had been around since the 1950s. In this method, photostats are used to produce lithographic printing plates, one for each color that will be combined into the final image. These plates are then inked, with the ink transferred through a roller or "blanket" onto the paper. With its versatility and relatively low cost, offset printing became the backbone of psychedelic poster production along with the printing of underground newspapers, which meant that longhair-friendly print shops were part of the local media ecology in places like San Francisco, Ann Arbor, and the East Village. Offset presses were probably responsible for the first widely distributed early acid sheets, even as a good deal of early printed blotter continued to be screened. And even when blotter kicked into a more properly industrial mode, silkscreens continued to offer a poetic and artisanal alternative, and are still used today for the occasional vanity edition. In other ways, though, the two processes were not that different, since both required photostats. Either way, makers were still faced with the painstaking job of hand-constructing stats out of carefully aligned grids of duplicated images and then photographically reducing those stats to the proper size for printing.

Whether screened or offset, the LSD blotter designs that emerged in the early 1970s represents a significant "intermedia" encounter: the material entwining of a powerful hallucinogen and a still renegade print culture. Marshall McLuhan had good reason to believe that the 1960s youth culture was a product of the new electronic universe, but for all the light shows and electric guitars, the Gutenberg galaxy still radiated its influences throughout the counterculture. Print allowed the scene to communicate itself to itself through newspapers, comix, broadsides, buttons, chapbooks, posters, even bumper stickers and clothing. This myriad of surfaces allowed new and distinctly countercultural approaches to graphic design to flourish. Critics Lorraine Wilde and David Karman note two important features of underground design from the 1960s that would feedforward into the strategies of 1970s blotter makers: density "of information, and of composition, across the visual field"; and "the rampant use of multiple modes of illustration, collage, and hand-drawing"—modes that, in blotter's case, were rarely combined in a single design but did characterize the format as a whole.[30]

LSD blotter is a singular genre of underground design. Like earlier if more visible countercultural print formats—rock posters, album art, and comix—blotter played a crucial role in collectively mediating the perceptual and mythopoetic features of psychedelic experience, but also in constructing and refining patterns and images that would themselves be looped around, through the feedback of set and setting, into people's trips downstream. Not coincidentally, psychedelic poster art, underground comix, and blotter art were all significantly—but by no means exclusively—developed in San Francisco. Indeed, we might consider blotter as a diminutive and sometimes derivative iteration of practices that go back to the *San Francisco Oracle*, *Zap* panels, and Fillmore marketing campaigns.

Consider one particularly oracular poster that appeared in October 1967, years before the first printed LSD papers hit the streets. Announcing an upcoming Winterland Halloween show, *Trip or Freak* (AOR-2.183) was a collaboration between three of the "big five" poster artists, Rick Griffin, Alton Kelley, and Stanley Mouse. It's Kelley's work with Lon Chaney's iconic *Phantom of the Opera* face that should catch our eye here: playing with grids, repetition, scale, and the popcorn grotesque, Kelley prophesied printed blotter. As if to seal the synchronicity, the small 5" × 8" *Trip or Freak* postcards that were produced alongside the posters were rumored to be dosed, with each Phantom holding a drop.[31]

The relationship between psychedelic posters and the concerts they advertised also helps clarify the logic of blotter. Poster designs were rarely tied directly to the band or the specific event; Wes Wilson's swirling typography or Rick Griffin's notorious flying eyeball could just easily announce the Doors as Jimi Hendrix. Like poster artists, and in contrast with the formulaic quality of more commercial "psychedelic" imagery, blotter designers drew from a wide range of image types and strategies, many of which had nothing to do with visionary experience. At the same time, while both poster and blotter artists were given free rein, the images they produced were not autonomous works of art but temporal, even festal gestures—they indicated, or advertised, a powerful experience lurking in the near future. Both posters and blotter were *expectant signs* that gestured toward an upcoming event promising revelation, delight, and elaborate visual effects. In the Anglo-Australian sphere, blotters were even sometimes called "tickets."

For many users, the psychedelic event on deck might be an informal gathering of friends, or a coven ritual, or a solo trip at the beach. But some blotter editions were also tagged to specific collective gatherings. Just as Owsley whipped up White Lightning for the Human Be-In, many blotter makers ran editions with particular events in mind—that summer's Rainbow Gathering (p. 183), say, or the local Renaissance Faire (p. 182), or Burning Man. Blotter's aura of imminent expectation also helps explain the potent role the medium came to play in magnifying the Grateful Dead tours of the late 1970s and 1980s. Transcending the rock performance racket of that era, the Dead promised and delivered immersive Dionysian events whose singular magic could be reliably enhanced with a ten-strip of tabs procured in the parking lot, their iconic promise sublimed into that night's nightfall of diamonds.

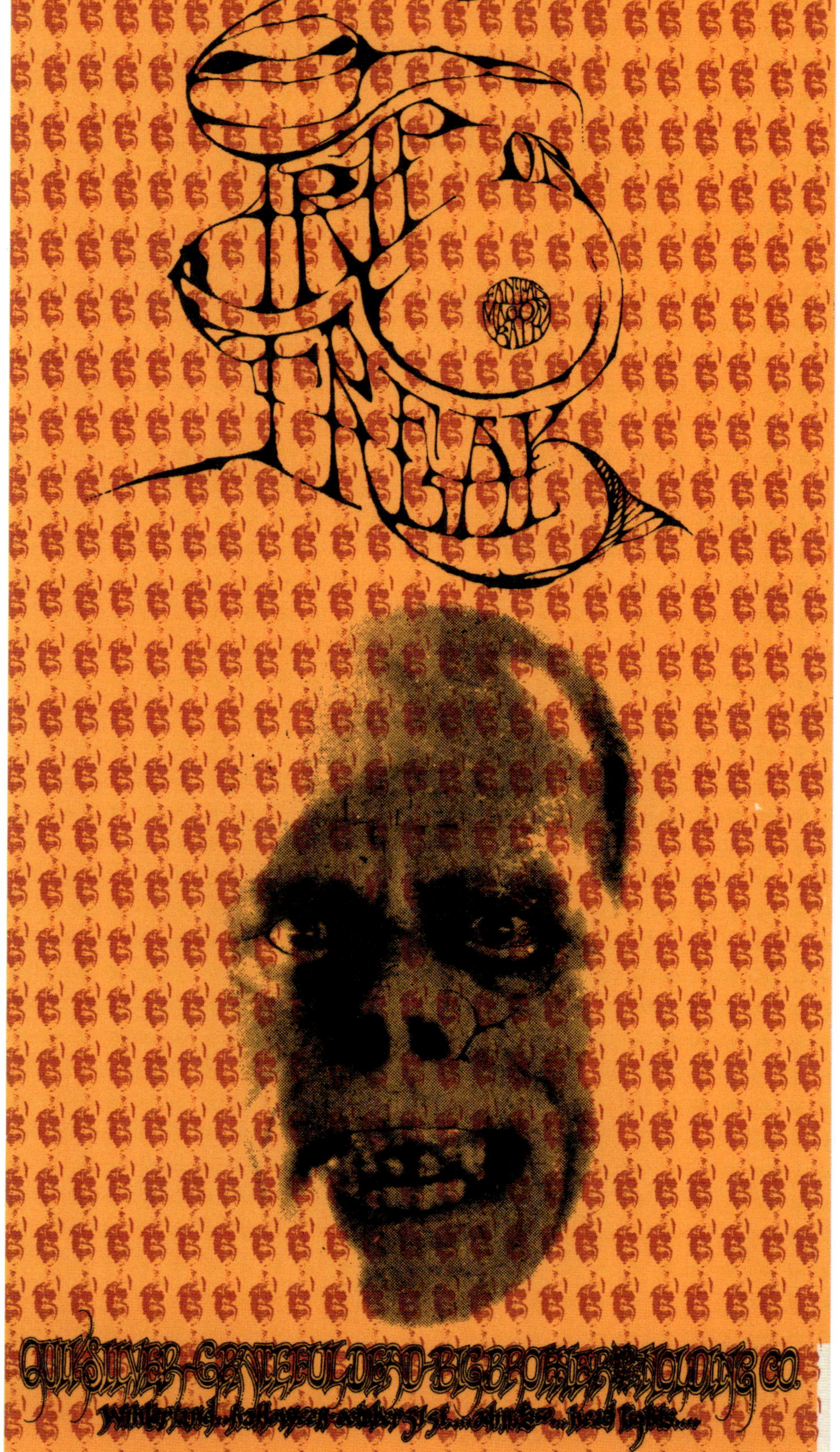

Trip or Freak, Rick Griffin, Alton Kelley, and Stanley Mouse (AOR-2.183), 1967. Hand flier, 3¾ × 7 in.

As we will see, underground comix artists also contributed a number of images to the blotter storehouse—occasionally with their actual permission. But blotter's real inheritance from comix and posters lies in social function and intent. As Wilde and Karman argue, the riotous novelties of San Francisco's psychedelic posters emerged in relationship to a very specific local community. Though in essence commercial advertisements, which like blotter sometimes parodied well-known ad campaigns, the posters "came from inside the intended audience for the events: the boundary between designer and audience transcended, melting the us/them dichotomy so built into conventional advertising."[32] These images reflected possibilities that everyone, including their makers, shared. All you needed was a ticket.

Gaining steam a decade later, blotter carried on the rock poster's insider communication, transmitting "symbols of a secret society" from outlaw acidheads to other outlaw acidheads. To recall Barthes's foody terms, while microdots or colored tabs may have *indicated* the load of LSD they carried, printed blotter *signified*. Rather than merely "packaging" the drug, blotter designs literally configured the substance itself, whose feisty molecules wrapped themselves around the very fibers of the printed paper. As such, tendrils of underground print culture were literally consumed along with the psychedelics themselves—even, at least sometimes, entering the warp and weft of the experience itself, impressing the phenomenology from the get-go like a signet ring: flying saucers, lightning bolts, Zonker from *Doonesbury*. By virtue of its illegality, to say nothing of its tight coupling to extraordinary experience, blotter kept a spark of hippie media's iridescent DIY immediacy alive and kicking within its tiny frame of perf marks.

Sheets to the Wind

The most likely candidate for the first printed blotter is *Mr. Natural*, one of a number of LSD sheets that appeared in the '70s and '80s featuring R. Crumb's funny, free-thinking guru character. The Midwest Research Institute's *Drug Atlas* includes a Kansas City example seized in July 1971—an orange four-way, costing $2.50—that shows the disreputable saint pointing to the sky (identified somewhat confusingly in the *Blotter Index* as *Mr. Natural #2*). "Sold as LSD," the *Atlas* reads; "reportedly gives a good experience."[33] Both *Microgram* and the *Los Angeles Free Press* reported further sightings in 1973, and by 1987, when the *Blotter Index* was published, five different Mr. Natural designs had been collected by the DEA.

Microgram does report one earlier example of "LSD paper"—a Raggedy Anne and Andy exhibit that may have simply been torn from a book and dosed. But *Mr. Natural* still seems like the natural first. Not unlike acid culture itself, the guru's antics combine humor, groovy spirituality, and an erratic and sometimes convulsive hedonism. Though first conjured by Crumb while living in Cleveland, the character is also deeply tied to Haight-Ashbury, and his appearance on blotter not only underscores the role that San Francisco would continue to play in the global acid scene, but probably directly hints, in the wink-wink manner of much blotter imagery,

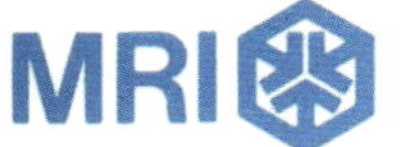

DRUG IDENTIFICATION REPORT

Identification No. KC-A46

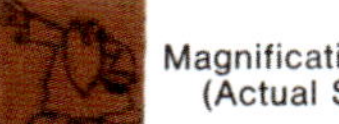

Magnification 1X (Actual Size)

While every effort has been made to faithfully reproduce the drugs analyzed, the photographs in this Atlas should be considered a quick reference indication aid only, and where treatment is to be administered a chemical analysis of the drug should be done.

Date of Acquisition: July 20, 1971.
Source: Resident.
Location: Kansas City, Missouri.
Price: $2.50.

Street Name: Mr. Natural.
Description: Paper square with printed design.
Weight: 34 milligrams.
Color: Orange with black print.
Other Comments: Sold as LSD, reportedly gives a good experience.
Ingredients Identified: LSD (Lysergic Acid Diethlyamide, "Acid"), approximately 100 micrograms per sample.
Other Active Ingredients: None.

symptoms

normal dose (~100μg. LSD)
Hallucinations, uncoordinated, disoriented, pupils dilated, euphoric state, dyssocial behavior, psychotic depression.

excess dose
Fatigue, tremors, dizziness, nausea, vomiting, rise in heart rate and blood pressure, stiff jaw muscles, flushing, shivering, chest pains.

antidote*

normal dose
calm the patient, converse, keep out of hazardous situations.

excess dose
Haloperidol, or trifluoperazine, administer as required. Amobarbital sodium, orally, reduces psychotic reactions.

*Antidotes should be administered only by a registered physician.

The Drug Atlas is published solely for the information and education of persons working with or interested in the problem of drug abuse.
MIDWEST RESEARCH INSTITUTE, 425 VOLKER BLVD., KANSAS CITY, MISSOURI 64110
Copyright—December, 1971, Midwest Research Institute

46

MRI DRUG IDENTIFICATION REPORT

Identification No. KC-A47

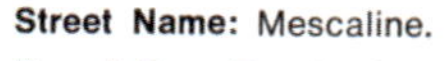

Magnification 1X (Actual Size)

While every effort has been made to faithfully reproduce the drugs analyzed, the photographs in this Atlas should be considered a quick reference indication aid only, and where treatment is to be administered a chemical analysis of the drug should be done.

Date of Acquisition: September 22, 1971.
Source: High School Student.
Location: Kansas City, Missouri.
Price: $2.00.

Street Name: Mescaline.
Description: Powder in capsule.
Weight: 302 milligrams (powder).
Color: Brown powder with black specks in clear capsule.
Other Comments: None.
Ingredients Identified: Morning Glory seeds spiked with LSD. LSD content 125 micrograms per capsule. No mescaline present.
Other Active Ingredients: None.

symptoms

normal dose (~100μg. LSD)
Hallucinations, uncoordinated, disoriented, pupils dilated, euphoric state, dyssocial behavior, psychotic depression.

excess dose
Fatigue, tremors, dizziness, nausea, vomiting, rise in heart rate and blood pressure, stiff jaw muscles, flushing, shivering, chest pains.

antidote*

normal dose
calm the patient, converse, keep out of hazardous situations.

excess dose
Haloperidol, or trifluoperazine, administer as required. Amobarbital sodium, orally, reduces psychotic reactions.

*Antidotes should be administered only by a registered physician.

The Drug Atlas is published solely for the information and education of persons working with or interested in the problem of drug abuse.
MIDWEST RESEARCH INSTITUTE, 425 VOLKER BLVD., KANSAS CITY, MISSOURI 64110
Copyright—December, 1971, Midwest Research Institute

47

The Drug Atlas, Edward J. Woodhouse and Gary W. Webb (Midwest Research Institute, 1973), 46.

at the origin of the hits themselves. Along with other comix images, Mr. Natural was a widely appropriated character, popping up like countercultural clip-art in fliers and underground newspaper layouts. In that sense, Mr. Natural had already become a kind of collective folk icon by 1971, one whose appearance on blotter only further underscores the link between the drug medium and freak print culture.

Though the institute holds many examples of early blotter and the photostats used to produce it, it is difficult to identify particular makers or determine the order of innovations, in the US or abroad. Though they were evidently circulating since the '60s, blotters formally appeared in the UK by 1974, when the *Freek Press* at the Windsor Free Fest reported the presence of orange and white sheets. A year later another blotter, this one "marked with a strawberry," and "weak or strong depending on the strength of your head," was gobbled at the Watchfield Free Festival.[34] For the most part, however, blotter in these earlier years rarely included any "marks" at all.

The absence of figuration made these sheets difficult to deal with. Ghost's original 5 × 20 litmus papers presented a convenient lattice of blue dots, an array that allowed heads to cut the sheets into properly sized individual hits. But a lot of the earliest LSD papers in circulation, hand-dropped and unprinted, were difficult to subdivide; if the spots were blurred or invisible, it was particularly challenging to know how much surface area corresponded to a hit and thus control for dosage. To make the implicit grid of LSD spots more visible on the sheet, some crews started to spot the acid onto graph paper. Though graph paper was commercially available, many of these explicit grids were manufactured within the underground; in an unconscious nod to the working processes Agnes Martin employed for her delicately woven canvases, blotter makers would lay down their homegrown grids with string and glue them by hand before photographing them for offset printing. Other grids were drawn with Rapidograph pens, or indicated with dots or printer crop marks.

Soon arrays of simple images began to stand in for these rectilinear grids, again not unlike Warhol's Campbell's soup cans. *Microgram* describes one early example from 1973: *Orange Bulb Acid*, a "new form of LSD impregnated paper" discovered in Canada. These small sheets of yellowish-orange card stock, measuring two by five inches, featured "98–108 small, closely imprinted electric light bulbs," each containing roughly 50 μg of LSD and selling for three bucks a pop.[35] Except for Ghost, who worked with the dosing machine described above, everyone still hand-dropped the LSD onto the paper, so each light bulb served as a good target for the spotter, as well as a handy guide for the tripper. Hitting the street the same year that Thomas Pynchon told the tale of "Byron the Bulb" in *Gravity's Rainbow*, *Orange Bulb Acid* offered another wry psychedelic meditation on the paradoxical materiality of illumination. The bottom of the sheet featured an impish slogan: "An immaculate conception from rumpled sheet enterprises."

Orange Bulb Acid announces the tension between the abstract sobriety of the grid and the iconic, satiric, and visionary potential of figurative imagery. This tension would become part of the essential dialectic of blotter art, which we will later describe as a psychedelic echo of modern art's mutation from high abstraction to pop. The silk-screened *Captain L*, which almost certainly dates to these early years, embodies this strange polarity. With its prominent graph paper grid (which was designed specifically for the sheet) and hasty execution, *Captain L* appears to be an early experiment in figurative blotter, one that disregards or even enjoys the awkward juxtaposition of mathematical regularity and the sort of hasty sketches cranked out by bored teenage stoners in the back of the class.

The sketch of *Captain L* takes up much of the sheet. Such full-sheet designs would continue to appear throughout the history of street blotter, and have become dominant in the vanity market. But despite the artistic freedom provided by all that space, most dipped sheets condense their imagery to the scale of the individual hit, or sometimes small clusters of hits. This format naturally favors the repetition of a single relatively simple image, which also helps maintain "brand identity" since the identifying marks remain intact at the medium's smallest transferable scale. Some of the most satisfying blotter grids, like *J. R. "Bob" Dobbs* (p. 137), develop Alton Kelley's strategy on the *Trip or Freak* poster in order to present a large image that harmonically supports a grid of smaller iterations of that

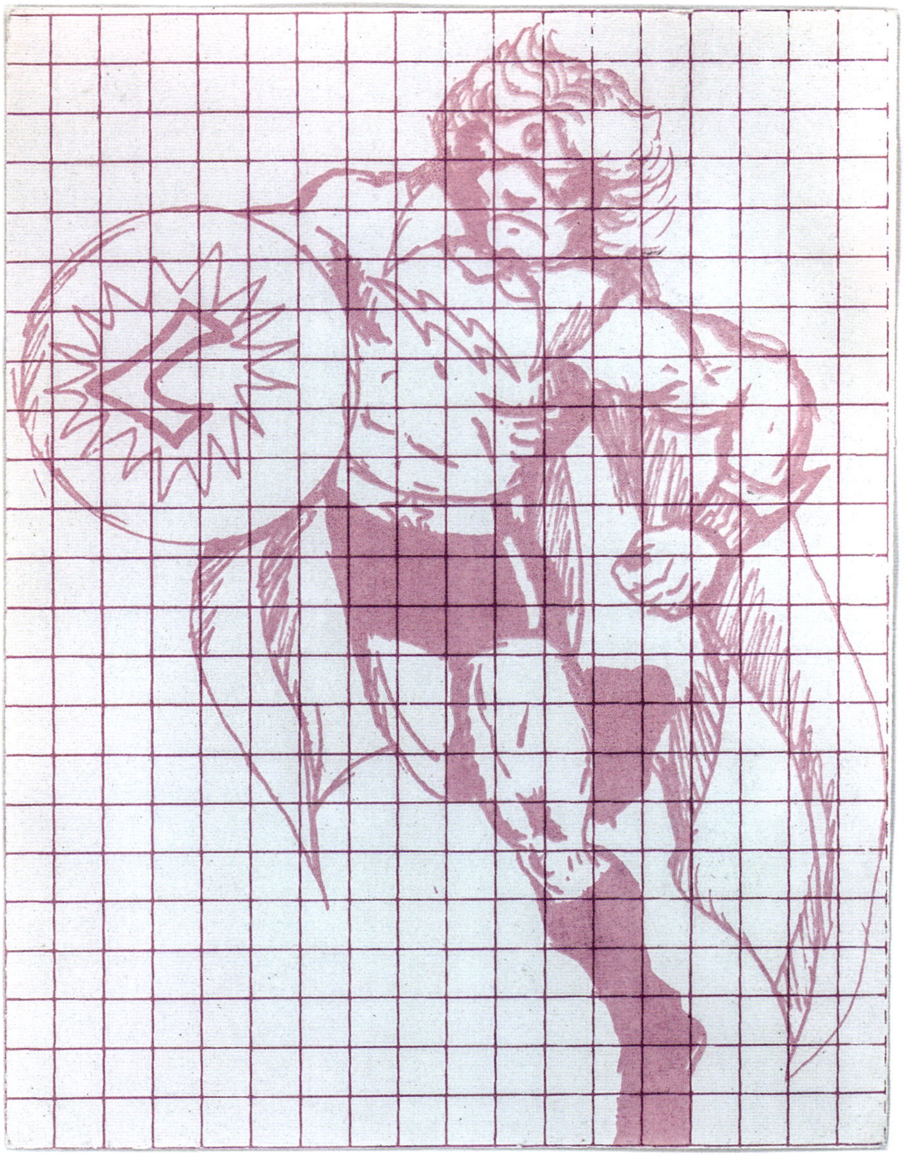

Captain L, San Francisco, mid-1970s. Cut-along sheet, 4½ × 5¾ in. The "L" may have referred to the lavender color of the original LSD crystal.

same image. (Such self-similarity across scale is found throughout the natural world, and familiar as well to many eaters of LSD.) Other blotters play more dynamically with the scalar tension between the hit and the full sheet. *LSD 60* (pp. 210–211) a celebrated vanity image by Stevee Postman from the early 2000s, accentuates the four-way hits in regions of the picture but elsewhere submerges them beneath the dominant macro image of a brain.

Whether made of repeated images or lines or dots, the visible grids on early blotter helped guide the user's hand when it came time to scissor or slice the larger sheets into individual doses. But sometime in the mid-1970s, an unknown producer started to perforate the paper before dosing it with LSD. As anyone who has ever torn out a check knows, die-cut perforations control the direction of the tear while otherwise maintaining the paper sheet's integrity. Similarly, "perfing" blotter made it easier

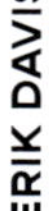

to break the full sheet into smaller units, while also allowing for more careful upstream management of dosage. Aesthetically, perfing materially transmuted the grid, shifting it from the printed surface of the paper to its penetrated depths. While grids of images remained dominant, they were no longer functionally necessary. Though perfing was never universally adopted by blotter makers, such die-cuts eventually became the signature feature that makes blotter "blotter"—even today, when blotter art is widely traded in the absence of LSD.

Perfing was a hassle for blotter makers. Local print shops, whether acting out of ignorance or collusion, would sometimes perform the task with professional die-cutting gear. Otherwise, blotter makers turned to a variety of cruder tools, including knives, pizza cutters, sewing machines, or simple stamp machines, which punched the paper rather than slicing it. Though home perfing was sometimes done one tedious row at a time, many producers chose to create a single "perf block" with multiple rows keyed to the final sheet's specific grid dimensions. These blocks could be run through a press along with single sheets, which would then have to be turned 90 degrees and run through again, often with a different block, to impress the full grid on the paper. One perf block in the III's collection utilizes the toothed strips found on tinfoil boxes, ten of which are attached to the block with photo tape.

Perfing blotter went hand in hand with another key innovation that emerged in the 1970s: dipping. Older methods of decanting drops of LSD onto paper, whether using an eye-dropper or a pin machine, were inherently inconsistent and time-consuming. Lab-grade pipettes were faster and more accurate than droppers, and continue to be used by some producers, but still don't really scale. Dipping whole sheets of paper into a bath of LSD distributes the material much more quickly, and—with some important caveats—offers good control over dosage. The guiding factor here is no longer the physics of the liquid drop as it grips the end of the pin or dropper, but rather the more dependable absorption rate of the paper itself.

The simplest dipping method involves laying perfed sheets flat into short-walled Pyrex cookie sheets filled with LSD in solution, and then drying them in air or on plastic. As you might imagine, the process can be messy, which makes tripping balls a real workplace hazard. Occasionally hoods were used, but a lot of dippers just handled the sheets with gloves, while more cautious characters used tweezers or similar implements. (The hand-stamped *Statue of Liberty* (p. 136) shows the impression of such a grip.) The sloppy factor was eventually solved with a more hermetic and exacting method: sealing the sheets in thick polyethylene bags along with the solvent, which is allowed to completely evaporate before the bag is even opened. With the proper calculation, multiple grams dissolved in the right amount of solvent can be distributed to fat stacks of sheets simultaneously. McCloud is aware of up to 400 sheets being dosed at one go using such "turkey bags."

These methods are not foolproof. Sometimes pipettes, or syringes with needles removed, are still needed to touch up zones of the sheet that haven't properly sucked up the acid. Other absorbency problems are linked to the water that already lurks in most paper stock, blocking the solution from thoroughly coating the paper fibers. Ideally, blotter producers heat and dry their sheets before dipping them, though this step is often skipped, resulting in uneven distribution of the molecule. Hanging the dosed sheets to dry also encourages the material to migrate. On the street, the outer strips of sheets are notorious for containing heavier concentrations of the drug.

Throughout the 1970s and beyond, blotter makers tried out different paper stock—Stonehenge, cotton, rag, woodchip—and experimented with size and grid arrangements. Mathematics was always a factor, given the overriding unit of the gram. For example, the largest format in the 1970s were 12-inch squares, usually perfed into a 20 × 20 grid of chunky hits. At the old-school dose of 250 μg a hit, each 20 × 20 sheet would receive 100 milligrams of LSD, with ten sheets making up the gram.[36] Such sheets were easily subdivided into four 10 × 10 grids, and were sometimes marked as such; *Mr. Natural #1* (p. 118) is a good example here. Aesthetically, the size and format of these early square sheets turned pieces like *Flying Saucers* (p. 167)—which used four hits as a unit of imagery—into unintended masterpieces of pop. But the more immediate affordance of this particular format is that it fit neatly into an LP record jacket, making for easy and discrete transport—as well as a fit reminder of the material links between the recording industry and drug culture, something also reflected in the common adaption of gatefold LP albums into trays to roll joints or deseed cannabis.

The album-sized proportion of the 12-inch blotter also set the stage for one of the more remarkable LSD blotter packages in the annals of the art. In the late 1970s, a single gram of LSD, divided between ten sheets, was distributed inside an LP jacket produced specifically for that purpose. The LP cover shows a lumberjack listening to a small record player that emits musical notes that float up into the sky, where hangs the name of the album: *Disco Hits.* The blotter sheets themselves, which reportedly had the rough heft of an actual LP when packed together, were themselves printed with an array of small round vinyl records.[37]

Disco Hits was by no means the only fancy package produced to house sheets of blotter, a practice that went back to Ghost's original Kodachrome spoof in the 1960s. Throughout the late 1970s and 1980s, many sheets were distributed in elegant and finely made containers as well as screen-printed envelopes. One of the most celebrated blotters of the era featured Mickey Mouse in his *Fantasia* guise as the Sorcerer's Apprentice. These sharply designed four-color sheets came perfed into a hundred units, each featuring their own budding rodent wizard. This was charming enough, but if you bought a gram, you'd get a red lacquered box that was also affixed with an image of Mickey, now surrounded by seventeen gold stars. Inside lay a bundle of forty sheets wrapped in a container of gold foil affixed with another image of the mouse, this time accompanied by the word "Sandoz"—alerting the discerning buyer that the batch was most likely made from LSD synthesized by the original Swiss sorcerers.

The popularity of *Sorcerer's Apprentice* suggested an important shift in the street market for LSD. In a *High Times* article that ran in 1981, Bob Stearne argued that the rapid growth of printed blotter in the late

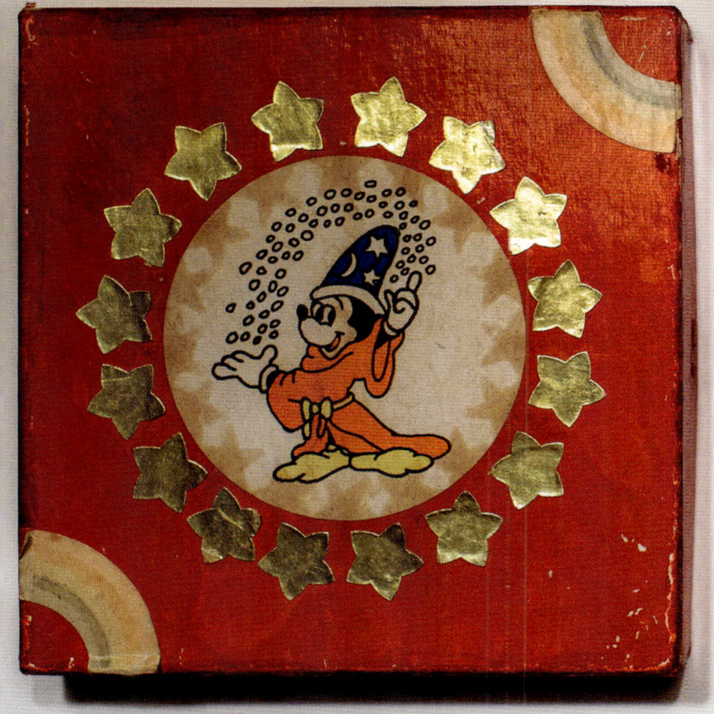

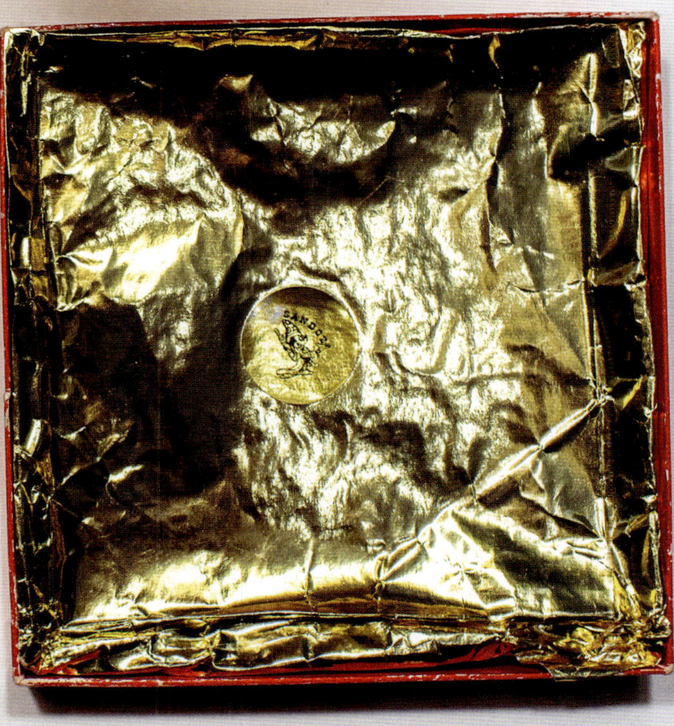

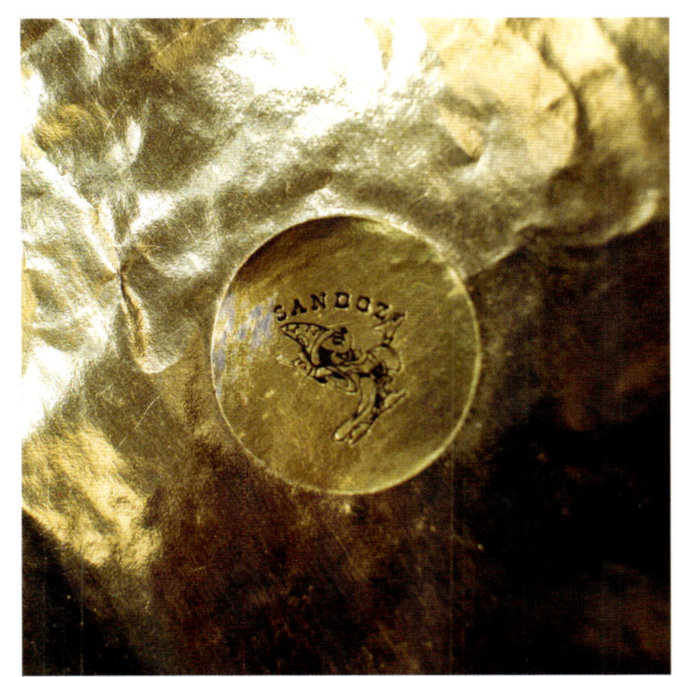

Sorcerer's Apprentice, cardboard container, San Francisco, late 1970s. 5½ × 5½ in.

Sorcerer's Apprentice, inner foil seal, San Francisco, late 1970s. 5 × 5 in.

1970s encouraged the return of real LSD "brands" for the first time since Owsley and Orange Sunshine. According to Stearne, the first new trademark out of the gate was *Red Dragon* (which also came in a green edition), a well-loved and widely distributed blotter that earned a reputation for quality at a time when street folklore still held the (basically false) notion that acid was adulterated with strychnine and speed. But another outfit then swiped the red dragon design for their own inferior product. In Stearne's view, the higher production values reflected in the Mickey blotter represented a strategy that some major players had turned to in order to protect their quality brands.

Stearne's specific claim is debatable, but the more general argument is true: whatever hippie idealism made it through the slog of the 1970s, the acid trade could get pretty cutthroat. Rip-offs, rats, and cons were common in the acid underground; Hells Angels and other ruthless biker gangs continued to be vital players; and more traditional forms of organized crime were known to sometimes seize parts of the market. In the years after the Berlin wall came down, Russian mobsters made aggressive and sometimes violent moves on the international acid market, though over time these mostly came to naught. Outlaws may be honest, at least some of the time, but they are still criminals.

Just how cutthroat the scene could be was proven in 1978 with the brutal slaying of Francis Ragusa in Oakland. A major West Coast LSD distributor, the regional source for Ghost's 5 × 20s, and well known for his Persian carpets and fancy suits, Ragusa was holding nearly 200,000 acid tabs and over a million dollars' worth of ergotamine tartrate—the primary starter material for LSD synthesis—when he was stabbed to death at home. Though the violence was only tangentially related to Ragusa's business, the murder disrupted the acid trade, which was already reeling from Operation Julie, the massive UK drug bust that had brought down Britain's huge microdot empire the year before. And there was more. After a solid decade of cooking and blotter manufacture, Eric Ghost was finally captured in upstate New York.

With Ragusa and Ghost out of the picture, the 5 × 20s dried up, which helped spark a fluorescence of blotter production at the close of the decade. Another galvanizing factor was the decision, made collectively by the families at the highest levels of the LSD trade, to significantly reduce the potency of the average hit. *Sorcerer's Apprentice* and *Flying Saucers* had all been 250 μg a unit. But the street market was changing; as McCloud puts it, things had moved from "Woodstock to the disco." *Red Dragon* was an example of the new weaker hits, pegged at 100 μg but often less, which were sometimes even called "disco hits" to indicate their new jam as party sparkle. There were other reasons for the shift as well. Reducing the dose decreased the likelihood of freakouts among new users, which allowed dealers to move into untapped territories while also lowering the heat on the overall trade. And, of course, more money could be made per gram.

Given the changing mathematics, the new dose dispensation required a corresponding shift in the grid dimensions of individual sheets. Matrices of 25 × 40 units became standard, popular in the increasingly

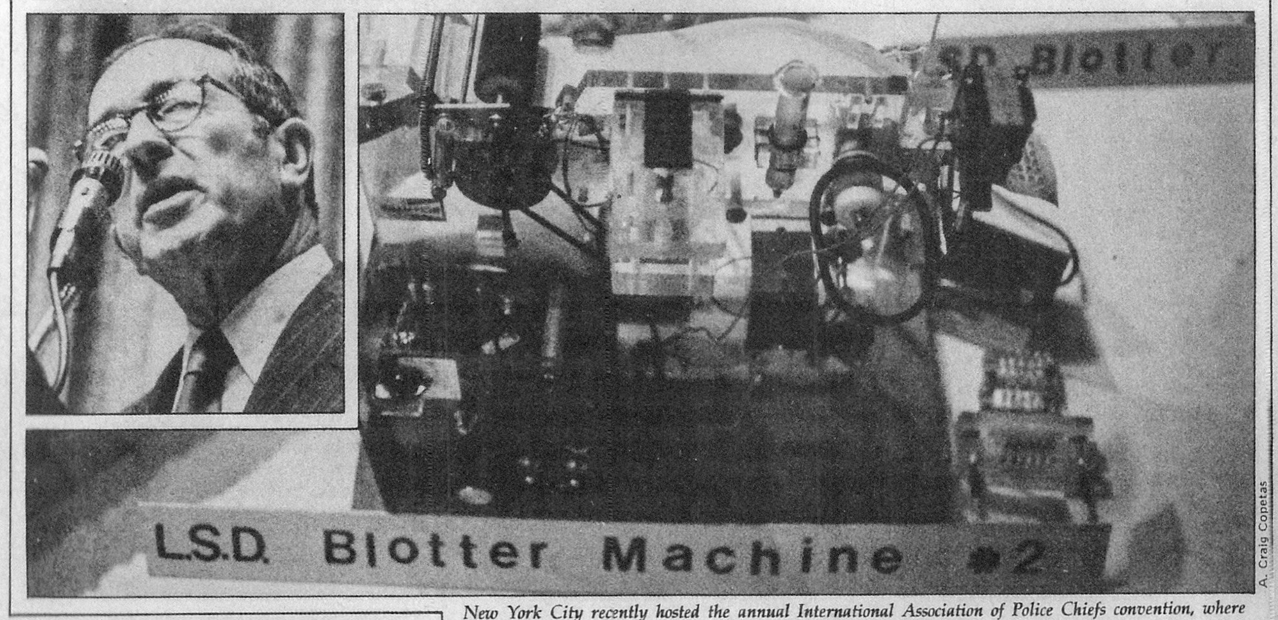

Colombian city of Cali, the cocaine capital of the Southern Hemisphere, said that "one might consider the legalization of the sale and consumption

not be an economic solution for Colombia, since we [the U.S.] will have laws to protect our national production."

he is considered to be a "futurologist" by the State Department. He lectures and writes regularly on the problems faced by future generations.

New York City recently hosted the annual International Association of Police Chiefs convention, where handcuff makers, bullet salesmen and heavy-arms dealers display their wares to the nation's top cops. Here (below) *a Drug Enforcement Administration agent strikes a pose in front of a display depicting the DEA's might. Confiscated LSD-making machine* (above) *put in years of glorious service printing out rolls of acid-dappled blotter paper. Attorney General Griffin Bell* (above left), *chain-smoking cigarettes, told the assembled police bigs that "marijuana ain't my problem, I got other things on my mind."*

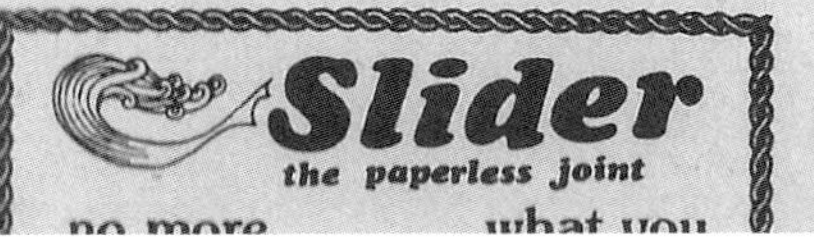

Eric Ghost's confiscated LSD blotter machine, 1979. Photograph from *High Times*, February 1979, 30.

independent European scene as well as in the United States. The 30 × 30 grid also become common, its 900 units easily subdivided into nine 100-hit squares, an arrangement visible on the later *Purple Jesus* (p. 196). (Eleven full sheets like this, plus a single separated "100 block," would equal the almighty gram.) As the market in disco hits developed, imagery flourished and diversified, with smaller boutique runs appearing alongside dominant lines from major players. Gels remained a beloved, if relatively minor part of the market, but tablets were down to a trickle, and by the end of the 1970s blotter dominated the scene.

Blotter was and is cheap, rarely exceeding $2.50 a hit or so, which meant that it actually offered less of a markup per unit that either tablets or gels. What disposed distributors to blotter was volume, ease of production and concealment, and speed of dissemination. Sheets are easy to transport, easy to mail, and easy to hide. When the notorious pranksters in the Tibetan Ukrainian Mountain Troupe descended on British festivals in the 1980s, they smuggled in sheets of acid-impregnated green cartridge paper that, because it resembled gasket paper, was stashed in tool boxes and laminated on-site with illustrated fascia brought in separately.[38] On the production side, blotter offered a number of advantages over tableting. Printing, and especially silk screening, used far less arcane and suspicious technology, and because the sheets were dipped after the fact—"asynchronously," we would say today—blotter makers could maintain some distance from the patently criminal production and distribution of the molecule itself. Blotters also weighed considerably less than tablets, though one of the most common reasons given for blotter's ascent—the passage of so-called carrier weight laws in the 1980s—doesn't really hold water.[39]

Illustrated blotter is also fun. Whether circulated on the scale of multiple sheets, sometimes called "pages," or as hits or "ten-strips" swapped outside the club, blotters are pleasant to handle: potent graphic fetishes that boast the gentle crispness of a thin matzah. Like chocolate bars with their grid of grooves, blotter asks to be fondled, torn and crumbled, nibbled. But like coins or stamps or show flyers, it also has the feel of ephemera you might want to hold onto for a while. As a crucial but underrecognized vector of underground print culture, illustrated blotter not only promises individual transport, but affirms participation in a marginal and collective demimonde that was and is sustained partly through an ongoing publishing effort, one that relies on print's capacity to build fanciful alternative worlds with mechanically reproduced signs. When Mr. Natural waltzed across the first printed blotter, he offered the ironic cartoon promise that the acid revelation just keeps on truckin', a promise you could participate in by eating the underground comix panel rather than just looking at it.

By placing illustrated blotter in the larger context of printed media, we get a better handle on its growth in the mid- to late 1970s, when "the" counterculture—never united in itself—splintered into the variety of subcultures that came to define the 1980s underground. As radical newspapers fell by the wayside, or became merely "alternative," the rebel DIY spirit moved into punk publications, flyer art, photocopied collages, and zines. This is why a savvy psychedelic freak like Mark McCloud started hanging out with edgelords like V. Vale of RE/Search and the Texas Dada punks of *Sluggo!* magazine. Despite its hippie origins, illustrated blotter comes to flourish in these later, more ironic and hardcore days, when underground print efforts sustained a satirical, surrealist, and anarchic space of anonymous culture-making and love-bombing in an increasingly confused, co-opted, and reactionary era. Criminality may or may not lend blotter "authenticity," but it does give it a great deal of outsider panache, one that long outlasted the hippie children's crusade. No wonder that Mark McCloud accepted Mr. Natural's invitation to a tea party.

The Hayes Street Gang

The most storied neighborhood in the history of freakdom is Haight-Ashbury. But what defines a neighborhood? Stand at the fabled corner of Haight and Ashbury and face north. Walk two blocks and you reach the Panhandle, a long, narrow, aptly named appendage of Golden Gate Park that hosted many a bongo romp and free pancake breakfast back in the day. Keep walking north and you enter another area of spacious and once rather run-down Victorian houses. One block up from the Panhandle, you hit Hayes Street, whose small clusters of commercial establishments, over half a century ago, provided a somewhat quieter, gentler alternative for the hippies, runaways, and other funky free spirits drawn to the Haight in its heyday.

By the early 1970s, Hayes Street's most venerable establishment was the Blue Unicorn. You could call it the first hippie coffeehouse, or, more accurately, the coffeehouse where beatniks mutated into hippies. Founded by bohemian refugees from North Beach, the Unicorn first opened on Frederick Street in the Haight in 1962 before moving to 1927 Hayes Street in 1965. Besides boasting the cheapest joe in town, the Unicorn served as a de facto community center, hosting poetry readings, chess meets, and gatherings of the Sexual Freedom League. It served food until the health department took too close a look at the kitchen.

In the 1970s, with the general scene in decline, the Unicorn remained an informal place for acid folk to meet and coordinate what McCloud calls "non-obtrusive LSD behavior." Even as the coffeehouse went through various hands and incarnations, it continued to host this rarified underground, which included a local crew of blotter makers, some of whom immortalized the cafe in the 1980s with a run of sheets featuring prancing blue unicorns. McCloud affectionately refers to this bunch as "the Hayes Street Gang," though they weren't a gang so much as a loose network of artists, printers, dealers, and esoteric freaks who hewed to the informal but Freemasonic ethos of the LSD underground.

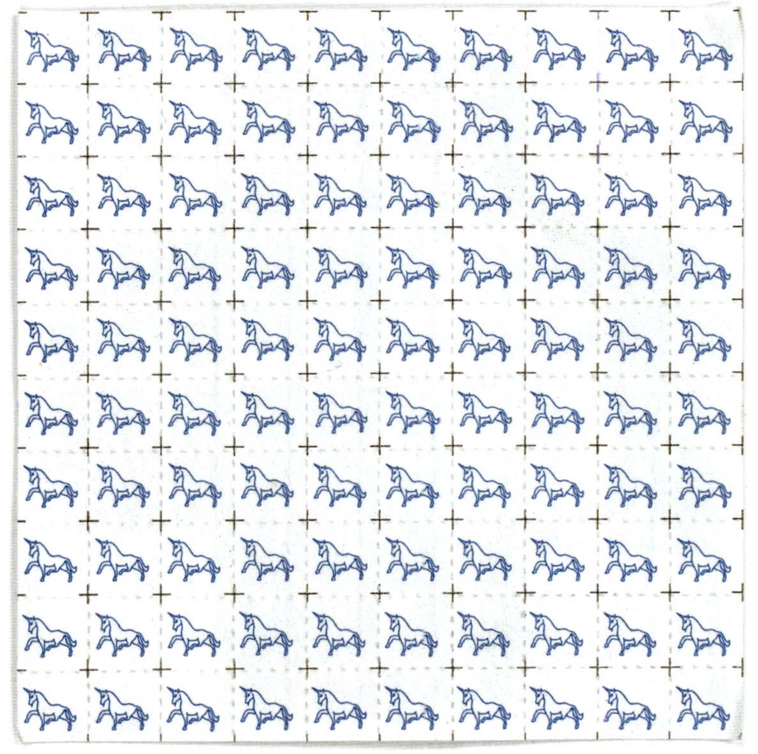

Blue Unicorn, San Francisco, ca. 1980. 3¼ × 3¼ in.

One of the earliest nodes in this blotter assemblage was Raymond Knight, who mostly went by Rocky. A gruff, imposing man from North Carolina, Rocky possessed the furious aspect of the bloodthirsty dharma protectors pictured on the Tibetan thangkas he liked to collect. He earned the handle "Rocky" for the intransigence he had once displayed when two armed hoods tried to pry the location of his hashish stash out of him. They shot him twice, but Rocky refused to budge.

Rocky ran the Floating Lotus Gallery, a tiny storefront on Hayes that he packed with visionary art, Tibetan mandalas, and a display of his old marksmanship trophies. Rocky also cranked out some of the earliest blotters in the 1970s, those large LP-sized silk-screened sheets with big fat hits. One standout featured a grid of labyrinths inspired by the classic Chartres design that appears prominently at San Francisco's hill-topping Grace Cathedral. Rocky also made the first sheet featuring the signs of the zodiac, which proved a popular motif over the years in part because he kept at it, trying to iron out the mathematical discordances caused by fitting twelve astrological signs into various blotter grids. When it came to the paper, Rocky refused to work with anything other than sturdy, 80-pound woodchip, preferred in part because of certain quasi-mystical ideas he held about how efficiently trees distribute water and nutrients.

In time, Rocky largely left blotter production behind as he climbed into the upper echelons of the LSD world. He grew particularly tight with an acid family based in Bolinas, a remote village at the Pacific edge of Marin County that had been colonized by bohemians. This crew was largely led by women, including Sarah Matzar, an important acid producer who spent a decade or so in the outer orbit of the Grateful Dead scene.[40] Matzar was the person who figured out that the indentations on some fluorescent light fixtures made a perfect mold for gelatin pyramids. A gifted artist and weaver, Matzar later produced blotter based on her own designs, including the charming *Camouflage* (p. 141). The code word for sheets of acid in her operation—which McCloud calls the "Bolinas Girl Gang"—was the marvelously unmacho "quilts."

Blotter makers related to the acid families in different ways. Some were tightly integrated into a single family that sold already dipped sheets at scale, or provided clients purchasing grams of crystal with undipped, pre-perfed blotter as a courtesy service—one that maintained control of the paper while also passing on some of the labor. Other blotter makers acted as independent agents, working with multiple clients and LSD producers, sometimes in competition with one another and sometimes in cahoots. Design ideas as well were decentralized. They might come from family-level producers, or distributors seeking to establish their brand identity with an "exclusive," or even just party people who wanted a special one-off for an event. Often the plans came from the blotter makers themselves, were executed by hired artists, and then pitched to multiple producers. The ideal product was a win-win marriage between compelling design and excellent chemistry, though the same design might get loaded over time with different crystal from different cooks, especially if the image proved popular.

As such, Hayes Street had plenty of room for the artisan approach represented by Tony Smith, a blotter maker whom everyone called Forester. He was from an accomplished East Coast family that was at once bohemian and genteel. His mother, Suzanne Bloch, taught lute and harpsichord at Julliard, and would sometimes perform in Renaissance costume. Suzanne's father was the composer Ernest Bloch, whose singular compositions were saturated with his Jewish heritage; her sister was good friends with Frida Kahlo. Forester's father, Paul Smith, chaired Columbia University's mathematics department and made important contributions to geometric topology—a rather psychedelic subfield devoted to intertwingled manifolds. One friend of the family was Albert Einstein, who sometimes played violin, poorly, with Suzanne. During one forest outing, little Forester peed on the great man's shoulders.

Paul's status didn't help Forester when the young man was busted selling a nickel bag of cannabis on the Columbia campus. Forester was already "experienced" at this point, having been turned on by no less august a figure than Timothy Leary, who dropped a sugar cube on his tongue during a peace march in 1967. After the weed bust, Forester

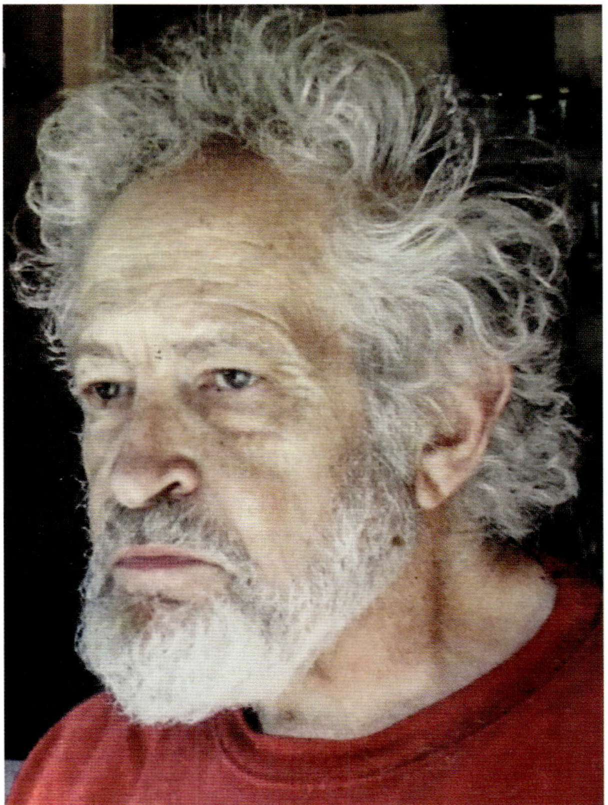

Tony Smith, a.k.a. Forester. Undated Polaroid photo.

hijacked the family station wagon and drove west until the car broke down and he hitched the rest of the way to San Francisco. Landing in the Haight, he immersed himself in the scene, becoming what his later business partner "Neil Benedict" called "a hippie in the true Digger style." He studied metaphysics and numerology, baked bread to give away, and lived in the Family Circus commune on Oak Street, where he had a kid with a witch-woman and then took off. He got into screen printing and opened a shop on 1943 Hayes Street eventually called Gilfeather Graphics, which made posters, T-shirts, signs, and greeting cards. Forester loved the outdoors—hence the nickname—and he named the shop after the road where his family had their country home, back in Vermont, where Forester once worked as a fire lookout and a gilfeather is a kind of local turnip.

Benedict, Forester's printing partner, was a younger man who didn't get to San Francisco until 1972. By that point, the bloom was definitely off the hippie rose; arriving as a teenager from the north woods of Wisconsin, Benedict found the Haight "almost post-apocalyptic." With a background in theater and media, Benedict was primed for the still-bubbling underground print scene, and enrolled in the graphic design program at San Francisco City College. Later he got a job at a pivotal Black community newspaper run out of the Fillmore, which also did printing for grassroots political campaigns and the Black Panthers. Benedict was one of the few white guys who worked there, doing darkroom tech, layout, and paste-up—skills that he would later bring to Gilfeather.

Benedict apprenticed with Forester, and together the two men refined the art of silk screening. They moved within a milieu of serious acid folk, but from Benedict's perspective, the decision to start making blotter grew out of their craft enthusiasm rather than any criminal aspirations. "It seemed like a good little side project," Benedict says today, "a great DIY, kitchen-sink operation that anyone could do." There never was a master plan. "Maybe someone else had one but from my point of view, it was just like, oh, here's another order to fill." Though LSD had been a profound spiritual teacher for Benedict, he did not share the acid evangelism that drove some producers and distributors, and he wasn't pleased with its drift toward the disco. "I considered LSD a sacrament, and at a certain point, it was no longer sacred."

One of Gilfeather's earliest blotter pieces was a grid of spades the two men screened around the middle of the 1970s, executed in both red and black. Oddly, they printed *Spades* on actual blotting paper, which had already been abandoned by most makers as a pointless annoyance. Because the sheets were unperfed, the spades were encased within a "cut-along" lattice of fat lines to guide the hand. In many of the subsequent unperfed sheets they produced, this lattice morphed into an elegant grid of variably sized blue dots, which McCloud suspects alluded to Ghost's original *Blue Dots*. Gilfeather productions featuring the blue dot grid include *Golden Dolphins*, *Snowflakes*, and the minimalist *Blue Grid*, which included only the cut-along lattice of points—a perfectly modernist integration of form and function. With *Snowflakes*, the duo also started to print little birthday-card-style envelopes to hold the sheets—an aesthetic decision that became quite popular and that Benedict now chalks up to marketability.

Marketability may have been a factor, but something like the joy of handicraft also played a role. Forester loved experimenting with his screens. He did loads of test runs, constantly refined the color, and made subtle alterations throughout a run. Such playful variations are a natural affordance of silk screening, of course, something exploited by pop artists like Warhol as well. Sometimes the Gilfeather team would outsource runs of a basic image to an offset print shop, but then screen different color layers onto the sheets for variety. There were other reasons to vary images as well. One of Gilfeather's more widespread and familiar icons was a peace dove, which appeared in many different color editions. But if you looked closely, you could see that the olive branch went through tiny changes between runs, with leaves appearing and disappearing. From his conversations with Forester, McCloud learned that these changes sometimes had a purpose: as with the different colors employed, subtle variations in the graphics allowed distributors to organize paper dosed at different strengths, and to track the paper as it made its way through the pyramid of dealers. If a bust went down and the specific variation could be identified, then the acid families could trace the problem back up the chain.

Soon Forester and Benedict started perfing their paper, a time-consuming process that screamed for automation. Luckily, a lot of old and heavy letter-press machines were getting junked in the 1970s. Forester and Benedict got their hands on a small flatbed proof press slated for the dump and figured out how to adapt the chase—the heavy steel frame that holds lead type—with blades and wooden shims to make an

Snowflakes, Gilfeather, San Francisco, late 1970s. Blotter: 4 × 5 in.; envelope: 5⅝ × 4⅜ in.

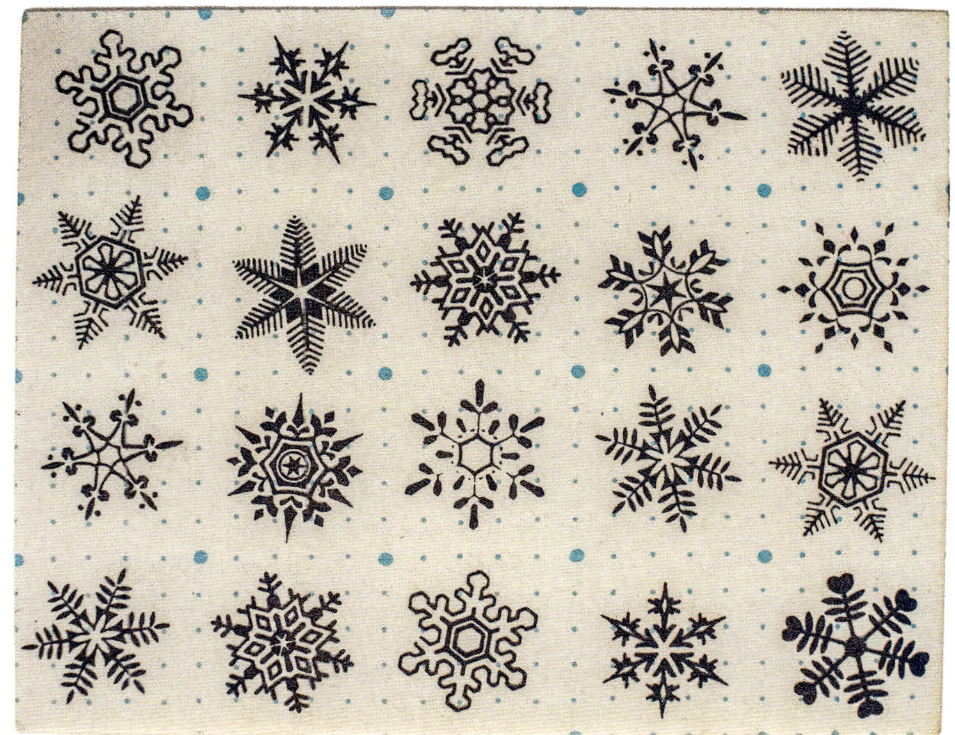

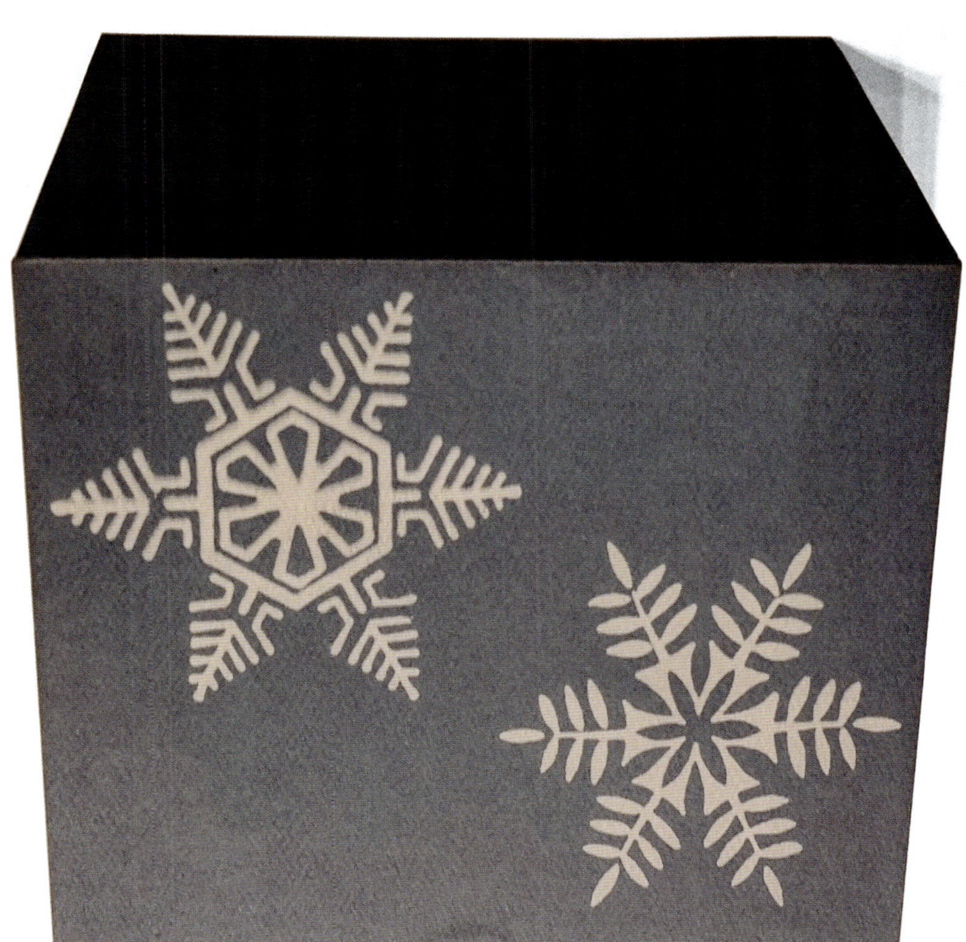

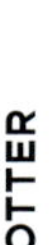

effective perforating form. Later, toward the end of his blotter career, Forester enlisted his teenage son to work this manual perf press after class.

The team also experimented with paper stock. Though some blotter makers preferred fancy art paper, Forester and Benedict found most of that stuff way too thick, taking forever to dry and requiring too much solvent down the line. But a lot of the commercial paper available was sweetened with dyes to make it white and bright, dyes that could interfere with the dipping process. Fluorescent additives also prevented manufacturers from using black light—which registers the natural fluorescence of LSD—to distinguish loaded paper from undipped stock. Inks too needed to be selected carefully and sometimes had to be loaded with additional metallic particles in order to survive their later encounter with "the sauce." That said, nobody wants to ingest a lot of metallic ink. Knowing they were essentially making tiny morsels of toxic food, Forester and Benedict tried to reduce their overall use of ink, outlining images rather than filling them in.

Horus, San Francisco, 1979. First edition, 9 × 11 in. Though this example is unmarked, the sheet was designed for perforation.

The two men made a lot of blotter over the years, their goods shipped and munched around the world. As a true hippie, Forester was explicit about the intent of his visionary art, explaining in a late interview that he wanted Gilfeather's designs to "elevate people spiritually and consciously, so that when they did get high on it their minds would *already* be attuned to a greater spiritual awareness."[41] As the product line developed, Gilfeather became something of a custom shop, doing special editions and smaller runs alongside large orders for the families. Some ideas were provided by mid-level dealers who wanted to put their own stamp on the grams they spliced out for the street. One young European fellow wanted to cross borders without fuss or fear, so Benedict put together a simple notebook of dosed graph paper that was bound with a light, low-tack adhesive and was easy to hide in plain sight. Most of the time, the pair came up with their own ideas, playful full-sheet designs like *Four-way Notes* (p. 132) and *Ants* (p. 158), or more minimalist pieces like *Highway 1*, named for the road that runs the length of California's coast.

Though these pieces are sharp and made with care, Benedict insists there wasn't much behind the designs, many of which were lifted from readily available clip art sources. Much of the imagery was not particularly "psychedelic" or countercultural—sometimes it was anything but. At the same time, psychedelic perception is notorious for its capacity to transform ordinary features of the world into oracular and animated signs, like Brian Barritt's encounter with the dancing Mr. Cube. As such, even frivolous blotter designs might carry additional layers of meaning, sometimes by virtue of their juxtaposition with the drugs they hold, and sometimes through hidden intent. Before he died, Forester told McCloud that he chose the suit of spades—historically derived from the pike or halberd, and whose ace was known as the "death card" in Vietnam—as a representation of ego death, the supreme mystic *desideratum* for the classic acid generation.

Then there is the matter of the pyramid. A number of blotters coming out of Hayes Street in the early years featured flat "cut-along" triangles, pyramids that you would instantly recognize as such because they were decorated with eyes. The most haunting of these was *Horus*, which

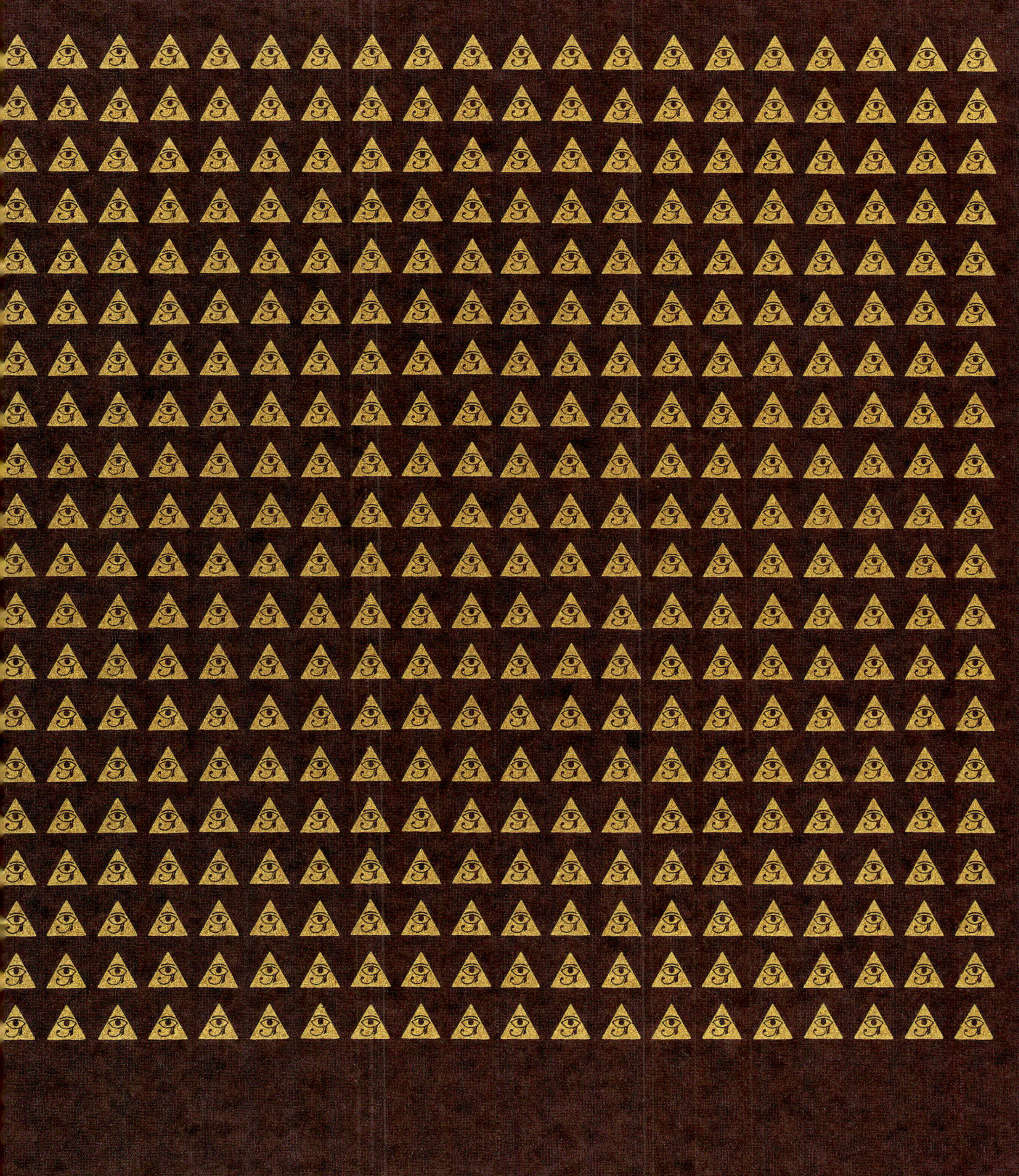

featured an Egyptian eye of Horus inside a triangle, initially gold and, in a later edition, black on beige. Acting like a hyperlink hidden in the III archive, *Horus* in turn invokes another enigmatic character from those years: "Manny Vogel," a whip-smart gay man from New Jersey who lived for a time in a converted cab dispatch garage near Polk Street, San Francisco's original queer neighborhood.

A generous fellow fond of disguises, the owner of numerous hippie crash-pads, Manny was an "acid lord" who sold a lot of loaded blanks but also contributed to the Hayes Street publishing effort. Manny was also a serious occultist. He studied Aleister Crowley and collected books on metaphysics, Rosicrucianism, and Kabbalistic lore (as well as many a tome on actual chemistry). He claimed to use occult methods, and maybe even sex magic, to enchant the chocolate pyramid confections he made and sold, which were so heavily dosed with cannabis that it probably didn't matter much one way or the other. Manny also served as the master of the Pyramid Club, an underground gathering of heads, mystics, and pansexuals that likely gave Manny the opportunity to break out the Masonic robes and props he also collected. For a while, the Pyramid Club met at an occult book shop Manny ran in the lower Haight before he decided he didn't want it anymore and simply gave it back to its original owner. Despite all this pyramid power, though, the actual image that inspired *Horus* may have far more quotidian origins. Benedict insists the icon was whipped up by a Gilfeather artist who specialized in commercial logos. On the other hand, another friend of Manny's points to the retail sign of Pyramid Liquor, a store Manny frequented out on Geary. That's the thing about some mysteries: they reverberate all the way through the banal.

Benedict and Forester were also acolytes of the freak occultism that was intertwined with Bay Area psychedelia and, to a degree, San Francisco's innovative sex culture. Forester read widely in witchcraft and Eastern mysticism, and used his Atari 800, an early personal computer, to investigate numerology in the early 1980s. Benedict, turned off by the myriad of newly minted spiritual groups that wanted to "reinvent the taco," immersed himself instead in the Theosophy and Rosicrucianism of an earlier generation. The two men's esoteric interests informed their handicraft as well; studying Kabbalah and hieroglyphs, they came to believe in a "language of symbols" that informed their work on underground logos. And they also owed their friendship to one of the more curious mystagogues of the Haight Street era: an enigmatic and notoriously corpulent friend of Manny's known as the Electric Buddha.

Born Richard Duran, the Buddha was from a small town in Idaho where his father worked as a pharmacist. He was an awkward young man, and fled home to join the army. He lived in Germany, then New York in the late 1950s, and ran a bookstore in Portland before moving to San Francisco. The Buddha was already on the scene during the Summer of Love, when he was listed on the masthead of *Vanguard*, the monthly magazine of a local gay liberation youth organization. His role at the publication? "Phallic Symbol." In *Amazing Dope Tales and Haight Street Flashbacks*, Stephen Gaskin describes the Buddha as a mind power guru and methedrine freak who vowed to shoot speed until he either attained enlightenment or destroyed his soul.[42] A good friend of Manny's, Duran ran crash pads and performed as sage and guiding light, especially to the unmoored young men he often wound up sheltering and loving. Benedict was one of these young men, and he became enamored with the Buddha's vibe, part esoteric hierophant and part mother hen. Benedict served as the steward at one of the crash pads, keeping the place as clean and uncrazy as possible.

At some point, the Buddha introduced Benedict to Forester, whom Duran had known since the days they both lived at the Family Circus commune. The introduction made sense. The Buddha had already been nudging Forester toward silk screening, and Benedict was a trained graphic artist who needed somewhere to pour his restless energy. Though there may have been no master plan, the arrangement likely grew out of Buddha's own enigmatic but likely significant relationship to the acid scene and the production of the earliest San Francisco blotter, whose sometimes peculiar geometric designs might have struck all manner of cosmic overtones in a mystagogic mind like his.

The Buddha was a print guy as well as a psychedelic metaphysician. In 1970, the same year he was hanging around with Crowley acolytes at the Richmond District's Kaaba Clerk House, including the future Ordo Templi Orientis Caliph Grady McMurtry, the Buddha published a chapbook called *Funk*. This proto-zine was stuffed with typewritten mystical riffs as well as esoteric and humorous collages, whose tone and content—"Was Noah the son of a space traveler?"—directly foreshadow the cosmic japes of the Church of the Subgenius years later. In the late 1970s, the Buddha contributed more essays and collages to an underground newspaper, alternately called *Stains (on Paper)* and *Astral Stains*, that was printed at Rip-Off Press and published with the help of Benedict, who did some of the darkroom processing late at night at his newspaper job in the Fillmore.

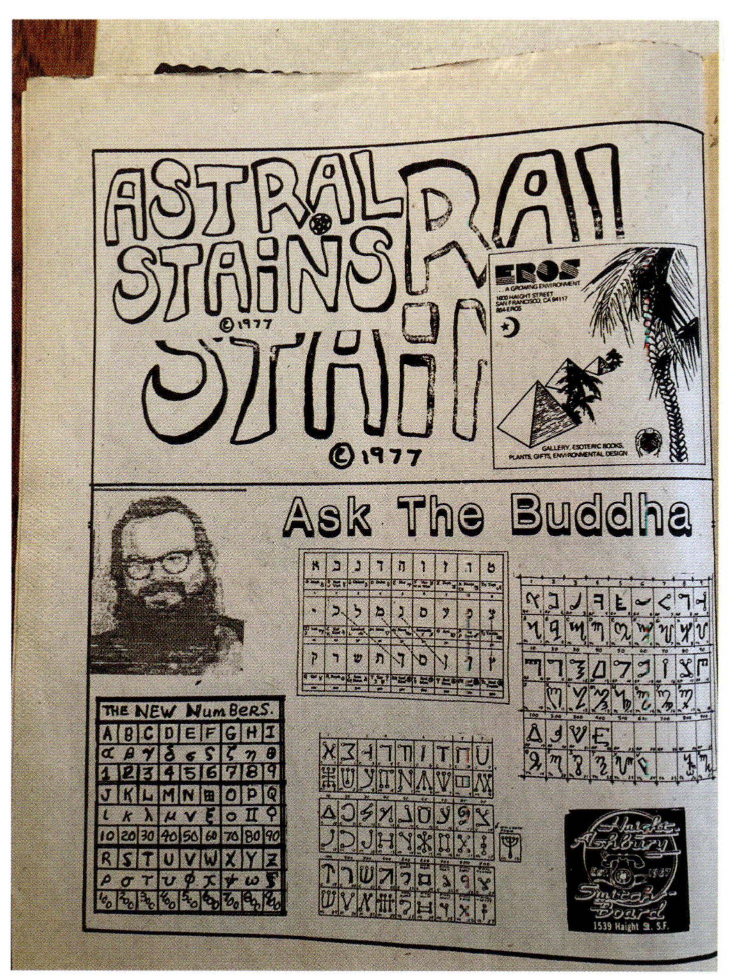

"Ask the Buddha," *Astral Stains* 1, no. 3, 1977

Forgotten except for occasional mentions in queer media archives, *Stains* is a marvelous spore print of the San Francisco underground in the late 1970s, an uncanny commingling of last-ditch freak mysterioso and the new art-damaged snarl of punk. Radical sex culture was one of the publication's themes, with lists of local gay hotels, free passes to glory holes in the Castro ("not valid after midnight"), and essays critiquing "Judeo-Christian" sexual mores, including the repression of adolescent sexuality. These threads were woven into a weird post-hippie tapestry that included articles on UFOs and Crowley alongside a cornucopia of colorful advertisements and occult graphics: magic squares, Egyptian pyramid diagrams, gematria keys, and cybernetic remixes of the Tree of Life. Occasionally Benedict, who did paste-up and ads, included pieces of clip art—like an acorn—that also showed up on Hayes Street blotter.

Manny and the Electric Buddha were not the only men straddling San Francisco's gay scene and the city's acid underground. As is clear to anyone familiar with the psychedelic antics of the Cockettes or the Angels of Light—legendary freak-drag performance crews of the high and holy hippie days—these worlds were once so tightly entwined that they were effectively indistinguishable. As one long-time San Francisco cannabis queer put it, "The first gays were hippies."

By the 1980s, some of the most delightful pieces of blotter art coming out of San Francisco were from the decidedly queer hand of Shep Mishkin, a jokester and love-bombing pothead known on the street as Grandpa. Jewish, and probably from the East Coast—Mishkin kept his cards close to his chest, even among friends—Grandpa lived for a while at the Castro Castle, a communal house run by cannabis activist Dennis Peron, who also very much enjoyed his LSD. Both men were galvanized by the city's AIDS crisis, with Grandpa joining a local aid agency that cared for the terminally ill called the Shanti Project. He also helped Peron establish the Cannabis Buyers' Club, the seed crystal of the medical marijuana movement. Gilbert Baker was another friend and fellow Castro communard. The celebrated creator of the LGBT rainbow flag, Gilbert received his vision for the now global banner while high on acid and glitter at a San Francisco nightclub. Years later, Grandpa issued a blotter based on Baker's flag (p. 164).

Lots of old school blotter hits were physically large. Mishkin was the first to seriously shrink the size of the hits; the smallest perfs in the III collection are a run of his tiny *Diamonds*, printed on very thin card stock and resembling glittering snowflakes. Ink-load was a consideration behind the size reduction, as was discretion. Mishkin was also drawn to the ludic power of cartoon characters on blotter, but didn't just steal them from the funny pages. His delightful *Pink Flamingos* (p. 176) features cartoon birds in human costume, including a cowboy with chaps and a leather daddy brandishing a whip. Mishkin was also responsible for *Dancing Test Tubes*, whose cavorting cartoon vials paid homage to the mascot of PharmChem Research Foundation, a nonprofit Menlo Park lab that tested anonymous submissions of street drugs and made the data publicly available.

After an acid lab that Grandpa was associated with got raided in the 1990s, he skipped out to Amsterdam, Europe's blotter capital, but returned after four years. Grandpa was never busted, keeping at his trade well into the 2000s; the last piece he made before he died was a celebrated pair of cherubs.

There were other crews who contributed significantly to the San Francisco blotter scene, about whom less is known, at least by Mark McCloud. Peace, Incorporated, which may have been partly based on the East Coast, were likely the first outfit to use computers, which gave them tighter control over color, whose ever-shifting values lend *Clowns* (p. 155)

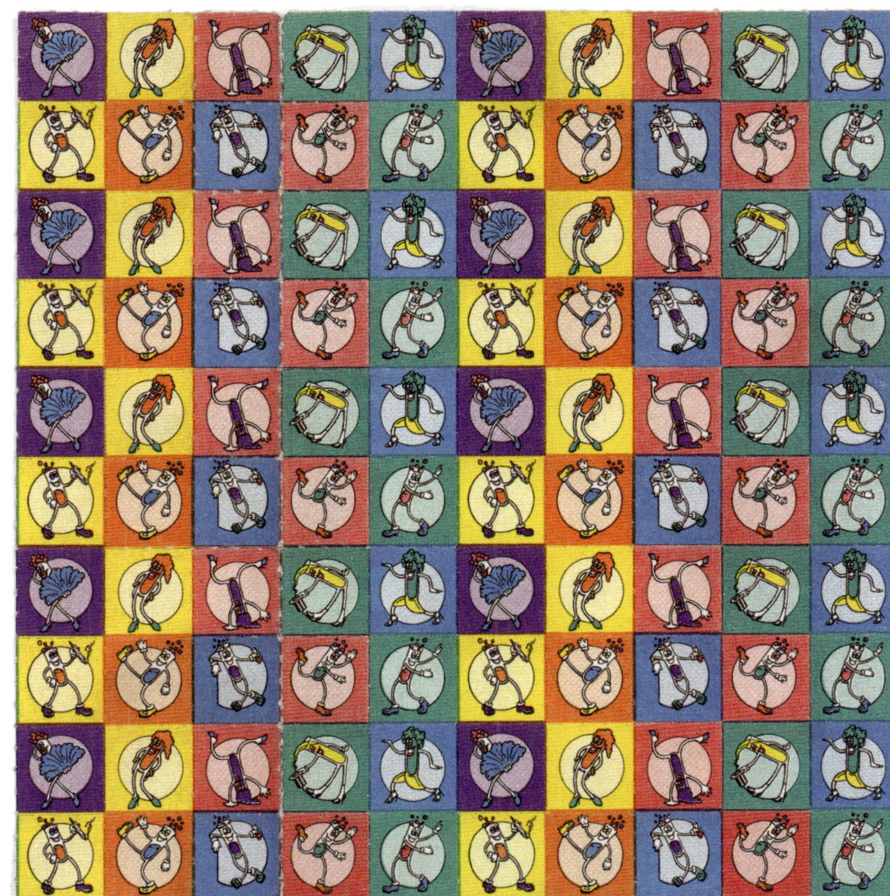

Dancing Test Tubes, *Grandpa, San Francisco, mid-1980s. 5 × 5 in.*

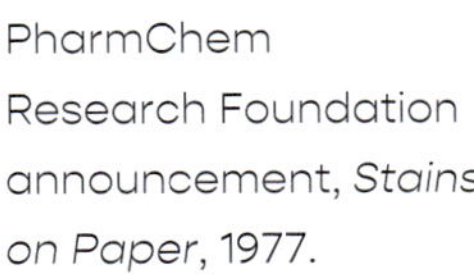

PharmChem Research Foundation announcement, *Stains on Paper*, 1977.

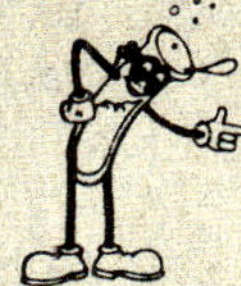

PharmChem Research Foundation

PharmChem Research Foundation is a private, nonprofit, public-interest research group that provides factual information about illicit and licit drugs. Samples from throughout the U.S. submitted to our **Analysis Anonymous®** drug testing service have demonstrated the continual appearance of new substances, widespread availablility of dangerously adulterated and poorly synthesized drugs and gross misrepresentation of street drugs.

Analysis Anonymous® drug testing service. Unbaised confidential information about the true content of illicit "street" drugs. To use this service, send one dose of the sample with $5.00 (cash or money order) and include either a 5-digit identification of your choice or a return address. (Please don't use numbers such as 12345 or 66666.) If possible, we'd like to know what the sample is being sold as, street price, origin of sample (city & state) and indicate whether any undesirable side effects are known.

To obtain results, telephone the laboratory between 4-5 p.m. (415/322-9941) 5 days after mailing and ask for a report using your 5-digit number.

The PharmChem Newsletter, published 10 times/year, available by subscription. Accurate reference material on drugs and drug use trends. Articles on current drug related topics as well as Analaysis Anonymous® test results. Sample copy available.

For further information call or write PHARMCHEM RESEARCH FOUNDATION, 1844 Bay Road, Suite 205, **Palo Alto** 94303. 322-9941.

an almost woozy surreality. Their *Chill Pill* (p. 4) presents a grid of TV sets, but if you look closely, you see that each tube on the sheet is broadcasting a different blurry image. There was also the group that McCloud calls the "Red Gang," named for the distinctive red cotton rag they used, which breaks up and fuzzes differently than most blotter paper.[43] The Red Gang put out a sheet featuring the trendy *Astrogirl* figure designed by Claudia Rey for the New York rave shop Liquid Sky. They were also responsible for one of the more pugnacious blotters of the era: a grid built from the official seal of the FBI, an ominous mandala that probably disturbed some acid eaters as much as it did law enforcement.

San Francisco was by no means the only source of blotter in the 1980s. A few outfits made their homes in New York and Florida, but Europe played an increasingly significant role. Underground acid labs had existed in Western Europe since the 1960s, with Ronald Stark's French operation supplying the LSD used for Orange Sunshine by the early 1970s, when Europe also became the primary source of the all-important precursor materials. But though a few labs continued to produce acid through the 1980s, especially in Amsterdam and Switzerland, much of the raw crystal used in Europe still came, one way or the other, from the West Coast.

Some blotters that circulated widely on the Continent and in the UK—like *Gryphon and Lion*—were made in the States but designed for export to Europe. When Antonio Piñeda got busted in Spain, he was holding copious sheets of *Conan El Barbaro*, a blotter issue produced in San Francisco in the wake of the 1982 Arnold Schwarzenegger film. But the globe-trotting Piñeda—a Salvadoran who attended Carlos Santana's high school in the Mission District, and later served as one of Ragusa's acid lieutenants—probably ordered the *El Barbaro* design with Spanish-speaking countries in mind. In the United States, the sheets were sometimes called "Mexican acid," a half-fantasized acknowledgment of the thriving psychedelic cultures south of the border.

Europe saw a lot of local blotter production as well, especially once the rave scene kicked into gear. At UK raves at least, inexpensive acid was always a popular alternative to overpriced ecstasy tablets, and by the early 1990s, the Inter City Firm, an often brutal English hooligan crew from East London, were reportedly offering a wide selection of different blotters for sale alongside the grams of crystal they were slinging. Other European operations were started by renegades from the States, some of whom had done time and needed to set up elsewhere after being released from prison.

One significant expat was "Acid Eric" Hodgman, who was born in Britain but lived in San Francisco during the psychedelic '60s, dealing Owsley tabs and announcing shows at the Avalon Ballroom. Hounded by the IRS, he hightailed it to India in the late 1960s, becoming a major fixture in the traveler freak scene whose home base lay in Goa. In the early 1980s, Hodgman, who sported a big beard and a colorful magian style, set up an LSD operation in Amsterdam. The famously drug-tolerant city had already become the continent's hub for acid, which was often distributed through already existing hashish networks. Hiring local artists and designers, Hodgman was responsible for popular pieces like *Purple Om*, a run of *Zippy the Pinhead* (different from the one included here), and, perhaps most notably, *Gorbachev*, which Hodgman released as a kind of glasnost spell just before the Berlin wall came tumbling down, and which subsequently became one of the most iconic blotters of the 1980s.

Assisting Hodgman in his efforts was Ed Visser, a Dutch blotter maker who produced some of the most arresting and celebrated European sheets of the underground era. Raised blue-collar, Visser didn't like school much and started working at a local printing shop when he was fourteen. With the exception of some wandering hippie years, he never really stopped working. In the 1970s, he helped make posters for the legendary Amsterdam club Paradiso, which showcased his clean, bright, and controlled aesthetic. Visser also liked acid. He first encountered blotter in 1971, when a nurse friend who worked for the controversial LSD psychiatrist Jan Bastiaans showed up at Visser's forest commune in Arnhem with dosed sheets she had swiped from the lab, hand-stamped units with red skulls they cut with scissors and enjoyed thoroughly.

Around 1983, Visser was asked to bring his professional skills to bear on the production of blotter. He had the chops: design and layout talent, knowledge of paper and inks, and a knack with machine perforation. The first sheet he designed featured a witch he lifted from a clip-art book, but he made his mark when he helped his pal Acid Eric honor Gorbachev. Visser adapted the image from a photograph that Hodgman selected, which he found on the cover of Gorbachev's book *Perestroika*. The printed design has the smooth quality of silkscreen, but was actually produced with offset, which Visser used to print in full color rather than relying on the usual CMYK dots. "I was designing and thinking as a silkscreen printer, but I made with it with offset," he says. Visser generally made 500-hit sheets with 20 × 25 rows of hits, but the mathematics meant

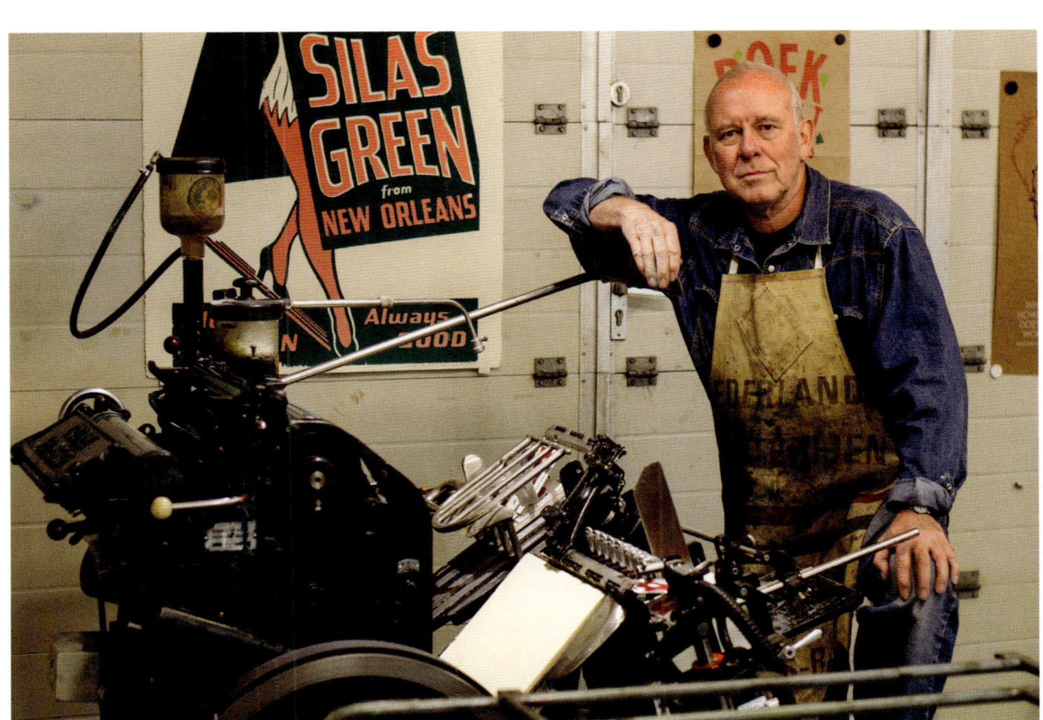

Ed Visser with his trusty Heidelberg Platen Windmill, 2020. Courtesy of Ed Visser.

that the final row of four-ways was cut horizontally in half. This seemed rude to the Soviet leader, so he added an extra row of twenty hits—a "freebie" for the street dealers, who could tear it off and still sell the expected 500-hit sheet.

Visser liked the exacting and meditative labor of assembling precisely measured grids of photographic reproductions and then reducing them for the print shop (who had no idea what Visser was actually up to). Early on, the blotter maker cottoned on to the need for alcohol-resistant ink. He also added value by sourcing highly absorbent blotter-type paper, which was still used in the late twentieth century by perfumers to present test samples to customers. For perfing, he used the Heidelberg Tiegel Automat Platen 26 × 38 cm letterpress, a.k.a. the Windmill, a demanding but excellent machine that Visser considers made for the job.

*Bike Rider 43 * 94*, Ed Visser, Amsterdam, 1994. 6⅕ × 7⅘ in.

The quality of Visser's work led him to work with multiple producers, and in 1993, he produced his most popular design: *Bike Rider*, a crisp and playful homage to Albert Hofmann released on the fiftieth anniversary of the good doctor's famous velocipedal lark. The run was so popular that it was immediately and widely copied by other outfits, which annoyed Visser, who thought consumers should know what they were buying. Thinking like a currency designer, he continued to employ an offset press for further variations of *Bike Rider*, but added wavy numbers with silkscreen and symbols screened with unusual glittery ink to stump black market mimics. For his screen prints, Visser used a mobile rig called the Black Box 1, which he also took to festivals and schools to demonstrate the art.[44] Today there are reportedly over a hundred variants of *Bike Rider* from Visser and others across the globe.

By the 1990s, the illicit blotter scene in Europe had exploded. But in the previous decade, much of the blotter gobbled around the planet still came from San Francisco, and a lot of that was crafted by the Hayes Street Gang. Like all participants in ongoing criminal operations, the San Francisco blotter makers faced the calculus of capture: how long can you keep working before you get popped? When a hit of *Horus* showed up on a *High Times* calendar in 1982, it sent a shudder down Benedict's spine. LSD convictions are a cruel business, and more so with the passage of mandatory minimum laws later that decade; while the core acid families remained largely unscathed, scores of lower-level distributors, dealers, and dippers did serious time. Because the paraphernalia that blotter makers crafted was at least one step removed from cooking and dipping, they had a bit more room to maneuver. To that end, Benedict kept himself in the dark about the deeper goings on, and insisted on keeping some distance between his print work and the sauce.

With Forester, it was a different story. Gilfeather had already turned to offset printing alongside silk-screening, presumably for the same reasons that other blotter makers had made the shift: to print more sheets with more efficiency. But at some point, Forester also started to dip blotter himself, using the turkey bag method, and in a sometimes slipshod manner that coated the surfaces of the apartment he maintained at the back of his shop with LSD, making it a notoriously tricky place to visit. Other mistakes were made as well, and one time an angry client

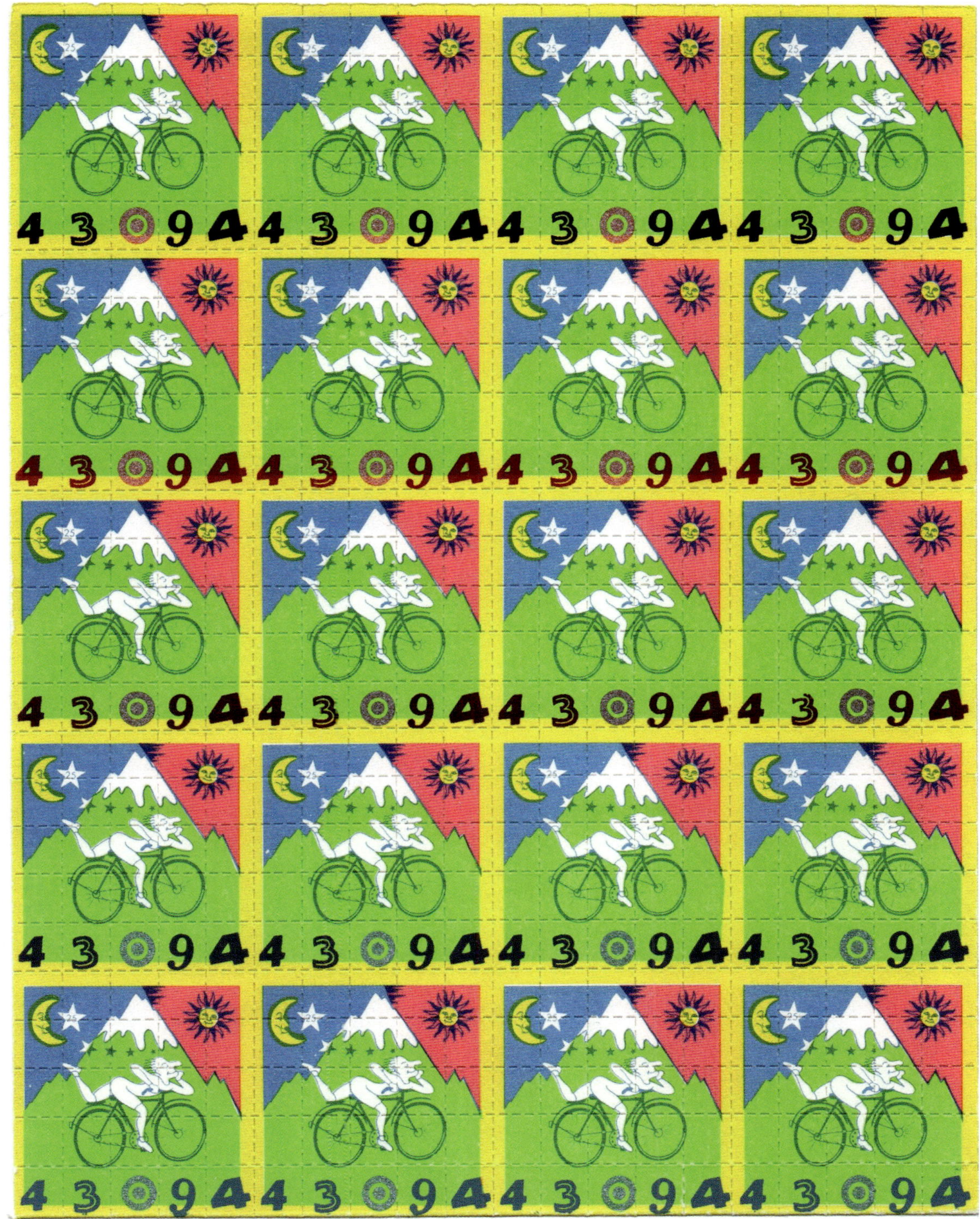

appeared at the shop with a gun. That was too much for Benedict, who went his own way, taking a few clients with him while remaining on good terms with his former partner.

In 1987, Forester got busted, set up like the proverbial bowling pin. He was convicted on three counts, including conspiracy to distribute, and sentenced to seven years, which he served in full at Lompoc and Boron, a minimum-security prison near Edwards Air Force Base known as "Club Fed." After Forester's arrest, Benedict quit the game entirely. Soon he found himself cranking out rock T-shirts for Bill Graham, which fell rather short of the dream. "In a way the whole blotter thing really tanked my fine arts printing career," Benedict says now. "It became a distraction, and then it kind of took over." Though utterly disinterested in hippie hagiography, Benedict remains proud of much of the work that Gilfeather did.

Down the Rabbit Hole

Forester was arrested the same year that McCloud mounted "The Holy Transfers," the SFAI gallery show that led to a surreptitious invitation to meet some local artists in the LSD underground. Needless to say, McCloud accepted the offer. But as McCloud met with and befriended various blotter makers and acid suppliers, it became apparent that a crisis of sorts was looming. A number of LSD crews depended on the steady and significant supply of undipped blotter coming out of Hayes Street, but that production had now effectively ceased.

Which is how Mark McCloud, lecturer in fine arts and avant-punk bon vivant, found himself involved in the production and creative direction of the very same underground craft he had helped put on the cultural map. For a renegade collector like McCloud, this was a dream come true. His main mentor in the trade was Rocky, who had by that point largely left blotter making for a gig up the chain, but who proceeded to both train and test the new blotter maker. He made McCloud drive up to an isolated barn in Sonoma County to retrieve the disassembled pieces of an ungainly perfing machine: an enormous manual flatbed etching press, operated with a big wheel, which McCloud barely managed to fit in the copious trunk of his 1969 Toronado. Rocky also passed on two perf boards—one with forty rows and one with twenty-five, which together made up a "1000 block" that produced a thousand hits per sheet. Using the boards and the press, which he set up in a basement on Page Street, McCloud set about his first task: perfing Forester's remaining stock, scores of Celtic knots, strawberries, and floating lotuses, the last an allusion to Rocky's old shop.

A few years later, McCloud started making his own designs. He got his hands on another perf board, a venerable 30 × 30 "900 block" from an old blotter maker named Fritz, who claimed to be an heir to the Russian throne and was responsible for old school sheets like *Surfing Shiva* (p. 163) and the first appearance of *Quinn the Eskimo*. McCloud liked the 900 block, which required only one board to perf, and stuck to that format for a long while. For his first image, McCloud decided to memorialize his harrowing Orange Sunshine trip from the early 1970s. Lifting a *Farmers' Almanac*–style illustration of a sun from the label of a

Mexican soda, McCloud laboriously prepared the matrix image for the photostat. He delivered it to a local Mission printer, along with boxes of yellow 80-pound woodchip paper, Rocky's long-standing preference. McCloud ordered a thousand sheets. Later, using the same printer, a young Asian-American guy who eventually took over much of his perfing work, McCloud would order up to ten thousand sheets at a time, pages covered with elephants, dancing condoms, Alices.

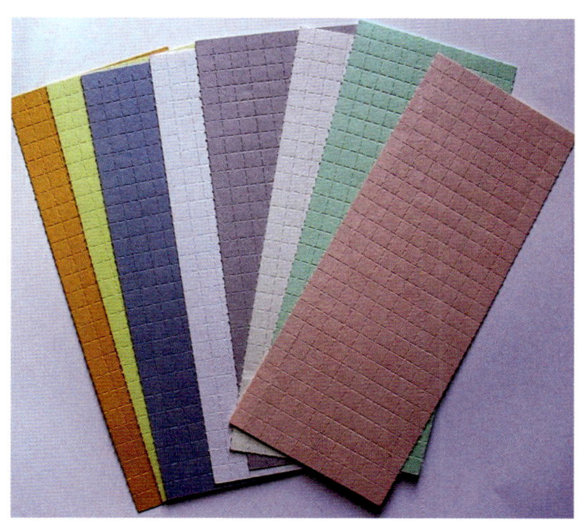

Blank sheets, early 1990s. 2½ × 6¼ in. each. Photo by Mark McCloud.

Many clients still wanted blanks, and so McCloud also provided clean perfed sheets in a variety of colors, the most popular possessing a minty hue known as *Shamrock Shake*. But the prints were a lot more fun. After meeting up at Burning Man, McCloud did a collaboration with the fringe illustrator Bill Barker, the man behind an enigmatic art-prank mail-order project known as Schwa. McCloud also crafted a condor design inspired by a Patagonian secret society, and adapted a low-rider cartoon he found in the Mission for the leader of a local motorcycle club: a hot-rod monster whose bandana he modified just to make it uglier (p. 190). One of the McCloud pieces most celebrated by later collectors was *Felix*, a grid of the grinning cartoon cat, his eyes a-popping, his name a wink-wink reference to an elite player in the global acid trade.

One of McCloud's steadiest clients was Magic Mike, one of many prominent acid traffickers who spent a good chunk of their year following the Grateful Dead across the land. This symbiosis should hardly surprise. Besides sustaining a psychedelic dance cult born in the Prankster Acid Tests, the Dead had been hanging around with acid makers since the days when Owsley built their sound system. By the end of the 1970s, when the band had established a more consistent cross-country schedule, Dead tour became the lifeline of LSD Americana in a country plunging toward new wave music, Reagan, and cocaine. For Deadheads, the parking lot was a reliably friendly place to score that evening's rocket fuel. But the loopy carnival that followed the band around also created a swirly cloaking device behind which acid movers and shakers could make contacts, try out product, lay sheets, and move large amounts of material around the country.

Mike was good at the game, good enough that, by the early 1990s, McCloud felt he had earned the right to his own line of blotter. What image did he want? Perhaps a variation of the dancing bears that had already graced so many Dead-themed blotters and fan-made tie-dye T-shirts? Or what about one of those rosy skeletons? Not this time: Mike wanted Beavis and Butt-Head. Though the duo were not exactly McCloud's cup of tea, he complied. He altered Butt-Head's AC/DC T-shirt to read "Acid Rock," and transformed his horns throw to a peace sign. While satirical cartoon characters had appeared in blotter art before, from Mr. Natural to Zippy the Pinhead to the animated Mr. Bill from *Saturday Night Live*, *The Beavis and Butt-Head Psychedelic Experience* hit a sophomoric note that prophesied the bongwater chuckles that would characterize much of the vanity blotter to come. The sheets also suggested that in the great acid dialectic of sacred and profane, the profane had gained the upper hand.

And one of the forces that kept that psychedelic dialectic dancing was precisely the Grateful Dead, whose popularity had mushroomed following the release of their top ten 1987 album *In the Dark*. The band was now selling out stadiums, whose parking lots temporarily transformed into Shakedown Street, a freaky full-service bazaar that served as an entertainment destination in its own right. As Jesse Jarnow explains in *Heads*, his vivid history of psychedelic America, this feral demimonde started to rile up the authorities; even the band—normally hands-off libertarians—issued a statement asking their fans to chill out. Acid busts had long been the snake eyes of the Dead-tour dice roll, reportedly inspiring a run of early 1980s blotter whose image—Snoopy wearing shades—cautioned Deadheads to keep a low profile. But now things were coming down hard.

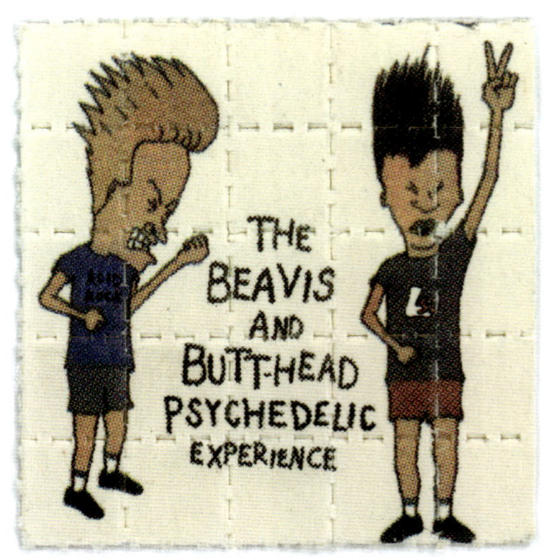

The Beavis and Butt-Head Psychedelic Experience, Mark McCloud, San Francisco, 1994. 1¼ × 1¼ in.

In 1992, the DEA unleashed the cheekily named Operation Looking Glass, a national campaign that targeted the acid networks that coursed through the Dead scene like mycelia. The Operation netted far more dealers than major distributors, and even some DEA agents at the time didn't believe it would do much to staunch the flow.[45] As part of the sweep, McCloud was arrested and charged with conspiracy to manufacture and distribute a controlled substance. Accused of being "The Cadillac Man," McCloud knew he was innocent of the charges, but he hired a powerful attorney, Doron Weinberg, and prepared for trial in Houston. After the prosecution spent days presenting their case, the judge, annoyed by the weak evidence and dodgy informants, immediately dismissed the jury and promised to get McCloud home by the weekend.

Though rattled, McCloud was hardly repentant. He soon shot back at the DEA's cruel and ham-fisted operation with a symbolic poke in the eye: *Through the Looking Glass* (pp. 199–200). Though not the first blotter to honor Lewis Carroll's Wonderland, nor the first to print two distinct but related images on each side of the sheet, McCloud's effort, which he produced with his wife and other assistants, was state of the art.[46] Set within a frame that underscores the square dimensions of the 900 block, McCloud's collage of John Tenniel's original Alice drawings inhabits a two-sided picture surface at once large and small, dense and spaciously twisty. The flat surface of the mirror suggests the flat surface of the blotter paper itself, which, when impregnated with LSD, becomes another sort of looking glass, inviting you to lose yourself in its nowhere plane. *Through the Looking Glass* also cemented a deal with Alan Dillard, a powerful acid player McCloud calls "Dealer McDope"; in the end, sixteen thousand sheets were printed, with millions of trips set loose into the land.

As McCloud climbed up the LSD pyramid, he continued to collect vintage blotter from his growing network of high-falutin acid folk. But it was tough at first. There just wasn't a lot of extant material from the early years. Specific blotter runs had mostly been small, and distributors had little reason to hold onto any examples, dipped or undipped. Many in the underground also viewed McCloud's attempts to archive this "folk art" with suspicion. He had to convince producers that he wasn't interested in their personal information, but just wanted physical examples and whatever stories they might toss in as a bonus.

Eventually the word got out, and people began sending McCloud envelopes through the mail, often anonymously. Manufacturers passed him leftover paper stock, or photostats that had been used for printing blotter long gone. Dealer McDope gave him an original hit of Ghost's *Blue Dot*, which had turned brown in the interim. A small collection of exceptionally rare examples from the 1970s—an early *Mr. Natural*, the first *King Tut*, the first *Eye in the Pyramid*—had been thrown into a guitar case and forgotten for over a decade before finding its way to the institute. Another significant haul came through an old associate of Rocky's, an underling who had been told to destroy a mass of lovely undipped paper but couldn't bring himself to do it.

King Tut, mid-1970s. 7½ × 7½ in. Likely the first Egyptian motif on blotter.

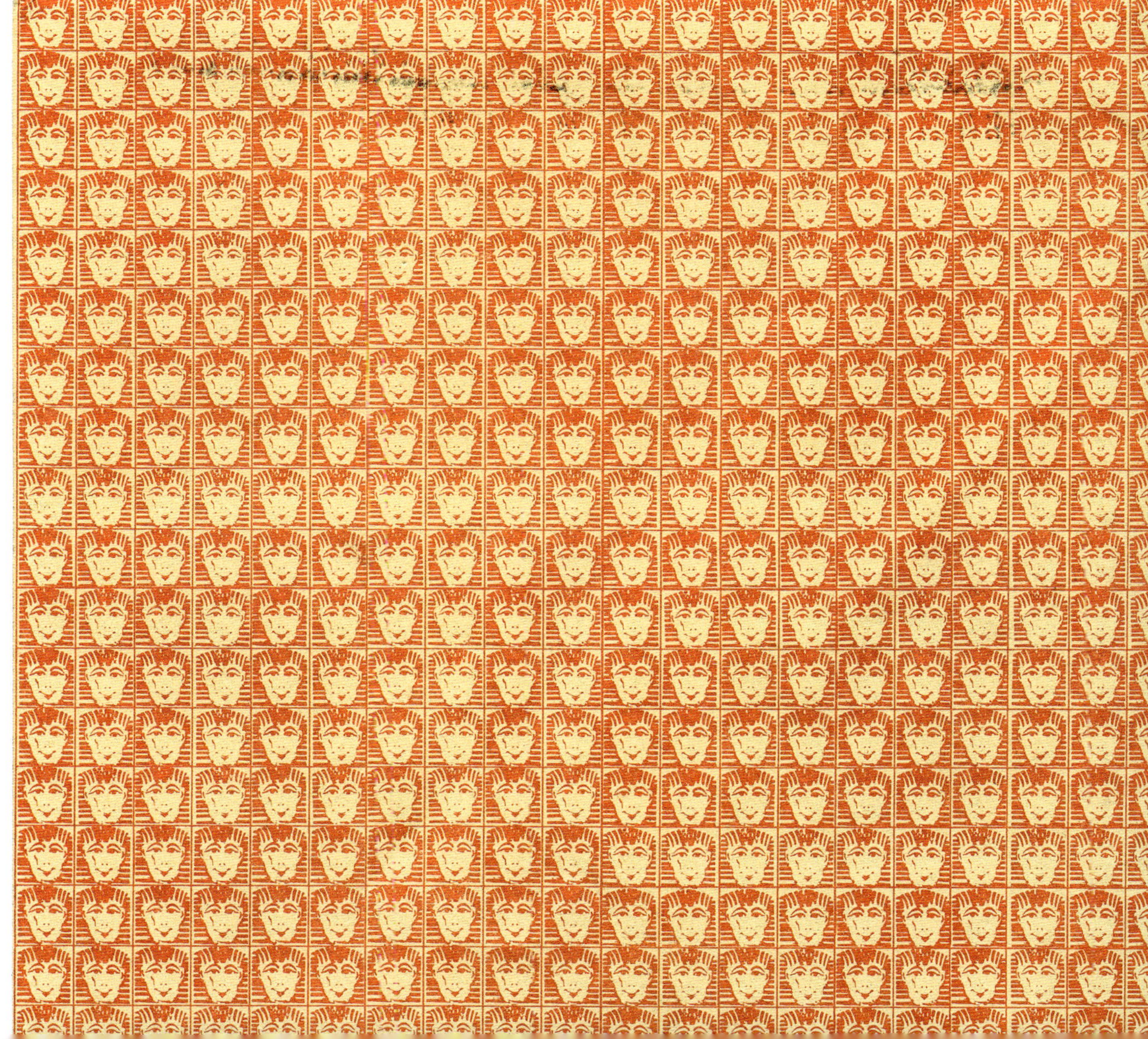

For one treasure hunt, McCloud used his connection with the legendary San Francisco civil rights attorney Tony Serra to arrange a dinner with Sarah Matzar, who had just gotten out of prison after admitting to a small charge following the bust of the Bolinas Girl Gang in 1993. Matzar was headed back to Guatemala, but told Mark that someday somebody would show up at his place with a couple of laundry bags of stuff, and that he should just pay them whatever they asked. She was right, and Mark added more blotter and photostats to his collection. Matzar's personal motivation, which entailed obvious risk, was entirely archival.

Throughout the 1990s, McCloud continued to work on the razor's edge of the black market, unknowingly setting himself up for a second and far more serious bust. In early 2000, after months of covert observation, a joint FBI–DEA force descended on the Institute of Illegal Images with hazmat suits, Hummers, and semiautomatics. McCloud had gotten a tip-off from a local homeless guy he often helped out, who told him that some men had dumped McCloud's trash in the trunk of their car around 3 a.m. the night before. But though the feds did not net all the incriminating evidence they might have, they took pretty much everything else: books, gels, handstamps, photostats, nearly four hundred framed blotters, and thirty-three thousand sheets of freshly printed undipped sheets. A SWAT team cuffed McCloud and tossed him the back of a cruiser and let him roast there at the scene while dozens of agents dismantled his home. The Queen of Hearts wanted heads to roll.

Illegal Images

Before the DEA packed up and left the institute that day in 2000, their agents were faced with the need to impose some order on the enormous haul of weird shit they now had on their hands. To itemize the framed blotters, which for all they knew were loaded with active acid, they affixed masking tape to the frames and hand-scrawled unique identifying numbers onto the strips. McCloud's painstakingly archived blotters, which the collector had both literally and conceptually framed as art, were about to become exhibits of another kind—the sort you submit as evidence to trial.

The slippage of the term *exhibit* points to an irony in the history of blotter: the agencies tasked with destroying the scourge of LSD were in essence the first collectors of the genre. Unlike users, who wanted to eat the stuff, the drug warriors wanted to preserve, study, categorize, and describe. The DEA publication *Microgram* enthusiastically listed new blotter exhibits culled from police and sheriff departments from around the country, and sometimes the world. These bulletins included scans or descriptions of images and designs, as well as details about size, material, and manner of production. While the initial chemical analyses of the exhibits were generally carried out locally, *Microgram* helped coordinate the broader effort to map the production and dissemination of blotter, including forensic or "ballistic" analyses that were beyond the capacities of local departments. A 1992 technical report out of the UK's Drugs Intelligence Laboratory described this sort of work as looking "for similarities and differences between the paper designs to assist in identifying trafficking routes and the eventual location of illicit production."[47]

Despite *Microgram*'s cool professional tone, however, an aura of nerdy fascination hovers around the newsletter, at least during its first few decades. Drugs breed fetishistic obsession, even among their adversaries. Occasionally, *Microgram* editors struggled over interpretive issues and critical taxonomies. Regarding a red animal that appeared on one sheet, the newsletter notes that the image "appears to be an heraldic figure of a lion on its hind legs with its forelegs upraised (rampant)." Another description of a perfed Escher captured the image's figure–ground ambiguity and its challenge to commonsense realism, describing the picture—whose Dutch source the feds did not recognize—as a "white fish on a green background, or green birds in flight on a white background." Similarly, while the blue globule that appears on a handful of tabs seized in Flagstaff in 1992 is described as a spermatozoon, the writer notes that "dissenters in the laboratory" argued that it was a tadpole or balloon.

As *Microgram* itself makes abundantly clear, LSD blotter hardly represents the only conjunction of street drugs and the printed image. The newsletter describes many large packages of cocaine or hashish decorated with emblems, either on the outside container or impressed on the material itself, like cakes of pu-erh tea. In the 1980s and beyond, heroin and other opiates in the New York tri-state area were generally sold in glassine bags hand-stamped with text or figures, often the logos of familiar brands like Prada, and, later, Starbucks and Target. Old-school LSD tablets were rarely impressed with designs, but ecstasy tablets have routinely featured imprints since the 1990s, often glyphs that work well with round pills: smiley faces, @ symbols, automobile emblems, letters, and many playful designs. In 2009, the Swiss artist Frédéric Post redrew hundreds of these images for his limited-edition art book, *Anonymous Engravings on Ecstasy Pills*.

In 1987, *Microgram* released the *LSD Blotter Index*, which was principally compiled by Edward S. Franzosa, a senior forensic chemist at the DEA's Special Testing and Research Laboratory. A Navy vet and former policeman, "Dr. Ed" earned a PhD in molecular spectroscopy and became a global expert in the forensic source determination of illegal drug formulations and packaging, including tablets, capsules, and blotter. Franzosa's lab tracked street blotters nationally, cataloging images as well as tracing sources of manufacture by identifying paper type or the unique bite of particular perf boards. But despite being collated in the spirit of pitiless repression, Franzosa's illustrated *Index*, which was scanned and released onto the internet by the Erowid Center in the early 2000s, is a joyful artifact for blotter fans and historians, though the reproductions are poor and there are reasons to doubt the accuracy of the LSD measurements in the exhibits.[48] Between the *Index* and the III archive, along with a few other indexes and technical papers prepared by European agencies also leaked onto the internet, we have a robust though necessarily incomplete record

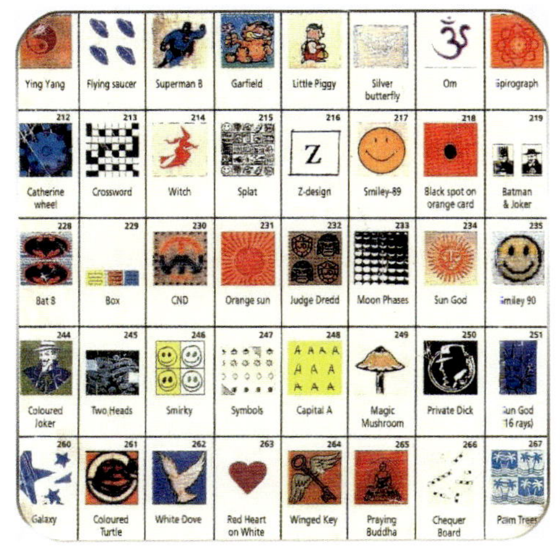

Law Enforcement Blotter Index, Europe, n.d.

of the images that vintage blotter manufacturers, distributors, and dealers chose to announce, enchant, and brand LSD on paper.

So what sort of picture do we get from all these images? It's all over the map. Despite the formal consistency of blotter grids, the designs range far and wide. For one thing, blotter makers employed many different *types* of images: doodles, cartoons, decorative patterns, religious symbols, corporate logos, high art appropriations, animal illustrations. These images were in turn executed with widely varying degrees of finesse, presented in both rich color and single tones, and produced through a variety of methods, from casual handstamps to four-color, computer-controlled offset prints.

Before diving into this menagerie of icons, it is worth dwelling a bit more on the commercial function of these black-market images. The obvious place to start is the nature of the illicit marketplace itself—but only if we remember that acid has always been a peculiar sort of business, one that we misunderstand if we reduce it to purely market terms. Some of the earliest purveyors of LSD, inspired by Diggerish sentiments, just gave it away, and many more sold it at or less than cost, convinced they were contributing to the transformation of humanity. In a 1968 ode to the acid dealer printed in the *East Village Other*, Timothy Leary describes the high bar the dealer must pass: "not only must his product be pure and spiritual but . . . he himself must reflect the human light that he represents."[49] Just like the acid chemists he knew, who prayed while they did their lab work, Leary declared that the "righteous dealer" should be a pure and radiant person—a Robin Hood, spiritual guerilla, and secret agent rolled into one. While this paean might read like mystic fluff, it not only captures the self-mythology that permeated the acid trade but accurately describes the praxis pursued—inconsistently, no doubt—by many dealers and distributors.

Even when the profits were rolling in, the LSD trade did more than simply line the pockets of a new breed of hip criminal entrepreneur. Like rock music, the LSD trade in the late 1960s also contributed to Jerry Garcia's hip economy. In this trickle-down freakonomics, again, profits by scene-makers were poured back into the scene through patronage and potlach. High earners sometimes sustained a large tribe of lifestyle shareholders through a kind of financial contact high—something the Grateful Dead continued to perform versions of throughout their long career. A key ideology of hippie commerce, the hip economy was of course mythologized and never practiced consistently. But it did produce visible and concrete effects, not only in hippie enclaves back in the day, but in more recent undergrounds. Until cannabis legalization, California's weed industry financially sustained untold numbers of fringe artists, activists, spiritual seekers, and slackers, who enjoyed both dealer largesse and the dependable wages of autumn harvest, when legions of urban freaks made their way to the Humboldt hills to trim bud.

Acid was the flagship drug of the hip economy, and even as the scene became compromised, or co-opted by other criminal forces, the acid trade's commitment to democratic access never disappeared. LSD has always been cheap in comparison with other drugs, with the cost of a single hit kept low and steady for almost half a century (though dosage has fluctuated along with the purity of the molecule). Part of this consistency is due to idealism, but part of it reflects the affordances of the molecule itself, which as noted earlier is so potent that it is effectively always produced in abundance. This makes the game more about dissemination than about per-unit cost, which in turn helps explain the fact that blotter eventually won the field despite offering less of a markup to street dealers than media like tablets or gels. Some consumers preferred it in part because they trusted it, and for good reason. Until relatively recently, blotter was rarely mislabeled or loaded with other drugs—the "LSD" you bought was usually LSD.[50]

So how did blotter images serve this illegal commerce? On one level, the designs just helped lubricate the flow, marking otherwise ordinary-looking paper with signs that declare an invisible specialness. Since undipped fakes were always a possibility, a tiny paper square featuring Zippy the Pinhead paradoxically seemed more reliable to some buyers that a blank white hit. Because these iconographic promises were coupled to particular batches of the molecule, which generally hit the street at once and often temporarily dominated supply, it is tempting to think of the designs as "brands." The concept certainly has its place. The production of a new and charismatic run of blotter would sometimes spark some of that old Owsley magic, transforming that edition's emblem into a popular marker of quality and reliability, just like Orange Sunshine or Clear Light. Over the decades, a good number of blotter designs achieved such dominance, like *Red Dragons* or *Gooney Birds* or, in the UK, *Purple Om*. According to a 1992 report from the UK's Drug Intelligence Laboratory (DIL), for example, nearly half of the blotter recently seized in the country were Oms, and over a quarter were the also ubiquitous *Strawberries*.

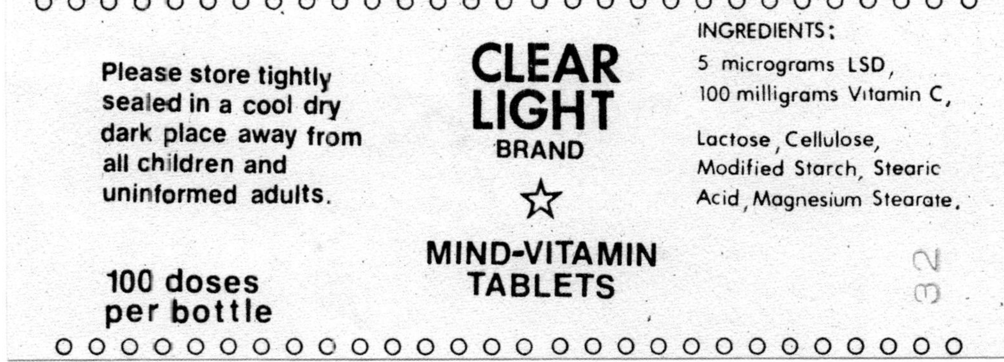

Clear Light brand label, 5 µg microdose LSD, ca. 1981. 1½ × 4¼ in.

The more you look at it, however, the more the concept of brand loses its stability, not unlike the Mr. Cube mascot that started to wiggle and dance when Brian Barritt was dosing sugar cubes back in the day. For one thing, it's not like street dealers and buyers are shopping for acid in an enormous LSD supermarket; a lot of the time folks just buy what their dealers are holding, and even "premium" brands don't necessarily fetch higher street prices. Over the decades, such designs were also easily and frequently copied by rival crews and dosed with different material—an act you could call "counterfeiting" if that term didn't evoke a domain of legally enforced product identity inappropriate here. In 1992, the same year that the DIL determined the popularity of *Purple Om*, police in Liverpool made a large seizure of unimpregnated Oms that "differed in a number of ways from the 'authentic' papers . . . and properly merit the description 'fake.'"[51] This illicit hall of mirrors—what exactly is a proper fake copy?—contrasts starkly with conventional commercial brands, which are dependent on the legal system to maintain consistent identity and longevity. Finally, even if you set aside the counterfeits, the acid market scrambled the stable relationship between brand and product. As Bob Stearne explains in his 1981 *High Times* article,

> Most middle-level LSD dealers buy acid in bulk and then produce their own "brand" of blotter acid using a stamp or silk screen to put their logo on the sheets. So there is often a variety of blotter acids on the market. They may look totally different from one another but they're all loaded with the same acid. Likewise, even if a blotter manufacturer obtains his LSD from different sources, he may distribute blotters that are standard in appearance.[52]

Recall that even the illustrious Orange Sunshine was loaded with different acid from different labs. While this variance didn't undermine the brand, it does render its meaning porous. The message of blotter is a postmodern one: the sign is not the signified, but its play does allow you to slip and slide.

The concept of brand also obscures the ephemeral nature of blotter. Most blotter designs were evanescent, riding the fast novelty waves familiar from trading cards or punk rock 45s. Often no more than a hundred sheets would be printed of an original design. In 1990, a British dealer was arrested in Amsterdam; along with sixty grams of crystal, he was holding almost a dozen different designs of blotter, including images designated as *Popeye*, *Witch*, and *Sad Ant*. Writing only two years after the arrest, the DIL reported that these compositions had almost entirely disappeared from circulation.[53] The incessant production of new designs meant that, while knowledgeable blotter buyers (and forensic police labs) could recognize continuities in format and thereby identify the producer behind them, the flickering images themselves scrambled identity more than maintaining it. Even producers who decided to stick with a popular design through multiple batches of crystal might be forced to suddenly cease distribution if their sheets were seized by police.

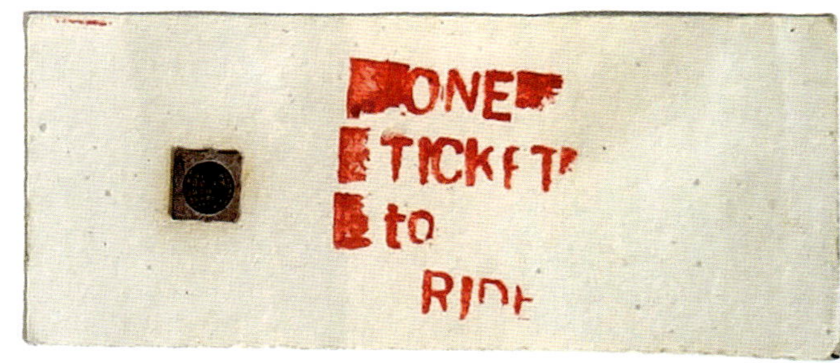

Ticket to Ride party favor, New York City, 1980s. 1 × 3 in.

The simple point here is that pieces of paper don't *need* to be illustrated in order to do the profitable job of disseminating LSD. People are buying the substance, not the images. That's why the distribution of blanks, perfed or not, and only sometimes colored, did not disappear with the rise of printed blotters, and in fact continued to be preferred by many dealers and consumers. Though blotter designs sometimes conferred a real market advantage, it is not clear whether this advantage economically justified the cost, labor, and risk associated with printing druggy designs. In other words, images on blotter are essentially *superfluous*. Their worth derives from a sort of phantasmagoric excess, an iridescent surplus of signs and patterns that communicate values—beauty, humor, swagger, magic, love—that outrun market logic. It is as if, through some psychedelic *Aufhebung*, blotter both absorbs and transcends illicit commerce, its images naturally and authentically blooming into printed media art—albeit a media art that, like acid experience itself, dissolves boundaries and resists easy classification.

Stains on Paper

When Mark McCloud hung tiny squares of LSD blotter on the gallery walls of the San Francisco Art Institute in 1987, he was framing these artifacts both literally and conceptually. But what exactly was the concept? The white walls and setting communicated contemporary art, while the magnifying glasses on hand suggested exhibits of coins or stamps, similarly teensy practical arts. As McCloud wanted to make clear, the blotters under glass were crafted by anonymous artisans working without hope of personal recognition and in the knowledge that some users won't notice or care much about their work. But by diverting these commodities from their intended use as a drug delivery device, McCloud freed their forms from their function, which was to deliver the goods at the very moment they ceased being objects in the world.

Now those forms are before you, pinned on a wall, or reproduced in a book, asking for engagement. The images are enigmatic, though also frequently quotidian, the pentagrams and UFOs more than balanced out by stars and clowns and soccer balls. The paper squares themselves vaguely resemble coupons, stickers, or stamps, but their psychedelic promise lends their material presence a more confusing and esoteric sense of power and ambivalence. Simply put, what *are* these things? Are they jokes or secret handshakes, confections or IOUs, artifacts or *objects d'art*? As signs, do they function like icons, indexes, or symbols? And if we are to consider them art, what manner of art?

We can take a hint here from a remarkable exhibit that opened at the Walker Art Center in Minneapolis in 2015. Called "Hippie Modernism: The Struggle for Utopia," the show gathered exemplars of countercultural art and design—inflatable furniture, guerilla television efforts, immersive environments, *The Whole Earth Catalog*—that both developed and unraveled aspects of modernist practice. In unpacking the title of the exhibit, curator Andrew Blauvelt observed that while hippies imaginatively embraced the premodern and the preindustrial, they also enacted modernism's fascination with new media and innovative *techné*, as well as the early avant-garde's "utopic dream of integrating art into everyday life."[54] Blauvelt argues that such hippie holism, found in urban centers around the United States and Europe, was explored most fervently on the West Coast of the US, which hosted scores of "hybrid experiments that eschewed and challenged disciplinary boundaries, often commingling art, craft, design, and performance." While "extending the notion of medium," these experiments also tended "to privilege individual experience as the basis of social transformation."[55]

Blotter fits the hippie modernist bill. A hybrid of art, handicraft, and design, illustrated blotter amplifies the "notion of medium" by fulfilling electronic media's bid to penetrate consciousness directly. Cheekily referencing its own performative capacity to alter and liberate human perception, blotter also fulfills its promise through a novel psychoactive technology, diverted from industry, that phenomenologically integrates cosmic aesthetics into everyday life. Blotter is thus a practical vector of hippie modernism that lasted far beyond the years covered in Blauvelt's show. And indeed, when "Hippie Modernism" was mounted at Berkeley's BAMPFA galleries in 2017, more examples of West Coast experiments were featured, including a few items from the Institute of Illegal Images. That same year, some of McCloud's blotters were also used in the London Design Museum's inaugural show, the tart and incisive "California: Designing Freedom."

But the question of blotter goes beyond contemporary design or media studies, into the very meaning of crafting images in the first place. By hanging his framed blotters on the gallery wall of SFAI, McCloud opened up the question of art, or art in modernity, a space of ambiguity and play that has always been infused—in ways that have finally come to be acknowledged in the art world—with fresh decantings of esoteric spirituality. Like Marcel Duchamp, a student of alchemy who is credited with putting a urinal in a gallery and calling it *Fountain*, McCloud was performing an old modernist prank by daring viewers to find aesthetics where they least expect it. But rather than a banal if elegant receptacle of human waste, McCloud presented scandalous drug paraphernalia, the grubby bubble-gum cards of a street trade largely associated, in the late 1980s anyway, with indulgence and deluded escapism.

Like *Fountain*, "The Holy Transfers" also interrogated the space of the gallery itself, which often serves as a hermetically sealed container for an idea of art that exists by virtue of excluding everything else. In particular, "The Holy Transfers" probed the largely excluded link between contemporary art and psychedelics. Here I am not talking about the nebulous genre of "psychedelic art," sometimes known as "visionary art" and including everything from Family Dog posters and expanded cinema to the popular canvases of Alex Grey and the hyperbolic architectures found in graffiti and related street art. As the critic Lars Bang Larson notes, from the perspective of the establishment art world, this sort of psychedelia represents little more than "a scandal of ephemeral form, hermetic imagery, and strange temporalities."[56]

In his book *Are You Experienced?* the art critic Ken Johnson offers a sustained and largely persuasive case that, despite this scandal, much of the art of the last fifty years demands to be understood at least in part through a psychedelic lens. Johnson isn't just talking about visual effects, nor about the fact that lots of artists took drugs and got something out of them. Instead, he suggests that the core value system communicated by so many contemporary artists boils down to a collection of hippie injunctions: "Distrust authority; oppose consensual reality; entertain possible alternative realities; be hyperalert to ways that culture and media shape consciousness; comprehend the interconnectedness of systems of power; explore alternative states of consciousness and multiple states of self; open up to spiritual experience; sympathize with the devil. . . ."[57]

Early in his text, Johnson quotes the conceptual artist Adrian Piper, whose austere, philosophically sharp, and highly political works do not generally register as trippy, but who partly credits her LSD use in the 1960s with exposing ordinary reality as a construct open to intervention.[58] In a remarkable passage, Piper integrates psychedelia into a continuum of

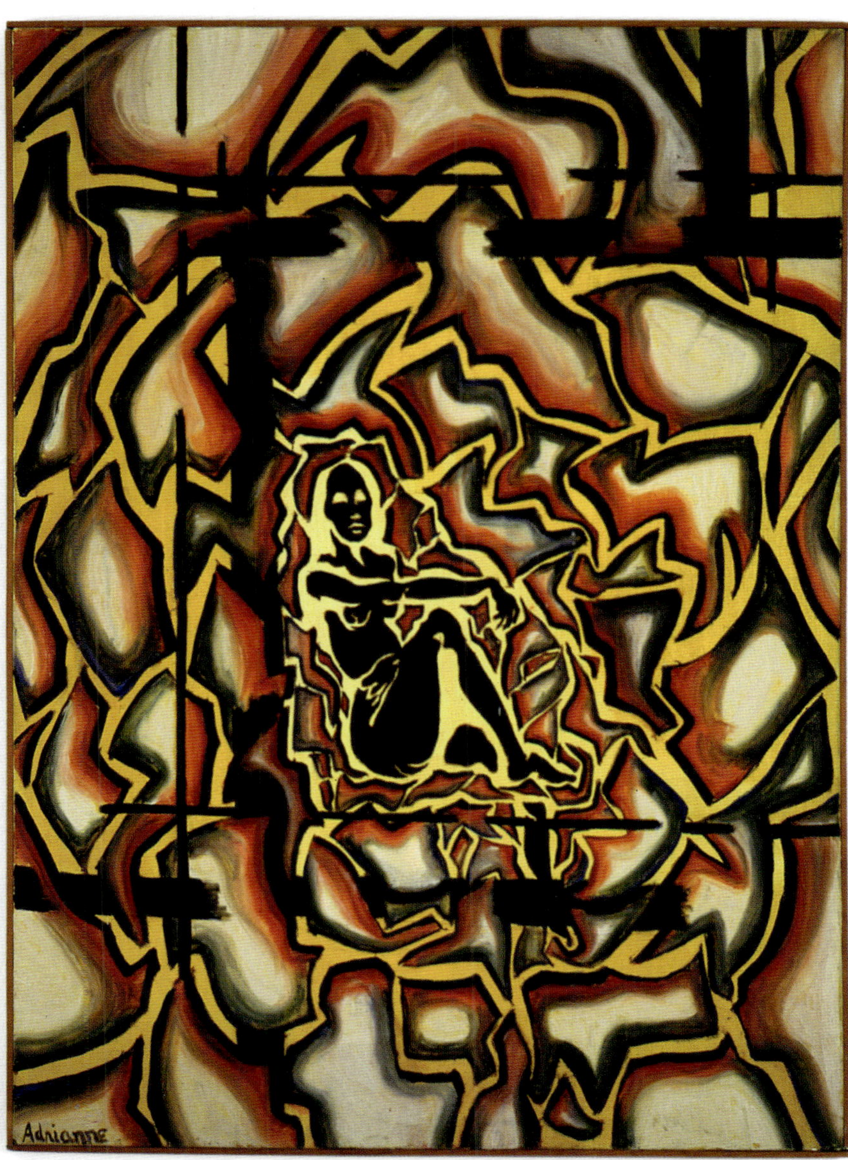

LSD Self-Portrait from the Inside Out, Adrian Piper, 1966. Acrylic on canvas.

modern art movements that dissolved and opened up the concrete possibilities of perception:

> Realism depicts the objects of ordinary conventional reality; Impressionism depicts the perceptual qualities of those objects broken up into light and color; Pointillism depicts the perceptual and formal qualities of those objects broken up even further into color and minutely small forms; Psychedelia depicts the cracking open of all of those perceptual and formal qualities; Minimalism expresses the underlying geometric essences behind those objects and their qualities; Pop Art depicts those objects shorn of the convention conceptual schemes that give them meaning; Conceptual Art expresses the breaking up and reconstitution of those conventional conceptual scenes and the objects (and subjects) embedded in them.[59]

As an artist exceptionally attuned to the social processes of othering, Piper here rescues psychedelia from the clutches of the frivolous, integrating it into the philosophical development and critical practice of modern art. Obviously Piper is not making a strictly historical argument. Instead, she is tracing a pictorial lineage of perceptual initiation that works through various art practices. While I don't believe that humble street blotter "belongs" in any substantial way to the canons of modern art, it does reflect and refract, almost synchronistically at times, elements of these same art historical processes.

In Piper's lineage, psychedelia initiates two almost contradictory responses, both of which help illuminate the aesthetics of blotter: minimalism and pop. With its ironic cartoons and sometimes garish silkscreens, pop art's resonance with LSD paper rings pretty clear. But the drug medium's echo of minimalism is also important, and equally if more subtly psychedelic. Here the most transformative thing in the world is a perfectly blank surface—page or canvas or gallery wall—charged with potential. This reminds us of a comparatively unique feature of classic LSD discourse: often the emphasis is not so much on hallucinogenic displays or visionary content, but on the limpid immanence of awareness itself, a "clear light" devoid of images. In *The Psychedelic Experience*, Timothy Leary and his coauthors Richard Alpert and Ralph Metzner characterize the first bardo encountered by the tripper as the radiant Realization of Voidness. There is no content here; instead, "liberation is the nervous system devoid of mental-conceptual activity." Part of the acid practice enjoined by the book is to extend this state, rich with electrical and other abstract fluxes of energy and lucidity, and precisely to *hold off visions*, whether frightening or heavenly. Once the clear light state can no longer be sustained, the tripper "must wander on into lower and lower conditions of hallucinations, as determined by his past games, until he drops back to routine reality."[60]

Roughly speaking, the earliest modernist gestures of abstract art were often animated by a transcendent and even mystical drive away from representation and inherited symbolism. As an often stern distillation of these earlier abstract moves, minimalism announces the artwork's separation from the things of ordinary reality, a gesture figured partly through what Piper calls "geometric essences." And one of these essences is most certainly *the grid*, which Johnson calls the "foundational armature of modern art."[61] Clinical and abstract, and nearly absent from traditional art history, the grid materializes the break that constitutes the self-consciousness of modernity in the first place. As the critic Rosalind Krauss writes in her seminal essay on the figure, the grid embodies the disenchanted formalism that characterizes modern science and technology; it is "what art looks like when it turns its back on nature." But Krauss also reminds us that some of the earliest practitioners of the grid form, abstract painters like Piet Mondrian and Kazimir Malevich, offered up highly esoteric interpretations of the lattice shape, writing of Spirit and Being rather than the efficiency of industrial design. As such, Krauss sees modernism as harboring an unconscious "ambivalence about the import of the grid, an indecision about its connection to matter on the one hand or spirit on the other."[62]

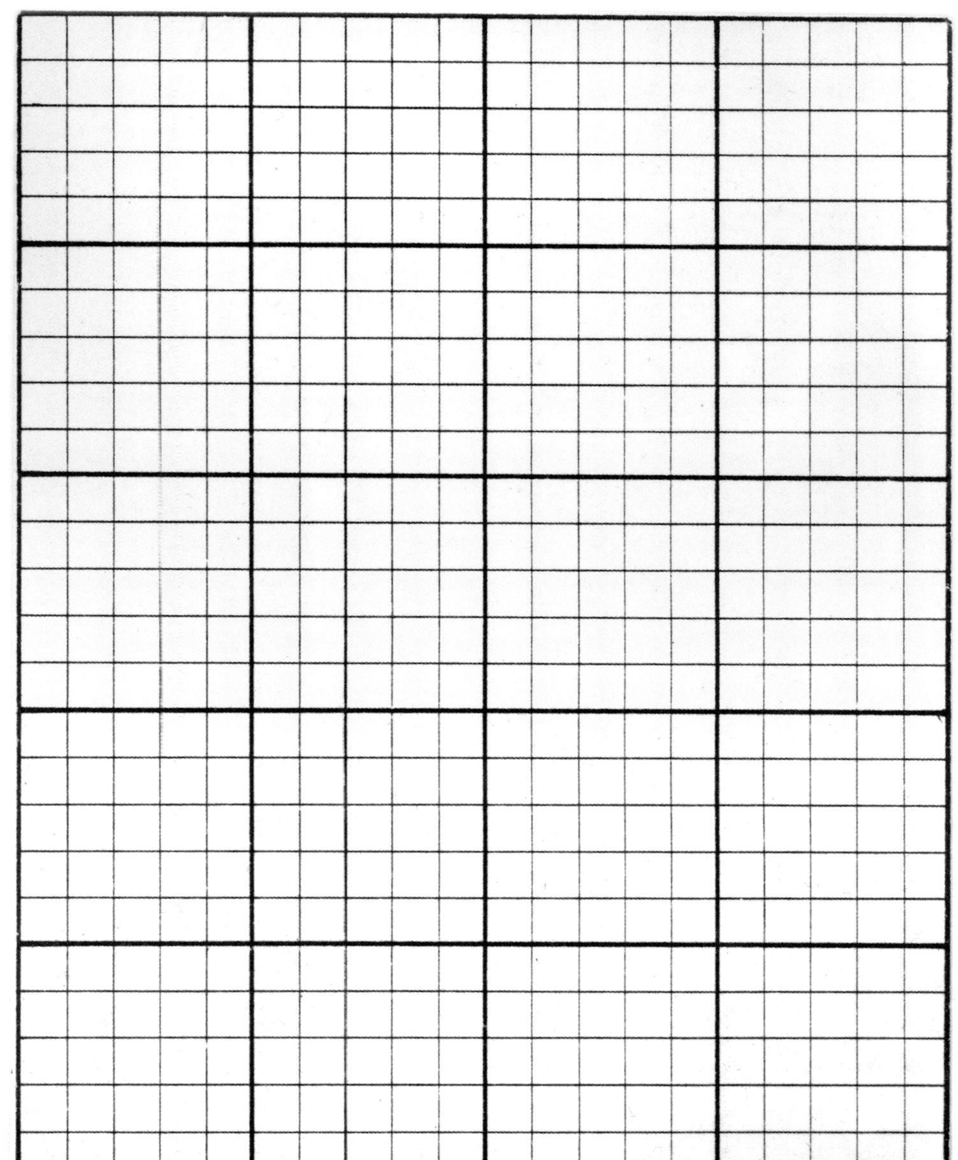

Grid, San Francisco, mid-1970s. Cut-along blotter sheet, 6 × 5 in.

Let's be clear: the first grid of blotter acid appeared because Eric Ghost wanted a practical and efficient way to organize the distribution of LSD at scale. But the aesthetic destiny of the form demands a deeper reckoning. Shorn of figurative imagery, sometimes blank as a gallery wall, the blotter grid already embodies the ambivalence Krauss describes, in perfect synch with the psychoactive it was designed to carry—a material molecule that, while produced through industrial methods and distributed initially by pharmaceutical combines, would come to serve as the twentieth century's most powerful technology of the sacred. Even the mythopoetic visions occasioned by LSD and other psychedelics, so deeply resonant with religious and mystical experiences throughout time, also feature evident material traces—effects not only of the drug but of the nervous system itself. In his classic book *Mescal and Mechanisms of Hallucinations*, from 1928, Heinrich Klüver established the influential idea of "form constants": universal visual patterns, associated with psychedelic and other trance states, that are derived from the organization of the visual system rather than the outside world. Among these entoptic figures, which include tunnels, mosaics, and lighting jags, are patterns described as "grating, lattice, fretwork, filigree, honeycomb or chessboard design."[63] In other words, *grids*. Alongside these patterns, as familiar to trippers as to abstract artists, Klüver also describes a hardwired hallucinatory phenomenon called *polyopia*, a condition that visually multiplies an object held in fixed attention, producing copies that often appear in rows and columns. Taken together, we might say that the basic character of printed blotter—a grid featuring iterations of an image across rows and columns—is not simply an artifact of drug delivery design but an unconscious expression of visionary mechanism.

Once the purely geometric blotter grid gives way to arrays of images, we have taken Piper's next step, from minimalism to pop. In 1962, five years before the "Trip or Freak" poster multiplied the Phantom's head across psychedelic San Francisco, Andy Warhol exhibited *Campbell's Soup Cans* at the Ferus Gallery in Los Angeles. Warhol had painted thirty-two small canvases in acrylic, each devoted to a different flavor—Cream of Celery, Pepper Pot, Tomato—of an otherwise identical product. At Ferus, the canvases were stacked on a long horizontal shelf like items in a grocery story, but the work attained its fame and notoriety in the form of the grid. Though each canvas was painted by hand, the designs were based on hand-traced silkscreen stencils; by the end of the year the artist turned to direct photographic printing to make his famous silkscreens, in part to streamline the process.

As significant in their way as *Fountain*, *Campbell's Soup Cans* not only intensified the question of industrial repetition in art but crystalized a visual crossroads in modernism: the transition between the implacable grid of early abstraction—which came to surround and organize the cans—and pop art's more ludic and ironic appropriation of all-too-concrete commercial and popular imagery. Though blotter itself is basically a commercial format, closer in this sense to the soup cans than the canvases, its classic grid format also embodies the tension between cold formalism and warm iconography, a tension that in both cases also reflects the mechanistic operations driving the satisfaction of consumer appetite, which selects a single desirable unit (or more) from an array of essentially repetitive choices.

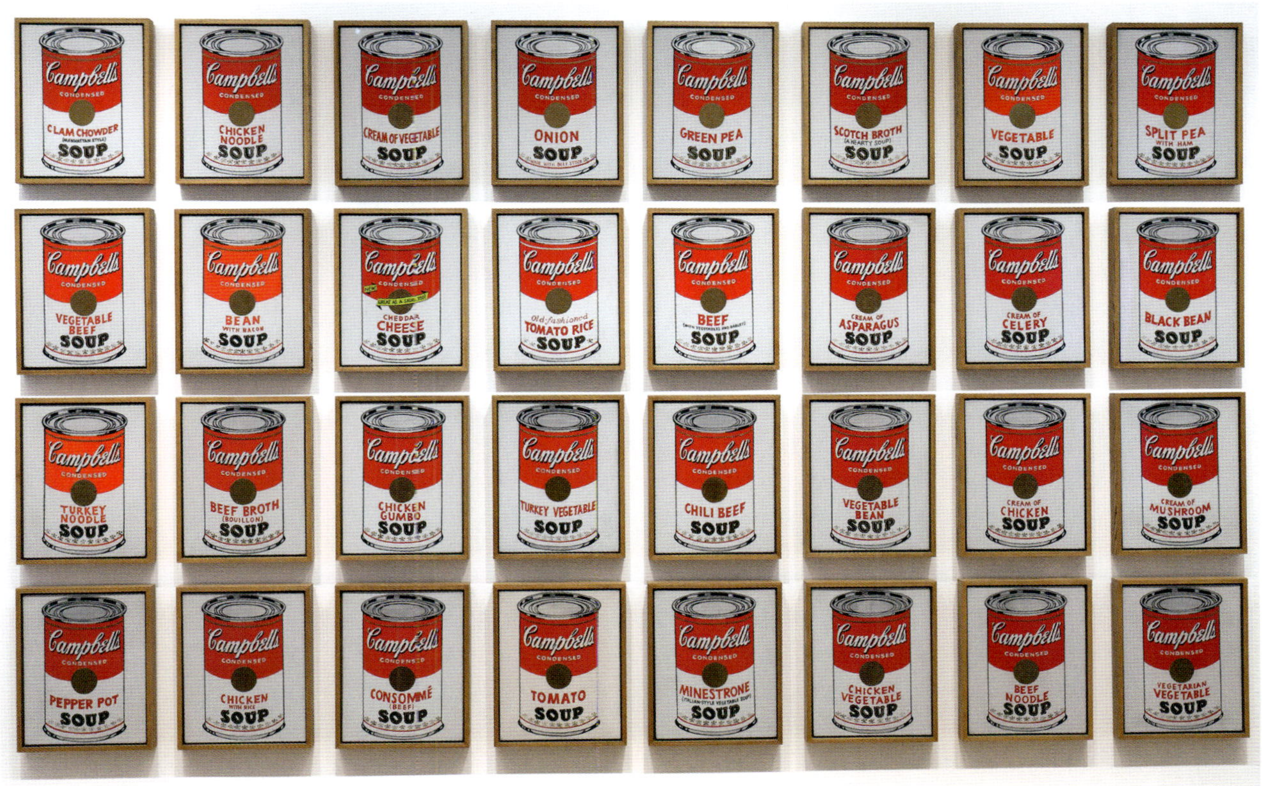

Campbell's Soup Cans, Andy Warhol, 1962. Acrylic with metallic enamel paint on canvas, 32 panels.

As a meticulously hand-painted silkscreen series, *Campbell's Soup Cans* also screws with the distinction between fine art's demand for uniqueness—a singular artist's singular artifact—and the logic of the copy that dominates industrial production. Typically, fine art reflects what Marcus Boon identifies as the "Platonic" logic that dominates Western thinking about the copy, in which the unique or original form stands above a host of inferior and ontologically degraded imitations. In his wonderful book *In Praise of Copying*, Boon contrasts this Platonic view, which is also enshrined in intellectual property law, with an exuberant, almost Dionysian mode of copying he finds in both traditional and indigenous cultures and a host of modern "tribes," from Situationists to punk rockers to early hackers, all of whom "constitute themselves through mimetic processes as a way of coming to power and collective joy." Here the copy celebrates the variations possible within the act of copying itself, making it "part of an excess or abundance, of a *more*."[64] Copying here is an affirmation of multiplicity, even to the point of dizziness. After all, if you iterate anything enough, it becomes phantasmagoric, uncontrollable, something between sacred and monstrous. Think of those Buddhist temples packed with thousands of identical statues, or the multiplying brooms in Disney's "The Sorcerer's Apprentice," or Alton Kelley's iterations of Lon Chaney's ghoulish skull.

Copying is intrinsic to blotter: aesthetically, technically, sociologically. The multiplication of identical images on a single sheet, and the subsequent multiplication of those sheets, reflects a kind of visionary excess that, in a rather psychedelic way, echoes across multiple scales and dimensions. Consider that blotter prints are coupled with molecules that themselves result from a kind of mimesis. For what is LSD manufacture itself if not a kind of copying? The very quest for "purity" idolized and idealized in the lore of the acid lab seeks to replicate a multitude of *identical molecules*, as cleanly separated as possible from isomer variations and other components of the reaction mixture. Absorbing these purified duplicates, the blotter image then repeats the basic promise of all commercial packaging: "trust me, the materials that saturate me are reliable and repeatable in their effects." Of course, while Campbell's Cream of Mushroom soup always tastes the same, the phenomenological "taste" of an individual LSD trip is anything but—a paradoxically "guaranteed novelty" that lends a certain irony to the formal monotony of the blotter sheet. At the same time, all trips are variations of tripping, organized according to a largely dependable metabolic arc and a host of recurring physiological, perceptual, and cognitive features—one of which happens to be the visual and vibratory repetition of forms and patterns, precisely the sort of giddy "traces" that the Houston collage artist Patrick Turk amplifies in his vanity blotter *Reincarnating no. 2* (p. 235), an image that is queasy with copying.

Street blotter makers also embraced mimesis beyond the production of single editions. Makers frequently recycled their own designs, varying colors and details, and sometimes using these variations to mark distinct batches of crystal. At the same time, different makers, then and now, would offer their takes on the same alphabet of images—dolphins, Saturns, dancing bears. Over time, these icons crystalized into blotter archetypes. Gilfeather cranked out a ton of doves, for example, but Forester didn't stick to a single design, drawing his birds from different sources, including Picasso. As noted, some popular blotters—like *Gooney Birds* or *Purple Om*—were also copied outright by rival acid gangs, the slight deviations on the "counterfeit" sheets noticeable only to hardcore nerds like McCloud or Franzosa. But again, while such copying made obvious moves on the street market, it is not always easy to separate economic competition from something like Boon's subcultural play. The Mickey Mouse lifted for *Sorcerer's Apprentice* was not an exact swipe from Disney, but rather an adaptation that, after proving popular, inspired a different acid clan to produce sheets that featured Goofy juggling a similar arc of magic drops—an arc that later recurs, in the form of asterisks, in a blotter honoring *Saturday Night Live*'s Mr. Bill. Such mimesis does not reflect thoughtless aping, but a kind of ribbing among rivals, or an amused fascination with LSD's own visual rhetoric of variation amidst repetition.

Mickey is one of the most recognizable brands in the world, which reminds us of another crucial aspect of blotter mimesis: appropriation. Like Warhol with his soup can labels, though without the alibi of gallery art, underground blotter makers freely swiped images from popular, commercial, and underground culture—sometimes with citation marks attached, sometimes without, and very rarely with permission. Many street blotters did feature totally original designs: simple patterns, homegrown cartoons, or unique and inventive compositions. But far more forged their icons by swiping them first. Makers snatched images from an extraordinary range of sources: video games, playing cards, heraldry, Asian iconography, low-rider culture, firecracker labels, TV, esoteric societies, pinup art, corporate logos, folklore, and federal insignia. Blotter makers also appropriated from their fellow freaks; when the legendary LSD chemist William Leonard Pickard was busted the first time, in Mountain View in 1988, he was holding reams of beautifully printed sheets that featured a collection of rock album covers lifted, without approval, from a book devoted to the San Francisco poster greats Mouse and Kelley. Even the history of art got swiped. Trippy masters—Bosch, Dalí, Escher, da Vinci—were copied in a spirit of homage not unmixed with the opportunism of giftshop merchandise. Other sheets alluded in more clever ways to contemporary trends, like the op art canvases of Bridget Riley or Yoko Ono's Fluxus sculpture *Ceiling Painting/Yes Painting* (1966). The latter piece, in which the gallery visitor must climb a ladder in order to see a diminutive painting of the word "YES" pinned to the ceiling, no doubt inspired one of the more delicate holdings in the Institute of Illegal Images: a single small sheet made of rice paper, its every individual hit embossed with the word "YES."

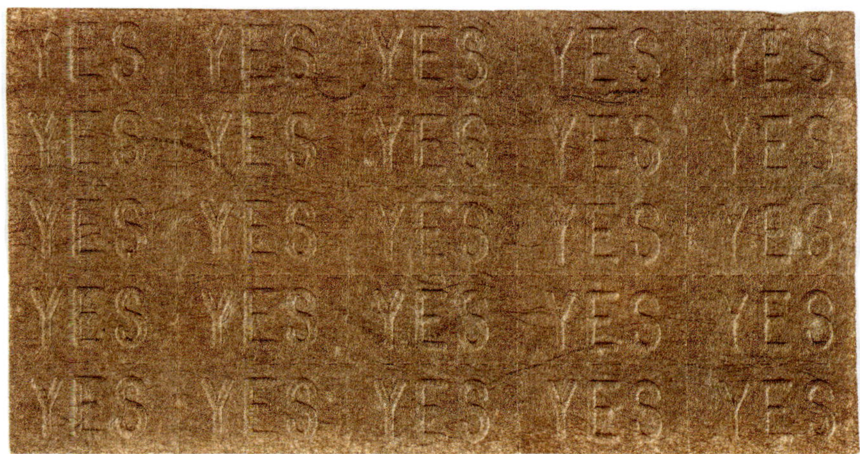

YES, Bernard Hassell, Sonoma, ca. 1985. Embossed rice paper, 2⅞ × 3⅞ in.

The diversity of these sources again suggests that blotter is less an art or a branded product than a wayward medium—a McLuhanesque mechanism for remediating a vast ecology of graphic meanings and materials. In this, the genre spiritually recalls the Verifax Collages that the West Coast artist and bohemian Wallace Berman produced in the 1960s. In these marvelous designs, Berman invited an extraordinary range of appropriated images to resonate within the repeated, mechanically reproduced frame of a hand holding a transistor radio, an image that itself was lifted from an advertisement. Similarly, the blotter format presented a skeletal visual framework—the grid, explicit or implied—that recirculated the slagheap of images that characterized contemporary visuality. This process also recalls Gary Anderson's now ubiquitous recycling logo from the early 1970s, which popped up on some small blue acid hits twenty years later. Translated to blotter, Anderson's hippie modernist icon of ecological

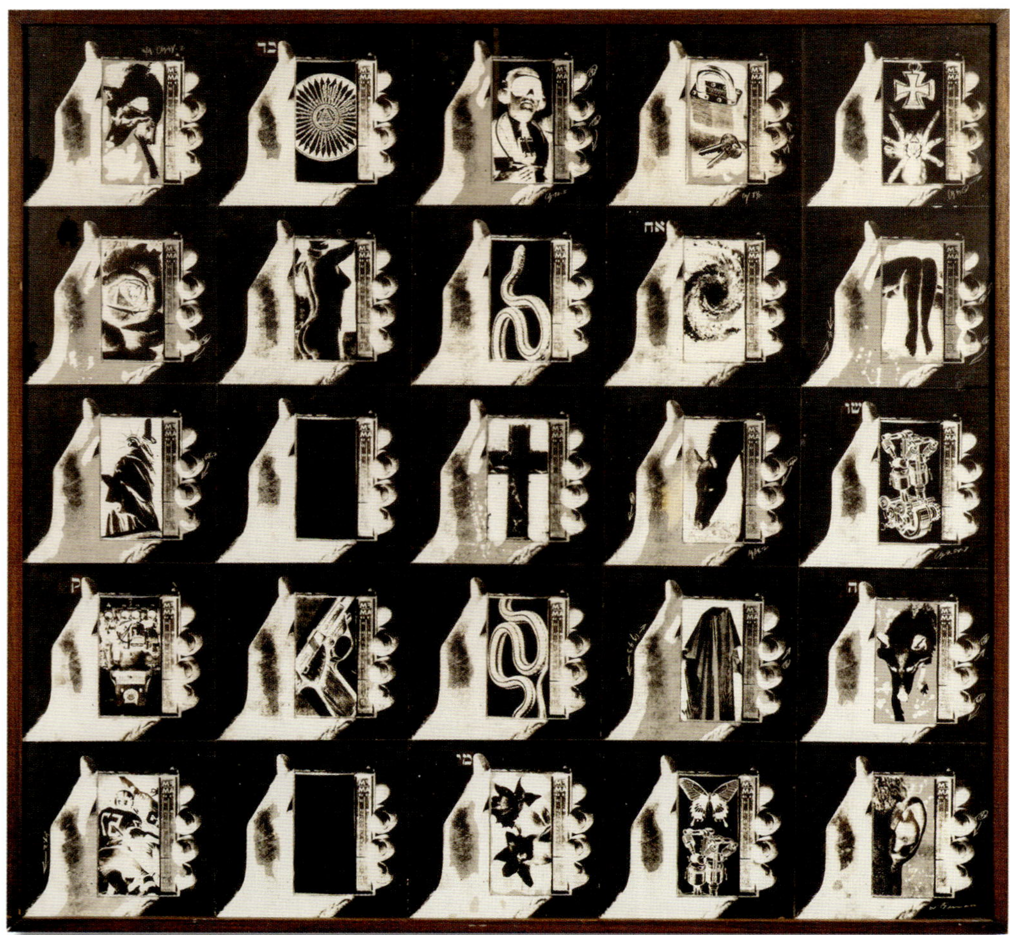

Untitled, Wallace Berman, 1966. Verifax collage. Courtesy of the Estate of Wallace Berman and Kohn Gallery.

feedback suggests a far more archaic law of exchange, a kind of karmic mandala capable of digesting both cosmic forces and consumer waste.

But while blotter can be understood as a street medium that leaned heavily and often lazily on appropriation, some pieces were executed with the sort of devotion, taste, and care that transcend the pulp semiotics of popular exchange. Even if the classiest of these issues do not quite achieve the escape velocity of fine art, they do scrape the stratospheric heights of handicraft. The same fellow who produced the Ono homage noted above, a brilliant British man named Bernard Hassell, was also responsible for *Japanese Crests*, widely recognized as one of the most elegantly designed street blotters ever. Hassell printed these precisely crafted sheets in multiple editions, and they came bound together in a small booklet that fit neatly into a glossy black slipcase. The *YES* rice papers also came bundled in stacks of fifty, "attractively packaged in small gift boxes of the sort one sees in boutiques," according to a newspaper account of Hassell's 1985 bust, which sent him to prison for half a decade. With restrained wit, these boxes were embossed with the word "ACME," the whole package wholesaling for around $3,600.[65] Another Hassell blotter batch even came wrapped in origami.

Though he outsourced the cooking, Hassell was the head of the whole operation, not just the blotter guy. Yet his work clearly transcended

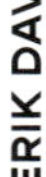

black market economics, reflecting a far more expansive aesthetic intent rooted in Hassell's own sensibility. As a child in war-torn London, Hassell had persevered through a terrible injury and emerged as an exceptionally strong and resilient person. He got psychedelicized in swinging London, where he attended art school before moving to California at the end of the 1960s. Like many, he hoped to turn on the world, and to do so in part by intentionally designing the one he actually lived in. Kat Harrison, who befriended Hassell in 1970s Sonoma County along with her then partner Terence McKenna, described Hassell's sensibility as "clean elegance." He approached all facets of his life with the same crisp and spacious ethos—his homes, his dress, his art and book collections, his social scenes and parties, his acid. It was not for nothing that, when his arresting officers asked Hassell his profession, he had the presence of mind to say he was an "interior designer." Even the machinery Hassell designed to produce his blotter was pristine and sophisticated. "That aesthetic came through everything—always pleasing, clean, and open," says Harrison. She adds that this aesthetic didn't just reflect Hassell's personal taste but spoke to a quality of spacious clarity in the LSD experience itself, "that clean, steely thing" that often gets lost in the garish rainbow tentacles of popular acid iconography.

Hassell's work reminds us that the most artful blotter productions should be seen, at least in part, as devotional offerings to the adamantine excellence that suffuses the greatest acid trips. The best makers, who like medieval icon makers offered their labor anonymously, extend this devotion to the unknown consumers of the drug, whose aesthetic enrichment is invited to begin before the molecules themselves are ingested. Making good blotter is, in this sense, like enhancing a gift by wrapping it wonderfully. For blotter makers still touched by acid idealism, such gifting is as much a matter of love as art.

In at least one case, that love was specific and literal. Later in this volume, William Leonard Pickard—a chemist, researcher, and bon vivant who was imprisoned twice for LSD manufacture, the second time serving twenty years for his role in the largest acid lab bust in history—tells the story of a handful of well-known and exceptionally produced LSD editions in the 1980s that were crafted for the love of a woman, a painter who lived at a legendary San Francisco arts collective called Project Artaud. Unfortunately for the acid chemist and blotter maker involved, the love was initially unrequited. The series of editions the man produced—including *Album Covers*, *Bond of Union*, and a reissue of *Japanese Crests* in eggshell blue—were designed to win that love.

Album Covers, William Leonard Pickard, San Francisco, 1987. Approx. 1 × 1 in.

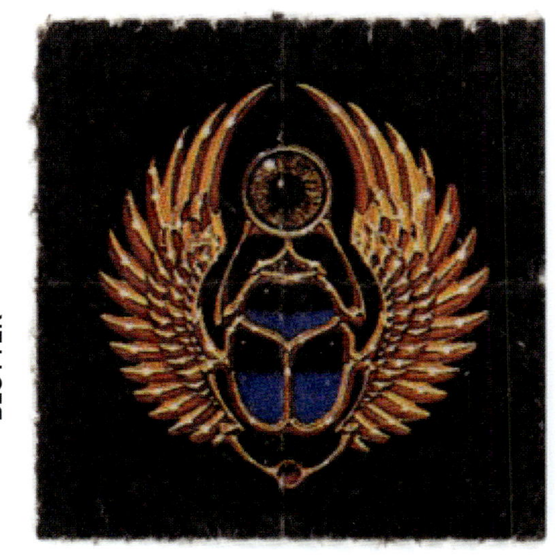

All these superbly printed blotter sheets were contained in glossy black rectangular boxes inspired by the packaging for Lancôme's Magie Noire perfume, whose original version included alchemical symbols set in deep crimson. The blotter boxes were also embossed, in silver, with the Zia sun logo adopted by the state of New Mexico, where Pickard's unrequited love was born, thereby signaling to her that the whole elaborate and expensive presentation was for her pleasure. In addition to cooking the acid, the chemist also devoted many lab hours to an inevitably money-losing batch of mescaline, which happened to be the woman's favorite drug. Here aesthetic aspirations extended to the molecules themselves, which Pickard describes as "massive beautiful fine crystals of mescaline hemisulfate dihydrate, one of the most beautiful substances one has ever seen." The chemist's elaborate and expensive offering did not trigger the hoped-for response, but the larger point was made: all kinds of motives drive the production of beautiful and excellent things, whether we consider those things art or artifact. And one of those motives is the desire to enchant both friends and strangers, to psychedelicize them, to turn them on.

Cartoon Archetype

Blotter acid is postwar paraphernalia, and as such reflects some crucial features of modernist design. Pattern and repetition undergird the form, crisp execution is key, and many sheets are decorated with abstract and minimalist motifs. But the heart and soul of blotter imagery is, well, *imagery*—those symbols, characters, and figures that the German psychedelic writer and wild man Christian Rätsch calls *Iconographia Psychedelia*. In a short essay for the journal *Entheogene*, Rätsch argues that these pictures reflect the "cognitive structures of LSD culture" and therefore suggest a deep mysticism that must be ferreted out through the proper exegesis. Many of the blotter symbols that Rätsch discusses—from the *Taiji* yin-yang symbol to UFOs—are obvious references to the sublimities of acid experience. But Rätsch sees such enchanted symbols everywhere. According to him, the acorn that graces one Gilfeather sheet recalls the sacred pagan oak groves of yore, while the strawberries that ruled Europe for a spell refer to the enigmatic paintings of Hieronymus Bosch, where they supposedly signify the fruit of the tree of knowledge, or possibly the magical mandrake. The octopus, in turn, reflects "a decentralized, expanded consciousness that extends its arms into all realms of being."[66]

Rätsch's interpretations probably tell us more about the hermeneutical excesses of psychedelic perception than about its cognitive structures. Even from a metaphysical perspective, he overweighs the sacred side of the sacred–profane dialectic that lies at the heart of the acid mystery—a dialectic that also characterizes the motives of many blotter makers, who were as interested in expedient appropriation and in-jokes as they were in esoteric symbols. As Neil Benedict commented in an interview, while samurai crests and Hindu yantras may be exotic and suggestive, they were also easily swiped from Dover books. And while some blotter images did reflect the archetypal punch of acid consciousness, others functioned more like badges of tribal identity, like the VW emblem, or the Rolling Stones lips, or the Starship Enterprise. Juxtaposing mainstream icons with a powerful and illegal psychoactive drug could also spark an easy countercultural *frisson*, which at its most extreme gave a sneering, punk-rock edge to blotters featuring the FBI seal or McDonald's golden arches. Once on blotter, even banal icons can be magically transformed into winking double entendres, as with the Rx symbol, or the Procter & Gamble mascot Mr. Clean, offering the ironic-but-not promise of "clean" LSD.

Mr. Clean also falls into perhaps the most important general category of *Iconographia Psychedelia*: cartoons and comic-book characters. As Mr. Natural's pioneering appearance on blotter reminds us, some of these illustrated personalities emerged from the underground itself, and were generally played for laughs, or at least a knowing wink. There is something funny about Mr. Natural trucking across a sheet of acid, an irony that derives from the conjunction of LSD—a mystical and sometimes utopian molecule in many corners—with a sarcastic but lovable cartoon guru that R. Crumb designed to take the piss out of such Aquarian aspirations. Similar miscreant giggles accompanied other countercultural icons that appeared on blotter, whether underground comix stars like Fat Freddy's Cat and Zippy the Pinhead, or weirdo mascots like J. R. "Bob" Dobbs, *SNL*'s Mr. Bill, and Beanie Boy, the snarling mascot of the SoCal skate punk band Rich Kids on LSD (who hired McCloud to produce the cover for their third LP, *Greatest Hits*). Blotter makers also reframed old-school illustrated characters into freak avatars, like Alfred E. Neuman, the Mad Hatter, and the Disney dwarf Dopey (get it?). In later years, blotter makers would come to celebrate more mainstream delinquents like Bart Simpson, the crew of *South Park*, and the aforementioned Beavis & Butt-Head. Clowns were a regular presence as well, sometimes pictured with menace intact.

All these funny folk compel a crucial question unasked by Rätsch: what does this edgy, sometimes aggressively profane humor say about "LSD-Kultur," at least in the years dominated by blotter? From one perspective, the appearance of Zippy the Pinhead on the sacrament confirms the golden age narrative mentioned earlier: acid trips were spiritually transformative in the 1960s, but degenerated into hedonic larks by the end of the 1970s. But this view profoundly misunderstands the role of humor and satire in countercultural consciousness and spirituality. As Christian Greer explains in *Angelheaded Hipsters*, humor is an essential source and feature of freak culture, at once dialectical, situational, and metaphysical. Laughter builds community for those hipsters who "get it," while also serving to deflate the pretentions of fellow travelers, whether naive hippies or arrogant, self-serious radicals. Humor also makes space for transcendental surprise, for the cosmic giggle, or for what Jack Kerouac called the "HOLY GOOF." LSD experiences can be pretty funny, in a way not always shared by other major psychedelics (ayahuasca may be sublime, but it is very rarely amusing). The oblique spirituality of the Merry Pranksters was all about the cosmic giggle, as was Art Kleps's more satiric Neo-American Church, which embraced playful nonsense as a prophylactic against portentous psychedelic metaphysics. Greer argues that as postwar bohemia changed and commercial society absorbed more and more of its features, this humor grew edgier and darker of necessity, which helps explain the sardonic Dada of many blotters from the 1980s.[67] But the play of the negative only takes you so far. By the end of the 1990s, even crude and satiric nihilism had found its way into mainstream TV animation; similarly, the

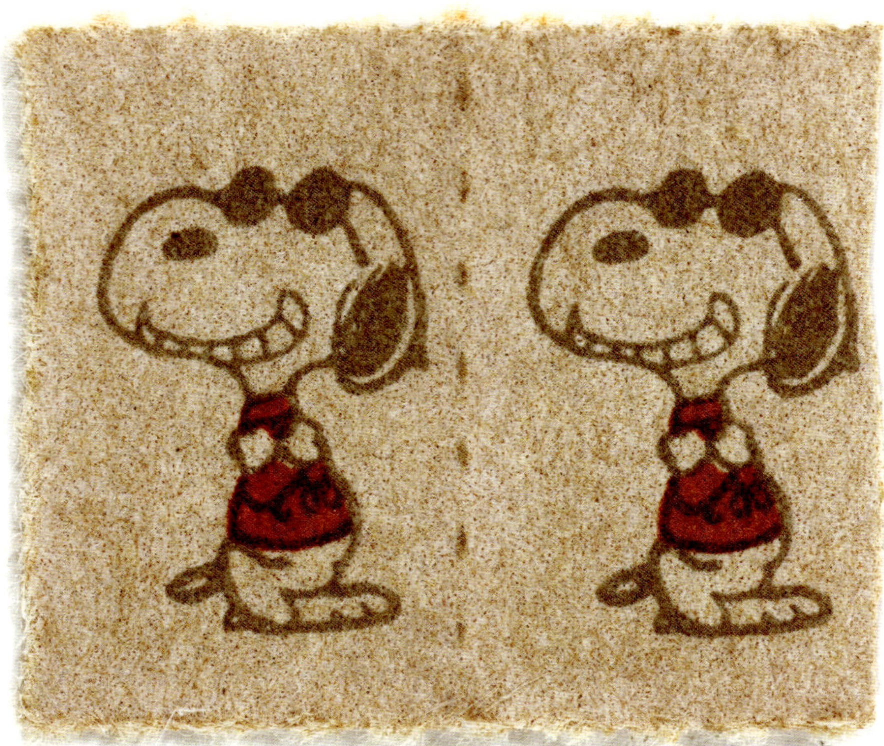

Snoopy, ca. 1981.
5⅘ × 5 in.

appearance of a Cartman or Homer Simpson on blotter barely raised an eyebrow. The edge was now everywhere.

Countercultural laughs alone do not explain the welter of mainstream cartoon and comic-book characters that invaded black market blotter sheets back in the day. While a few of these appropriated figures radiated a certain stoner aura—Bullwinkle, *Doonesbury*'s Zonker, or Woodstock from *Peanuts*, named for the festival—many had no associations with freakery. Popeye, Mighty Mouse, Pink Panther, Porky Pig, and Tweety Bird all showed their familiar mugs on blotter; Donald Duck and Snoopy proved particularly popular, each inspiring multiple designs. Greer might call these appearances examples of "vernacular sacramentalism," the playful celebration of the notion that, as Philip K. Dick once claimed, "The symbols of the divine show up in our world initially at the trash stratum."[68] This is also an acid insight: deeper symbolic meanings lie beneath the sometimes tawdry icons of popular culture.

Superheroes popped up as well: the Batman and the Joker, Judge Dredd, and multiple Supermen. Such heroes had also played an important role in countercultural consciousness. Captain Marvel strongly influenced the young Ken Kesey, who later dubbed himself "Captain Flag," while the cosmic wormholes of Steve Ditko's *Dr. Strange* panels mapped a delirious visionary cartography for the Merry Pranksters and other heads. After all, the very idea of a superpower—a supernatural ability generated through weird science or evolutionary forces—resonated with the psychedelic hope that a chemically aided paranormal mutation was at hand. In the late 1970s, even Timothy Leary appeared as a spaceman superhero on the cover of *Neurocomics*, published by the San Francisco comix outfit Last Gasp, even as Superman graced the cover of Psychic TV's overtly druggy 1988 twelve-inch "Tune In (Turn On the Acid House)."

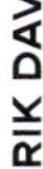

Other blotter superheroes were homegrown. As mentioned above, the lavender *Captain L* sheet stands as one of the earliest figurative blotters, while a Hermes-meets-Silver Surfer character sometimes known as *Captain Yin Yang* (p. 191) appeared on some European tabs that the art critic Carlo McCormick literally found on the street in Amsterdam. Familiar superheroes mutated as well—on the first Superman sheet, the Man of Steel has grown as soft and corpulent as Vegas Elvis. And one of the punchiest freak-pop blotter silkscreens of all displays an elegantly three-dimensional version of Shazam's lightning bolt insignia. Along with the graffiti-styled shadow effect, this design takes on extra meaning given the long-standing linkage of LSD and the iconography of electricity. Examples here include the Rick Griffin poster that inspired Owsley's White Lightning tabs, as well as the thirteen-pointed bolt that adorns the Grateful Dead's famous "Steal Your Face" logo, another Owsley creation and one that also wound up on blotter.

Similar tripster wit characterizes the most exuberant example of a mainstream cartoon to appear on blotter: Mickey Mouse in his aforementioned guise as the Sorcerer's Apprentice. When this blotter hit the streets in the late 1970s, Mickey had long served as a wholesome icon of middle America. But "The Sorcerer's Apprentice" film itself, included in *Fantasia* from 1940, reminds us that Mickey also embodied what Walter Benjamin called "the ambiguity of situations which have both a comic and a horrifying effect."[69] For all its comedy, the mouse's Faustian fuck-up also telegraphs the sort of out-of-control feedback loops that modernity forges between power, labor, and increasingly autonomous technologies. Mickey's appearance on Sandoz-saturated blotter is thus doubly ironic. On the one hand, we have a tongue-in-cheek celebration of another magical product of the Promethean West—LSD, whose drops Mickey appears to be conjuring between his hands. But this figure casts another shadow: the fact that the LSD trade itself also involves risky youngsters stealing the fire from heaven and replicating enchanting molecules that have a life of their own.

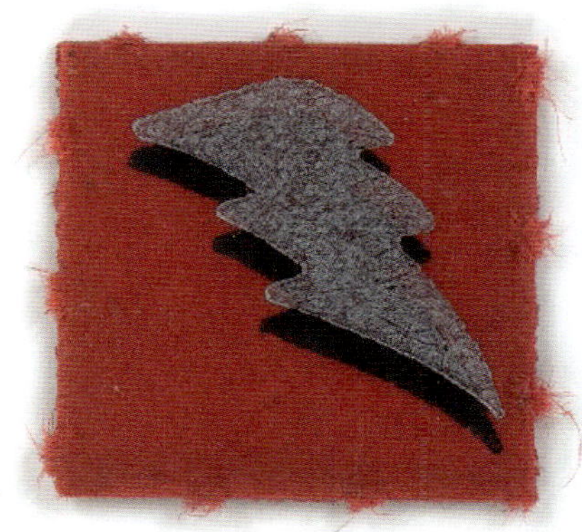

Lightning Bolt, Berkeley, ca. 1983. Single hit, ⅜ × ⅜ in. Cotton paper.

Appropriately, the afterlife of this particular blotter grew to absurd and fantastic proportions. By far the most powerful and persistent urban legend associated with blotter LSD was the "Mickey Mouse Acid" rumor, later known as the Blue Star Tattoo scare. According to the urban legend specialist Jan Harold Brunvand (1986), the story began in the early 1980s, when Mickey was circulating on the street. According to the tale, which was spread through fliers or leaflets, dealers had started directly targeting children with temporary "lick and stick" tattoos that were dosed with drugs. Ann Stuart Berry, then director of Drug Prevention and Education for Young Children, warned parents to look out for "brightly colored paper tabs resembling postage stamps that have pictures of Super-Mouse [*sic*] and other Disney characters on them."[70] The fliers warned that even briefly touching the papers could get you high. The rumors reached such intensity that even the drug warriors at the DEA tried to calm things down, informing the public that no evidence suggested that dealers were focused on kids, or that any child had been injured by touching an "LSD-laden 'tattoo.'" Nonetheless, the legend lumbered on for decades, like a zombie. Part of its longevity may reflect the unsettling liminality of blotter itself: little cartoon vectors designed to enter the body, their contents absorbed through tongues and stomachs.[71]

That said, there are deeper and more organic links between the phenomenology of LSD and the peculiar life of cartoons. Acid can turn your eyeballs into blobs of Silly Putty that lift forms from the surface of the world, twisting and exaggerating them into animated and sometimes goofy caricatures. And somewhere between these vibrating organic forms and the angels and demons that haunt deep visionary experience lies the "cartoon continuum": a zone of acid visuals populated by pop culture archetypes, graphic animism, and a paradoxically sacred irreverence. While many blotters could be said to reflect aspects of the cartoon continuum, the dimension itself seems to open its doors in *Crazy World* (p. 130), a Gilfeather blotter from the late 1970s. The picture itself came

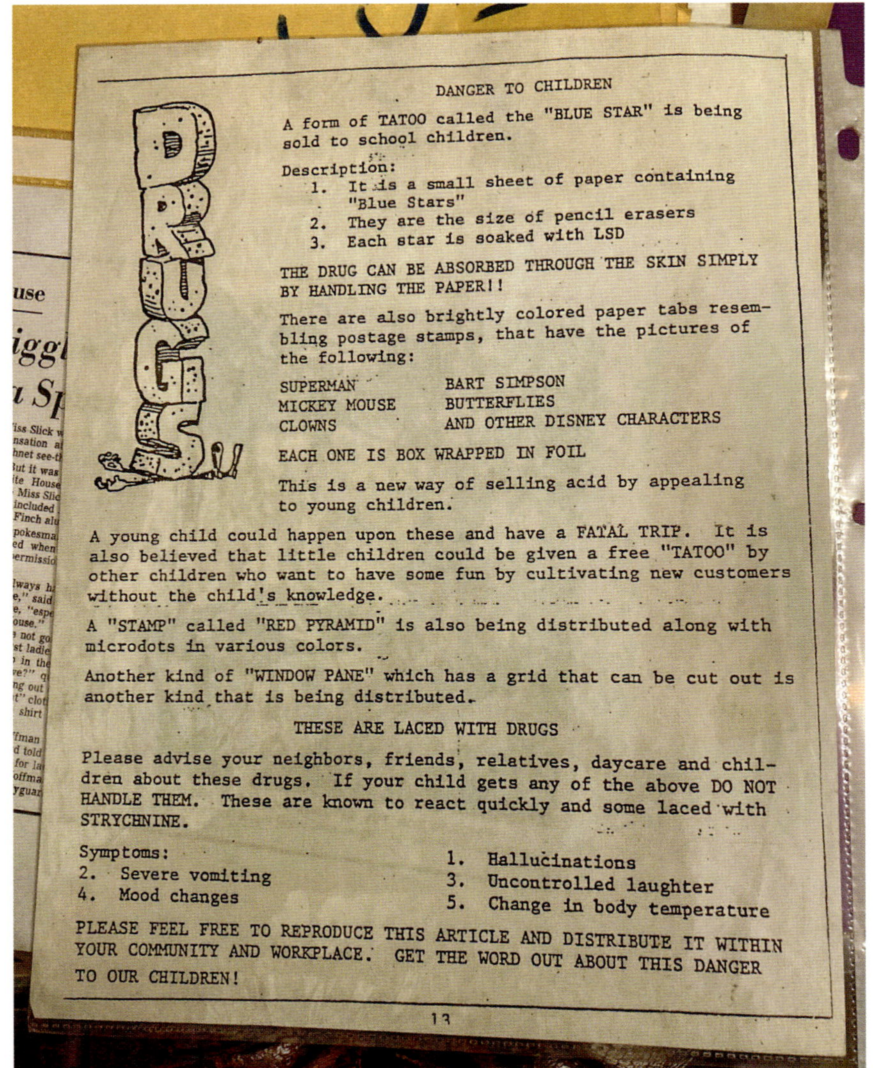

DANGER TO CHILDREN

A form of TATOO called the "BLUE STAR" is being sold to school children.

Description:
1. It is a small sheet of paper containing "Blue Stars"
2. They are the size of pencil erasers
3. Each star is soaked with LSD

THE DRUG CAN BE ABSORBED THROUGH THE SKIN SIMPLY BY HANDLING THE PAPER!!

There are also brightly colored paper tabs resembling postage stamps, that have the pictures of the following:

SUPERMAN	BART SIMPSON
MICKEY MOUSE	BUTTERFLIES
CLOWNS	AND OTHER DISNEY CHARACTERS

EACH ONE IS BOX WRAPPED IN FOIL

This is a new way of selling acid by appealing to young children.

A young child could happen upon these and have a FATAL TRIP. It is also believed that little children could be given a free "TATOO" by other children who want to have some fun by cultivating new customers without the child's knowledge.

A "STAMP" called "RED PYRAMID" is also being distributed along with microdots in various colors.

Another kind of "WINDOW PANE" which has a grid that can be cut out is another kind that is being distributed.

THESE ARE LACED WITH DRUGS

Please advise your neighbors, friends, relatives, daycare and children about these drugs. If your child gets any of the above DO NOT HANDLE THEM. These are known to react quickly and some laced with STRYCHNINE.

Symptoms:
1. Hallucinations
2. Severe vomiting
3. Uncontrolled laughter
4. Mood changes
5. Change in body temperature

PLEASE FEEL FREE TO REPRODUCE THIS ARTICLE AND DISTRIBUTE IT WITHIN YOUR COMMUNITY AND WORKPLACE. GET THE WORD OUT ABOUT THIS DANGER TO OUR CHILDREN!

13

"Blue Star Tattoo" information sheet, 1980s.

from the hand of John Flores, a local San Francisco illustrator originally from Italy who, for once, gave permission to the blotter makers to reproduce his work. Here we see dozens of characters, drawn from underground comix, cartoons, and Hollywood, hurtling their space vehicles through a surreal crossover multiverse saturated with figures drawn from commercial illustration and what McCloud calls "the LSD astral plane."

But there is yet another motive for the prevalence of cartoon characters in blotter. Many of these characters are also animals, and animals, including mythical beasts, are without doubt the most copious single category of figurative images found in the III archive. Such creatures come in all shapes and sizes and styles: bunnies from illustrated children's books, crude handstamps of dancing frogs, naturalist drawings of snakes and owls, corporate logos like Penguin Books and Mobil Oil's Pegasus, fabulous beasts like gryphons and unicorns, and lots of dolphins and dragons and doves. Additionally, a number of blotters feature less charismatic critters, like flies and ants, the latter of which wander across one Gilfeather sheet in an asymmetrical circuit pattern.

Sometimes the transformative symbolism is clear, as with Pegasus or alchemical salamanders. Other times, animals serve more totemic roles. The formidable Texan artist Jim Franklin, for example, had already remade the armadillo into a hippie Lone Star mascot when some blotter clients from Austin—San Francisco's freak sister city—commissioned an armadillo sheet from Gilfeather (p. 123). Similarly, most of the bears found on blotter were insignia of the Deadhead tribe. Owsley's nickname in the scene was Bear, which inspired Bob Thomas to add some bears to his cover art for 1973's *History of the Grateful Dead, Volume One*, a.k.a. *Bear's Choice*. (Thomas's design was based on a standard 36-point lead printer's slug that had been in use for at least a decade.) For Deadheads, dancing bears play the cuddly yin to the dread yang of the skeleton, though the ever-opinionated Owsley insisted that the bears were actually *marching*. Some bear blotters veer toward Hallmark kitsch, while others are roughly rubber-stamped, like the indulgent ursid in *Party Animal* (p. 144), identified by the DEA as a "bear-devil."

What lies behind this blotter bestiary? Like cartoons and other kid stuff, animals represent a relatively accessible escape from the lonely adult rationality that imprisons many modern human minds and in turn drives some of them to take drugs. Animals represent and offer "animist" digressions from the disenchanted aspects of modernity, and therefore serve as fit avatars for a psychoactive domain that can literally animate the world, bringing forms to life and rendering philosopher Gregory Bateson's underlying "pattern that connects" into an in-your-face source of messages, signs, and conversations with the nonhuman. While they represent the more naturalistic side of LSD's mysterium, beasts also embody what William Blake called "Animal forms of wisdom"—allies in ecologies that link nature and the self.

As you might imagine, blotter's *Iconographia Psychedelia* also includes many explicitly religious and occult symbols. Earlier we discussed Manny Vogel's esoteric *Horus*, only one of a number of blotters featuring Egyptian imagery; other notables include a Mouse and Kelley scarab and a three-colored pharaoh lifted from a playful Rick Griffin panel in *Zap Comix* (p. 150). While the aura of these blotters can be traced in part to popular Egyptomania—the "Treasures of Tutankhamun" tour in the late 1970s, or the Dead's 1978 Egypt shows—they also draw from a perennial occult fascination with the ancient kingdom. *Star Anubis Skull*, for example, was reportedly associated with the Church of Satan, still headquartered at the time of the sheet's release in San Francisco's outer Richmond, where Church leader Anton LaVey lived in an Edwardian house painted entirely black. Another explicitly esoteric blotter design featured a dense kabbalistic pentagram lifted from Éliphas Lévi's *Dogme et Rituel de la Haute Magie*, a founding text of modern occultism that came out in the 1850s. This blotter (p. 120), which was packaged in a classy envelope, was unusual in that the ink itself was dosed with LSD; a reverse printing of the same pentagram on the flip side of the sheets assured an even distribution of the drug.

Purple Jesus/Carbon Jesus, Mark McCloud and Alex Grey, San Francisco, 1992. 7½ × 7½ in.

Occultism was a core current of the acid milieu, of course, and many a pagan, witch, and ceremonial magician enjoyed their psychedelic accelerants. But the esotericism suggested by some blotters also reflected the secret society of the LSD underground itself, whose furtiveness only intensified when psychedelia faded as a dominant countercultural framework. Consider an elegant pair of rare, limited-edition blotters that bore explicitly Masonic and Rosicrucian imagery (p. 172). These were crafted around 1990 by a former Ragusa lieutenant named Walter Bloch, who designed them with an old-school psychonaut elite in mind. At a time when the strength of the average hit was declining precipitously, making even the "disco doses" from the late 1970s seem relatively strong, Walter's blotters were heavy-duty four-way hits that hearkened back to a more adventurous era of Akashic meltdown. Though the sheets didn't announce their dosage, a key of sorts lay in the image, which in both cases featured a red dot roughly where the cut-along lines would cross on a properly subdivided four-way.

Other sheets bore more explicitly religious imagery, though once again we should be wary of drawing sacred conclusions too hastily. Blotter makers loved punchy logos, and the faiths of the world have a surfeit, like the Islamic moon and star, or the *Taijitu*, or the Sanskrit Om—all of which appeared on sheets over the years. Other editions hosted full theophanies of gods and goddesses, like White Tara, Ganesh, and the Virgin of Guadalupe. Perhaps the most iconic religious blotter resembles an actual icon. *Purple Jesus*, also called *Carbon Jesus* on the street, was lifted from an oil painting by the visionary artist Alex Grey. Grey crafted the image in 1987 for an unreleased LP made by the house band of the Church of the Little Green Man, a parodic freak faith founded by the artist Mike Osterhout. When McCloud purchased the original painting, from the then largely unknown Grey, he paid $1,000 for it, more than the asking price. Then he sent it to Argentina, a gift for his mom. A few years later, without asking Grey's permission, McCloud translated the conveniently shaped image into a few thousand 7.5"-square, 900-hit sheets and released them into the wild. (There were two versions, a full-sheet single reproduction and a grid of nine Jesuses, both of which included the wooden

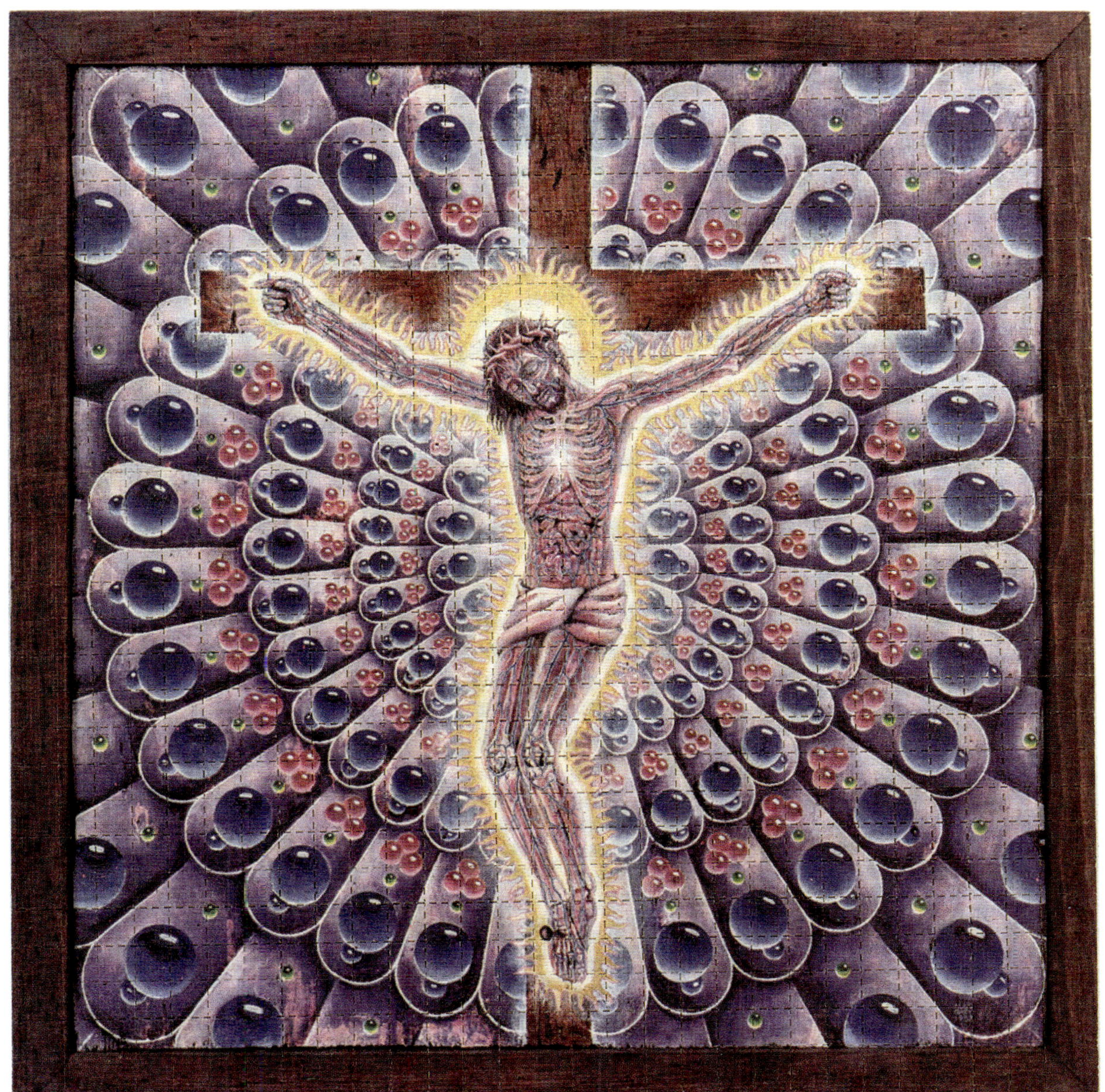

frame.) Grey wasn't particularly amused when he found out, but he came to appreciate McCloud's canny merchandising of his work, which proved popular in the Dead scene and beyond, becoming one of the more memorable blotters of the 1990s.

Who is this Jesus? How should we frame the figure, when the frame itself literally forms the cross he bears? Is Grey's depiction, part Matthias Grünewald and part Robert Williams, *religious*? Incarnating a battered and blue version of the luminous biological bodies that are Grey's trademark, here the crucified god-man seems to dangle between the holy and the weird, suspended at a criss-crossroads that, like the Church of the Little Green Man, or the earlier Church of the Subgenius, finds its sacred in the profane, or rather in the bizarre and incandescent coupling of the sacred *and* the profane. As Jason Sexton writes in *Boom*, Grey's acid icon represents "the humanity of Jesus juxtaposed with astral glory radiating from his body and shining through his heart, along with the explicit connection of Jesus to LSD and the psychedelic community." Far from a blasphemous transgression, then, this blotter Christ memorializes the original Jesus freak, who remains as central to the acid pantheon as Shiva or Buddha. As McCloud told Sexton, "If you take acid long enough, you've gotta deal with Jesus."[72]

McCloud was raised Catholic. His father was knighted by the pope into the Order of St. Gregory, and his mother remained devout until her end, which is why she got the Grey painting in the first place. When McCloud first took communion as a youth in Argentina, he fully expected a transformative experience, a "one-on-one with the Maker." He gave a complete confession beforehand, and sincerely consumed the sacrament. But after swallowing the host, nothing happened. One of his friends even got in line twice, just to make sure their disappointment wasn't a fluke. "We got burned," McCloud says. "No magic. So I said, well, I'm going to find where they hid this, you know? I was on a quest for the host."

In McCloud's spiritual narrative, he got what he wanted with that tab of Orange Sunshine he swallowed back in Santa Clara, which introduced him to God and Satan and the vibrating eons in between. Though he came to reject organized religion, except maybe the Church of the Little Green Man, McCloud believes that tripping is sacred, or at least a "healthy spiritually emancipating act." But in another way, McCloud holds fast to his boyhood faith, because his core personal metaphor for blotter is not food or numismatics but the communion host.

Leaving the mystery of transubstantiation aside, the host already presents a powerful media metaphor that illuminates some of the subtle spiritual connections that acid blotter makes between object, experience, and image. While some communion confections feature blank surfaces, in many Christian communities the wafer is stamped with the emblem of the local church or diocese, and sometimes with a dove. At the same time, the manufacturing and imprinting of the edible object is not sufficient to lend it sacred power, which requires a separate operation. Consecration "doses" the wafer with the Holy Spirit, and its consumers eat it in the expectation of grace. In this way, the host differs somewhat from the magical and healing spells that, in traditions around the world, are inscribed on small pieces of paper that are rolled up and consumed. Tibetan popular medicine, for example, includes many such edible mantras, some of which are printed with wooden blocks. While these spells are sometimes blessed by tantric lamas, impregnating them with something like the priest's consecrating power, the inscribed spell itself is considered efficacious. But with the Catholic sacrament, the symbolic inscription is only incidental; the power and effect lie in the actions and words of the priest, and through him the Holy Spirit. "By themselves, wafer and paper have the status of liturgical implements," says Claire Fanger, a historian of religion and magic. "You might want them to be attractive and appropriately decorated, but they aren't holy in themselves."[73]

This distinction raises the central question of illustrated blotter: do the images make a difference or not? Do they phenomenologically inflect the spirit of the psychedelic, or do they remain empty packaging? If these icons do make a difference, how do we characterize this effect—is it a spell, a prayer, a costume? As Owsley proved when he stained the same crystal with different food coloring dyes, which took on different associations once they hit the street, the look and feel of the carrier media does shape the lore and thus the "set and setting" that inform the experience of LSD. In that sense, if all other conditions are the same, it does make a difference whether you eat a flying saucer or a dove or Bart Simpson's slingshot. At the same time, there is a limit to such influence, just as there is a limit to set and setting, or the placebo effect. Images can only take you so far into the invisible, or the infinitesimal.

Given Mark McCloud's investment in the art of blotter, you might think that he would insist on the talismanic significance of its imagery. And he does, but only to a point. "The trip is about the beanstalk, not the magic beans," he says. The aesthetics of blotter cannot be confined to the material object; it is "completed," he says, by personally turning on, an act that is ultimately more iconoclastic than iconophilic. "You don't want to make them into the golden calf," he says. Instead, he invites students of the art to note that if you place a well-made and properly perfed sheet of blotter before a lamp, you can see the light through the perforations. "Speaking as a blotter artist, no matter how involved you are with the supremacy of your vision, you can hold that sheet up to the light and see through it absolutely. You can see the transparency of the shadow on the wall that is the image itself, and you can see through it to the other side."

United States v. Mark McCloud

In March 2001, thirteen months after McCloud's home was raided and his archive and person seized by federal law enforcement, the blotter maker and collector found himself in a US District Courthouse in Kansas City, hearing a young bulldog attorney named Michael Oliver make the case against him. There was a lot of evidence. In addition to the blotters taken from McCloud's Mission home, including his framed collection and 33,000 boxed sheets that McCloud himself had manufactured on rag paper, the prosecution also presented dozens of street blotters, loaded with acid, that they claimed could be traced directly to the perforating machine they had confiscated from McCloud's home. Oliver described McCloud not simply as a blotter maker, but as the source of the LSD itself—a kingpin personally responsible for a good chunk of the acid circulating in America.

The dosed blotters in evidence came from around the country, but *United States v. Mark McCloud* took place in Kansas City because the acid dealers busted there—dealers now acting as witnesses for the prosecution—had been working near an elementary school. This allowed prosecutors to toss in an extra, morally compromising charge to the two counts of conspiracy to manufacture and distribute LSD that McCloud was already looking at. The proximity to schools also dovetailed with Oliver's argument that some blotters in McCloud's collection, like *Sorcerer's Apprentice*, proved that acid dealers like him were directly targeting kids.

The feds, who had already spent millions on phone taps, analysis, and months of surveillance, made it clear: they wanted Mark McCloud to spend the rest of his life in prison. About the only silver lining for McCloud in the prosecution's case was his codefendant: Nick Sand, the legendary Orange Sunshine cook who had indirectly gifted McCloud with his life-changing trip back in Santa Clara. McCloud had never met Sand, who was not present in the courtroom and whose trial was scheduled for a later date, but he always wanted to. If McCloud had to face the music, at least he was doing it alongside one of his heroes. The other bonus was the courtroom appearance of the DEA chemist and *Blotter Index* compiler Edward Franzosa, who testified that the particular bite marks on the street blotter proved that they were perforated with the same machine found in McCloud's house. McCloud was okay with this testimony in part because he respected Franzosa, whom he saw as a fellow blotter obsessive.

McCloud's defense attorney was again Doron Weinberg, who often fought public corruption cases and would later defend Phil Spector, unsuccessfully, against murder charges. Savvy and dramatic, Weinberg also hailed from outlandish San Francisco, but the lawyer knew that he and his client were not in Oz anymore. When Weinberg began his defense, after three days of relentless prosecution, he faced a suspicious and highly unsympathetic midwestern jury. He made no attempt to hide the fact that McCloud was a drug user and a freak, or that McCloud was responsible for printing and perfing an ungodly amount of blotter paper. But Weinberg insisted that the witnesses were corrupt, and that absolutely no evidence linked McCloud to the actual LSD that later impregnated some of his sheets. None of the blotter confiscated in the Mission, he underscored, was loaded. But in order for this crucial fact to really hit home, Weinberg also needed to explain why anyone would produce so much paraphernalia without intending to dose it with drugs. In other words, Weinberg needed to convince the jury that blotter had value in and of itself, which meant arguing that at least some people believed it was culturally significant on its own. As a Kansas City reporter covering the trial put it, "The decision to convict or acquit ultimately became a question of art."[74]

Nick Sand, Nicolás Rosenfeld, 2016. 7½ × 10 in.

Of course, one person's art is another person's pile of trash—especially, perhaps, in Kansas City. Who cares if McCloud had already organized blotter art shows in California and New York City? As Oliver argued, these could be written off as nothing more than a smug cover for illegal activities. Could little pieces of paper with Mickey Mouse and lightning bolts on them really be considered *art*? What the defense needed was a persuasive authority in contemporary and popular art practice, and Weinberg and McCloud knew just who to call: Carlo McCormick. A New York–based critic, McCormick contributed to reputable organs like *Artform*, *Art in America*, and *Art News*. He had also written the groundbreaking catalog essay for McCloud's "Holy Transfers" show in 1987.

But Weinberg didn't put McCormick on the stand as an expert witness. Doing so might have led the prosecution to dig up a rival art authority whose conservative views would in turn have cast McCormick as a bullshitting East Village hipster. Instead, Weinberg called McCormick as a character witness. The critic explained that he had met McCloud over twenty years earlier at SFAI, and knew him as a ceramicist, visual artist, and professor. McCormick lectured at McCloud's MFA

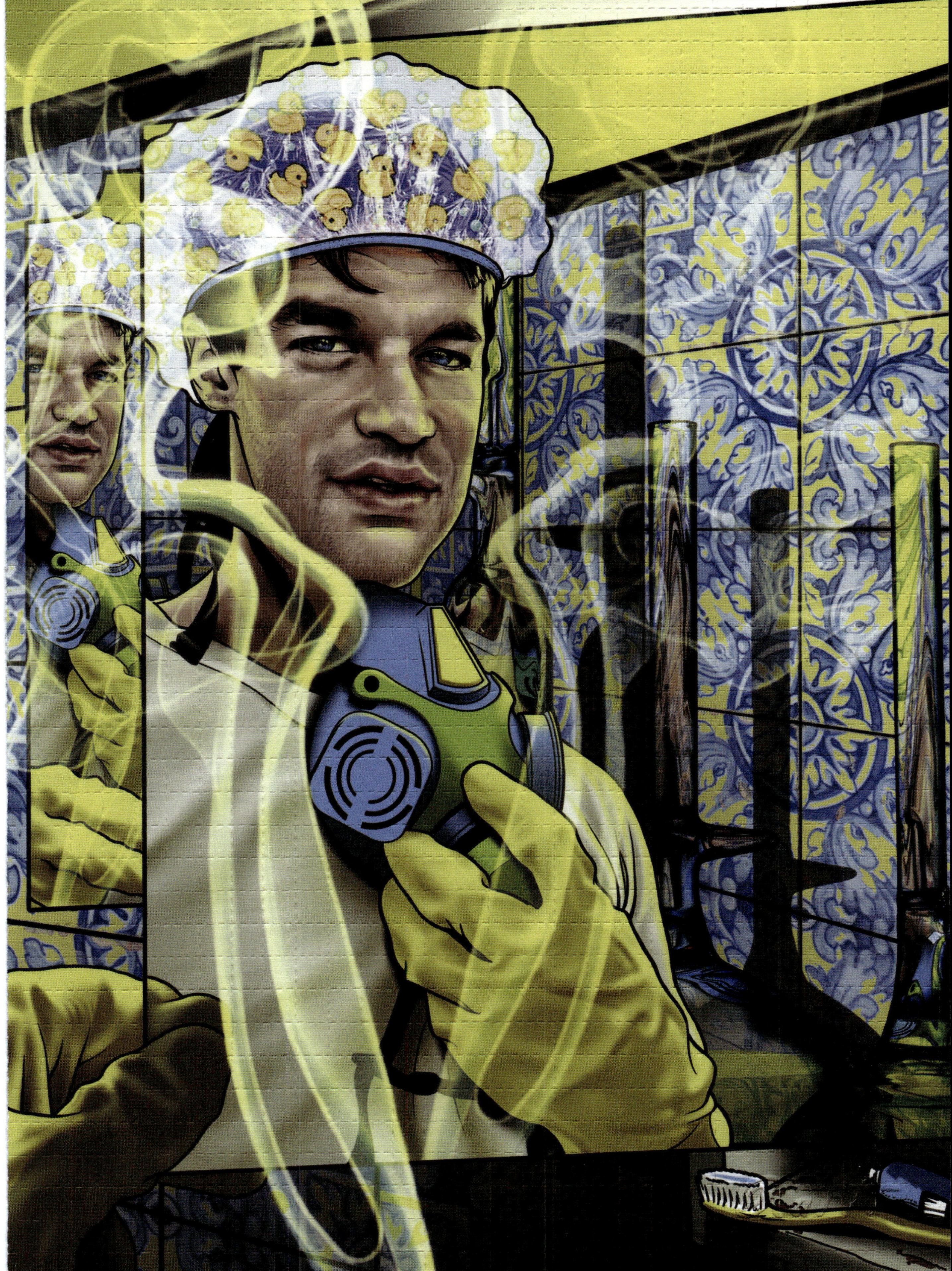

class at Santa Clara and worked with him on some gallery shows. As the testimony unfolded, Weinberg allowed McCormick to also establish his critical bona fides, and to drop in crucial observations about the contemporary art world—especially the fact that the sort of appropriation that landed Mickey Mouse on a small square of perforated paper was widely recognized as a vital strategy of modern and contemporary art. As an example, McCormick mentioned Andy Warhol, an iconic figure even in Kansas City.

Oliver aggressively cross-examined McCormick, accusing him of being paid for his appearance. "The DA was incredibly arrogant and belligerent, and he made mistakes," McCormick now says. "He asked me open-ended questions he didn't know the answers to, and then had the temerity to have a fight about art with an art critic." When Oliver asked McCormick how a sheet of paper bearing the FBI logo could possibly have artistic value, McCormick didn't miss a beat: "That would be considered art all throughout the art world, sir." Soon McCormick had the jury laughing. Rather than idealize the art world, the critic made fun of it, exposing a shifty scene where creativity and commerce merged in peculiar ways. While the number of sheets that McCloud had produced seemed incriminating, McCormick explained that the overproduction of prints was common for artists like Picasso or Chagall.

For this line of argument to really stick, however, the defense had to show that there actually *was* a market for undipped blotter. Luckily, McCloud had been quietly selling both defanged street blotter and fresh clean sheets for a while. Compared to the popular market for vanity blotter just around the corner, McCloud's efforts were modest, and had more to do with establishing blotter as an art object and collectible than with making real money. After his SFAI show, he sold a few framed hits to other curators. As he got his hands on more material, including growing numbers of complete sheets that had been diverted undipped from the street trade, he began passing on items to a guy at ArtRock, a gallery in San Francisco that, like Psychedelic Solution in Manhattan, was spearheading the market for classic and contemporary psychedelic rock posters. Illustrated blotters and trippy poster art are kissing cousins, after all, and soon McCloud was mounting small shows at the gallery. Later, when he started making his own blotter, McCloud would set aside a box or two, wait for the street distribution to run its course, and then pass the virgin paper on to ArtRock, who started listing the stuff in their catalog. At the trial, ArtRock head Phil Cushway testified that he had purchased as many as 12,000 sheets from McCloud over the previous decade, all for resale, usually pegged around $35 a pop.

At some point, the ArtRock catalog also started including signed blotter sheets, which often listed for hundreds of dollars each. But unlike normal art prints, the autographs did not belong to the blotter artists themselves but rather to psychedelic illuminati like Ken Kesey, John Lilly, and Grace Slick. These "signature blotters" became the autographed baseballs of psychedelia, drawing their fetishistic power from the marriage of legacy drug celebrities with colorful contemporary paraphernalia. In effect, the legends of the counterculture, their game days mostly behind them, got to personally "sign off" on artifacts of an ongoing if less beguiling drug scene that was in turn ennobled through those very signatures. For obvious reasons, the actual blotters signed were not impregnated with LSD, though the editions those sheets were drawn from were, initially at least, destined to be dosed. What signature blotters did instead was replace the usual psychoactive molecules with the semiotic charge of heroic charisma and, over time, the magic of market appreciation. Eventually the most desirable signature blotters traded for many times more money than the sheets would have been worth if they had been soaked with acid.

The origins of signature blotter are murky, but the fellow who always claimed credit for the idea was Thomas Lyttle, a gourmet chef and weird scene habitué from Florida. Lyttle also published *Psychedelic Monographs and Essays*, one of the few serious (if sometimes far-out) journals of psychedelic studies available in the late 1980s and early 1990s, when nobody cared about psychedelic culture beyond heads themselves. Lyttle befriended McCloud, who gave him the lowdown on blotter and helped him build a collection. Lyttle then commissioned McCloud to produce six new blotter designs that would be reserved exclusively for the signature and collector market that was just beginning to bud.

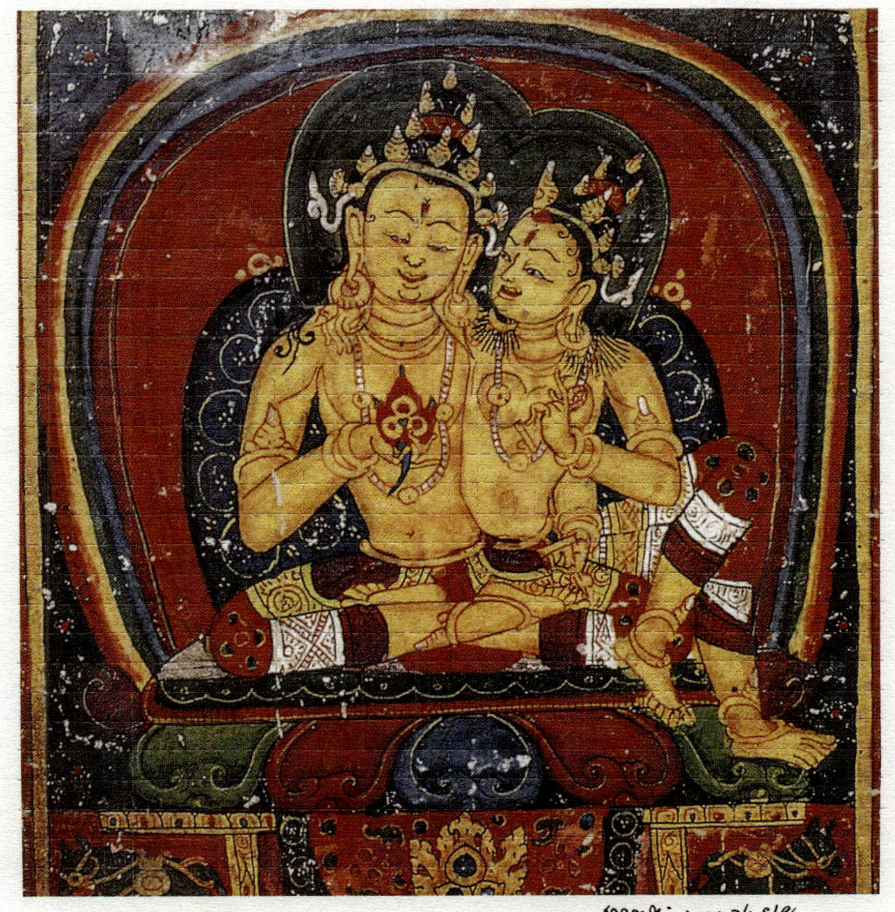

Ratnasambhava, Thomas Lyttle, 1996. 9½ × 9½ in. Drawn from a fifteenth-century Tibetan *tsakali*, or initiation card. Signed by Allen Ginsberg (above).

McCloud went to town on Lyttle's order, developing new designs with his team, including the artist Dana Smith and his now ex-wife Alexandria Martin. McCloud also enlisted the Pizz, an LA lowbrow artist and tiki lord who crafted two memorably goofy images based on McCloud's suggestions: a swirly-eyed Mad Hatter, his clock striking thirteen, and *Alfred E. Pluribus*, a perverse melding of a winged dollar-bill pyramid with a cartoon Cyclops eye and Alfred E. Neuman's instantly recognizable gap-toothed grin. But after McCloud produced the sheets, the notoriously mercurial Lyttle changed his mind and decided to make six of his own. These largely inferior images—which include an appropriated *ukiyo-e* geisha and some fractal designs now locked eternally in the curdled aesthetic amber of the 1990s—are the first real "vanity blotters": perforated sheets whose entire purpose is to be signed, sold, and traded among collectors. Over the years, Lyttle used these and other vanities to capture signatures from a raft of personalities, including Allen Ginsberg, Ken Kesey, Alexander Shulgin, Robert Anton Wilson, and Ram Dass.

McCloud's six blotters did not go to waste. Instead, he released them onto the street, where they were enthusiastically consumed. He also got up to his own signature campaigns. After taking the liberty of making blotter based on Grey's *Purple Jesus* painting, McCloud convinced Grey to number and sign 500 undipped sheets. McCloud then approached Timothy Leary, the most incandescent of all psychedelic luminaries. Leary signed 250 sheets of *Heavenly Blue*—a McCloud production, named for a breed of Morning Glory, that featured a flower plucked from the "Blue Rose" poster that Stanley Mouse made in 1978 for the final Dead show at Winterland. Suitably matted and framed, signed sheets of both *Purple Jesus* and *Heavenly Blue* were then sold through the Greenpeace booths found at Dead shows in those years (proceeds were split). Other signature blotters were used to raise funds for the prisoner campaigns organized by John Beresford, a much-loved mensch who had worked with LSD as a psychiatrist in the 1960s but gave up his license in 1991 to advocate for convicts incarcerated for psychedelic offenses.

Even Albert Hofmann, who looked askance at the drug scene, signed a few fundraising blotters, albeit for his own nonprofit Albert Hofmann Foundation. McCloud once again supplied the paper for the campaign, but like Beresford, and in the wake of his own experience with Operation Looking Glass, McCloud was also thinking about the plight of psychedelic felons. So rather than mail off some of his own blotters to Hofmann, McCloud provided the foundation with a handful of *Heraldic Shields*, an array of blue escutcheons featuring Templar crosses and lions rampant. These had been produced by an acid distributor named Kevin Baron shortly before he got busted, something that McCloud did not mention to the foundation. This was symbolic magic on McCloud's part—another way to erode the boundary between outlaws and the professional class. For obscure and possibly esoteric reasons, Hofmann signed the sheets upside down. A couple were sent to Leary to sign as well, which annoyed Hofmann, who didn't particularly care to be associated with the Pied Piper of LSD. These sheets have been called the Holy Grail of signature blotter, and one of them sold for over $10,000 in 2016. But Baron's

Heraldic Shields made money in other ways as well. Like Leary's *Heavenly Blues*, thousands of these sheets were also dosed and circulated in the underground. Eventually Interpol dropped in on Hofmann, alerting him of the fact and suggesting that he might want to stop signing contraband.

The more that blotter became established as an art and a collectible, the more ambivalent its social character became. Again, what *is* this stuff? This ambiguity was also exploited by Doron Weinberg in order to undermine the prosecution's case against McCloud. "How does [the evidence] prove anything other than Mark McCloud distributed untreated blotter art?" he asked in his closing argument. The key term here is "art." By establishing "blotter art" as an actual thing in the world, Weinberg was able to separate McCloud from the acid underground. To emphasize his point, Weinberg performed a nice bit of theater. The visual hub of the trial was McCloud's telltale perforating machine, which sat there in the middle of the courtroom floor like some hellraiser manual printing press: a three-and-a-half-foot-tall hand-cranked laundry wringer whose rubber rolls had been replaced with PVC pipe, and whose pokey floating perfing bed allowed a skilled practitioner—like the sinewy ex-stripper from Oregon whom McCloud regularly employed—to crank out thousands of perfed sheets in a weekend. For his closing arguments, Weinberg placed a sign right on top of the machine: "Beyond a Reasonable Doubt."

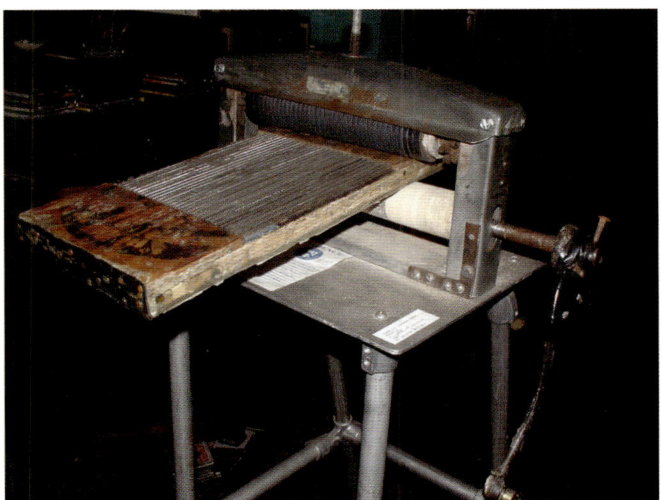

Hand-crank perforation machine, constructed by Fritz, Mark McCloud, and Tim North. Adapted from a laundry wringer and a previously existing perf board first fashioned in the 1970s.

After eight days of trial and ten and a half hours of deliberation, Mark McCloud was acquitted and set free. "I want every LSD prisoner let go," he said a few days later, "whether they were a snitch or not. I want their property returned and a public apology from these people who took our right to consciousness without permission."[75] The feds were required to return all the materials they had seized, though they held many items back, including McCloud's collection of acid gels and some of his most valuable signature blotters. At least his archive of framed street blotters was returned, with their identifying labels still affixed. McCloud has never removed these bits of tape, which he now considers part of the artifacts themselves—sticky residue of the snaky path that LSD media has traced between illicit paraphernalia and art on the wall.

Mirror, Mirror

The more you think about vanity blotter, the curiouser and curiouser it becomes. Consider the term itself, which was coined by McCloud toward the end of the 1990s, when the market for undipped blotters illustrated with original designs, sometimes signed by legendary heads and sometimes not, started to kick into gear. Then and now, folks interpret the term as a kind of diss, a belittling way to refer to artists or makers who deign to indulge in perforated paraphernalia that serves no actual psychoactive purpose. But that was not McCloud's intent. Once blotter abandons its function as a drug delivery device, McCloud believes, it transforms into a kind of visual ode—a praise song and confession of aesthetic debt that celebrates and reflects LSD's own beauty, power, and convulsive grace. In other words, it is the molecule's own vanity that is being served by the artists and designers of art blotter. Their sheets hang like illuminated mirrors in the honeycombed palace of Dame Acid, magnifying her weird and iridescent glory.

With vanity blotter, the medium truly becomes the message. Or at least, it becomes another medium, joining art prints, posters, T-shirts, decals, coffee mugs, coasters, mouse pads, and skateboard decks as a pop printing surface whose images are prized for their looks, their trendiness, and their function as totems of identity. Like the concert posters and street art interventions to which it is loosely allied, vanity blotter aspires to be an art market, settles for being a collector's market, and happily pursues pure and sometimes unscrupulous commerce when it can get away with it. But despite its bid for legitimacy, or at least free and open traffic, vanity blotter retains aesthetic and material ties to the black market that irredeemably stains the medium. The aura of the illicit clings to the stuff like bongwater stink to a frat house carpet.

As we have seen, the images that appeared on vintage street blotter were sourced from all over the place: decorative designs, commercial logos, old books, the doodling hand of drug users. Relatively few of the images are particularly "visionary," though they are sometimes made so through context. But just as Deadheads came to wear a tie-dye uniform that was not at all evident in the scrappier 1960s, so too do today's vanity artists largely adopt a recognizably "psychedelic" sensibility. Though lacking clear definitions, this style can now be understood as a sort of stuttered pop surrealism that draws variably from lowbrow, 1960s psychedelia, visionary art, rock posters, fantasy illustration, underground comix, street art, tattoo designs, and hippie memorabilia. It's a rich stew, and at its best, vanity can be disruptive, gorgeous, and quite witty. Over the last quarter century, the sass and tactile charm of the format has attracted many well-known artists with already successful careers on the fringes of fine art: edgy visionaries like H. R. Giger and Gary Panter, celebrated poster artists like Frank Kozik and Emek, street artists like Banksy and Shepard Fairey, psychedelic painters like Stanley Mouse and Alex Grey, and new-school visionary artists like Amanda Sage and Android Jones. But while many vanity blotters are based directly on works that exist outside that specific form, scores are made specifically with the genre in mind.

So who made the first piece of vanity blotter? No doubt high school trippers have been cooking up fake blotter designs in their third-period notebooks since the drug delivery device hit home. But the first art-for-art's-sake blotter was made, appropriately, by a bona fide fine artist. Fred Tomaselli grew up in the drug-saturated fun zone of 1970s Santa Monica before moving to New York City in the 1980s. Then and now, he approached art as a "reality modification device," a transcendental probe into the conundrum of consciousness loosed in an uneasy world of enigmatic artifacts. Tomaselli eventually established himself in the gallery world with a dazzling signature style perhaps too classy to be dubbed "psychedelic": vibrant collage paintings of birds and trees and exploding cosmic geometries, their resin-cloaked surfaces incorporating unusual materials like pills and cannabis leaves.

Like a lot of downtown artists, Tomaselli took in Mark McCloud's blotter show when it ran at Psychedelic Solution in early 1988. As the artist put it, the show "popped my brain." He saw that, by putting blotter in a frame, McCloud had not only identified a vital vein of contemporary folk art, but had also transformed the use value of a drug medium into an aesthetic material all its own—a canny appropriation not unlike Tomaselli's later reuse of pills and weed as collage materials. Tomaselli also recognized the modernist convergence of blotter aesthetics with the minimalist grids he already admired in Donald Judd and Carl Andre. Inspired by McCloud's show, and meditating upon the utopian desires that drive so many modern subcultures, Tomaselli designed *Youth Culture Rebellion Blotter Acid* in 1990. Each perforated hit is marked with a yellow mandala composed of tribal icons: an Om, a smiley face, a pentagram, a peace symbol, an anarchy monogram. He also threw a dollar sign into the mix, to ironize the batch in an era of triumphant neoliberalism.

Tomaselli went on to make other blotters. About a decade after *Youth Culture*, he collaborated on a limited-edition art book with the author Rick Moody, whose text, the short story *Phrase Book* tells the sad tale of a young woman who takes seventy-five hits of acid and winds up in a psych ward. For the book, Tomaselli produced a perforated blotter sheet featuring a jagged image of ants in combat—another contribution to the blotter bestiary, reminding us once again that animals are the most alien minds that most of us ordinarily encounter. Five years after *Phrase Book*, Tomaselli became obsessed with a photo on the front page of the *New York Times*, a shot of the former WorldCom CEO Bernie Ebbers clutching the hand of his wife after being convicted of $11 billion worth of fraud. Tomaselli applied his colorful hyperdimensional collage magic to the image, producing the first of what would become an open-ended and deeply hallucinogenic series of doctored *Times* front pages. The Ebbers one received special treatment, however; working with Creative Time, a nonprofit public arts organization, Tomaselli created a blotter edition of the page, whose perforations were performed by some Boston head that Carlo McCormick knew. Since then, Tomaselli has made a few blotter-inspired watercolors, including *Black Acid 2*, a vivid abstract grid that adorns the gatefold of the avant-mystic British band Cyclobe's 2014 LP version of *The Visitors*. Most collectors haven't seemed very interested.

"All the News That's Fit to Print"

The New York T

VOL. CLIV . . . No. 53,155 Copyright © 2005 The New York Times NEW YORK, WEDNESDAY, MARCH 16, 2005

Ex-Chief of WorldCom Is Found Guilty in $11 Billion Fraud

Ebbers Has Become Highest Executive to Be Convicted

By KEN BELSON

Bernard J. Ebbers, the former chief executive of WorldCom, was found guilty yesterday in federal court of orchestrating a record $11 billion fraud that came to symbolize the telecommunications bubble of the 1990's and the excesses that were uncovered in its aftermath.

The seven women and five men in the jury reached a verdict after deliberating for about 40 hours over eight days. Mr. Ebbers was convicted of securities fraud, conspiracy and seven counts of filing false reports with regulators. Each count carries a sentence of 5 or 10 years.

Mr. Ebbers and WorldCom, through the acquisition of dozens of phone companies, helped to create the rush for telecommunications stocks in the 1990's. They were at the center of a swirl of scandals that cast doubt on corporate accounting methods, the role of Wall Street analysts, and investment bankers who sold stocks and bonds to investors.

WorldCom's phantom growth caused once-mighty telecommunications companies like AT&T to cut prices and slash costs in the crippling race to keep up, from which they never fully recovered. And MCI, which WorldCom acquired with its lofty stock in 1998, was tainted by WorldCom's bankruptcy, was forced to let thousands of workers go and may soon be acquired.

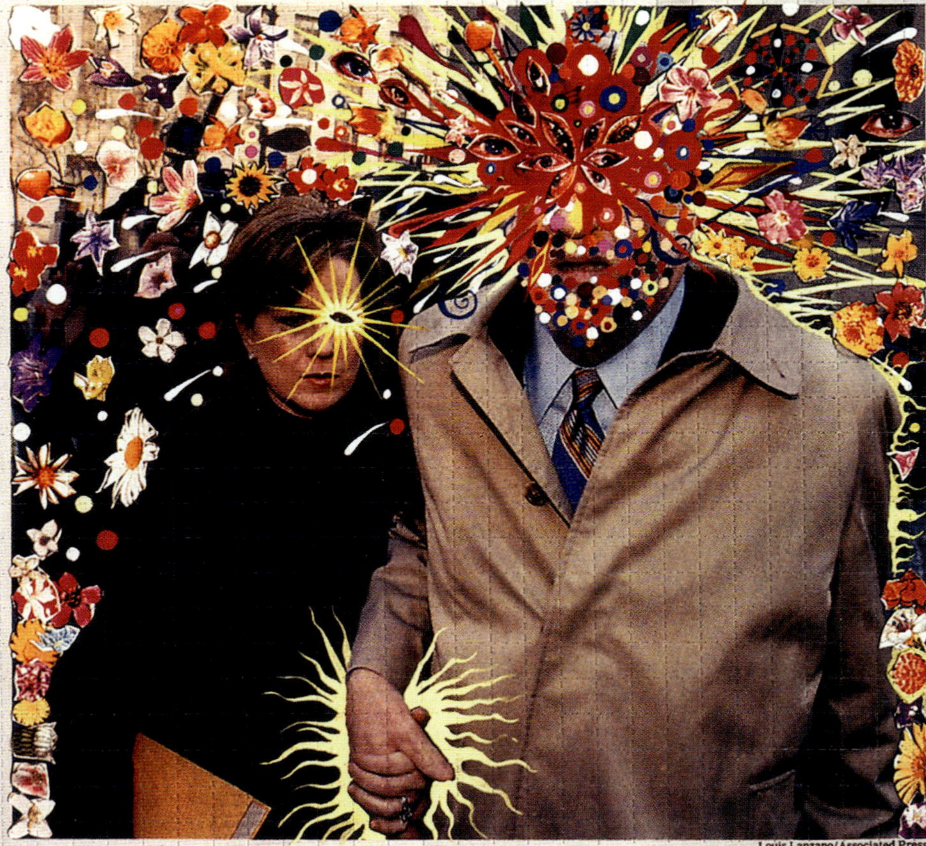

Louis Lanzano/Associated Press

Bernard J. Ebbers and his wife, Kristie, left Federal District Court in New York yesterday after he was convicted of securities fraud, conspiracy and seven counts of filing false reports with regulators.

Guilty, Fred Tomaselli, 2005. 12½ × 12½ in.

Another early vanity blotter also appears on and as an album cover. In 1993, the Canadian electronic music producer Richie Hawtin released a legendary album on Novamute under the name Plastikman. *Sheet One* is a masterpiece of minimal techno, an endlessly undulating fabric of sinewy melodic pulses and galactic atmospheres whose beats don't pound so much as subtilize. Besides foregrounding the psychedelic subtext of a lot of club music, *Sheet One* also invoked LSD visually. The front inlay of the CD is a 20 × 20 perforated blotter grid whose individual hits reproduce the Plastikman logo; these undipped sheets were also slipped into some of the LPs as well. The allusion was convincing enough to occasionally cause trouble—police outside Dallas arrested one young man and held him almost a week for possession of the disc.

Sheet One and *Youth Culture Rebellion Blotter Acid* were isolated foreshadowings, but the vanity era really started to take off in the summer of 1995, when McCloud threw his biggest ArtRock Gallery show to date. "Timothy Leary in Wonderland" featured the original intelligence agent himself, dwindling but still grinning, and autographing, among other pieces, one of the blotter editions that McCloud had originally made for Thomas Lyttle. As with all of those editions, McCloud had given *Leary Profile* (p. 204) special treatment, hiring a classy printshop in Vermont to print the sheets on high-quality watermarked art paper. Principally designed by McCloud's collaborator Dana Smith, *Leary Profile* featured the elder Leary in profile against a grid of block letters that spelled out SMI^2LE, his cyberdelic post-'60s rallying cry—an acronym for space migration, intelligence increase, life extension. Musical notes pour out of his head, while skulls striate the shoulder of his coat, invoking an important lesson from Carlos Castaneda's *The Teachings of Don Juan*: that death lies just over your left shoulder. Leary could hardly argue the point, since by the time of the show he knew he was dying from inoperable prostate cancer. Much of the money raised from the ArtRock sales went to his heath care expenses. "I feel like the Pope signing the communion wafer," Leary reportedly said at the time. When the sheets hit the street, which they inevitably did, the skulls were said to be double-dosed.

Leary's autumnal Wonderland appearance drew attention to the still rather obscure world of signature blotter. But equally significant was the show's synchronistic opening: August 9, one day after the death of Jerry Garcia. The blotter show became part of the impromptu wake that consumed San Francisco that week, as throngs of sad hippies gathered to bid fare thee well to a dewdrop guitar sage whose death also signaled the imminent collapse of the LSD distribution network in the United States. While the demise of the Dead was followed by other druggy jam bands and other networks, Garcia's passage marked the end to the long strange post-'60s acid era that in many ways was incarnated in blotter. Never again would a single musical outfit be tied so snugly to both the mythopoetics and the material circulation of a major psychoactive drug. But even as LSD dissociated itself from the Grateful Dead to forge new symbiotic relationships, so too did vanity blotter peel away from the format's psychoactive raison d'être.

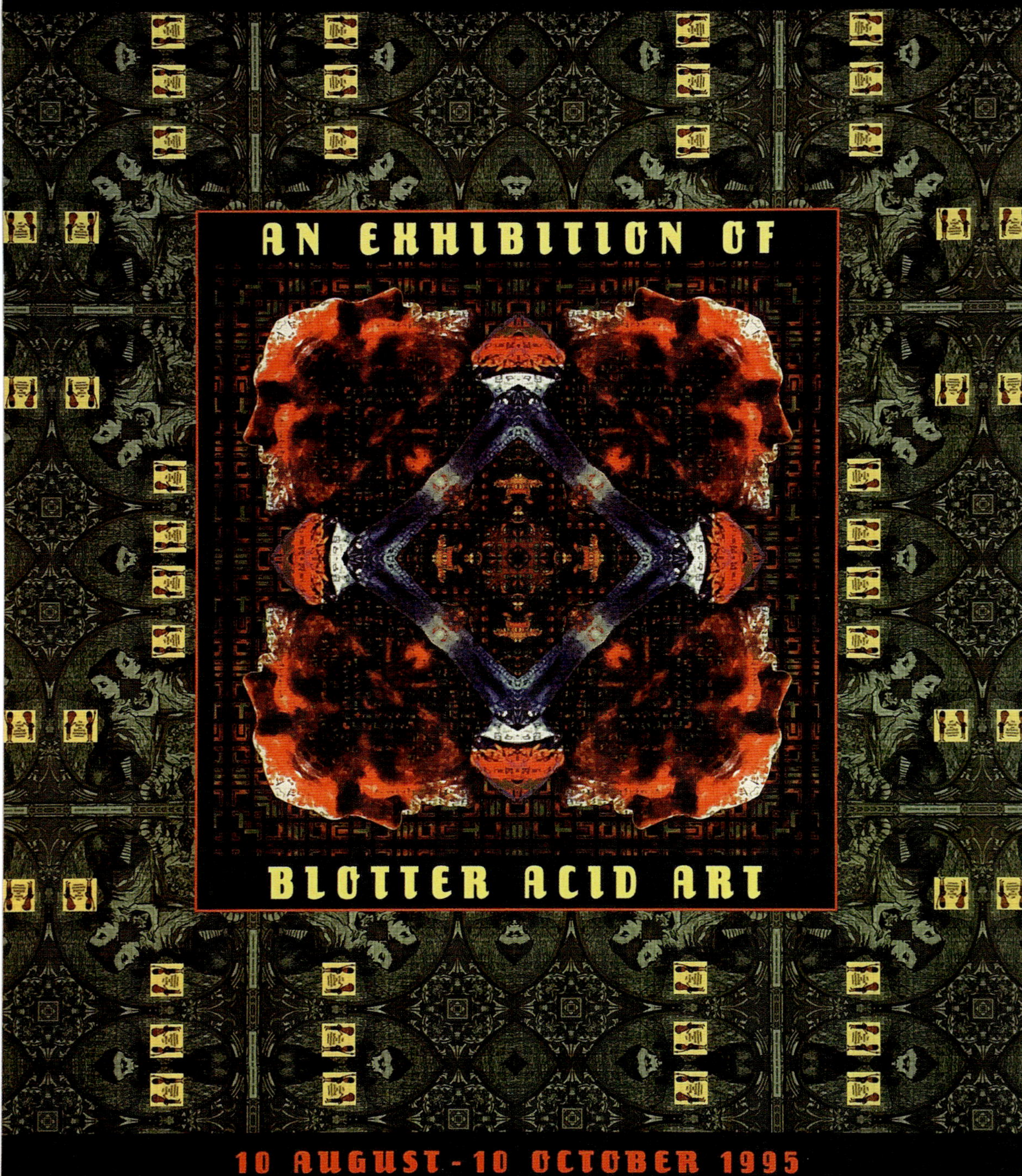
TIMOTHY LEARY
IN WONDERLAND
AN EXHIBITION OF
BLOTTER ACID ART
10 AUGUST - 10 OCTOBER 1995
DR. TIMOTHY LEARY HOSTS A RECEPTION 5-9PM 10 AUGUST
ARTROCK GALLERY 1153 MISSION STREET S.F.

Timothy Leary in Wonderland, Mark McCloud, 1996. Poster, 13 × 19 in.

As mentioned above, Tom Lyttle produced the first batch of vanity blotters expressly designed for the psychedelic collectors market in the mid-1990s. (McCloud's original batch of designs got dipped for the street after Lyttle rejected them, so they don't count.) Given the carelessness of most of his images, Lyttle was evidently more interested in signatures than in art per se—indeed, to provide more visible acreage for those value-multiplying autographs, his blotters included an unperforated white border around the central grid of individual hits. Ken Kesey was one of the luminaries who signed these and other undipped sheets, and Kesey's son Zane, who already sold Merry Pranksters books and merchandise, cottoned on to blotter's extraordinary markup potential. Zane began purchasing sheets wholesale for his dad to sign and selling them through his mail-order business, Key-Z Productions.

Dipped or not, blotter was exceptionally portable—an affordance directly linked to the format's origins as contraband. This also made it an easy thing to add to the mix of wares offered in the merchandise booths that festooned the various events that colonized the void left by the death of Dead tour and its thriving parking lot scene. These multiday gatherings included national music tours, like the Furthur Festival, as well as the sort of regional events that would soon bloom into powerhouse events, like the Bonnaroo Music and Arts Festival. According to Matthew Rick, who started selling signed Kesey sheets for Zane at festivals in 1998 and later became a major producer and vendor in the vanity scene, it took some guts to openly sling blotter in these environments, especially for folks weaned on the sketchiness and paranoia of Dead tour. Rick made sure to always travel without cannabis or other substances.

In 2000, the same year McCloud was busted, a Louisiana entrepreneur and professional printer named John Blackburn stuck his finger into the air, felt the way the wind was blowing, and opened blotterart.com. Blackburn was no Deadhead, but he did love the look and feel of classic street blotter and wanted to try his hand at making his own. A technical wizard who had attended MIT, Blackburn also worked a straight job at a professional printshop in Bossier City, which gave him access to a large Heidelberg offset lithography press. With persnickety perfectionism, Blackburn began printing high-quality vanity sheets that he perfed, also superbly, with a machine he modified from an old clamshell hand press. Over time, he came to work with a variety of up-and-coming artists, including the rock poster maestro Frank Kozik, the tattoo artist James Clements—who offered sugary pop surrealist riffs on stock Alice in Wonderland characters—and a friendly psychedelic lowbrow artist from Oklahoma named Rick Sinnett, who had already been printing and perfing small runs of his own vanity pieces. Blotter art was turning into art blotter.

The early 2000s were the golden years of online retail, and blotter proved a perfect commodity for eBay and other internet marketplaces. Between the web and the merch booths at the burgeoning festival scene, Blackburn and his associates started to clean up. Sinnett, who started vending blotter at the first Bonnaroo festival in 2002, regularly sold sheets for twenty bucks, a delicious markup for a perforated piece of cardstock

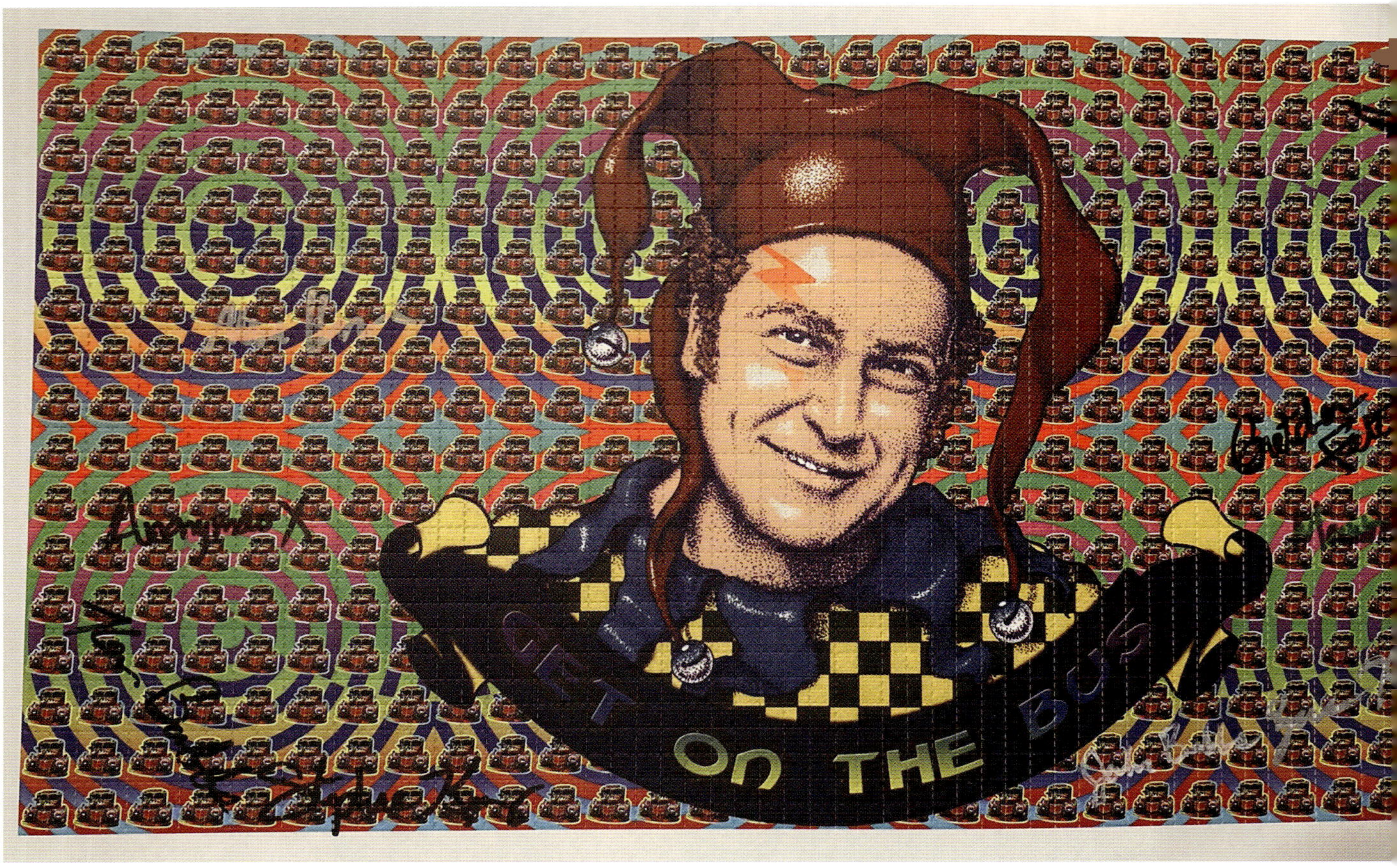

Get on the Bus, Zane Kesey and John Blackburn, mid-2000s. 8 × 16 in. Adapted from the cover of *Spit in the Ocean* no. 7.

that cost around fourteen cents to produce. For charismatic stuff, like an *Easy Rider* sheet signed by Peter Fonda, Sinnett might get $500 to $1,000. But it wasn't just hippie nostalgia that did the trick. Sinnett, who had watched the sort of lowbrow art celebrated in *Juxtapoz* magazine expand into a vital and collectable genre, wanted to move vanity beyond swirly psychedelia. He produced an original piece with the visionary Mexican-American artist Daniel Martin Diaz, whose esoteric lowbrow-adjacent imagery blends alchemical diagrams, Mexican retablos, and early scientific illustrations. Though Diaz's signature didn't mean much to a typical Deadhead, his haunting cosmogram *Mystery of Faith* (p. 208) still fetched a grand for Sinnett when he sold it to one of the many elite psychonauts who started collecting blotter around the millennium.

By allowing the actual artists to sign their work, vanity blotter recapitulated a crucial shift in the history of Western art: the era in the 1500s, when painters who had previously labored as anonymous religious artisans began signing their work and emerging as singular "artists." But old-school street blotter sheets, whose authentic ties to the black market made them collectable even without signatures (or, needless to say, acid), also grew in value. Blackburn sold vintage stock along with vanity, some of which he sourced from outside collectors. But with nothing really to stop him, he started printing and selling replicas of street blotter, including lots of Mark McCloud's stuff. These copies were not only unauthorized, they were presented with a hazy provenance that led many buyers to believe

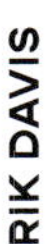

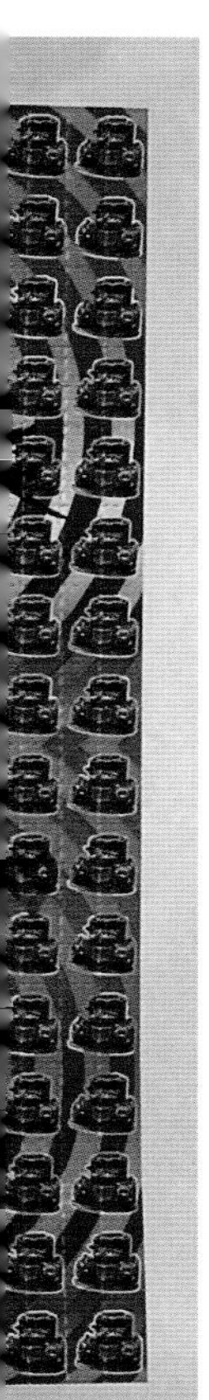

they were getting the real deal. And because Blackburn was such a good printer, you needed to be a real nerd to tell the difference.

Blackburn got grief for all this, especially with McCloud staring at life in prison. But the alley cat was out of the bag: from 2000 until today, the blotter trade has been saturated with bootlegs and false advertising, not to mention massive copyright infringement and a frequently kitsch culture of mimicry and low-hanging ripped-off memes. This should surprise no one. Blotter is an outlaw form, or at least a delinquent one. Pirates too are outlaws, and in an economy of signs, one thing that pirates like to swipe is other people's creative work—especially when those other people are outlaws themselves, as in the case with street blotter makers. At the same time, it's important to remember that, as a medium, blotter is *always already iterated*. Its aesthetic force derives, at least in part, from the vertiginous delirium of the copy. So once the blotter format was separated from the "Real" of actual LSD, the stuff naturally started to replicate itself, like Jean Baudrillard's pure simulacra, or like poor Mickey's maniacal broomsticks.

That said, the budding blotter market remained rather recherché for quite some time. The fact that blotter was unquestionably drug paraphernalia whether or not it was dipped held most folks back, even as that clandestine association lent the products a tantalizing aura—a gritty fusion of charisma and scandal, dash and stain. A helpful FAQ on Blackburn's site advised buyers on the slippery ontology of their purchases:

> **Can I be arrested for Blotter Art?**
>
> **Yes! Although the artwork itself is not illegal, you can still be arrested because it does look identical to the artwork that drug dealers sell on the streets. The police will then have to test the artwork to see if it contains any traces of LSD, which it does not. . . . Our recommendation is that you frame this art and keep it at home on display. . . . Also, if you try to sell (or even give away) this artwork as if it were real LSD, you can be arrested and convicted of possession and distribution of a Controlled Dangerous Substance, even though the artwork contains no illegal substance! Therefore, we recommend that only those who enjoy and appreciate these items for their artistic value bother to purchase them. Blotterart.com accepts no responsibility for the misuse of our items.**

This final admonition reminds us that vanity blotter was tainted not only by its cultural associations with a controlled substance but by its material potential to be dipped and sold *as* that substance. Even free from scheduled molecules, vanity blotter was and is a psychoactive medium that can never be entirely cleaved from the street.

When Mark McCloud was acquitted in 2001, the news hit the scene like the crack of a starter pistol: undipped blotter was officially "art." What Matthew Rick calls a "space race" was on, as budding blotter makers—mostly untrained in either fine or practical arts—tried to figure out how to print and perf the stuff themselves. McCloud himself also got into the act. In 2002, he opened Blotter Barn, a website that showcased many images from his collection and offered collectors limited edition prints, numbered and signed by McCloud. These scans were initially produced with a large drum scanner owned by a local underground film collective, though improvements in technology eventually allowed McCloud to offer some striking large-scale blow-ups. Over the years, Blotter Barn also offered limited edition books, including the 1.5-inch square *Blotter Barn Hits*. But the site stayed away from anything perforated.

Like McCloud, who brought fine art values to his reproductions, some of the new blotter makers on the block wanted to keep the bar high. They worked with good artists on original images designed primarily for blotter rather than being adapted from poster art or other sources. Tripatourium.com, which hit the internet in 2002, emphasized quality and collectibility, offering limited editions that were not only signed by the artists but numbered, something Blackburn didn't do. Like Lyttle, the outfit also surrounded their perforated sheets with a blank white border, this time rather obnoxiously emblazoned with the company's URL. In place of nostalgia, Tripatourium showcased lowbrow edgelords like Trevor Brown, Naoto Hattori, and Paul Booth, as well as unhippie-but-trippy musicians like Mike Patton, the Melvins, and Devo's Mark Mothersbaugh. Tripatourium also explicitly invited the druggy multitude into their online gallery. "Too many times are there great pieces of merchandise priced far out of reach of the average human," declared the site in demotic prose. "Through our service we will offer limited edition items priced for the average collector."

Zane Kesey also got into the act, though he took the format in a different direction. Once he realized how much more a signed Kesey blotter was worth than a signed Kesey book, Zane started working with Blackburn on a line of Prankster-specific images, including a swirling homage to Furthur, the legendary International Harvester school bus the Pranksters drove across America. Though Ken died before he was able to sign any of these sheets, Zane could read the tie-dye on the wall. He started producing his own blotter with uncorked abandon, lifting imagery wholesale from '60s artists and the Deadverse, copying vintage blotter designs, and generally wallowing in the rainbow muck of the hippie imaginary. Meanwhile, scores of other blotter producers with even fewer skills or scruples flooded eBay with their wares. Within a few short years, these producers significantly drove down both the price and quality of blotter. The bottom of the barrel was getting dangerously overscraped.

The demands of the ongoing LSD trade made things even more wobbly. Take *LSD 60*, one of the most iconic and valuable blotter issues of the 2000s. In the late 1990s, a Californian named Jon Hanna started organizing the Mind States conferences, a series of cross-disciplinary psychedelic gatherings that attracted heady heads, avant-shamans, underground therapists, and a small coterie of legit researchers with only a gleam of the coming renaissance in their eyes. For the 2003 Mind States, Hanna decided to produce an original blotter, printed with soy-based inks on hemp-blend paper, that would commemorate Albert Hofmann's discovery of LSD's psychoactivity sixty years before. The plan was to get a handful of sheets signed by conference speakers and other psychedelic illuminati, and then

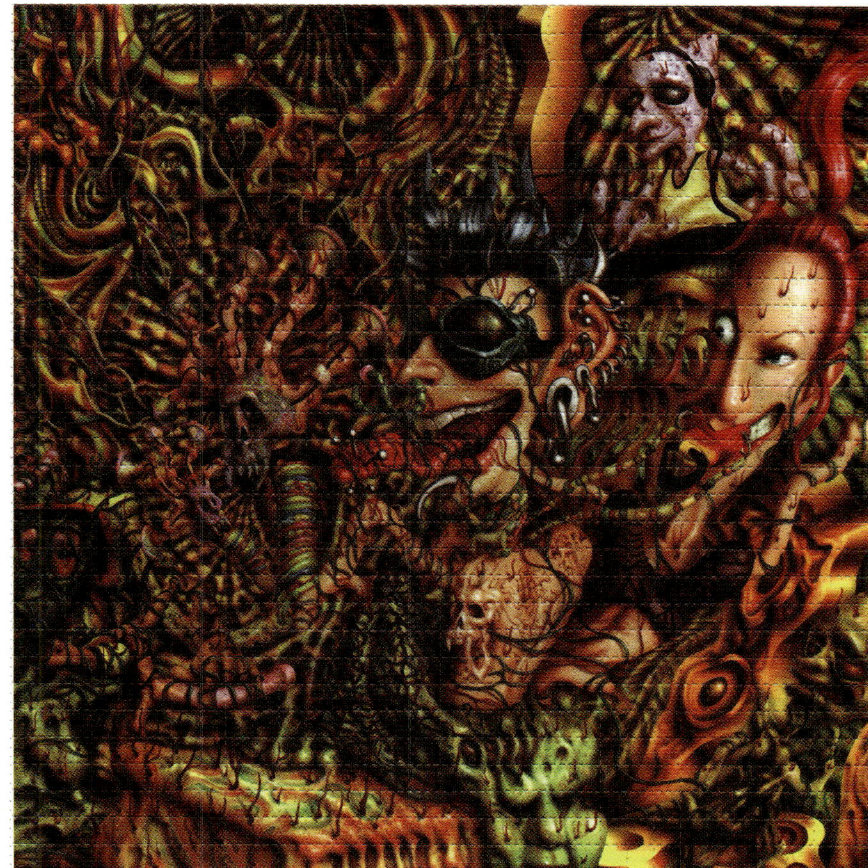

Tripping, Naoto Hattori, Tripatourium.com, 2003. 9 × 10 in.

use them to bring in money for Erowid, the preeminent online drug information site, and MAPS, the Multidisciplinary Association for Psychedelic Studies. Hanna approached the digital artist Stevee Postman, and together they hashed out a vibrant image of a lotus-flower brain whose weird beauty prophesied the twenty-first-century psychedelic science to come.

By 2003, most of the signature legends—Leary, Kesey, Lilly, Ginsberg—had died. But there was still one Great Man standing: Albert Hofmann himself. Hanna asked MAPS' Rick Doblin for an introduction, but Doblin refused, explaining that, as noted earlier, Hofmann had been warned off signing blotter by the Swiss authorities. Hanna persisted, writing a letter to Hofmann that his mom, whose parents were both Swiss, translated into German. Charmed, Hofmann said yes, and signed sixty-three prints that Hanna sent him, sixty of which Hanna later numbered, most of which he distributed to Erowid and MAPS. One of the unnumbered extras was additionally signed at the conference by Stan Grof, Ralph Metzner, Myron Stolaroff, and Nick Sand—an autographed sheet eventually dubbed "The Legends of LSD" blotter. Over the next few years, Erowid raised thousands of dollars from their slips of printed cardstock. In 2010, "Legends" helped bring in $10,000 to the nonprofit, who more recently thanked a new $50,000 donor with the gift of their final signed Hofmann print.

Postman's piece was a hit among collectors, and a number of individuals and online resellers purchased stacks of sheets from Hanna at wholesale prices. In 2004, a wild-ass chemist from the West Coast named Casey Hardison was arrested in England for manufacturing LSD, DMT, and 2C-B. Shortly after Hardison's arrest, a vanity dealer forwarded Hanna some police photographs of Hardison's lab, one of which showed an evidence bag stuffed with a fat stack of *LSD 60* sheets. These may or may not have been dipped, but a few years later, poking around drug forums online, Hanna stumbled across a glowing review of the Mind States blotter—or rather, of the high it engendered, which was apparently strong and clean. Though concerned about the diversion from frame to street, Hanna was philosophical about it. "I suppose the art form has come full circle."

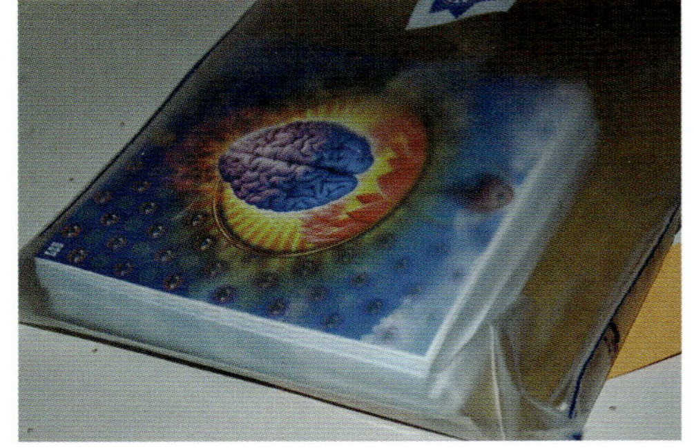

Police photograph of *LSD 60* blotters seized from Casey Hardison's lab, United Kingdom, 2004. Courtesy of Casey Hardison.

By the mid-2000s, the fledgling market in art blotter thus faced illegitimacy on two fronts: its proximity to felonious commerce, and its precipitous decline in quality. Whether silk-screened or offset, vintage street blotter carried the same matte finish prized by fine art printers and rock poster illustrators. These standards remained very important to finicky vanity producers like Blackburn, Hanna, and the Tripatourium crew. But many newcomers were happy to use inkjet or laser printers; others would stoop to photocopiers, or printing jpegs downloaded from the net at 72 dpi. Digital printing also provided a distinct economic advantage over old-school printing methods. Because the metal plates necessary for lithography are somewhat expensive to produce, offset print runs require a relatively high volume to make any money. But for the cost of a single offset run, the new kids on the block could digitally crank out far more designs, increasing the variety of their wares as well as dropping their dependence on expensive machines.[76]

Once you have the sheets in hand, it's usually pretty easy to tell the difference. Standard inkjet and toner prints possess a glossier finish and a thicker, more plastic skin, and they lack offset's characteristic rosette pattern. But you can't see these features online, and you still have to know what you're looking for. Many collectors had and have no clue, or just don't care. The blotter scene never developed the strict hierarchies of value produced by the sorts of experts and gatekeepers who shaped the rock poster market, which included devoted gallery curators like Castor and Cushway, canon builders like Paul Grushkin, Gayla Lemke, and Dennis King, and collector-nerds who could craft the sort of the forensic apparatus that Eric King developed in his remarkable multivolume *Collector's Guide to Psychedelic Rock Concert Posters, Postcards and Handbills—1965–1973*. With low barriers to entry, copious piracy, and critical discourse restricted to fractious, sophomoric, and frequently dissembling online forums, blotter was and remains a marginal, even outlaw genre, sodden with bootlegs, crude materials, and tripster kitsch.

Not that some blotter makers didn't try to up the ante. When Blackburn decided to quit the business around 2010, he sold blotterart.com and all its stock to Paul Guest, a warm-hearted blotter freak from South London who came up DJing acid house parties in the 1990s. Known as Monkey to his many pals, Guest produced new blotters with artists like John Coulthart and Banksy—informally, in the latter case—and rigorously followed the classic production methods: offset press, vegetable-based inks, and properly perfed chlorine-free paper. He also worked hard to school collectors, and to source and distinguish authentic vintage from the pirate copies clogging the pipes. "These are the originals!" his site would declare alongside a listing. "Not Copies!!! Don't settle for less, demand the best . . . this is it!"

But even this quest for quality has a paradoxically illegitimate side. Vintage blotter looks and feels more satisfying than cheap inkjet, but it also takes the form it does because that's what the underground figured out was the best format for a paper LSD delivery device. Old-school authenticity, in other words, is not just an aesthetic standard but a measure of street utility.[77] The inks on a lot of vanity will not withstand an ethanol solvent, and most folks agree that eating thick tabs of plasticized pigments rather than lightly printed paper is just gross. This means that, by reproducing the technical features of vintage blotter, good quality vanity can be easily and even ethically repurposed to carry LSD (though even mediocre stuff does the trick in a pinch). These days, good vanity is also increasingly used to carry other drugs, as the old semiotic standards give way to a host of molecules, some potentially dangerous: benzos, or Shulgin alphabetamines, or the heavy-duty bromo-dragonfly.

The upshot of all this is that, rather than transcending the underground, vanity blotter has come to largely replace the production of blotter destined for dipping. (Artisanal street blotters aimed entirely at the black market are still produced; the two-sided *Toltec* (p. 218) is a beautiful example.) Though too distant from crime to court arrest, vanity makers do find themselves in a bind sometimes, like the time that Interpol came knocking on Paul Guest's door, demanding to know who bought all those sheets of *Cat in the Hat*. Observers also report that a significant portion of the blotter confiscated in acid busts these days can be traced directly to Zane Kesey, who, following the much-lamented demise of Monkey Paul in 2022, has become the largest blotter producer and perfer on the planet. But there is not a lot the authorities can do. Kesey, whose production standards have improved significantly over the years but whose garish digital front page still screams at you like a MapQuest website from old, jumps through all the right hoops. But even he acknowledges that "if someone orders three hundred pieces, I know they aren't just putting them on their wall."

There is no way around it: there is something suspect about blotter, a stain that is both a blessing and a curse. As Matthew Rick puts it, "blotter is the last underground art form that's going to stay underground, simply because you're creating something that looks like and functions like a felony." In other words, blotter is *ontologically* illicit; it is, as Rick says, "drug paraphernalia by its very existence." So even as blotter stokes and reflects consumer and collector desire, there is something irredeemably tainted about it, as if the perforations that define the form puncture whatever cultural legitimacy it might gain. "Pop culture can take the edge off of anything eventually, but you can't take the edge off of this stuff," says Rick. "It doesn't matter how far down the rabbit hole you go. Disney is just not going to make a blotter edition."

Keeping Tabs

Like so many niche scenes in the age of the internet, vanity blotter is a vibrant, dynamic, and sometimes lucrative cultural zone that remains largely invisible to everyone else. Given its panoply of artists, producers, collectors, aesthetic genres, and feral symbols, vanity deserves a vaster overview than *Blotter* can provide. The sample of pieces included in this book, all drawn from the III's archive, are not representative of the overall genre, which includes a good deal of poorly made bootlegs, doofus memes, and hasty trash. Instead, we have mostly selected notable works that push or refract the envelope of psychedelic art and that engage and reframe blotter's material history as both a countercultural medium and the black-market avatar of LSD-25.

Given the weight of its associations with LSD, vanity is a necessarily self-conscious form, at once delinquent and playful, its inevitable nostalgia sometimes opening to rich historical reflection. One particularly knowing example here is the first piece of vanity made by Joe Roberts, a.k.a. LSD World Peace, a reclusive San Francisco artist who channels pop culture icons and psychedelia through the bold tongues of Basquiat and outsider art. *Green CERN* honors a number of the iconic blotters found on the III's Blotter Barn website, feeding them into a nervous and obsessive mandala of the urban profane. Roberts draws some of his jagged buzz from Gary Panter, the great second-generation underground comix artist whose work in *SLASH* and *RAW* unfurled a fast, edgy, expressionist vibe more punk than freak. In 2017, Panter created an installation for the Marlborough Contemporary called *Hippie Trip*, a meditation on a Mt. Shasta head shop he visited as a teenager in 1968. Amid the installations' blacklight posters, comics, beads, and hand-cast candles, Panter presented a series of art blotters that resurrected the humble handstamp (p. 219)—a perfect formal expression of the artist's appreciation for the scratchy, provisional texture of pulp psychedelia.

Like so much recent pop culture, vanity often takes a referential stance littered with winks, and scores of makers over the last quarter century have drawn their references from cartoons. Many vanities stumble down the path of mashup yucks, subjecting classic cartoon characters to a simplistic stoner *detournement*. Others honor, or merely pirate, the numerous animation shows—like *Ren & Stimpy, SpongeBob SquarePants* and *Adventure Time*—that have for decades served as popular culture's most dependable source of satirical psychedelia, both subtle and overt.[78] One of the first vanity sheets to really go viral was Randal Roberts's 2009

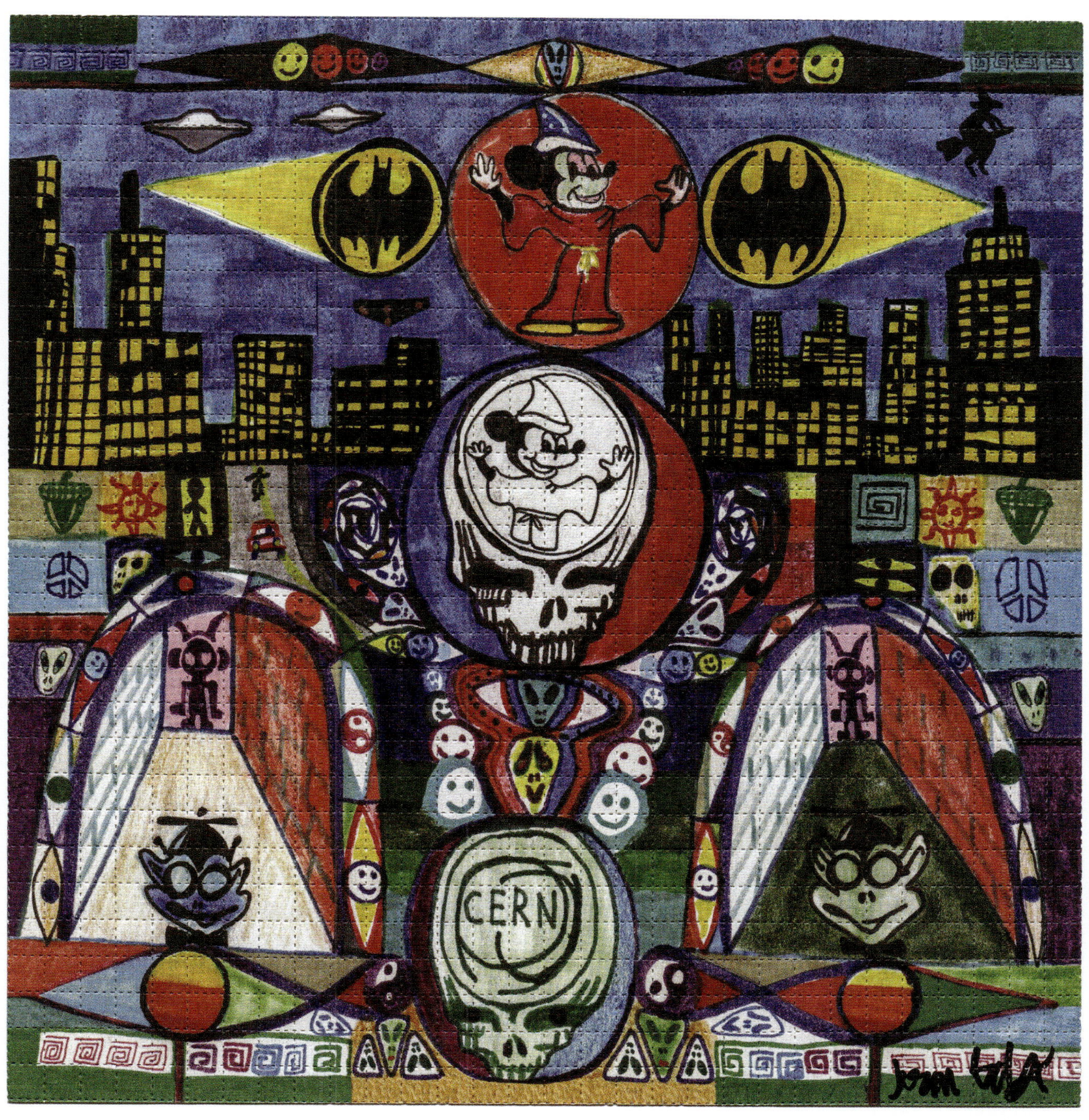

Green Cern, Joe Roberts/LSD World Peace, 2018. 7½ × 7½ in. Signed.

Portrait of Homer (p. 214), which subjects the Simpsons character to a tactile swarm of acid damask. The LA gallery artist Mark Dean Veca has spent much of his career subjecting familiar cartoon characters like Yosemite Sam and Tony the Tiger to even more visceral and oozy transmutations, and this work inevitably led to a series of blotters, including a *Strong to the Finich II* series based on E. C. Segar's Popeye characters, as well as a dizzying take on Mr. Natural.

Other vanity pieces play more reverently with earlier hippie styles. Callie Fink, a young artist from Orange County, takes up one of the supreme demands of classic psychedelic graphics: the attempt to represent the unfolding multidimensional shuffle of the high-dose cosmic grok. *Ascension* (p. 234) recalls the galactic geometries of comix mystics like John Thompson and Paul Kirchner, as well as the big-boned LP phantasmagoria of Mati Klarwein. But the star child that looms over Fink's scene speaks for something more newly androgynous, even posthuman. Like Fink, the Houston collage master Patrick Turk, who builds 2D and 3D pieces out of meticulously layered and repeated pictures sliced from books, avoids the easy vertical symmetry that seduces far too many "visionary artists." In *Reincarnating no. 2,* his blotter-only piece from 2021, Turk takes a familiar element of psychedelic phenomenology—the stuttering visual echo often called "trails"—and replicates it into an unnerving and serpentine Busby Berkeley dream. And for her piece *LSD Is the Bomb (The Dirty Deceiver)* (p. 222), Isabel Samaras draws from the pop patterns and color schemes of actual '60s fashions to ironically send up Jack Webb, whose *Dragnet* cop show returned to the airwaves from 1967 to 1970, allowing gruff Sgt. Friday to take on the longhairs.

Samaras's piece is a lysergic time-slip that actually serves up something new, unlike the copious vanity blotters that simply repeat already worn-out hippie motifs. But even this iterative nostalgia underscores the fact that vanity carries acid history in its perforated bones, history it both reveals and subtly conceals. So while Tina Carpenter's *Anonymous Bosch Flower Power* (pp. 226–227) remixes Bernie Boston's iconic snapshot of 1960s protest—the placement of a carnation in a soldier's rifle during 1967's March on the Pentagon—the piece also subtly refers, as Mariavittoria Mangini discusses later in our volume, to a legendary Hayes Street acid figure. Argentina's Nicolás Rosenfeld also shines light on a less visible hero, serving up a brilliant portrait of the Orange Sunshine chemist Nick Sand that refracts Sand's marvelous insolence through LSD's sometimes rubbery hall of mirrors. (Rosenfeld is also responsible for *The Passion of Mark McCloud,* found at the start of this book.) More recently, Ryan Kerrigan flashes back to the no-hitter that Dock Ellis pitched for the Pittsburgh Pirates against the San Diego Padres on June 12, 1970. Ellis had taken LSD that morning, forgetting he had a game to play later that day. Ellis pitched superbly despite losing his grip on time and being largely unable to see the batters. A testament to acid's sometimes uncanny enhancement of physical performance, Ellis's "LSD no-no" is also a key moment of Black psychedelia. There are a number of goofy Ellis blotters out there, but Kerrigan's piece psychedelicizes the pitcher's 1973 Topps baseball card with elegant

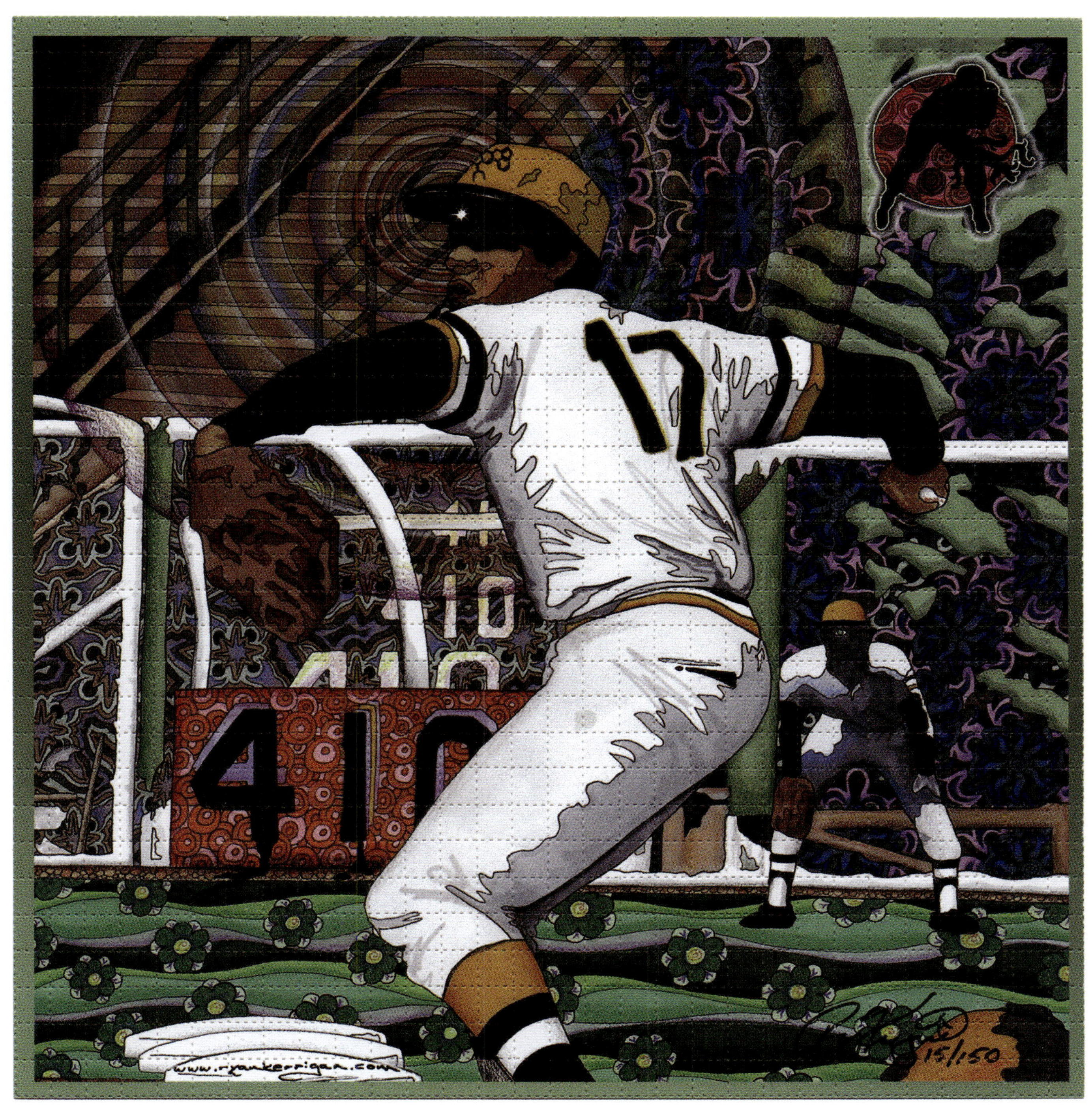

Dock Ellis, Ryan Kerrigan, 2021. 7½ × 7½ in. Signed.

restraint, recalling both the expressionism of 1970s sports illustration and the third-eye clarity of clean LSD.

As we've seen, illustrated street blotter has always been a kind of meta-medium, a knowing conjunction of drugs, art, appropriation, and design. Vanity blotter, self-consciously reframing itself as an artistic object disaggregated from drugs, just adds another twist to the tale by recapitulating and extending acid history, lore, and aesthetics. Both literally and figuratively, blotter serves as an avatar of LSD-25 (though it bears repeating that today's black-market paper is often dosed with other psychoactive molecules). This makes blotter a particularly interesting lens through which to view today's much-hyped "psychedelic renaissance." Over recent decades, a perfect storm of clinical researchers, psychotherapists, venture capitalists, journalists, wellness entrepreneurs, and decriminalization activists has radically transformed the medical, cultural, and regulatory profile of psychedelics in the United States. This process is inconceivable without the historical catalyst of LSD, which is far and away the most influential psychedelic in modern postwar history, and one that remains widely available and widely consumed. But LSD has been largely marginalized in the contemporary discourse around the promise of psychedelics, a process that is reflected in the strange and even uncanny status of blotter art.

There are three main reasons for Dame Acid's comparatively low profile today. One is that, for both therapists and clinical researchers, LSD is kind of a pain in the ass. Though the substance has been widely studied for decades, and continues to play a central role in some breakthrough research, LSD takes a long time to metabolize.[79] Acid trips easily last a half a day or longer, which increases the person-hours as well as the chance for things to go screwy with subjects or clients. If you are an entrepreneur who wants to efficiently scale a new psychoactive medicine, these are not the affordances you are looking for. Underground therapists have a long history of working with LSD, of course, but these were and are not "mass" protocols. Though some new psychedelic companies backed by venture capital are researching LSD analogues and applications, most are focusing on psilocybin and other molecules.

There is another reason that professional therapists, clinical researchers, and mainstream advocates downplay LSD these days: public relations. Today's psychedelic proponents and marketers have a vested interest in crafting a new psychoactive narrative that is freed from the outlaw taint of the counterculture. By downplaying LSD, the sorry debacle of freakouts, flashbacks, free love, and acid-fueled rebellion can be sidestepped or written off as a distant memory no longer relevant to today's bright and shining era of last-ditch mental health (whose own capitalist shadow side is routinely swept under the carpet). The bête noire here is of course Timothy Leary, who gets blamed in some contemporary research narratives for destroying the first wave of psychedelic science by preaching direct drug democracy to the hoi polloi. Indeed, Leary often gets more grief than the many MK-Ultra white coats who performed clandestine psychedelic torture under the aegis of the CIA. But even this makes sense: Leary was not just a Pied Piper but also a professional turncoat—an uncomfortable reminder to today's expert

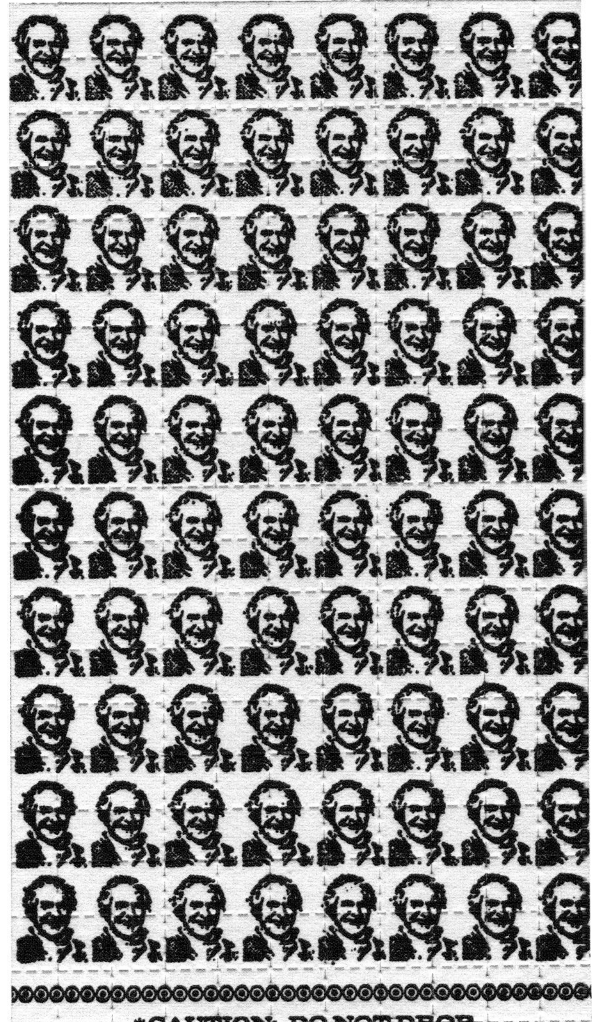

Timothy Leary blotter from Hunter S. Thompson, *Mistah Leary He Dead* (X-Ray Book Company, 1996).

class that some people, even those who have achieved the high status of teaching at Harvard, have more fabulous fish to fry.

There is a third reason for acid's muted contemporary presence. Recent decades have seen an ecological shift in the cultural and spiritual imaginary that frames psychedelic substances and the set and setting that informs people's experiences. Though MDMA, ketamine, nitrous oxide, and synthetic DMT play important roles in today's psychedelic cultures, spiritual authority has come to be vested more intensely in plants and fungi—ayahuasca and psilocybin mushrooms principally, and to a lesser extent ibogaine and mescaline-containing cacti. Many fans of smoked 5-MeO-DMT, for example, prefer to hassle poor *Bufo alvarius* toads during their mating season rather than consume an easily synthesized near equivalent of the animal's secretions. The fact that all these substances are coded as "natural" rather than "synthetic"—an old debate in the underground, usually generating more heat than light—gives them a charismatic animism that LSD lacks, despite its chemical similarity to the morning glory seeds that ancient Mesoamerican cultures used and called *ololiuhqui*. The name of a popular movement to legally liberate psychedelics—Decriminalize Nature—exploits the way that plant medicines and fungi symbolically address contemporary anxieties around climate crisis, environmental imbalance, and technological alienation. My hunch is that contemporary trippers also far more readily attribute an animating spirit to shrooms or ayahuasca than to LSD, though there may be phenomenological reasons for this as well, having to do with LSD's arguably more lambent and mirror-like illuminations.

An ethnobotanical bias follows this organic one. Ayahuasca, psilocybin-containing mushrooms, *Salvia divinorum*, iboga, huachuma, and peyote are rightly seen as inextricably connected to indigenous frameworks of ritual practice, plant wisdom, and ancient cultural traditions, even though some of these traditions—like Santo Daime and the Native American Church—are themselves largely syncretic products of mixed-up modernity. But history is not the point. For psychedelic seekers of the global north, anxious to escape or redirect an unsustainable civilization that seems to be hurtling off a planetary cliff, Indigenous forms of earth wisdom and healing offer hope and balm, whether or not this perception arises from romantic primitivism or a respectful insight into the extraordinary intelligence and heart of these ancient folkways (or a bit of both). As such, plant preparations and fungi associated with Indigenous cosmovisions or mestizo medicine have come to rule the psychoactive symbolic, especially when measured against a synthetic molecule birthed in a pharmaceutical lab lodged in the heart of an industrialized West—a West whose comparatively pampered progeny the drug went on to seriously mutate.

For all these reasons and more, LSD does not play a leading role in today's psychedelic theater of healing, hope, and hype. In some basic ways, it remains illegible, the invisible elephant in the room. But in the looking glass world of visionary culture, where Jungian enantiodromia is the rule, the marks against acid may also be sigils of a deeper, diversionary magic. With the exception of the microdosing fad—whose importance to the creative class at least ensures the black-market supply of squeaky-clean LSD—acid is not going to get a glossy makeover by the wellness industry. Acid is just too funky, too jangly, its sacred transmissions too stained with the profane. But the very associations that make acid tough to rebrand—from mind-control spooks to goofy Phishheads—can also be seen as apotropaic spells that protect the molecule from the simultaneously anodyne and predatory narratives of the metastasizing psychedelic industry. Despite its industrial birth in the R&D kitchens of the System, LSD may paradoxically remain wild. And even vanity blotter retains a trace of this furtive Outside.

LSD's industrial origins also have nothing to do with cultural appropriation. While the ergot alkaloids that birthed the lysergic acids are attached to older traditions of popular use, these practices are found within Europe. Other than the periodic outbreaks of deadly and daemonic ergotism, the most plausible "ancient tradition" associated with psychoactive ergot are the Eleusinian Mysteries, which ran for a millennium just outside of Athens, and whose hallucinogenic *kykeon* Albert Hofmann himself suggested might have been based in part on ergot from a *Claviceps* species—a thesis, once ignored by mainstream historians, that has recently gotten some serious archaeobotanical support. In other words, LSD is a European mystery, or a Euro-American mystery, or a Euro-American-Californian mystery. This is not to argue that it *belongs* to the West; rather, it belongs to the planet, since the regime that minted and mediated the drug was and is part of a global order whose international transport networks alone helped ensure that tiny little molecules of LSD on tiny little pieces of printed paper were smuggled into some of the remotest corners of the globe. Like the Beatles, or YouTube, LSD belongs to the world.

Many leaders and activists in what equity bros call "the psychedelic space" are demanding that Indigenous groups not only get a seat at the table but also a healthy cut of the industry repast. Such reciprocity efforts are far more than cosmetic. They concretely acknowledge the enormous debt that all psychedelic people owe to those savaged but vital communities, whose healers and medicine wizards developed and continue to maintain visionary plant and fungi traditions for centuries and presumably millennia. But we also owe a debt to the hippie freaks, renegade chemists, pranksters, midwives, healers, dealers, guitarists, poets, mystics, burners, artists, and DJs of the deep acid underground. However half-baked, dangerous, or even batshit their practices, these folks—often low-profile by necessity—still hold powerful medicine for those of us psychedelicizing ourselves within WEIRD societies: Western, educated, industrial, rich, and (more or less) democratic. These folks are our "ancestors"—even the Hells Angels, or the bad brujos in the CIA. Acid history may look like a profane mess, but it is also a sacred struggle, and like all such esoteric agons you have to approach it elliptically, through patterns and symbols and tricksy media that might only send you further into the forests of whatthefuck. That's the deeper message of the Institute of Illegal Images, which is not just a collection of artifacts but a wayward memory palace, an iconostasis of initiation and synchronicity, a comic-book collage of igniting signs, and the inevitable cracks between them.

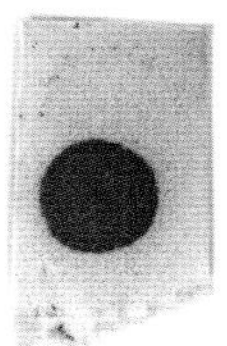

5 × 20/Blue Dot, Eric Ghost, Manhattan, 1968. Single cut-along hit, approx. ⅝ × ⅜ in. This rare item was a gift to the IIl from Alan Dillard.

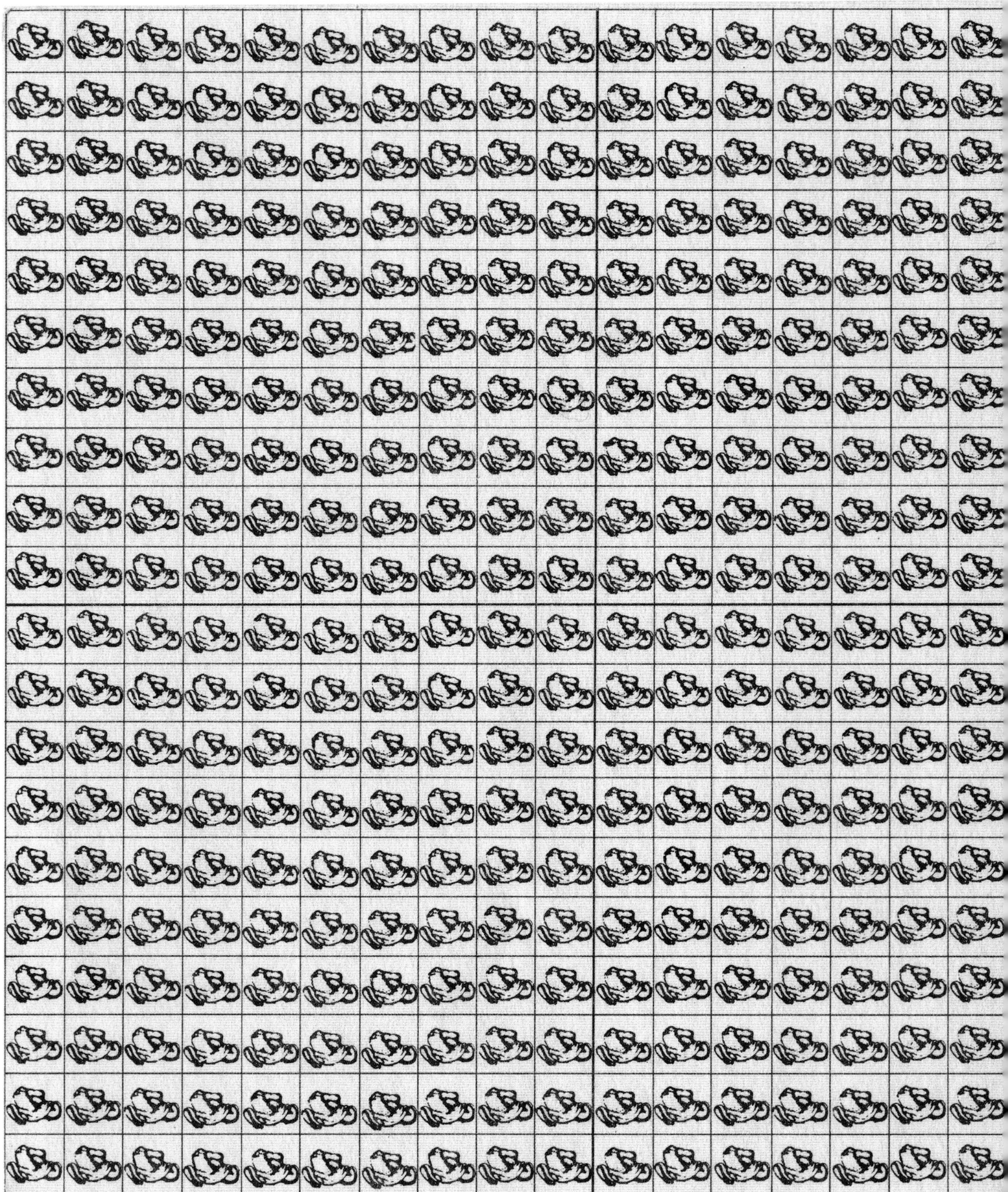

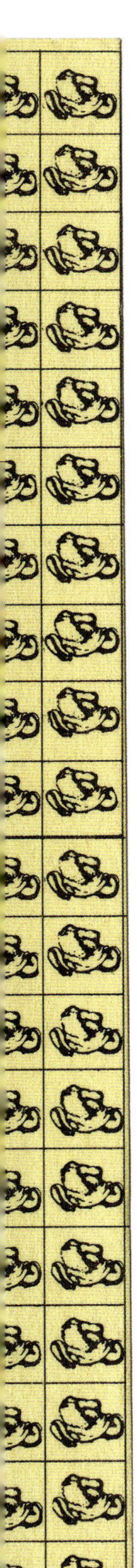

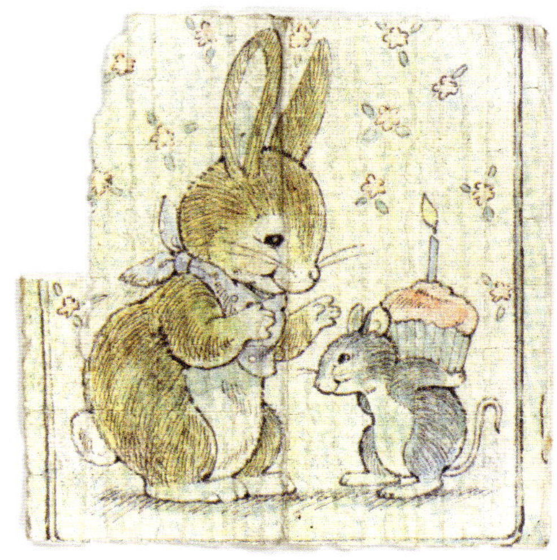

Mr. Natural #1, San Francisco, mid-1970s. Cut-along sheet, 7½ × 7½ in. A classic "400 block" format, with four well-defined ten by ten grid sections containing 100 hits each.

Bunny Birthday, ca. 1976. 2⅗ × 2⅗ in. One of the first full-color blotters, possibly removed directly from an illustrated book.

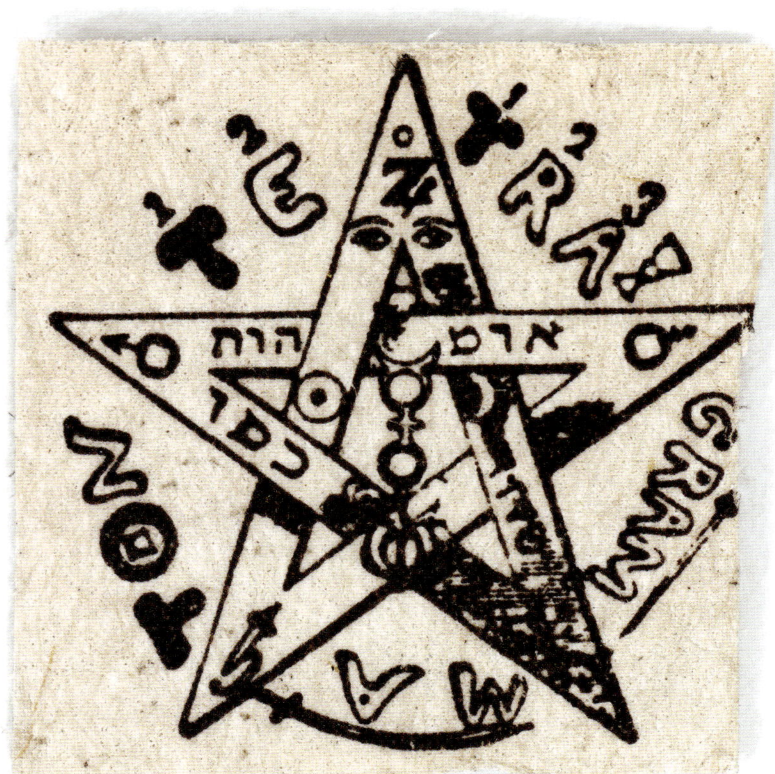

Tetragrammaton, San Francisco, ca. 1977. Single four-way ½ × ½ in. hit. Printed on the reverse side in reverse tones. Image originally appeared in Eliphas Levi's *Dogme et Rituel de la Haute Magie* (1854, 1856).

I didn't know there was any acid to be had, but T says something about the end of our magical group and goes out into the garden. She returns with a muddy tobacco tin, smiles and cracks it open.

Inside are two foil-wrapped blotters. They have pentagrams on them, black on white, nicely drawn, with interlaced sides, and the word *TETRAGRAMMATON* curving 'round the outside. The familiar pentagram shape—we've been using that symbol daily to bring our wandering minds into sharp focus. As for the Tetragrammaton, the Hebrew code name for the God whose name can never be spoken . . . For the last six months we've been shinning up and down the spheres of the Qabalistic Tree of Life, from Malkuth to Kether and back again, as David Bowie phrased it, and the Tetragrammaton encapsulates all that in its four sacred letters.

We look at each other and yes, it does seem like a good idea for us to take the acid.

It is good and clean, and surprisingly strong considering it's been buried in the garden for who knows how long. We ascend to the unstructured brilliance of the Unmanifest, then back down through the archetypal colors of the inner worlds.

Both of us are hoping that somehow the group's good times will return; but even well-preserved blotters that hint at the true name for God can't dissolve all the obstacles. I leave in the early morning, trees in bud, a pre-echo of spring 1983.

Dave Lee

Wallpaper, San Francisco, ca. 1975. Cut-along sheet, 5¾ × 5¾ in. Note that the pattern includes a variety of nested square shapes, aiding the later division of the sheet.

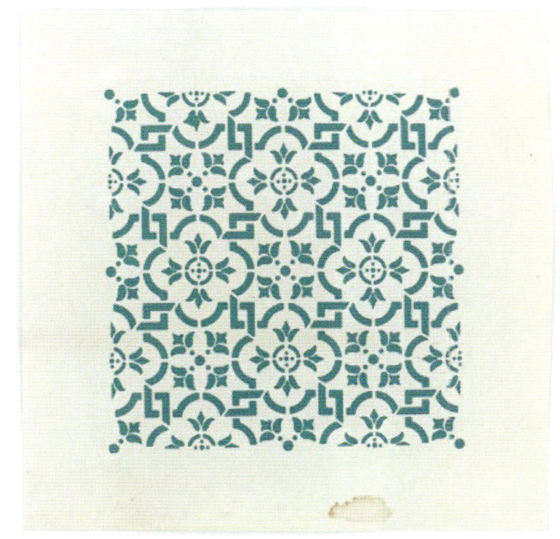

Maze, San Francisco, mid-1970s. Photostat, 7¼ × 7¼ in.

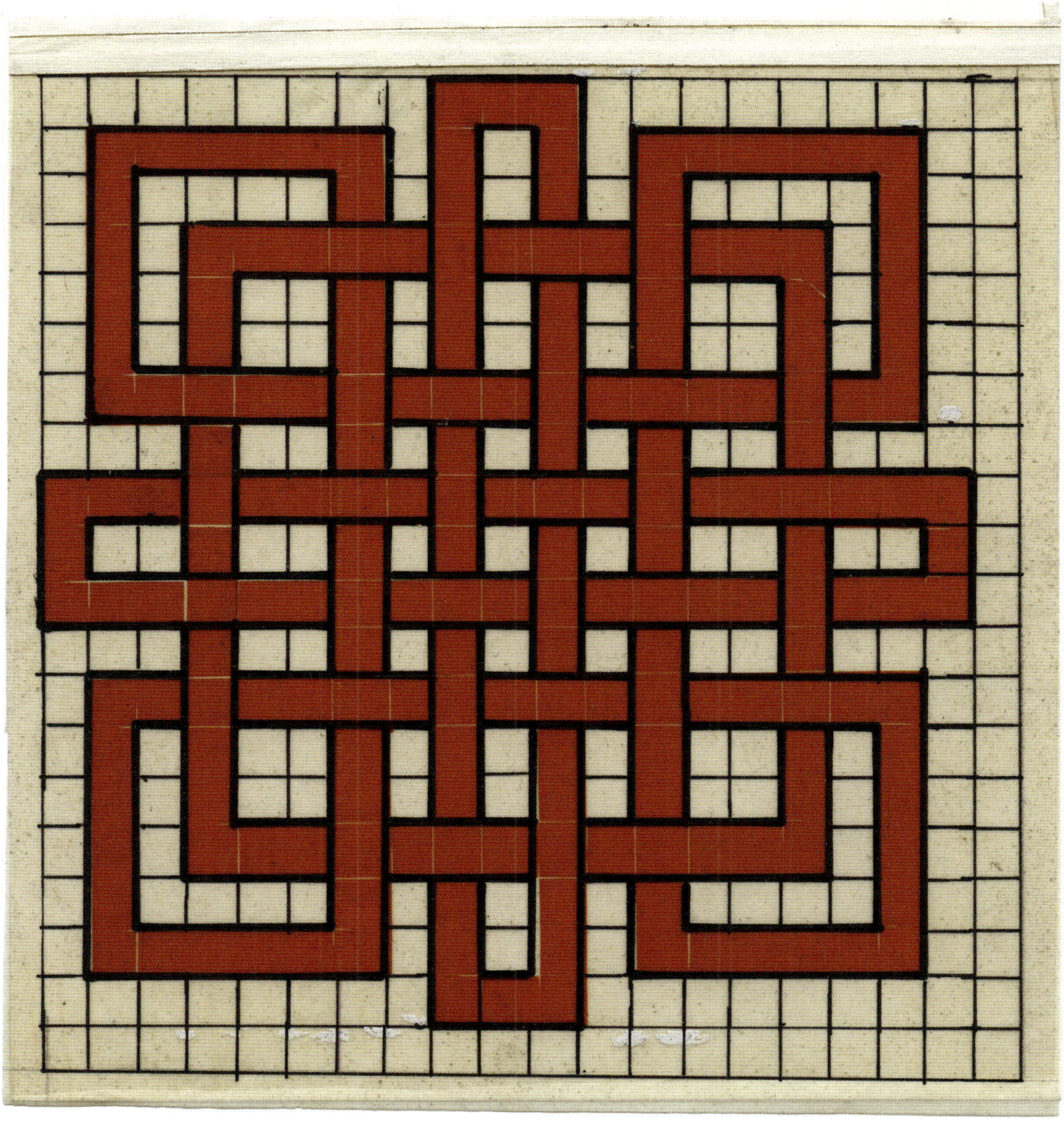

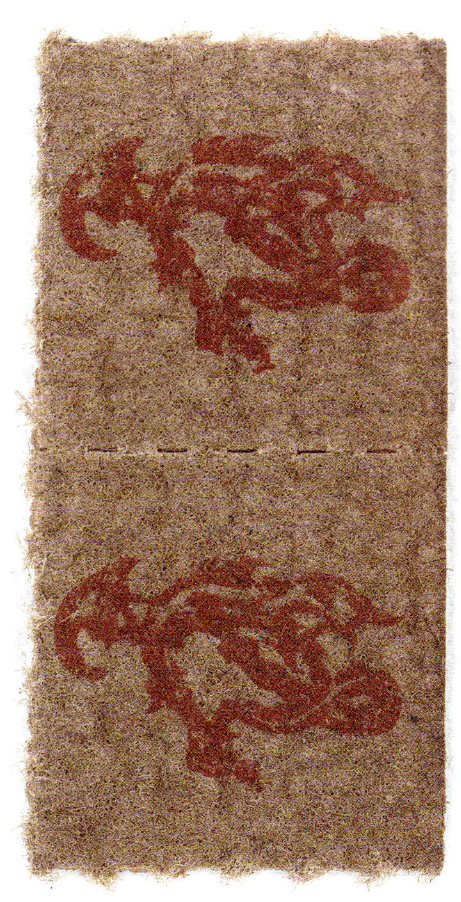

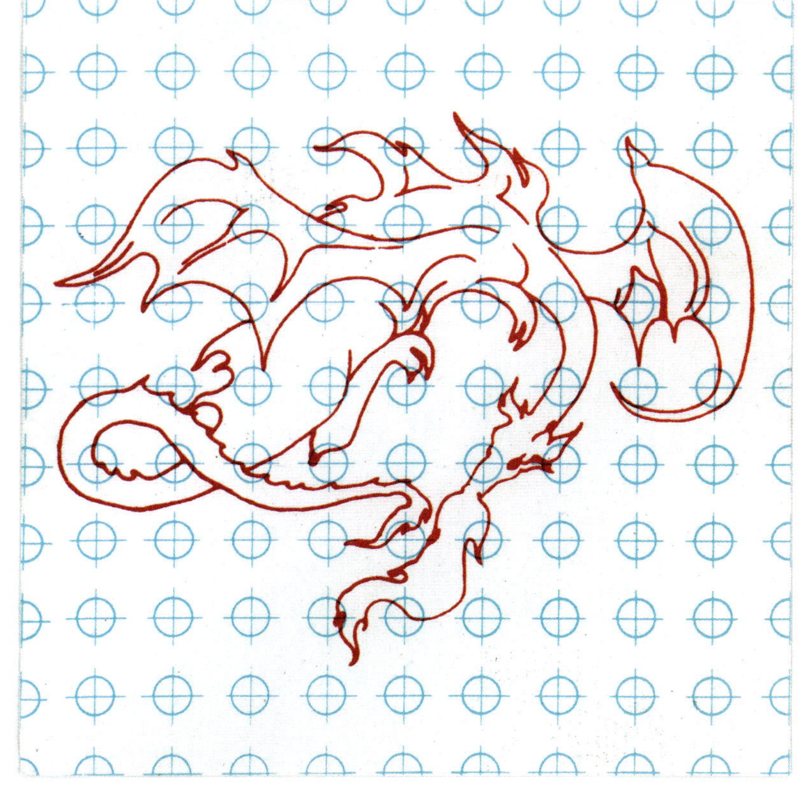

Red Dragon, San Francisco, 1978. ¼ × ½ in. This sinewy design was the work of Susan Mattison, a hippie art student from Detroit who was asked to "draw something cool." She avoided shading so as to limit the ink on the paper.

Red Dragon, reissue, ca. 1991. Cut-along, 4 × 4 in.

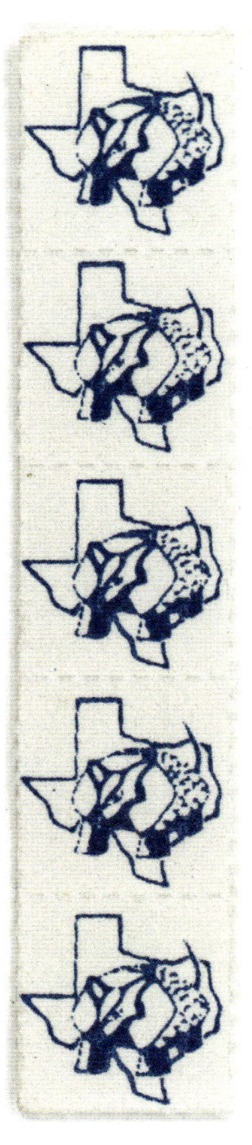

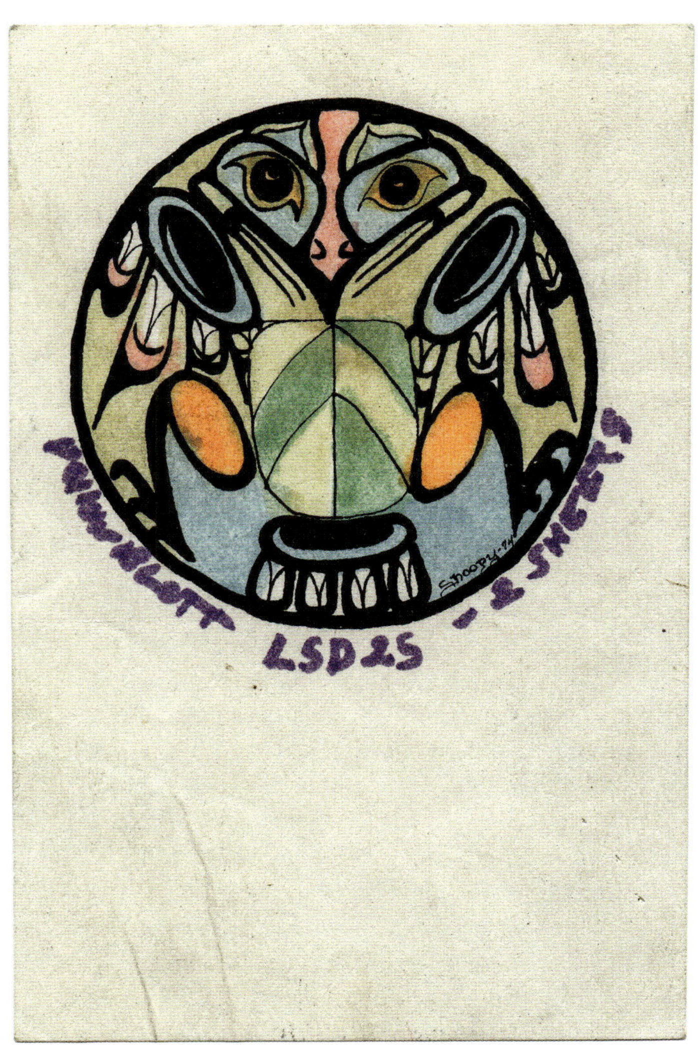

Texas Armadillo, San Francisco, ca. 1978. Based on imagery drawn from the legendary Austin, Texas, illustrator Jim Franklin. Five four-way hits, ½ × ½ in. each.

Handmade one-off blotter, 1974. Cut-along, 3 × 2⅜ in. Colored with ink and watercolor.

Super-duper, late 1970s. Cut-along, 9 × 9 in. The first Superman blotter.

There is a serious and a playful dimension to this Superman blotter. On the serious side, "Superman" definitively entered the American English lexicon with George Bernard Shaw's play, *Man and Superman* (1905), itself a reflection on Friedrich Nietzsche's philosophy of the evolving Superman (*Übermensch*). Nietzsche had developed the figure in *Thus Spoke Zarathustra* (1883), a work he believed would help catalyze the evolutionary transformation of humanity itself.

The American Superman countered the later Nazi reframing (and distortion) of Nietzsche in almost every way. Created in 1938 by two young Jewish men from Cleveland, the writer Jerry Siegel and the artist Joe Schuster, the Man of Tomorrow came to embody not fascism and antisemitism but democracy, or "truth, justice, and the American way." One can certainly make too much of this humorous blotter image of a slightly paunchy Superman flying in opposite directions in great numbers. But one might note that individuals who have ingested LSD have reported endless psi-phenomena or experienced "superpowers." The project to put psi or real-world superpowers back into psychedelics is best displayed in David Luke's marvelous *Otherworlds: Psychedelics and Exceptional Human Experience* (2017), which goes to great lengths to explore the paranormal dimensions of the psychedelic experience, including the motifs of entity-encounter, precognition, psychokinesis, and telepathy.

What really makes the present image oh-so-1970s, however, is its simultaneous affirmation of this "super" background and its equally clear refusal to take itself too seriously. Hence the "duper."

Jeff Kripal

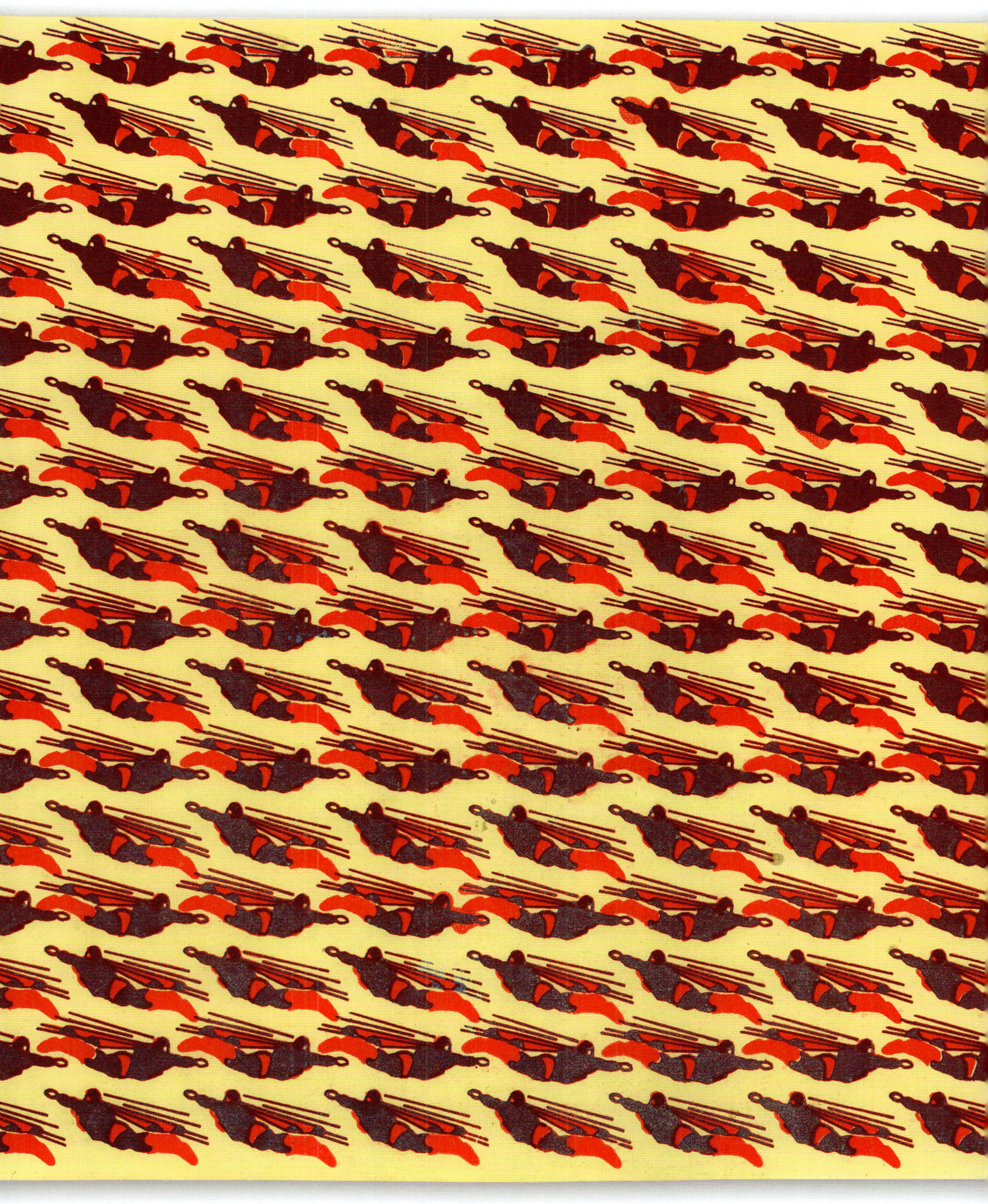

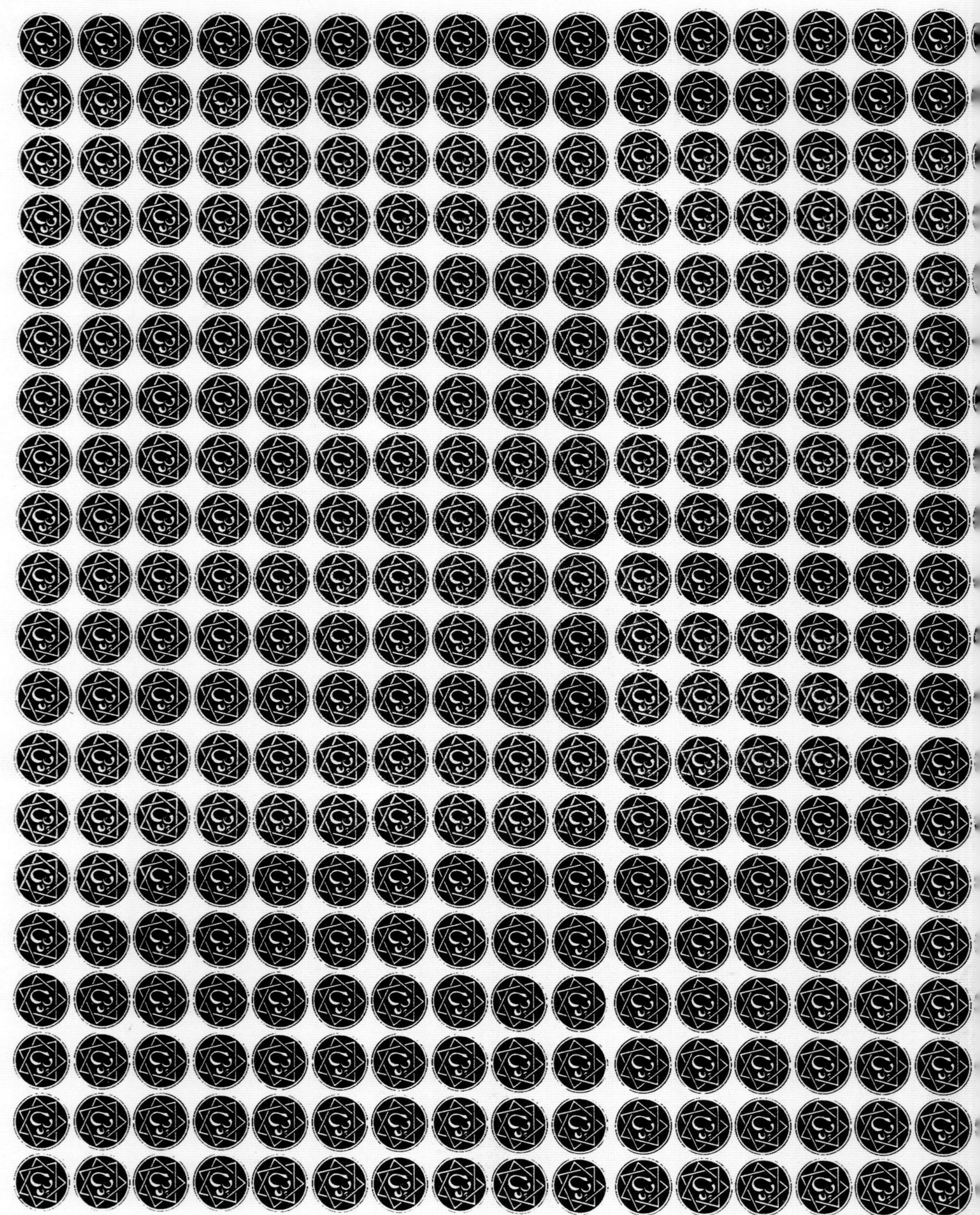

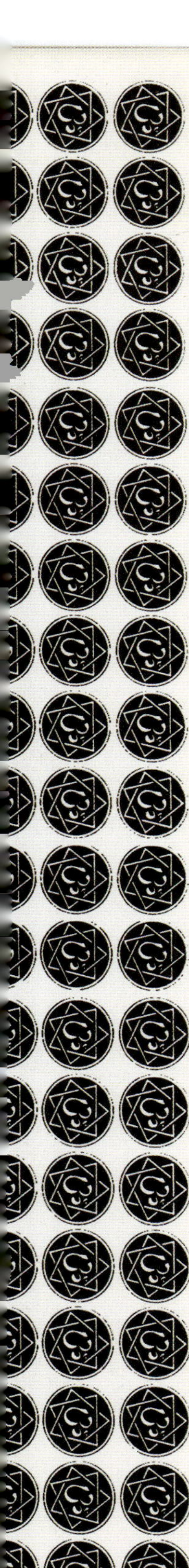

Om Seven Star, San Francisco, ca. 1978. Cut-along sheet, 12 × 12 in.

Magic Cubes, San Francisco, late 1970s. Irregularly perforated sheet, 6 × 7½ in.

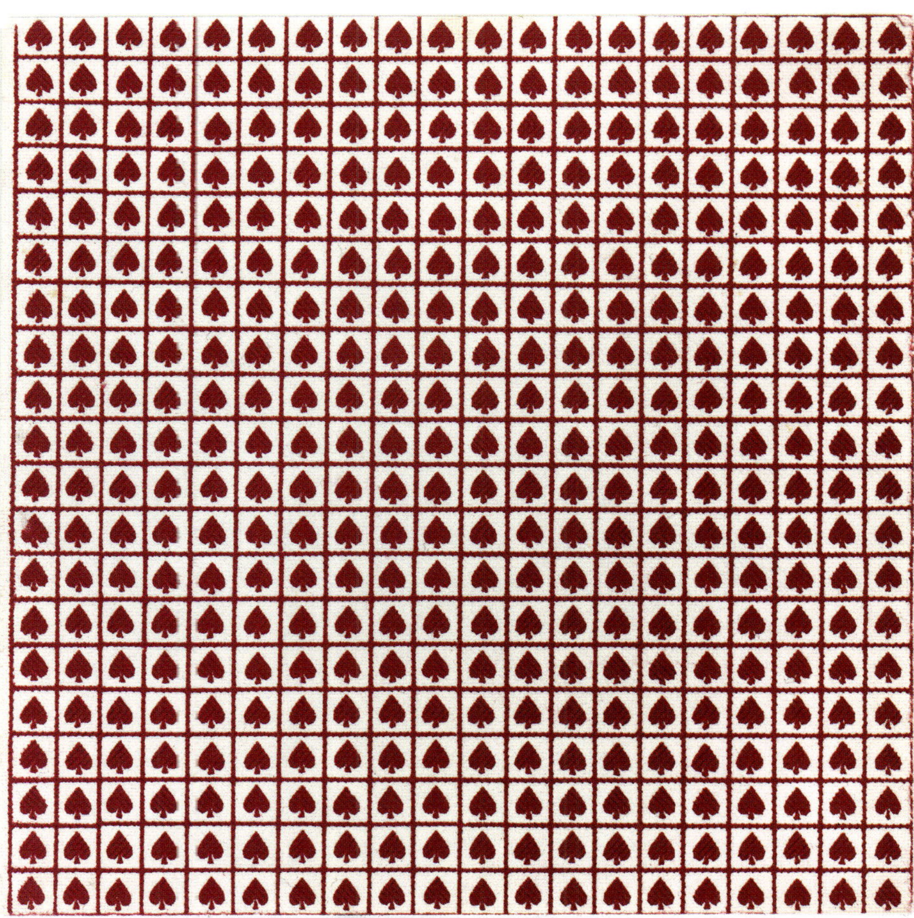

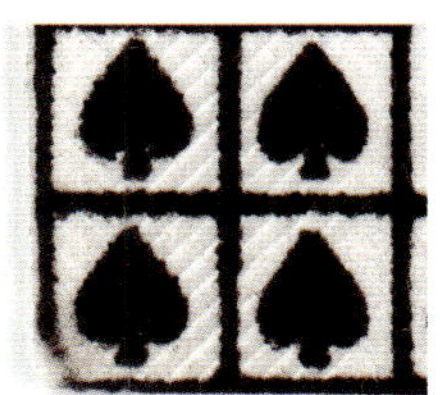

Dark Star, Pyramid, mid-1970s. 7½ × 7½ in. Perforated only in a single direction. Cut from a larger sheet.

Spades, Gilfeather, San Francisco, ca. 1977. Cut-along, printed on actual blotter paper, 5 × 5 in.

Spades, Gilfeather, (detail).

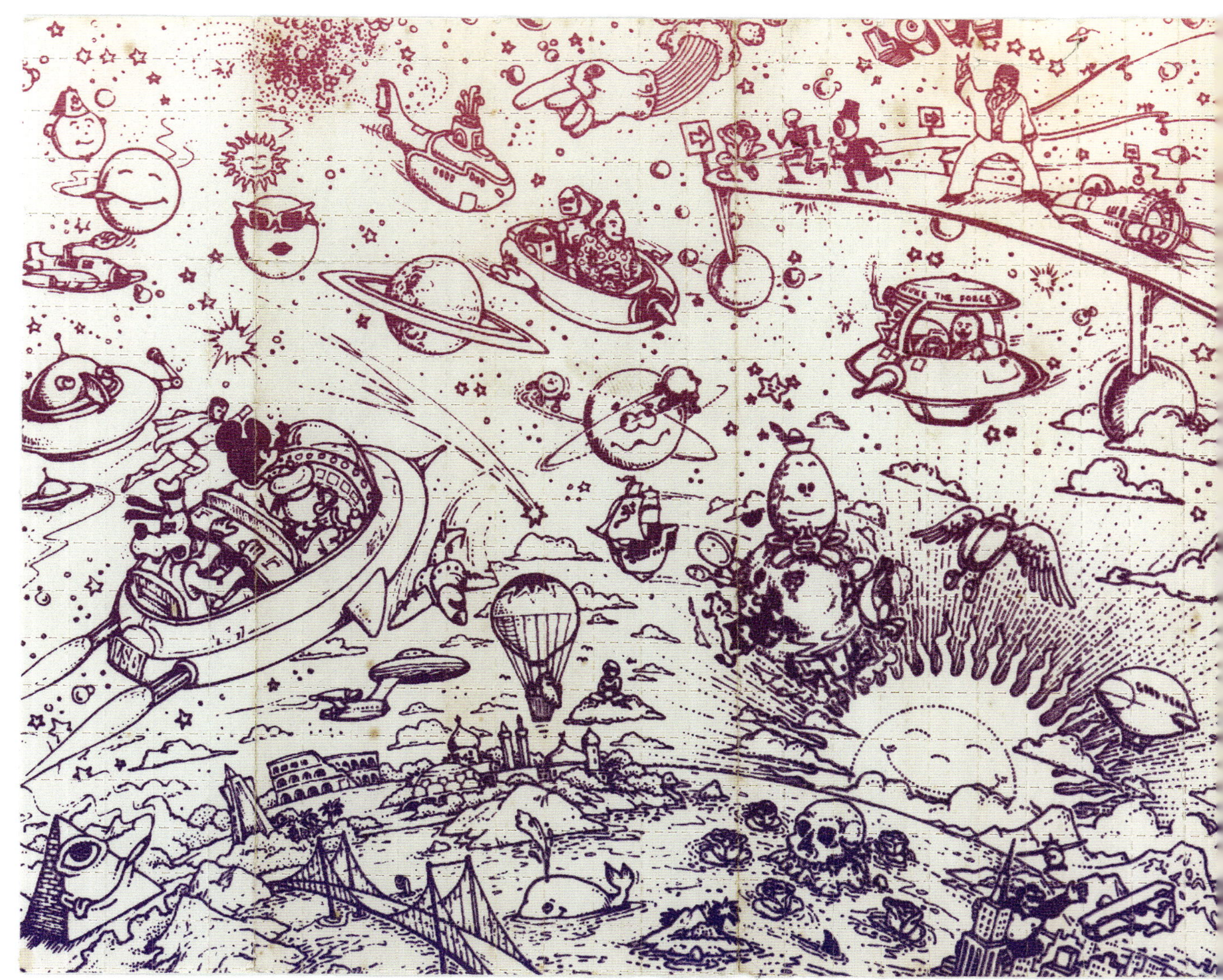

England was a gray place for a child in the 1970s. Hypnotic cartoons on *Sesame Street* and kaleidoscopic comic strips like *Captain Marvel* pointed me to America—and beyond there to outer space. In my suburban home I meditated on what these places were like and how to get to them, as well as fantasizing about having superpowers.

This blotter artwork captures the 1960s playfulness and recognition that childhood wonder is an essential tool for psychonauts. From a distance you see a bustling landscape of travel, intrigue

Crazy World,
Gilfeather, San
Francisco, 1977.
5⁹⁄₁₀ × 7½ in. Based on
an original image by
Italian–San Franciscan
artist John Flores.

and adventure. Close up, it's a zoo of iconography with an inspiring disdain for copyright.

Drawn from the Beatles' *Yellow Submarine*, the boat, the sinister glove, and cartoon John Lennon make a welcome appearance here—animations that warped my prepubescent psyche. More underground imagery startled me during visits to small, dark comic shops with sticky carpets. With my arms full of Marvel back issues, my eyes were drawn to the unnerving imagery on the walls, including Bill Griffith's *Zippy the Pinhead*. My pocket money didn't stretch to smuggling this weirdness home. I was also transfixed by photos of San Francisco surrealists the Residents in tuxedos and eyeball heads. I spent years speculating about the stories and sounds behind these visuals.

The mind-expanding artwork I absorbed like a drug as a child confirms the worst fears of conservatives about long-haired hippies subverting youth. In my case, the inquisitive wonder triggered by these visuals proved to be perfect training for the psychedelic experience itself.

John Eden

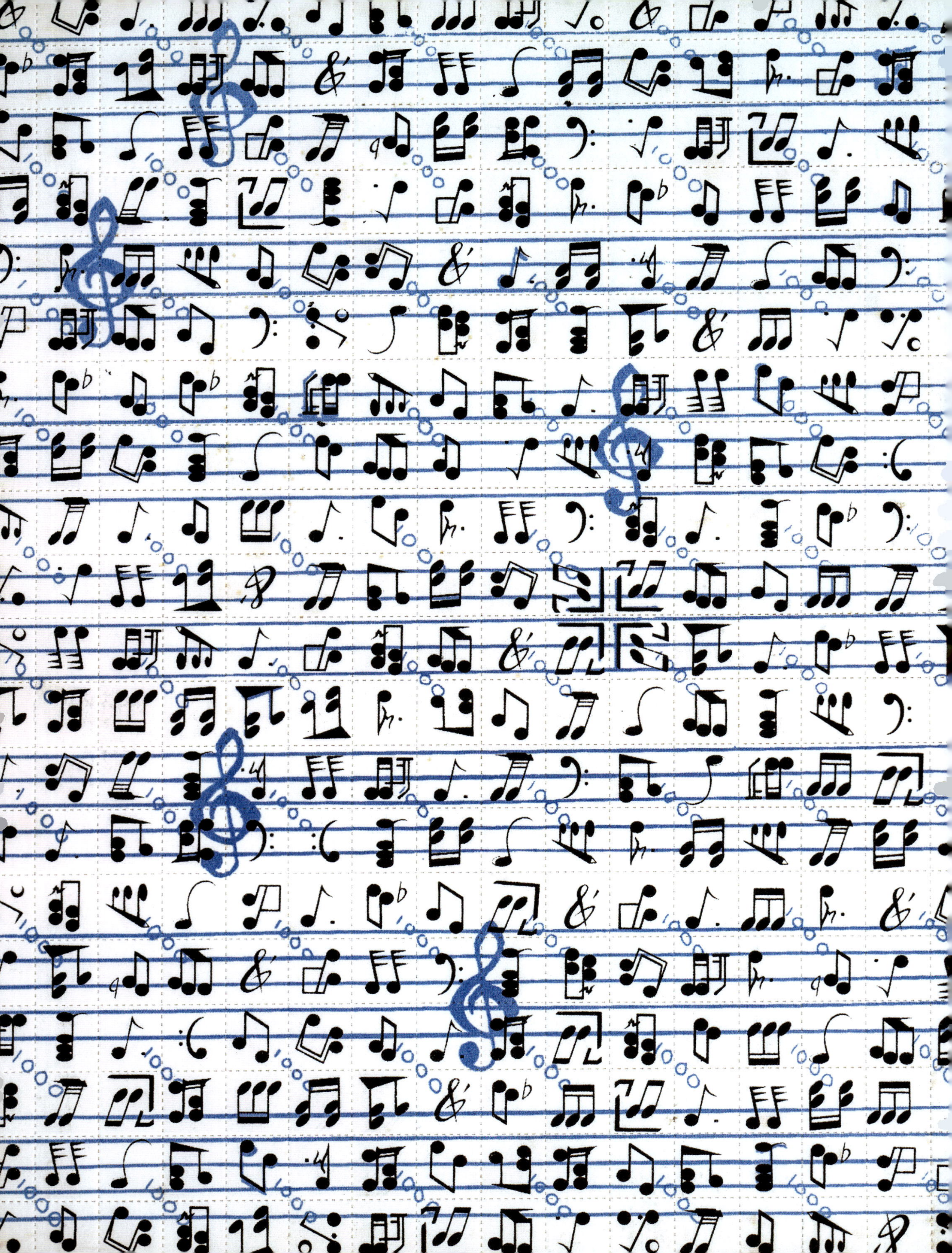

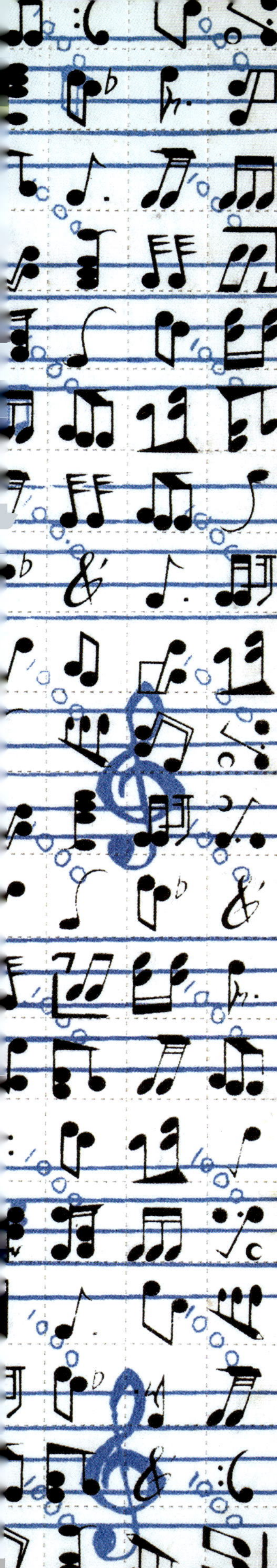

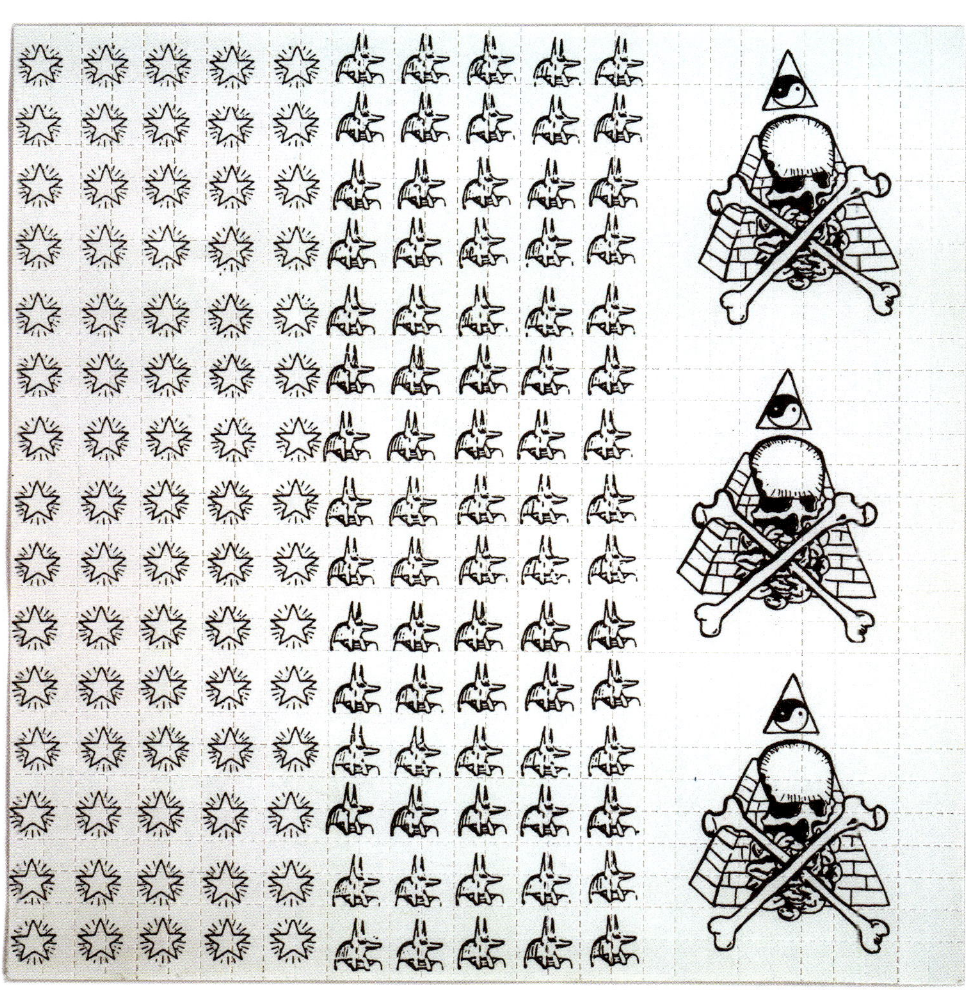

Four-way Notes, Gilfeather, San Francisco, ca. 1978. 10 × 10 in. The numeral "1000" reminds the user of the stronger "old school" four-way dosage of the sheet.

Star Anubis Skull, San Francisco, early 1980s. 7½ × 7½ in.

Blue Array, Gilfeather, San Francisco, ca. 1980. Cut-along, 4 × 5 in.

All drugs embody the mystery of how an often modest or humble materiality holds the tiny invisible molecules, whether amines or alkaloids, that produce such powerful changes of consciousness in us. Think of the peyote "button" or Maria Sabina's "little saint children." Sheets of LSD blotter make the synthesized molecule both visible and sensible, dosed in micrograms or millionths of a gram, a literal blank sheet to be marked at will.

Early LSD sheets were produced using litmus paper, the drop of the LSD on the sheet turning acid blue, the shape of the dot tracking the liquid's saturation of the paper and authenticating it. The blue dots on these sheets are printed onto the paper, perhaps paying homage to the earlier litmus sheets. Again, I'm struck by the modesty of the dot, and the playful irony of the dot's indexing of the baroque richness and vastness of the acid trip. The dot, in geometric terms, is as far as you can go in terms of being there before disappearing into the void. It's the minimal mark of being.

Early psychonaut René Daumal, high on carbon tetrachloride, asked us to imagine "an immense circle whose circumference reaches the infinite and which is perfect and unbroken except for one point; subsequently this point expands into a circle that grows indefinitely, extends its circumference to infinity and merges with the original circle, perfect, pure and unbroken, except for one point . . ." That point is us.

Marcus Boon

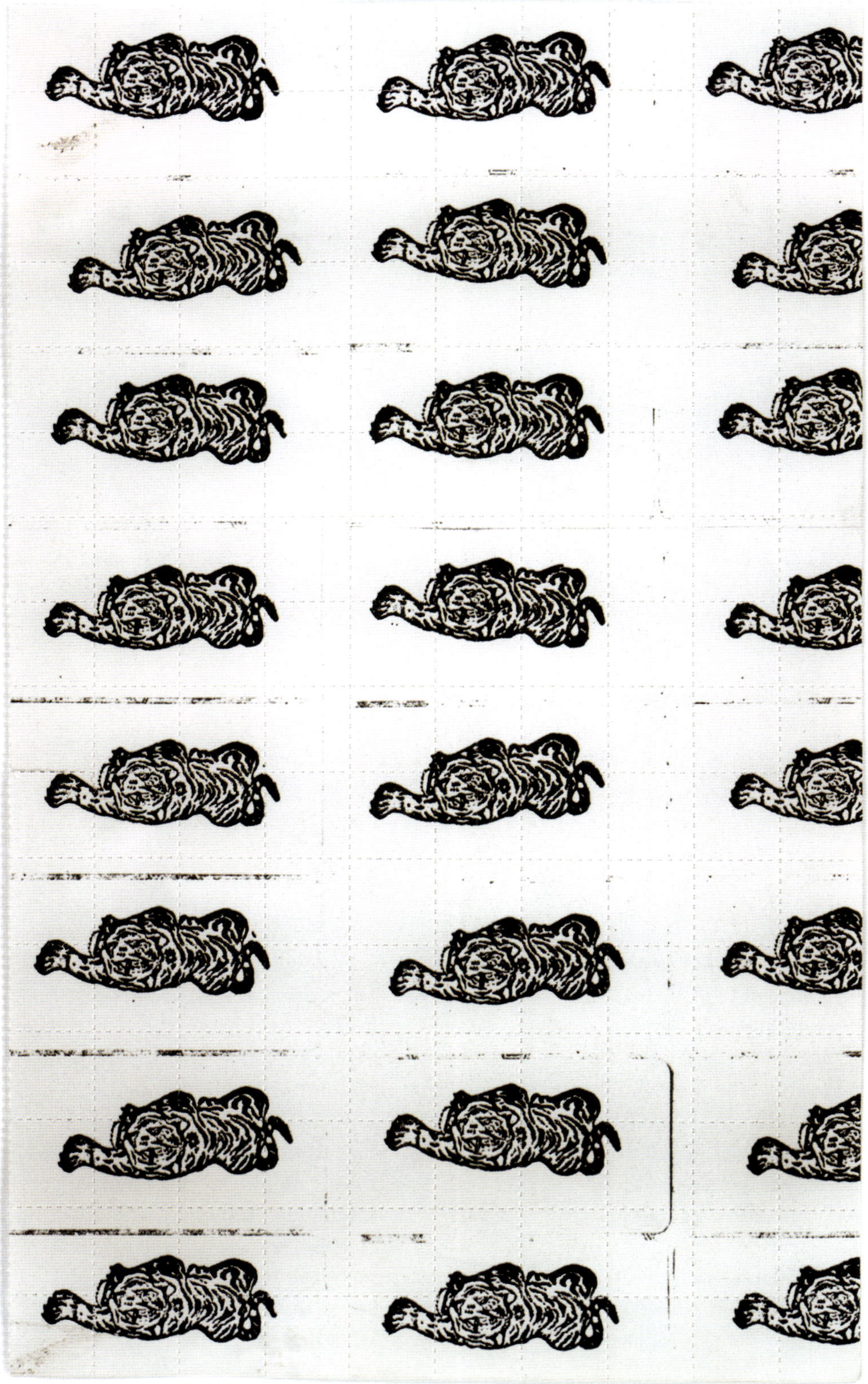

Tiger, Santa Cruz, ca. 1980. 5 × 8 in. Printed to resemble a crude handstamp; a cat's paw is featured on the reverse side.

Black Cat, Texas, ca. 1981. Four hand-perforated hits, approx. ⅘ × ⅘ in. Copied from a popular brand of firecrackers.

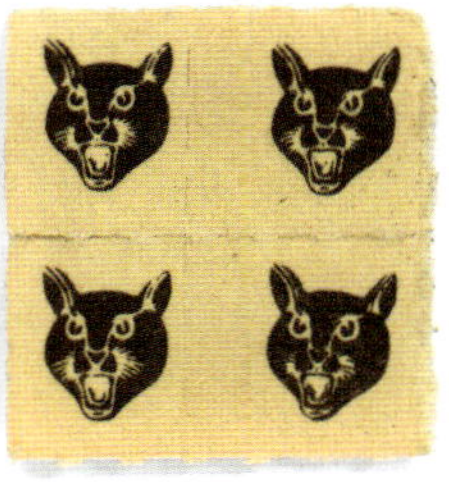

Statue of Liberty, New York City, early 1980s. Handstamp, 1¼ × 2⅛ in.

This was classic New York City issue blotter, signature for the era, popular and potent. New York was always a gritty kind of trip, far from the bucolic idyll of rural mindscapes, cluttered with sensory overloads and agonistic turns.

For all she stands for, from the most heroic ideals to the tawdriest schmatta, the Statue of Liberty has always had a particular appeal to the arts, her image rendered by a diverse pantheon from Norman Rockwell and Alfred Hitchcock to Florine Stettheimer and Andy Warhol, and as a site of trespass protests for women's rights (1970), Puerto Rican independence (1977), the release of Black Panthers (1980), and the cessation of anti-immigrant policies (2017 and 2018). As her message of inclusivity and tolerance as well as her symbolism of female strength have increasingly become a new front of the culture wars, and her promises continuously undermined, her visage has become ever more appealing to women artists, as well as artists at home and internationally, drawn to her ever more doubtful impersonation of American ideals.

But here, in this preciously self-crafted and anonymous bit of blotter, hand-stamped and hand-dipped—on some you can still make out the tweezer marks where the sheet was held—we get both an esoteric link in this long chain of collective memory and a prescient foreshadowing of how Lady Liberty's split meanings and divided loyalties have become a crucial node through which culture can at once reify and subvert her myriad meanings.

Carlo McCormick

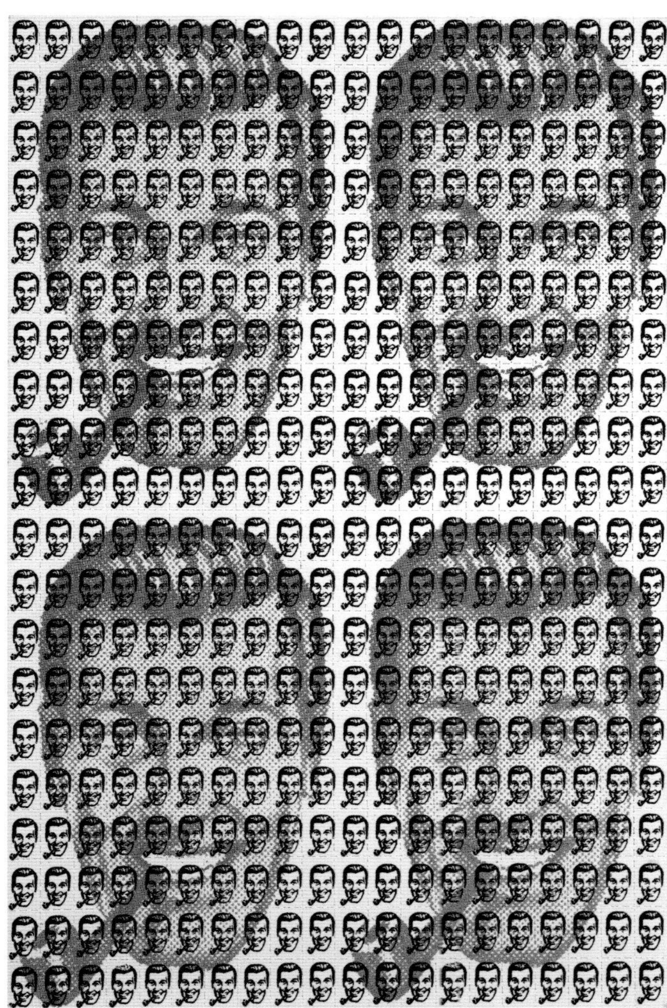

J. R. "Bob" Dobbs San Francisco, early 1980s. 5 × 7¾ in.

The face of J. R. "Bob" Dobbs, known as the Dobbshead, is the central icon of the Church of the SubGenius, created in 1980 to act as a "big tent" for psychedelic people who found themselves exiled—at least intellectually—by the War on Drugs. Originating as an unattributed piece of advertising clip art from the 1950s, "Bob" was appropriated by the founders of the church, "Rev. Ivan Stang" (b. Douglass St. Clair Smith) and "Dr. Philo Drummond" (b. Steve Wilcox), its copyright acquired by the church after the publication of *SubGenius Pamphlet no. 1*, the blistering, conformity-critiquing booklet that launched the church.

It seems likely that the Dobbshead acid sheet first appeared at the SubGenius World Convention hosted November 20–22, 1981 in Dallas, Texas. Such latter-day acid tests became the central touchstone for the SubGenius movement, which hosted local, regional, and national "Devivals" throughout the year.

The Dobbshead became one of the late twentieth century's most recognizable pieces of psychedelic iconography, second only to the dancing bears and "Stealies" associated with the Grateful Dead. Abetting this, the earliest SubGenius fanzines included instructions on creating DIY graffiti stencils of "Bob." American cities were subsequently hit with successive waves of Dobbsheads. As a ubiquitous cultural phenomenon, "Bob" deserves to be recognized as the progenitor of more widely celebrated street art, specifically Shepard Fairey's "OBEY Giant" stickers and the stencil work of Banksy. Unlike these more commercial artworks, though, the Dobbshead represented a psychedelic religious worldview diametrically opposed to normal society.

J. Christian Greer

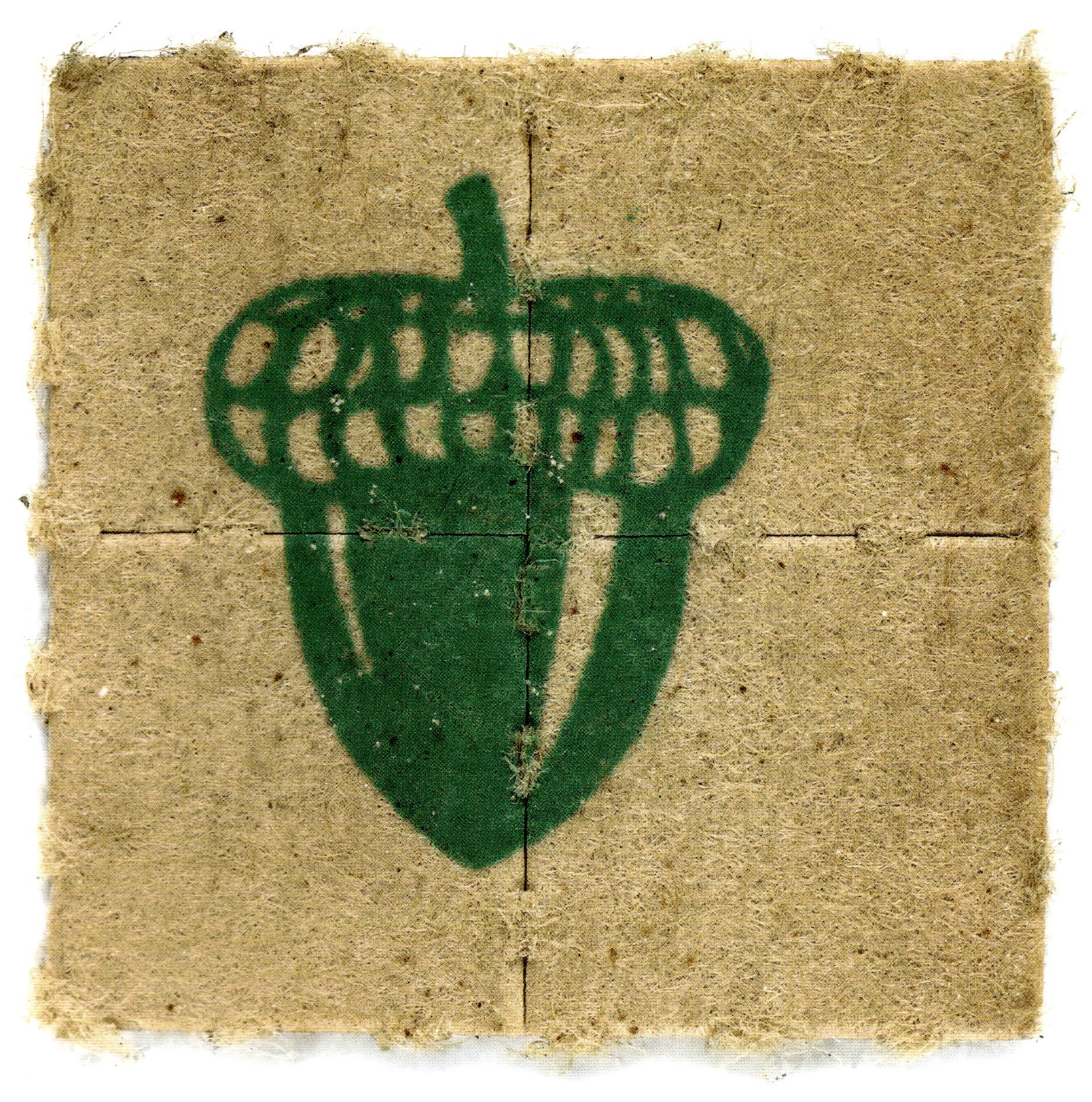

Acorn, Gilfeather, San Francisco, ca. 1981. ¾ × ¾ in. The envelope for this item declares "Forests Are Forever."

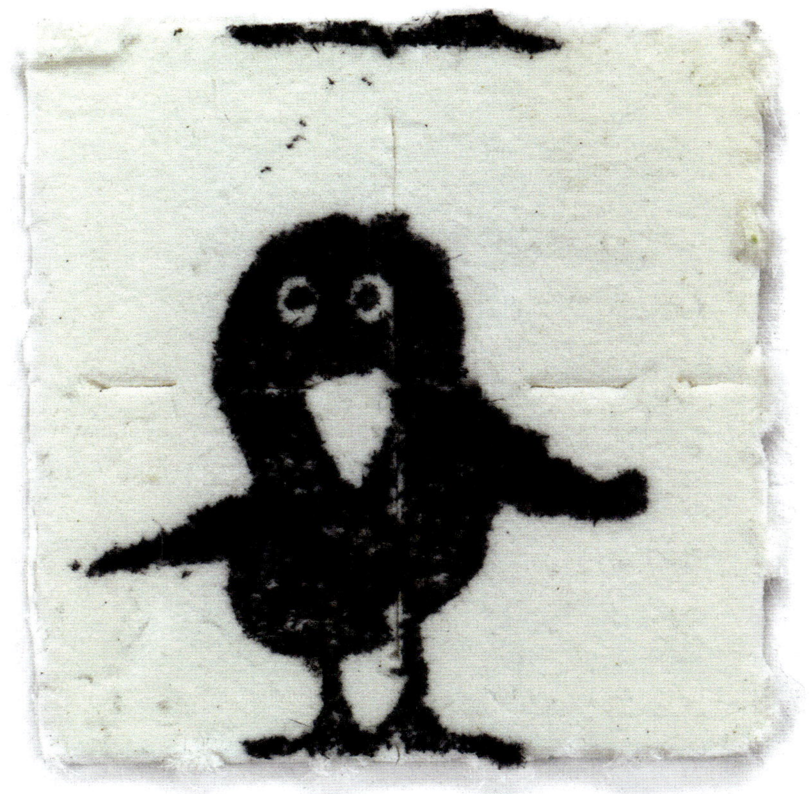

Blackbird, ca. 1983. Four hits, ½ × ½ in. Though it resembles a handstamp, the image was printed.

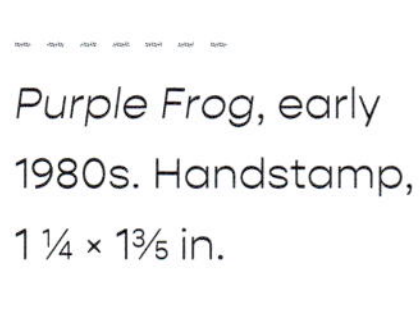

Purple Frog, early 1980s. Handstamp, 1 ¼ × 1⅗ in.

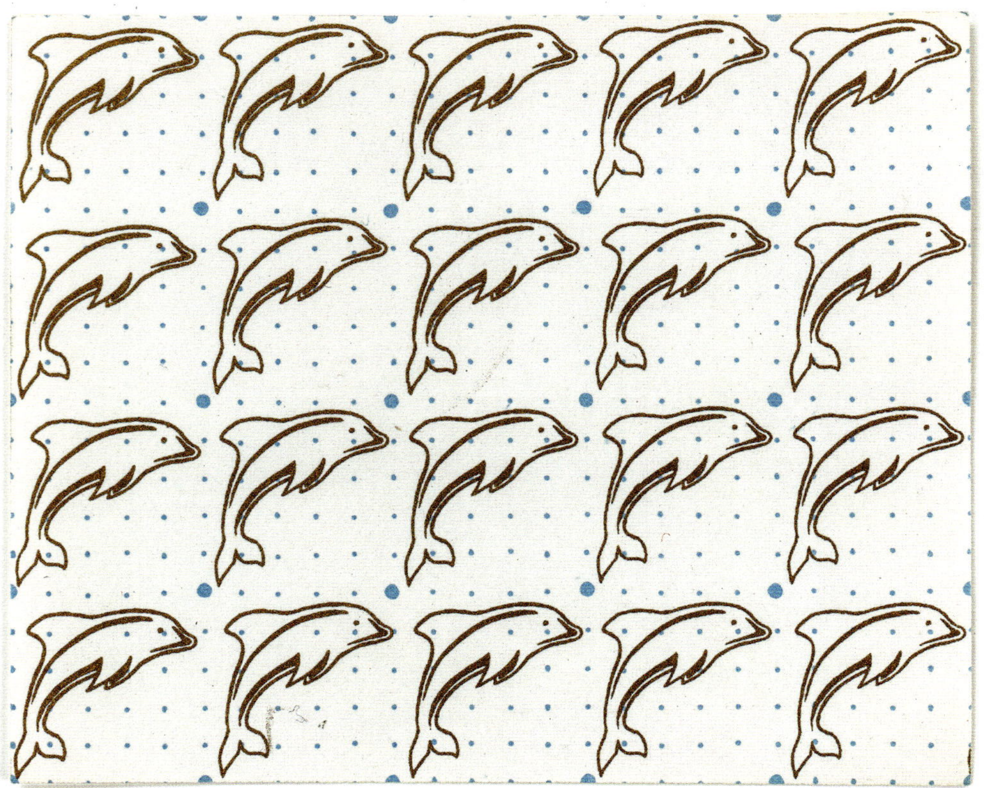

Golden Dolphins, Gilfeather, San Francisco, ca. 1980. 4 × 5 in. Note overstamp with *Blue Array*.

Camouflage, Sarah Matzar, Bolinas, mid-1980s. 6¼ × 10 in. This design appeared in scores of different color combinations.

Beyond its beauty, blotter art serves as a brand according to the original, medieval purpose of branding as a proof of origin. Like the icon burned into the hide of a calf, the branding of a bottle of beer or sack of grain meant that someone was taking responsibility for the quality of the product.

Blotter art is no different. The quality of the chemical and the quality of the trip is known, right down to the batch. And anyone taking acid in New York in the early 1980s knew that *Golden Dolphins* could be trusted. It wasn't as clean as the green pyramid gelatin that was going around at the same time, but nothing ever quite was.

My friend Stephen and I only got four hits at first, barely enough to make out the back of one of those golden dolphins, from a dealer named Joe who sat at the corner table downstairs at Max's Kansas City. But when we learned they were made locally, Stephen traced them to a graduate student at Columbia University, who claimed he was involved in their manufacture. We must've gotten fifty hits—two full squares of the repeating double-dolphin pattern—that lasted us the rest of our college careers.

Golden Dolphins were a classic, one of the few identifiable, beloved formulations of acid during the decidedly unpsychedelic era of Ronald Reagan, yuppies, John Lennon's death, and Iran–Contra. They were the New York arts counterculture of 1980, in physical, chemical, and visual form.

Douglas Rushkoff

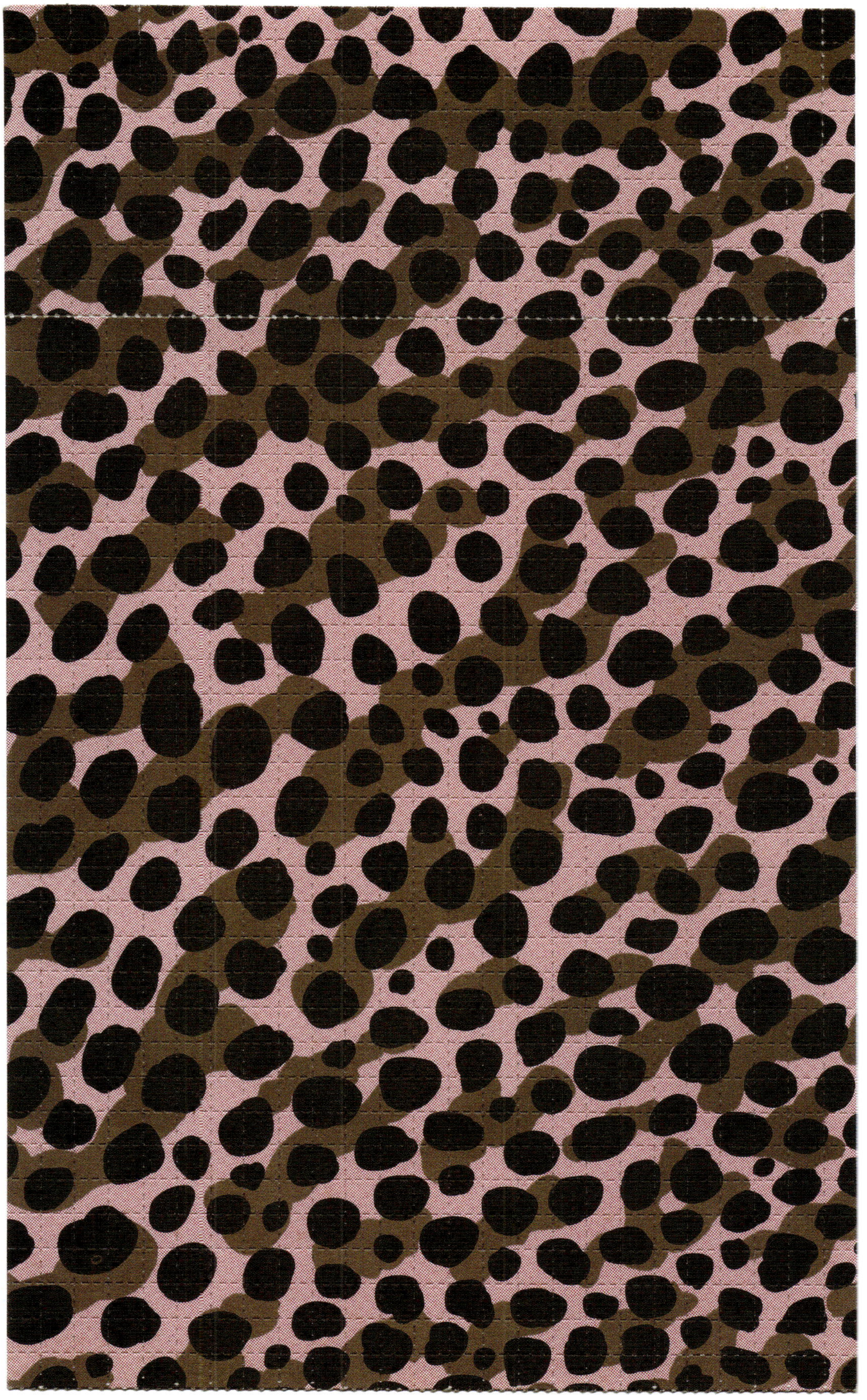

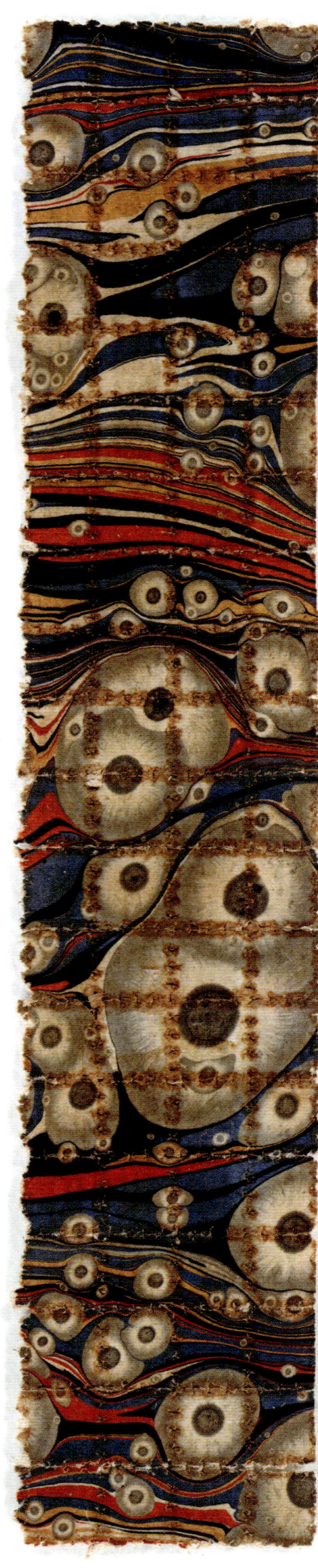

Suminagashi, ca. 1982. 1 × 5 in. Likely perforated with a pizza cutter. The paper itself may have originally served as book endpapers.

Steal Your Face, late 1970s. 2¾ × 2¾ in.

The skull-and-lightning-bolt design first flashed into the mind of Bear, a.k.a. Owsley Stanley, while careening down a road through a Northern California rainstorm—a vision of a disk split by a lightning bolt. He stenciled it on the Grateful Dead's gear as an easily identifiable icon to help find their road cases in jumbled stacks of bands' identical boxes at festivals. Later, he asked his close friend, the artist Bob Thomas, if he could come up with a way to write "Grateful Dead" beneath the circle in lettering that appeared to form a skull. Bob couldn't get the writing to

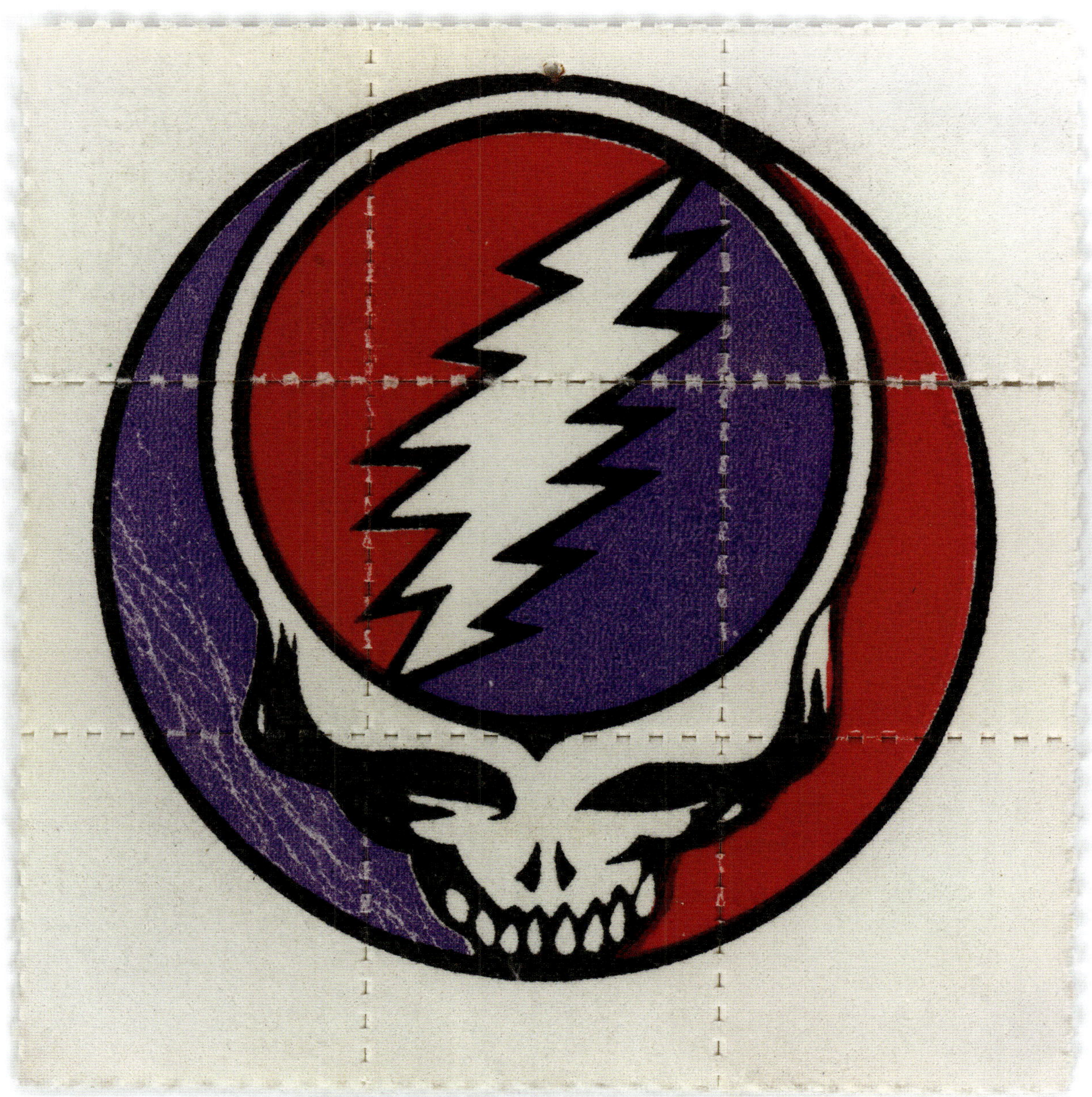

work out, but what he drew instead turned it into iconic art.

Bear loved art. And Bear loved acid. But many people are surprised to hear that Bear *hated* blotter. That may seem strange, since blotter's acid-on-art is as synonymous with LSD as Owsley's own name. Bear's exactitude meant he found the quality of blotter sorely lacking. "Acid is polar," he'd grouse. "When blotter dries, it migrates all over the place, and there's no telling how much is on any square." Moreover, it would get rubbed off the surface and degraded by light, so that by the time that little magic tab finally met an eager tongue, much of what might have been simply no longer was. Indeed, Bear hated inferior forms of LSD distribution so much that he pioneered a process to make tablets that were evenly mixed, so you could accurately titrate your dose—half a tab was half a hit. Of course, Bear's idea of a "proper dose" was perhaps a bit heavy-handed for most folk, so predictable divisibility could be a good thing. When Bear handed you something, it was generally advisable to start by taking half!

Starfinder Stanley

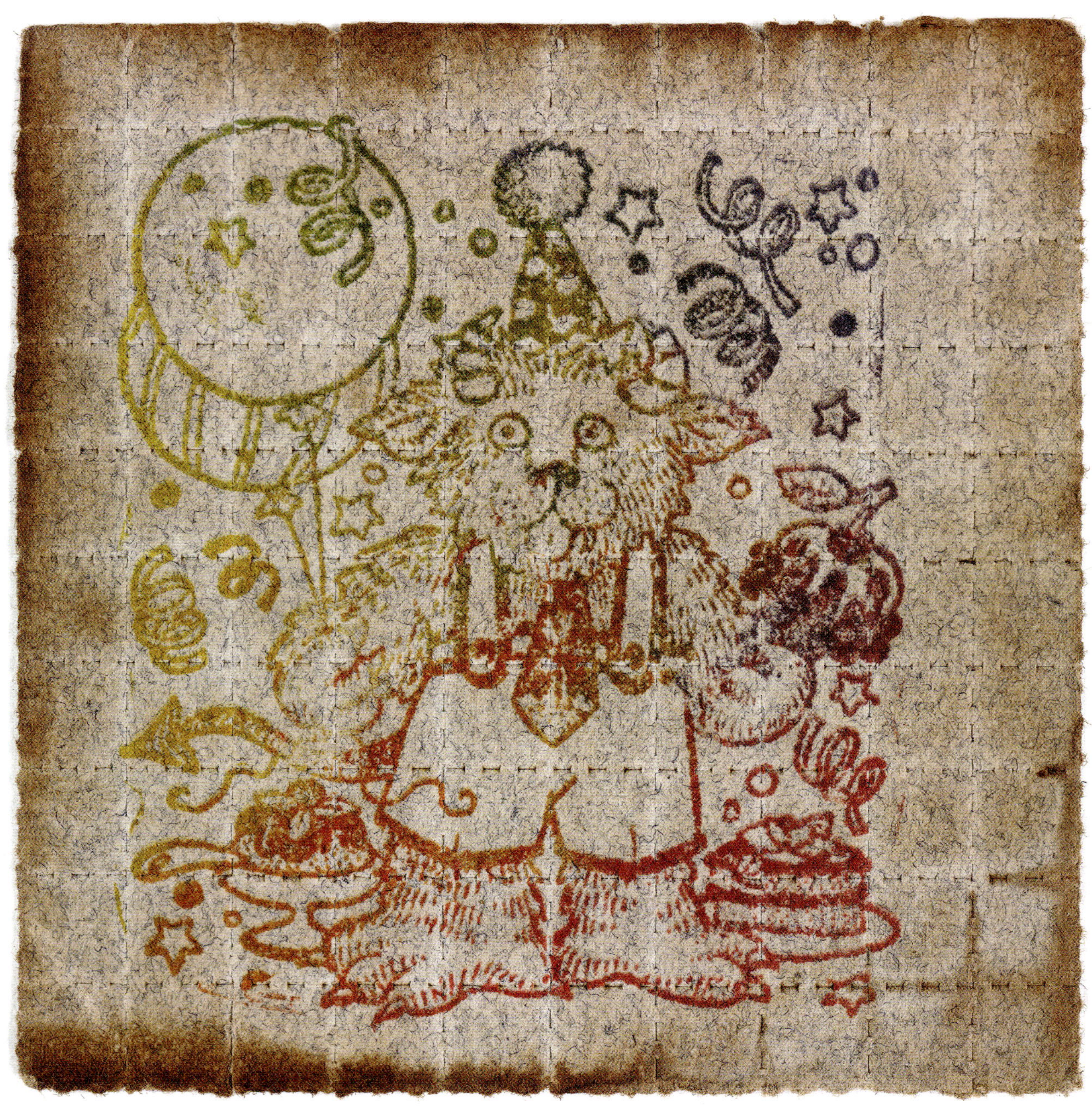

Party Animal, ca. 1983. Split fountain ink, 2½ × 2½ in. Unbalanced dip. Purchased in line for a Grateful Dead show at Berkeley's Greek Theatre in 1983.

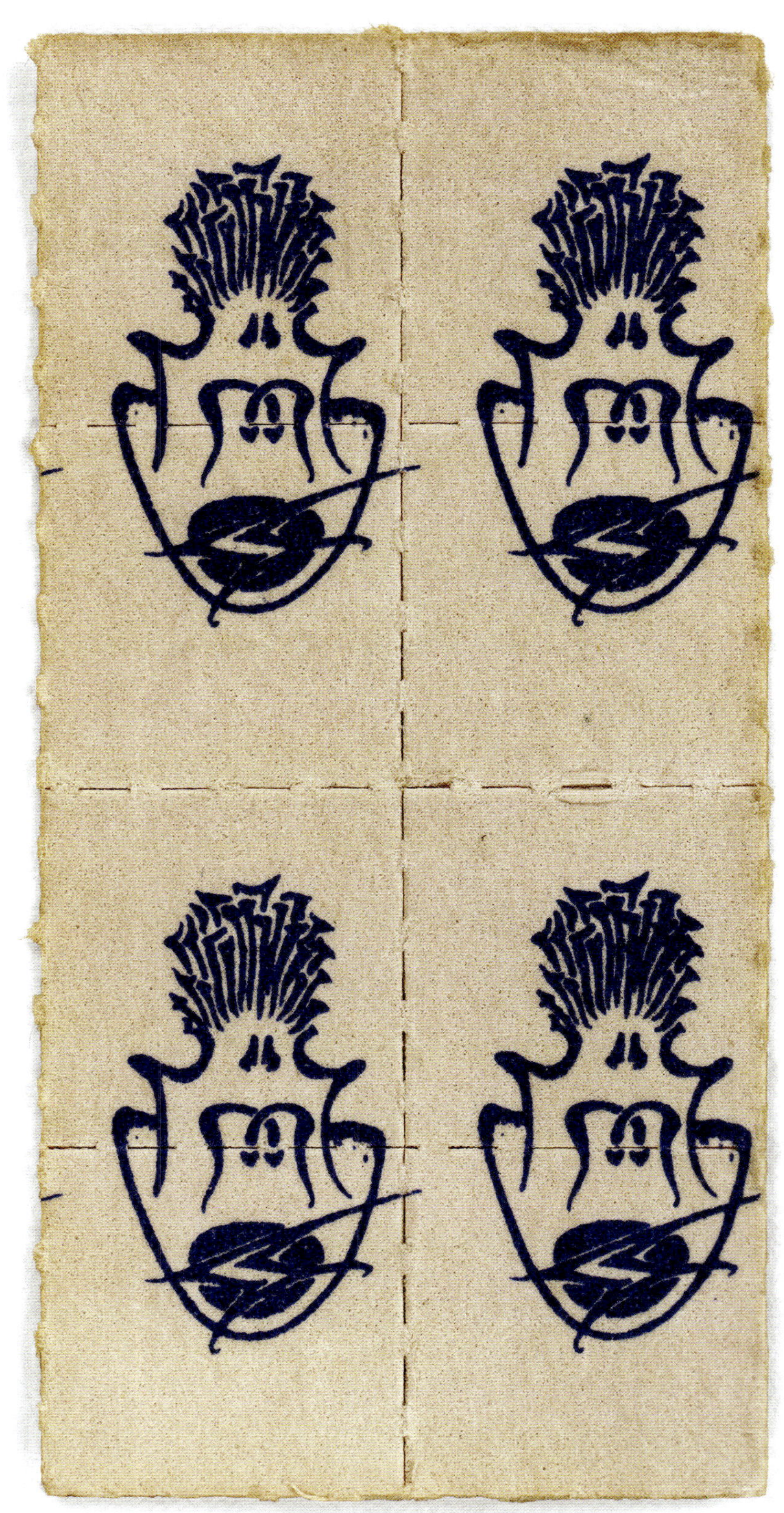

Baby Ganja, ca. 1982.
¾ × 1½ in.

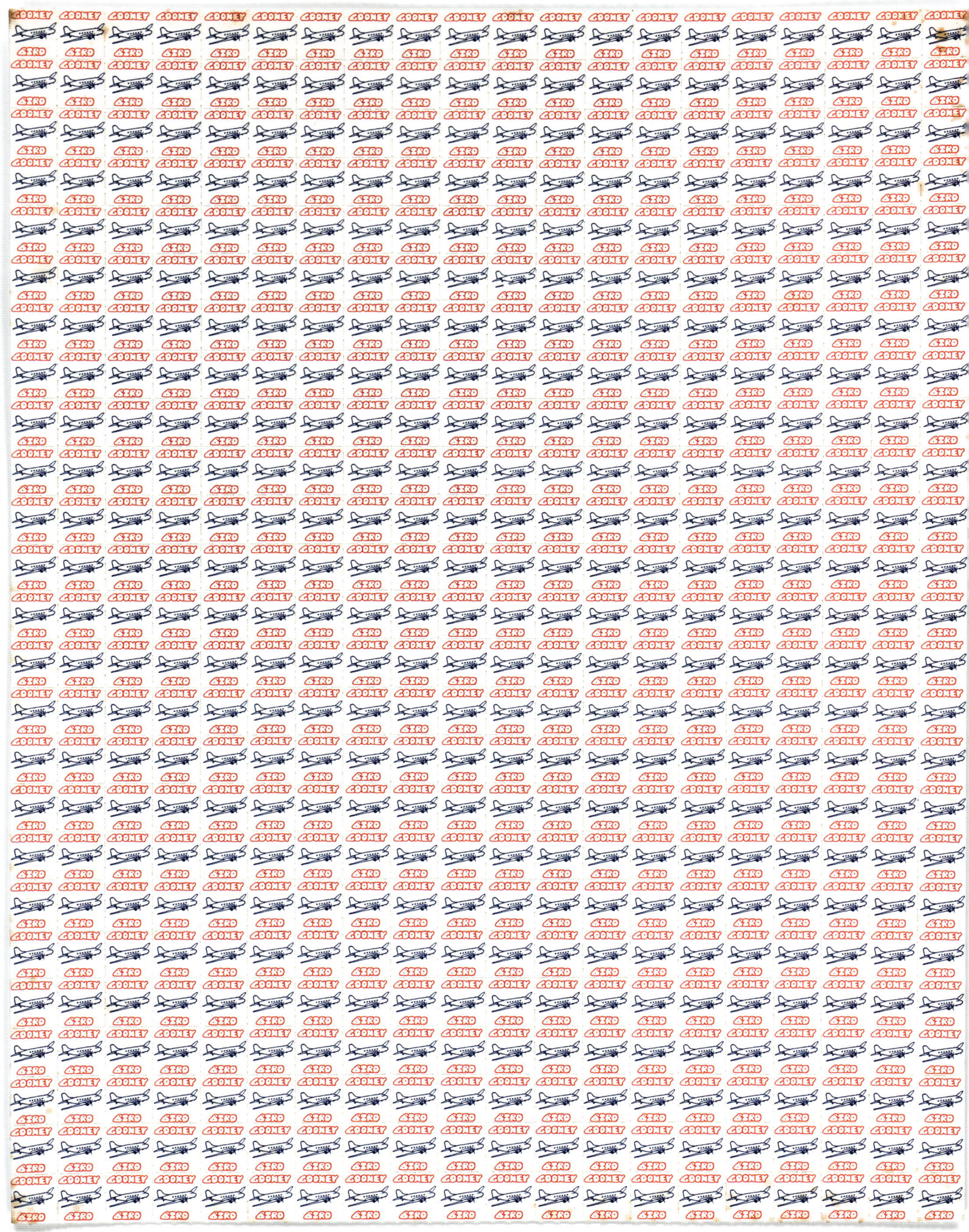
GOONEY
BIRD

Gooney Birds, BMT, Berkeley, ca. 1982. Sheet, 7⅜ × 9⅜ in.; single hit ⅜ × ⅜ in.

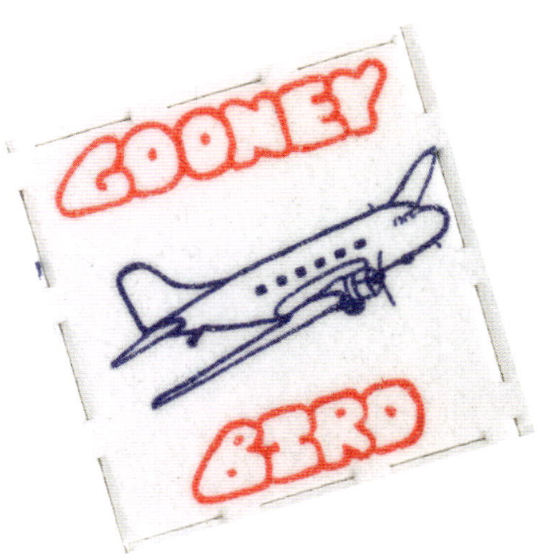

For many of us who began to acquire an advanced psychedelic consciousness in the mid-to-late-'80s, often on tour with the Grateful Dead, Gooney Birds were "the first." Not the inaugural LSD consumed, nor maybe even the strongest, but the initial recognition of acid that carried a mark of quality. Call it a blotter brand you could trust. I was introduced in Saratoga Springs in June of '88 and hung out for the next year. Even the blotter's art was somewhat related to its trustworthy qualities. Gooney Birds acquired their sobriquet from the cartoon airplane depicted on them, the popular Douglas DC-3, recast during World War II as the C-47, which gained its nickname when the reliable long-range transport became the first military plane to land on Midway, an island 1,000 miles northeast of Hawaii inhabited by a large albatross colony.

The intake of Gooney Birds never required more than a single dose; the long trips open to both unexpected mind exploration and rhythmic acuity. It was great for dancing, the come-down smooth as honey, and the sleep after adding its own wonderfully odd, colorful postscript; yet it was also untroubled, ruining me for a future of speedy LSD sessions. My last memory of eating Gooneys is in September of '89—a final dalliance with LSD innocence before things got more intense, an onset of understanding that the gained lessons weren't going to make it easier to exist in society and simply flying away was a hollow option.

Piotr Orlov

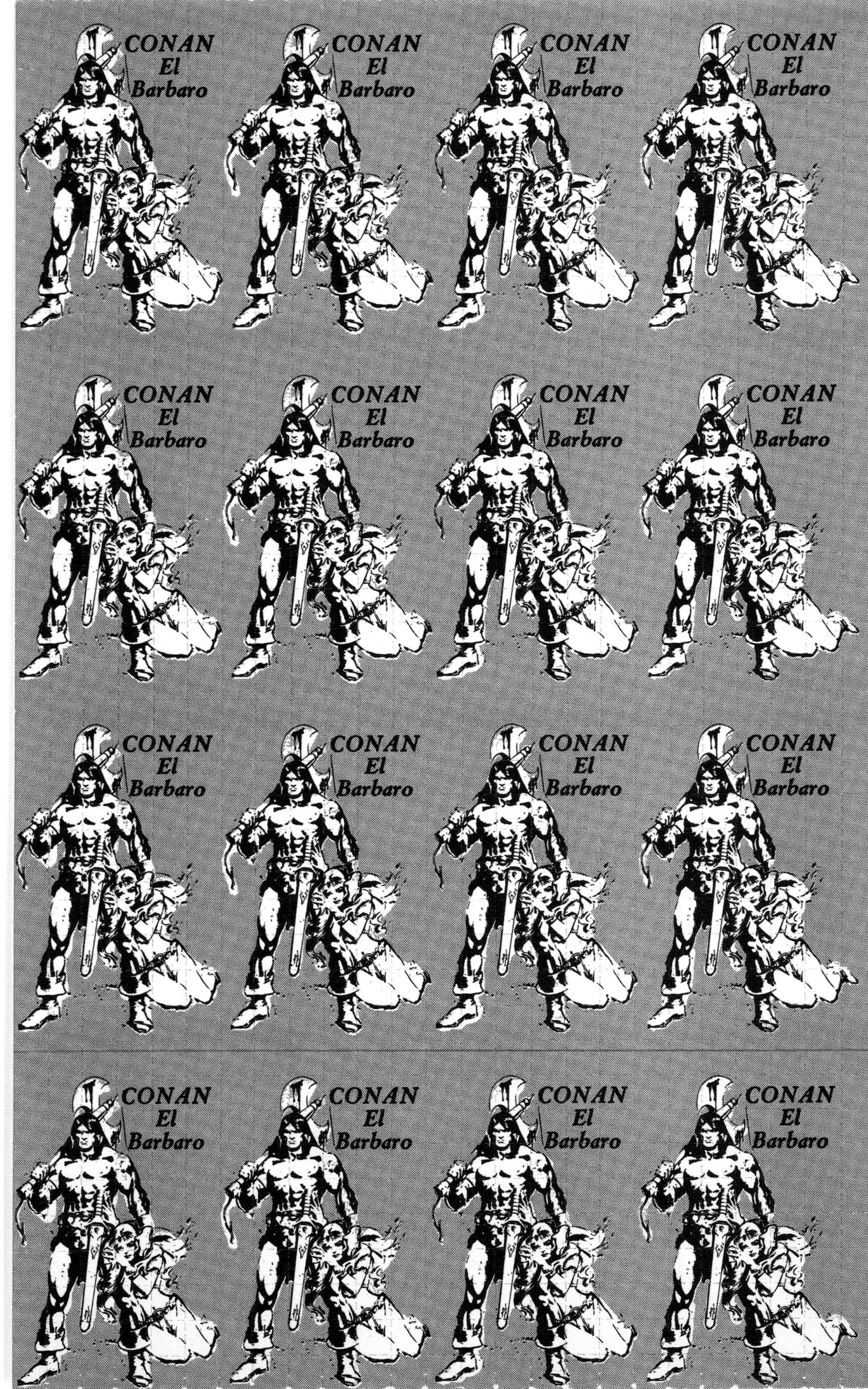
CONAN
El
Barbaro

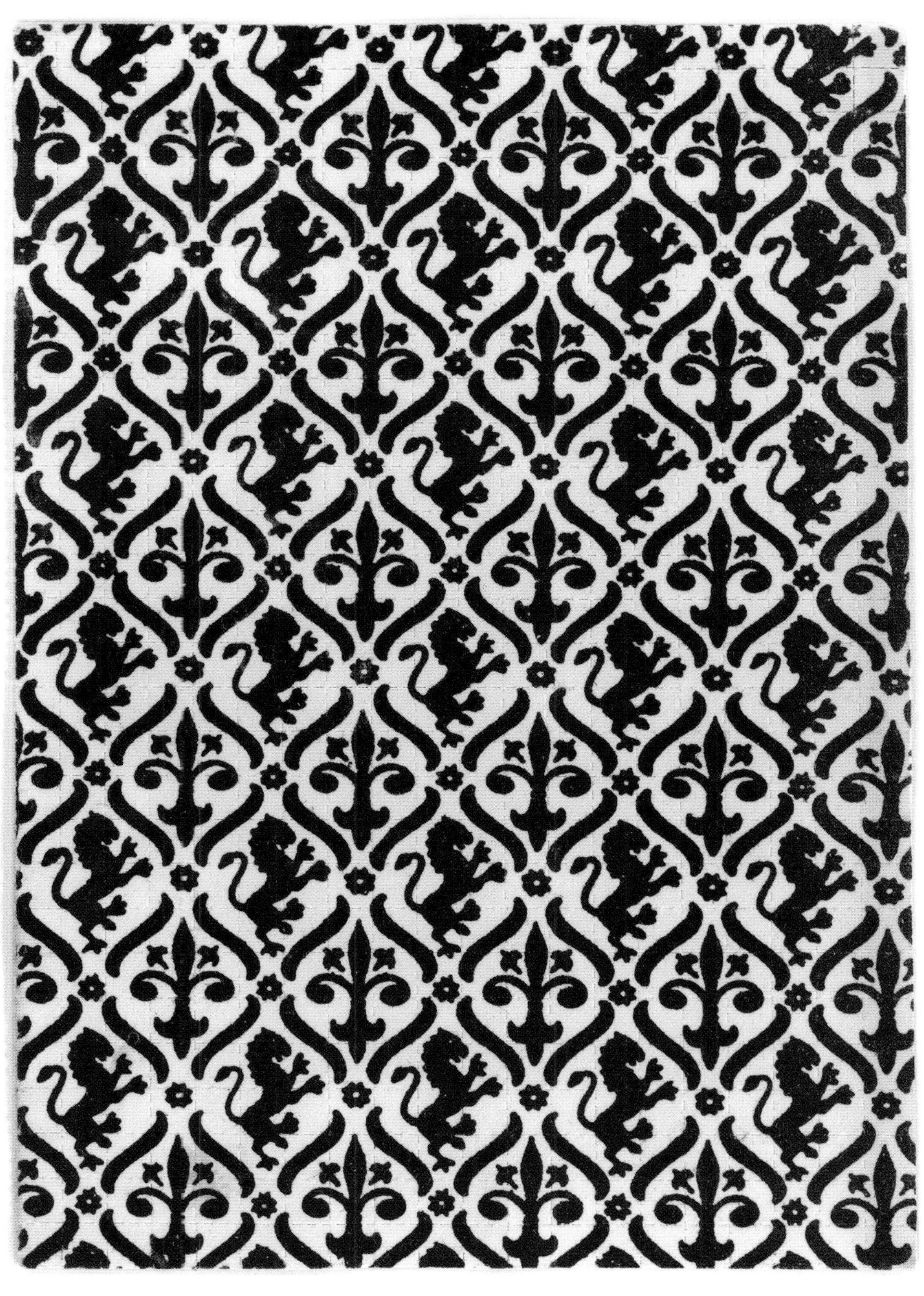

Conan El Barbaro/ Mexican Acid, San Francisco, ca. 1981. 6¼ × 10 in.

Lion Rampant, ca. 1980. 5 × 7 in.

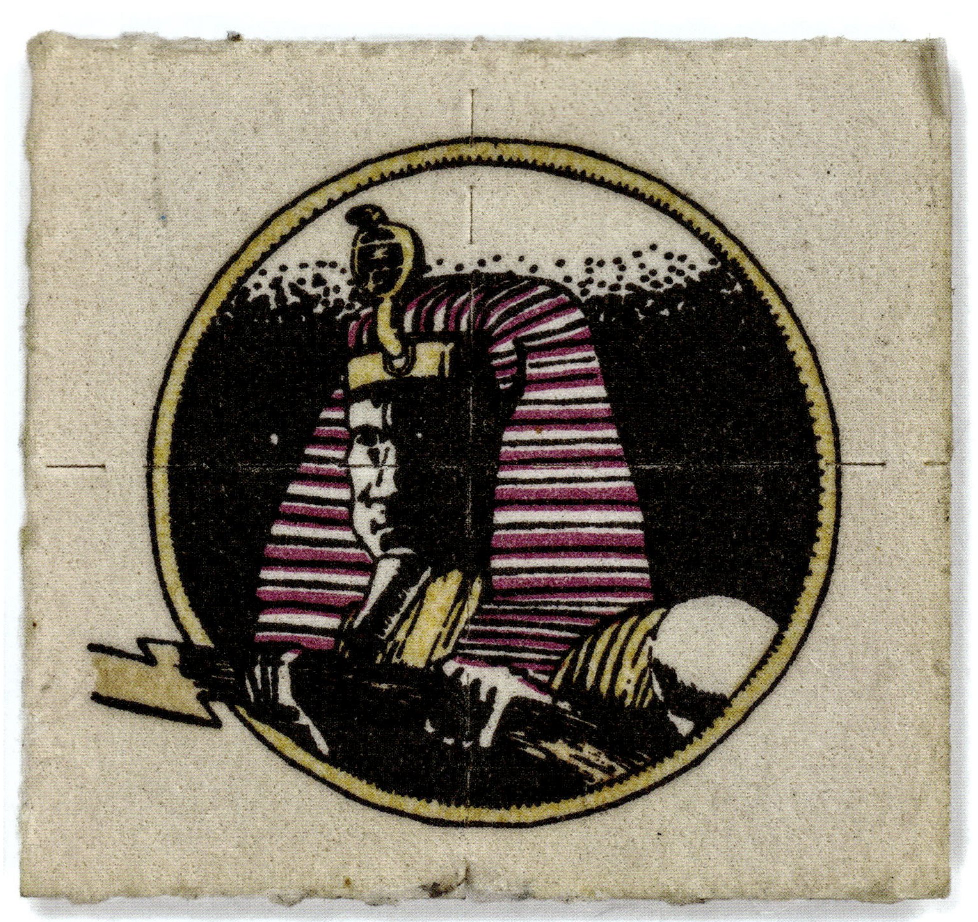

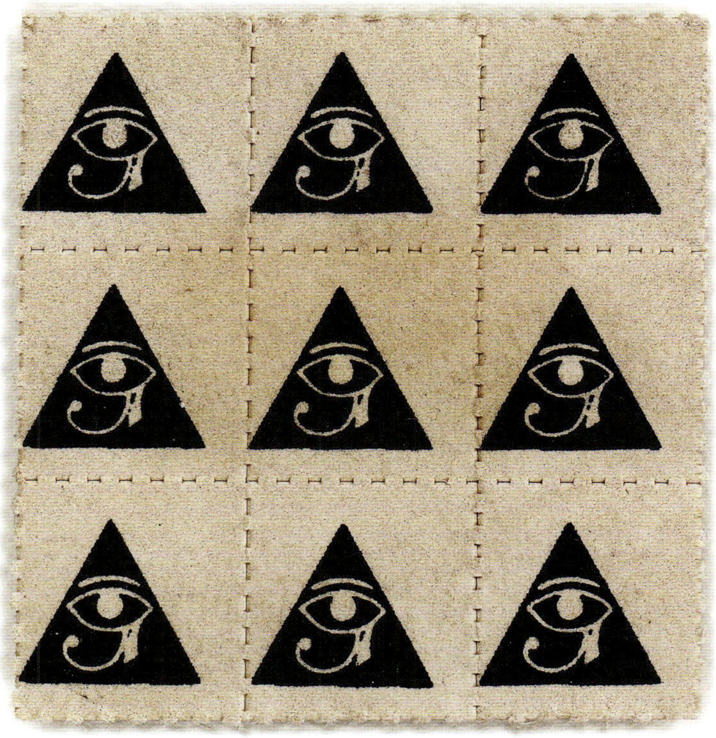

Sphynx/Pharaoh Acid*, San Francisco, ca. 1982. Single hit, ¾ × ¾ in. Sourced from Rick Griffin, “Ain Soph Aur,” *Zap* no. 3, 1969.

Eye of Horus, Pyramid/Gilfeather, San Francisco, ca. 1982. 1¼ × 1¼ in.

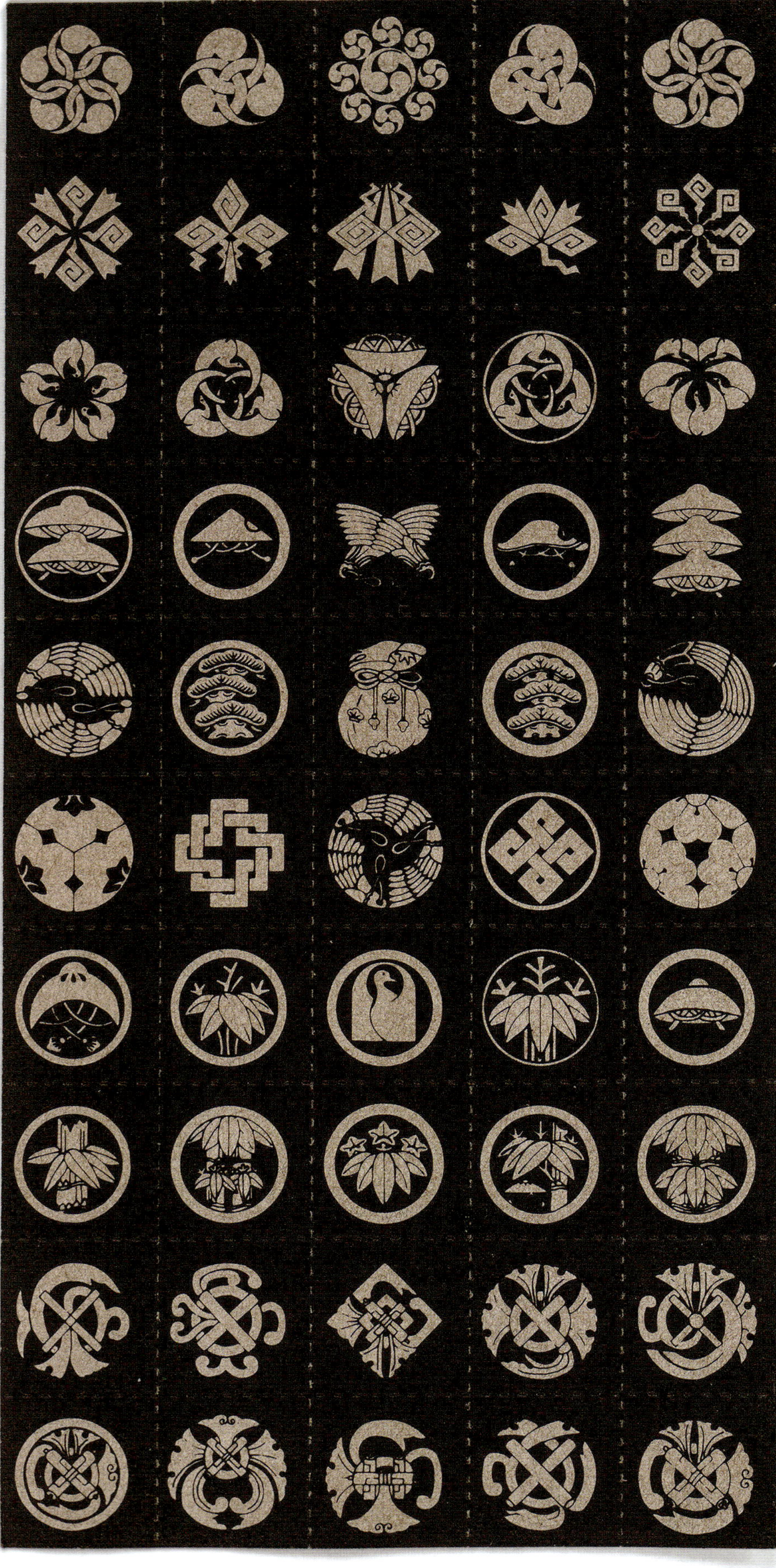

This little packet is my favorite ever presentation of the Supreme Sacrament in blotter form. Known on the street as "samurais," these came fifty to a page, in a folder a little smaller than an index card. The blotters themselves were protected by a shiny black cover featuring a seal that resembled three mushrooms (which were really hats) centered in gold on the face. These folders then came in a box, and in each box, one folder had a higher dose than the others. These were touched with gold so that the user would recognize the difference.

At the time that these blotters were produced, the designs themselves were available in several Dover Press publications that were intended to be used like clip art. Almost all of the seals depicted here can be found in *Monsho: Family Crests for Symbolic Design* by Isao Honda (1963). Each seal represents a Japanese badge or crest known as *mon*. Historically, *mon* are more like trademarks than heraldic devices, having been introduced as battle insignia, but eventually being produced for brothels, actors, and brands of sake.

Although it is possible to interpret the design components and identify their origin, they are mostly commonplace elements: birds, plants, a feather duster, a purse. The second row, however, represents five different depictions of a thunderbolt, which I consider to be the most evocative image for this extra special delivery. These were made at 4,000 hits to a gram, an honest 250 microgram dose.

Mariavittoria Mangini

Japanese Crests/ Samurai Shields, Bernard Hassell, Sonoma County, 1982. 2 × 4 in.

Japanese Crests, reissue, mid-1980s. Single hit, with gold flake trim, ⅜ × ⅜ in.

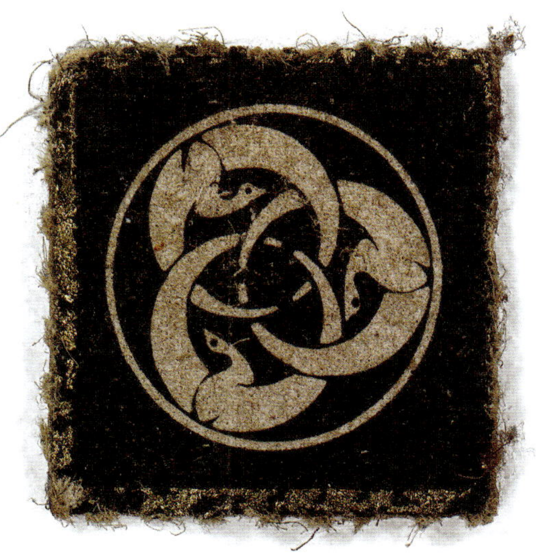

Blue Dove, Gilfeather, San Francisco, early 1980s. ½ × ½ in.

Third Eye Smiles, Fritz, San Francisco, mid 1980s. 7½ × 7½ in. Design created by a local roller derby queen.

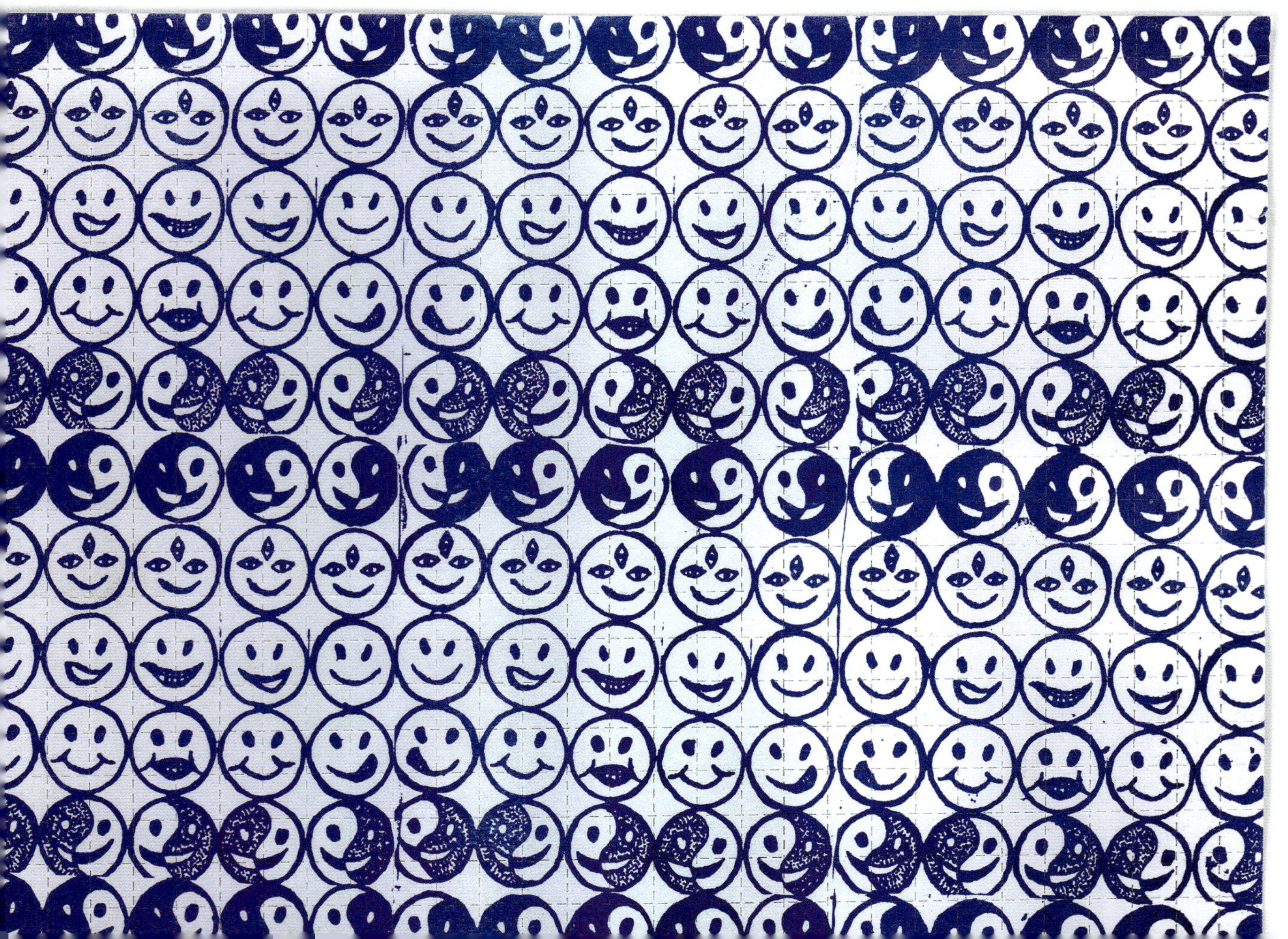

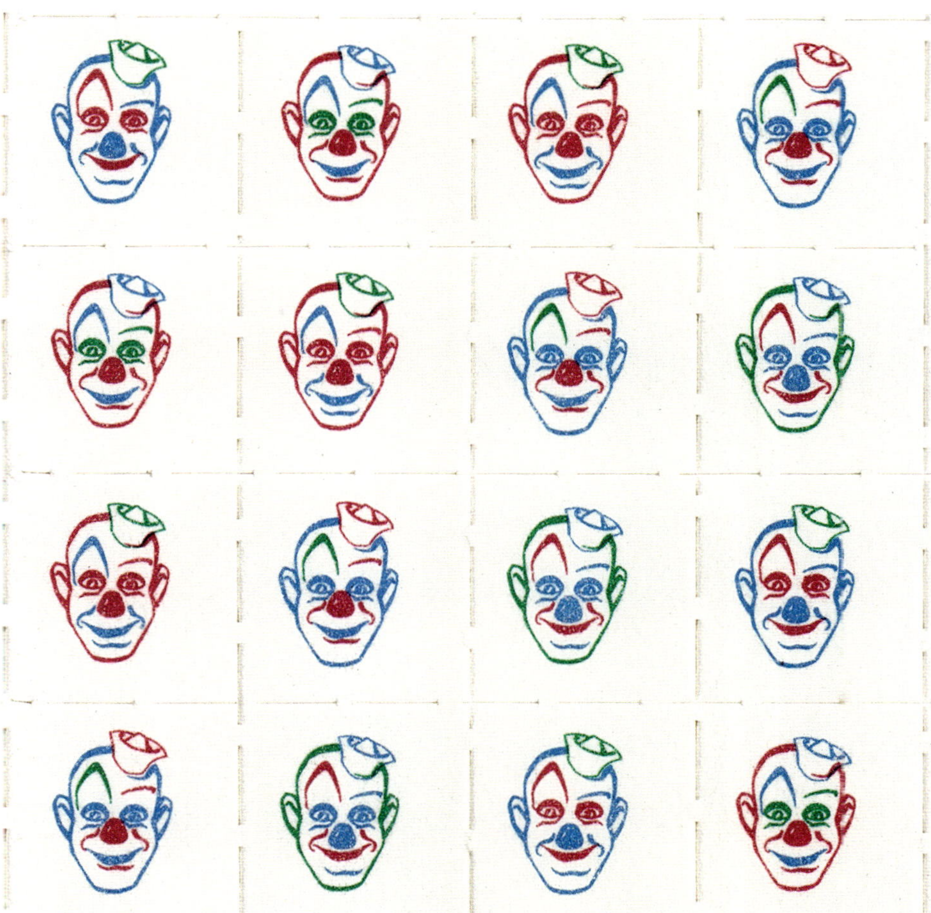

Clowns, San Francisco, Peace, Incorporated, 1981. 1½ × 1½ in. Represents an early use of the computer to control color.

I moved to New York in 1980. Tripping in my new unexplored home, a vibrantly decaying metropolis, certainly was a far cry from the set and setting I was used to back on the West Coast. Ashrams, spiritual lectures, and communing with nature gave way to nightlife, conceptual art, and urban survival skills. Some of the blotters I would get from friends back west had typical symbols of the New Age movement that had actually kind of chafed me by the late '70s, marketing that greater spiritual growth that was the promise of psychedelics fifteen years earlier. It was all somewhat out of kilter with this belly-of-the-beast universe I was grappling with as the '80s madness unveiled a noir side of humanity to me.

When a sheet of *Clown* blotter showed up it offered a totally different subliminal message as one tore off a few tabs. Were these clowns leering at me? Winking? Laughing with me or at me? Uncle Clowney—with his perplexing cocked eyebrow, leering smirk, and shifting visage—became the better-fitting new icon for my journeys into the neon-colored, jaded post-punk underground of NYC in the early '80s.

Jacaeber Kastor

Leviathan, San Francisco, ca. 1985. 2½ × 2½ in.

It's an irony of history that blotter acid and minimalist art both emerged in the late 1960s. Artists like Donald Judd and Carl Andre set to work stripping art down to the basics, reducing it to Cartesian grids in an attempt to alter perception. Meanwhile, the counterculture produced different kind of grids, always guaranteed to alter perception. Spongy LSD blotter, perforated into gridded doses and branded in pop, folk, and sacred imagery was produced and consumed around the world. A decade later, the polymorphic imagery repressed during minimalism slowly returned to art. Maybe all the acid sloshing around in the art world had something to do with it? It turns out that blotter acid was the ultimate work on paper.

One blotter I saw but never experienced was a black drawing of an octopus on a white background and spread over a hundred perforated squares; its expression implied it was on to something very intense. Likely it was produced before we fully understood the strange intelligence of cephalopods. With independent brains spread through their limbs, and the ability to communicate by changing shape, texture, and color, some consider octopi to be an alien life form. When scientists recently gave antisocial octopi a dose of MDMA, the octopi began to snuggle with one another, just like humans. Cephalopods are amazing! And delicious, although I no longer can bring myself to eat them. But I might be persuaded to gulp a square of octopus blotter to plug into some alien intelligence.

Fred Tomaselli

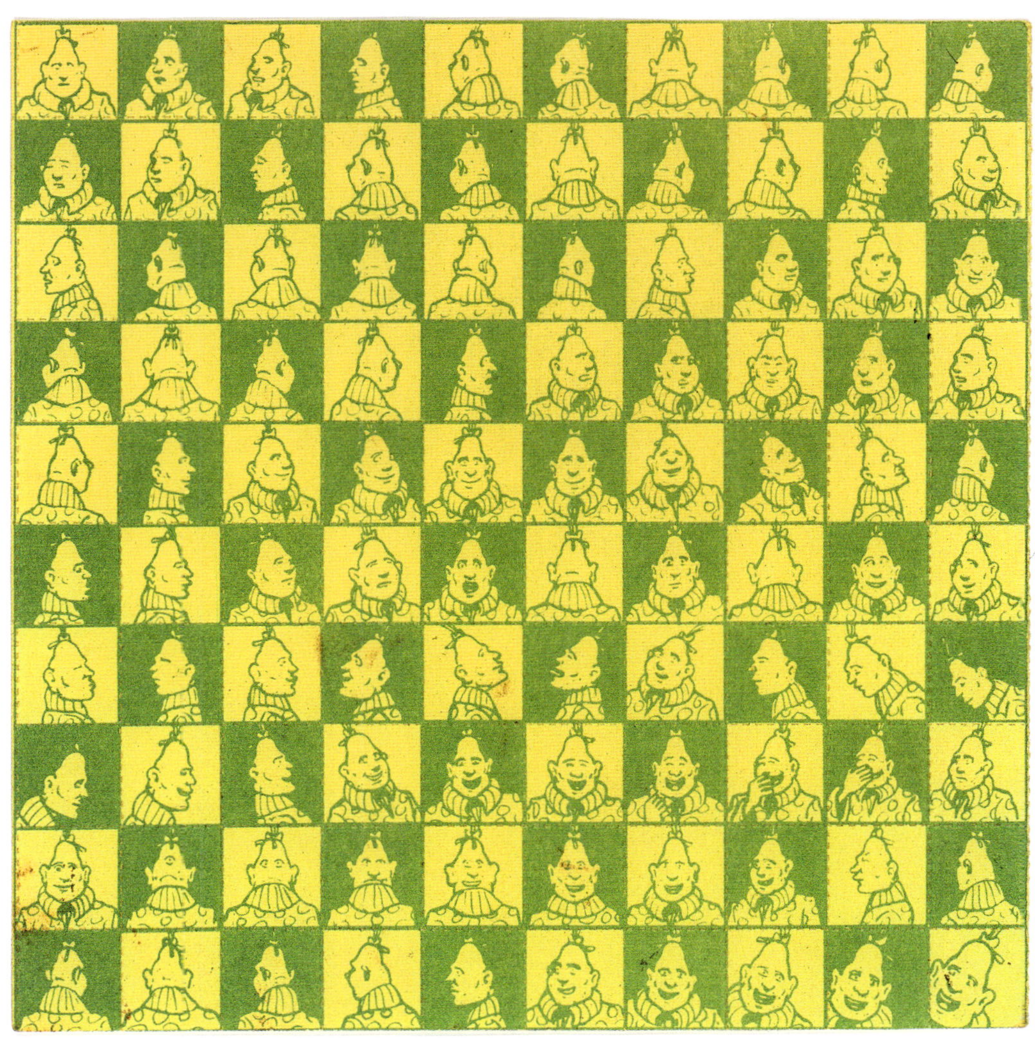

Zippy, San Francisco, 1982. 5 × 5 in. Sourced from the inside cover of Bill Griffith's *Zippy Stories*, a 1981 collection published by Last Gasp.

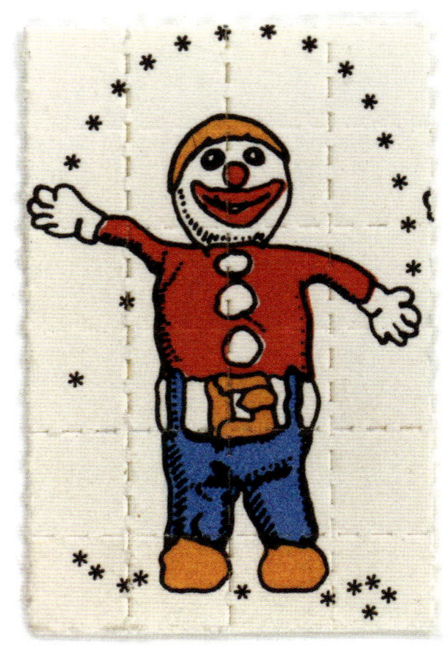

Mr. Bill, Santa Cruz, ca. 1982. 1 × 1½ in.

Ants, Gilfeather, San Francisco, mid-1980s. 2½ × 2½ in.

My Little Arthur, Alan Dillard, San Francisco, mid-1980s. 7½ × 9½ in., less missing hits. One of the first dot-matrix blotter prints, dosage conveniently announced.

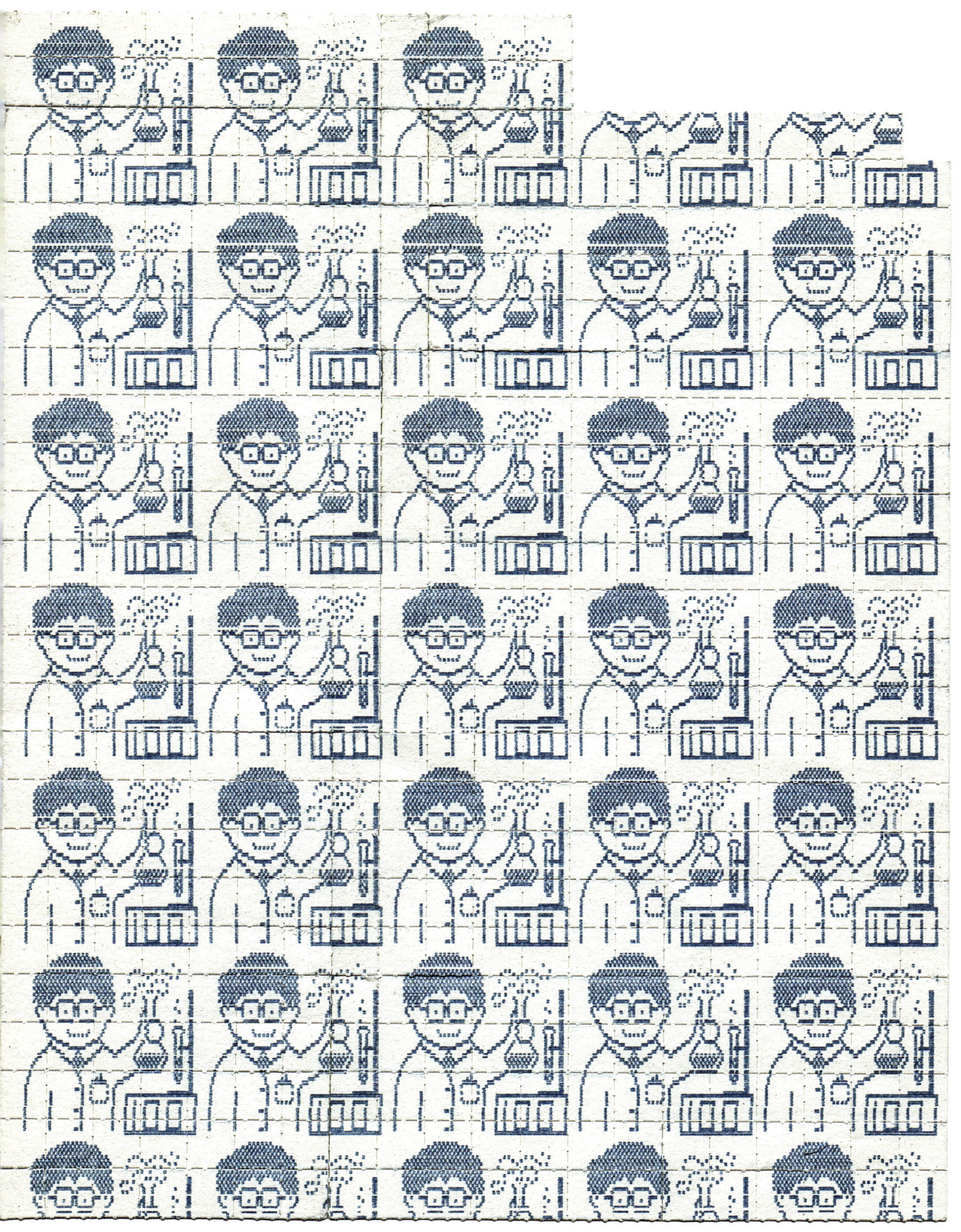

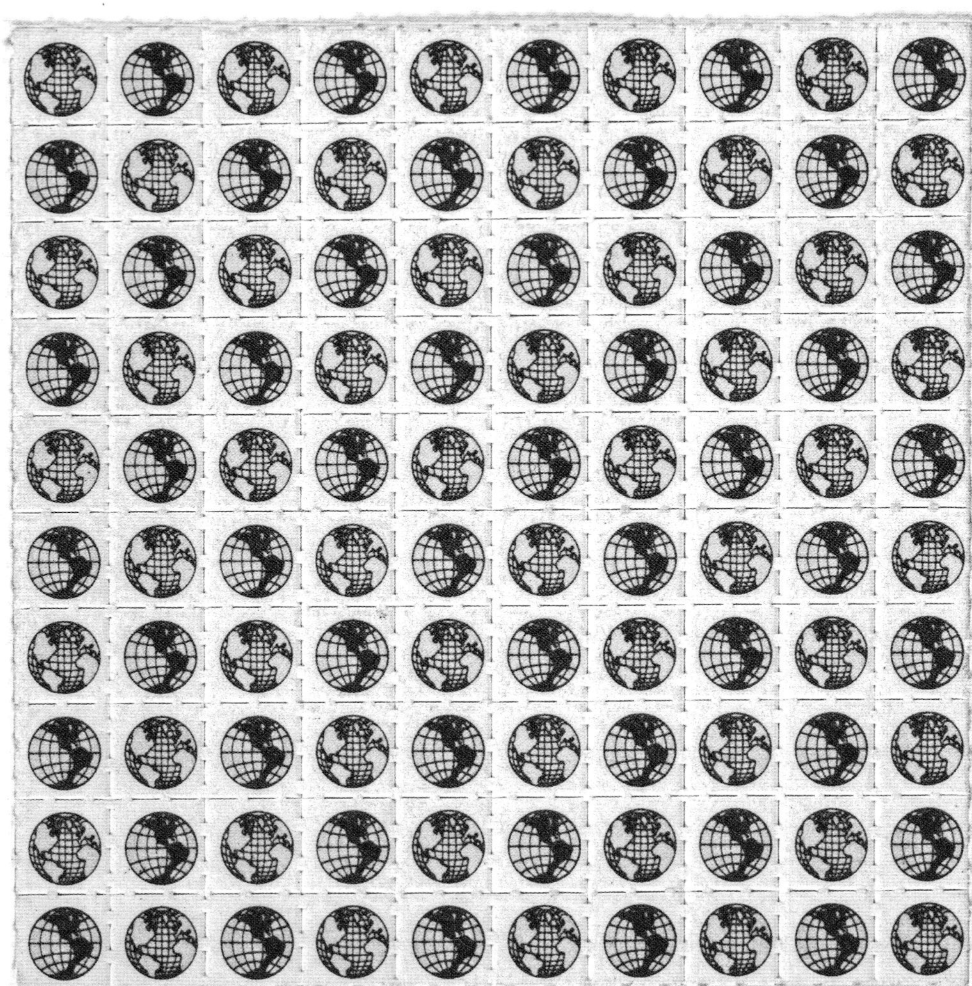

Globes/Hemispheres, San Francisco, ca. 1985. 2½ × 2½ in. Computer-set.

***Hemispheres* changed my life.** I was living in Japan in the '80s, which meant zero acid was available. I had left a wild and wonderful scene in the States a year earlier, and some friends from there eventually put together a huge package of tripping art and sent it to me. Paintings, collages, cutouts—all kinds of hilarious, raging works of madness, dripping with lysergia. But there was one special item in there: a tiny metal box, painted all over in gold, with a plastic see through window in the cover. Inside, surrounded by op-art patterned paper, was a dried June bug, masquerading as a scarab beetle. It was an uncanny, exquisite, tongue-in-cheek bit of wonderment from a world left behind, and it transported me into a sense of intimate connection with my faraway friends.

Then a sly thought entered my head and I delicately picked up the June bug. Underneath were hidden three hits of blotter; a type I had never seen before. It depicted hemispheres of the globe, which felt oddly appropriate with me on the other side of the planet from where this gift had come. A friend and I took it a few days later, and it turned out to be *that* trip—the one you never come back from.

Michael Taft

Barrel of Monkeys, early 1980s. Single hit, ⅜ × ⅜ in.

Fly in the Anointment, early 1990s. ½ × ½ in.

Plumed Serpent, 1984. 2½ × 2½ in. Rumored to be printed with chlorophyll.

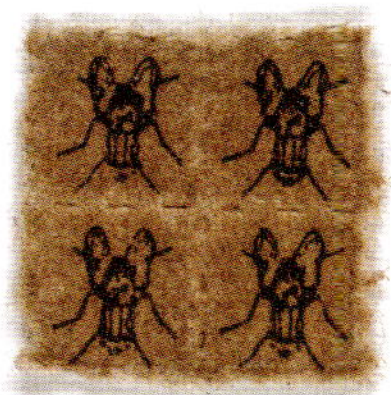

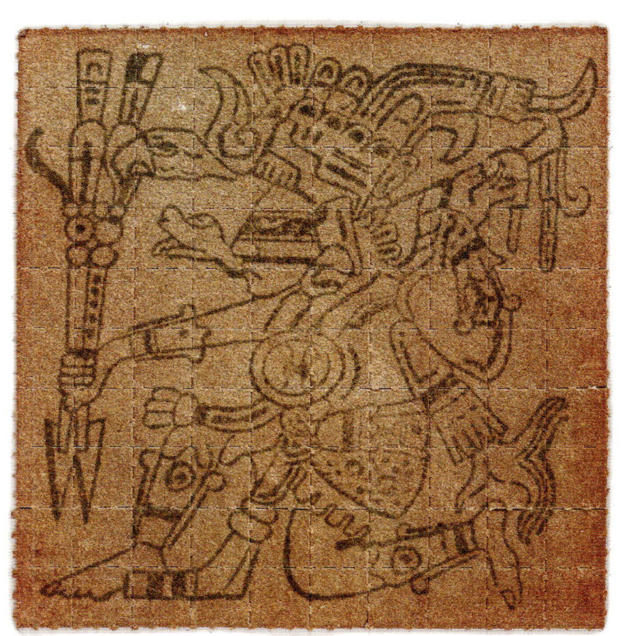

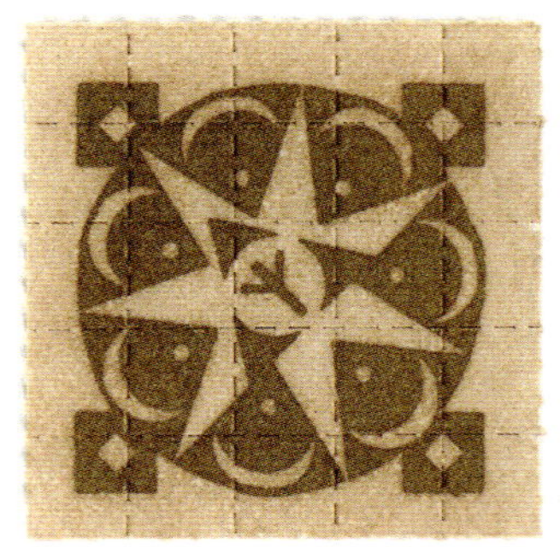

Far L Phantasmals, Pyramid/Gilfeather, San Francisco, ca. 1984. 1¼ × 1¼ in. The Elder Futhark rune in the center is Algiz, "Elk," considered by some modern esotericists (and *völkisch* nationalists) to be the "life rune."

Scholars argue whether it is something like language, or cooking, or empathy that defines humanity. Perhaps something even more singularly characteristic is our desire for transcendence. This obsession exists across the world in both socially acceptable religions and underground psychedelic cults. In colonial Western discourse, the religious and the psychedelic were often kept separate, but twentieth-century visionary artists often sought to collapse this artificial binary.

Here we see Baba Ram Dass, one such boundary breaker. A renowned Harvard psychologist, Ram Dass left his tenured position to embrace the life of a mystic guru, here shown as Nataraja, an incarnation of Lord Shiva as a divine dancer. The dancing Lord Shiva represents a blissful, playful orientation toward all the fluctuations of life, an orientation that Ram Dass thought could revolutionize and save stress-stricken modern Western humanity. In his iconic 1971 book, *Be Here Now*, he asked his readers, "Shiva's dance of life / Do you do it from uunnnkkk / Or do you do it from aaaahhhh!! / Do you surf through it all? / Or do you carry it around like a load?"

In this particular work, the artist perhaps sought to transmit this very attitude to the seekers about to begin their psychedelic voyages. Instead of going through their journey bent down by the weight of their thoughts, they should dance into eternal bliss with the rhythmic, boundary-breaking, transcendental energies of Ram Dass and Lord Shiva powering through them! We can only hope that the transmission was successful.

Anuj Gupta

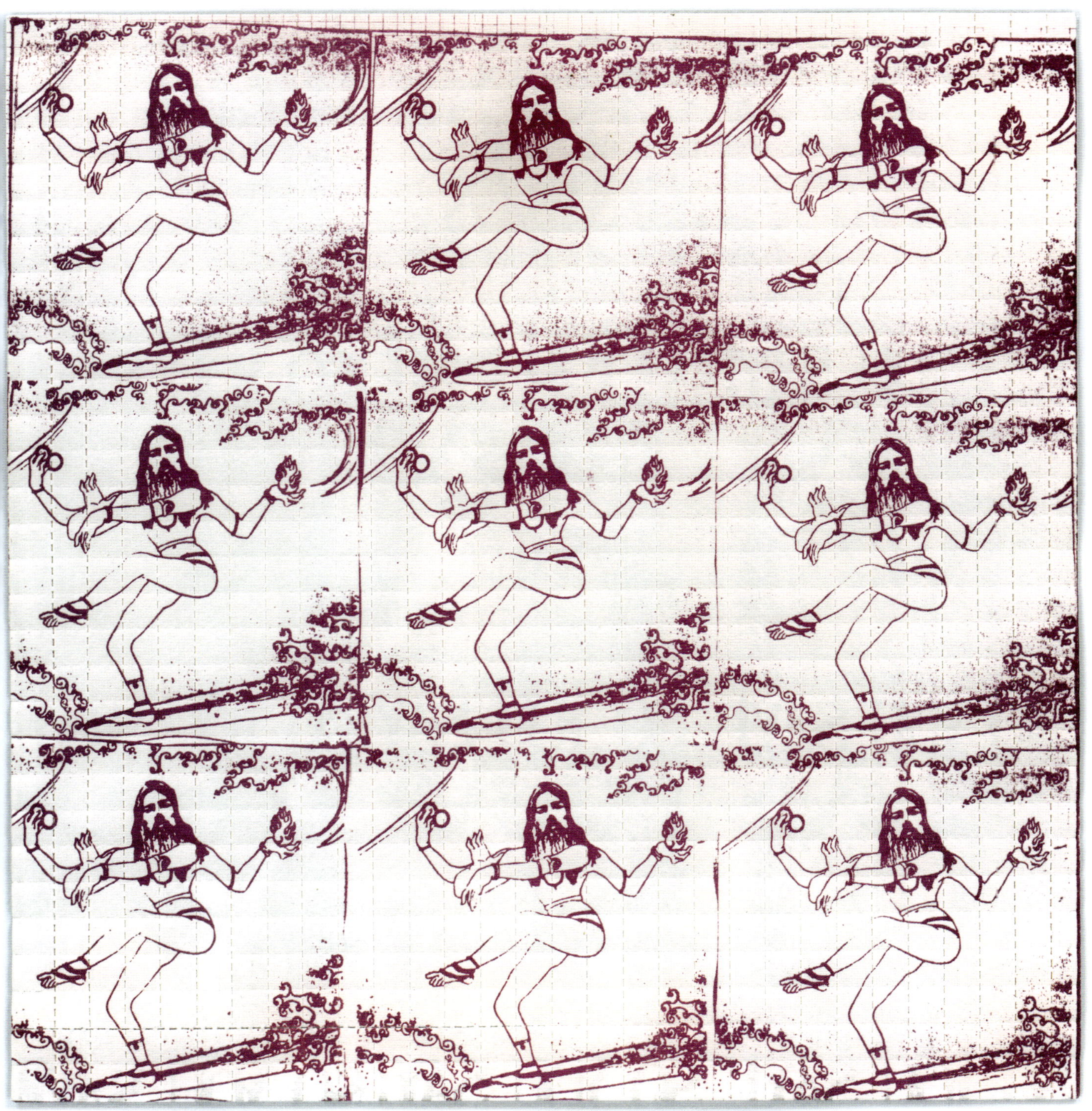

Surfing Swami, Fritz, San Francisco, mid-1980s. 7½ × 7½ in. Image drawn from Ram Dass, *Be Here Now* (1971).

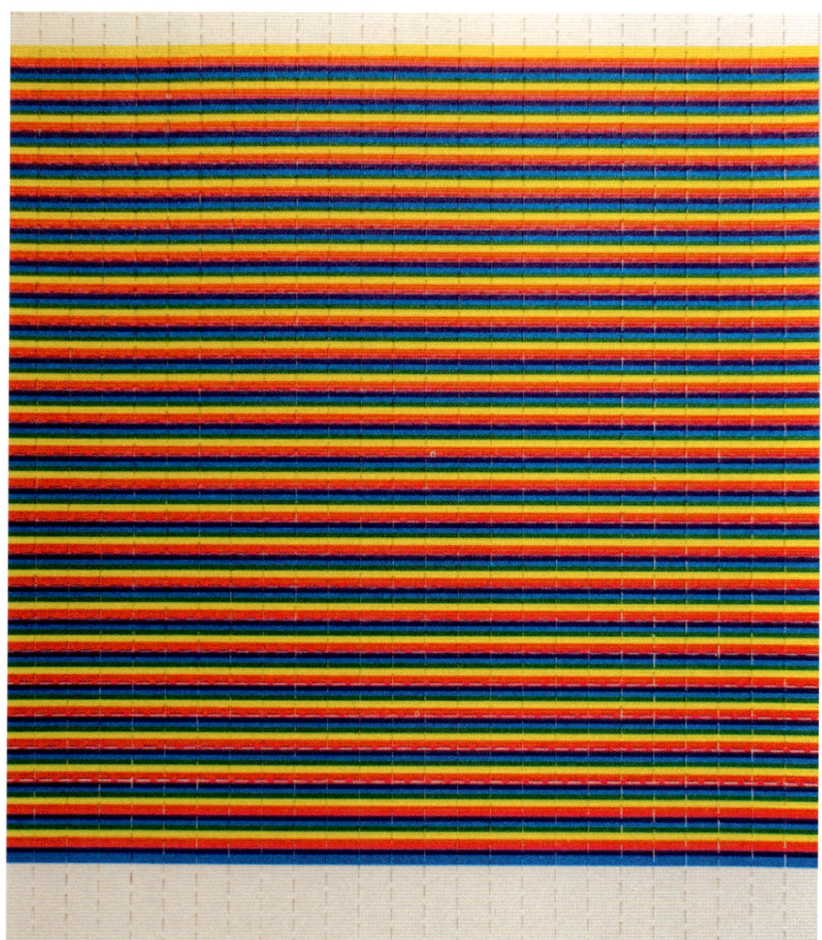

Rainbow Flag, Grandpa, San Francisco, mid- to late 1980s. 4 × 4½ in. Based on Gilbert Baker's famous LGBT rainbow flag.

Rainbow Targets, Grandpa, San Francisco, ca. 1984. 6½ × 7½ in.

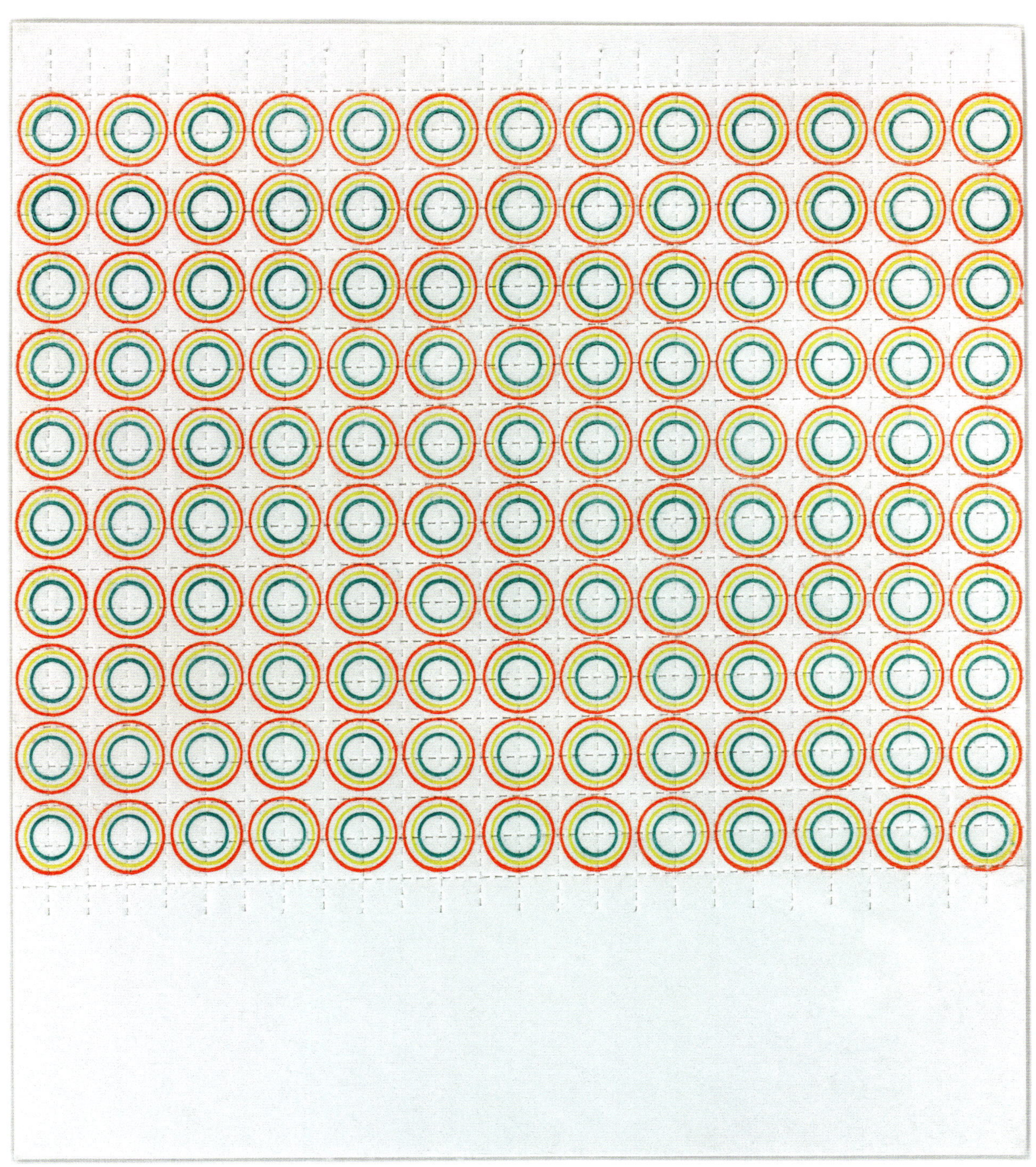

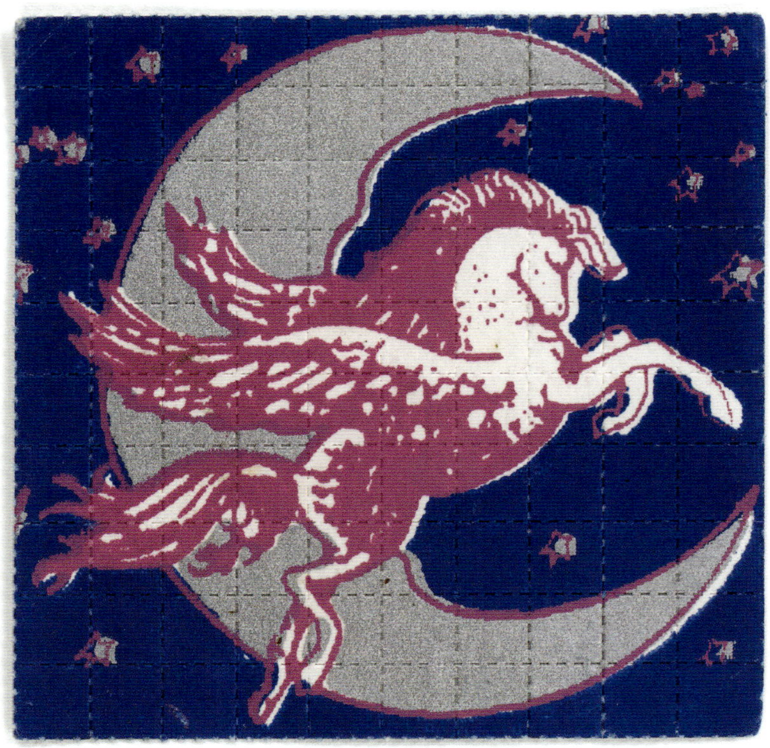

Pegasus Moon, Santa Cruz, 1985. 2½ × 2⅜ in.

Pink Pegasus, ca. 1984. Single hit, ⅜ × ⅜ in.

Flying Saucers, San Francisco, ca. 1987. 6 × 6 in. A later edition of a popular design, these were printed with 1987's Harmonic Convergence, a coordinated global New Age meditation celebration, in mind.

Visionary psychologist Carl Jung called the flying saucer "a modern myth of things seen in the sky," and it remains one of the twentieth century's most iconic images, emblematic of the "other" and all that entails. It was immaterial that the flying saucer depicted on blotter sheets in the 1970s was taken from the classic but decidedly faked photographs taken by American contactee George Adamski in 1952. They might not have physically landed, but they were here, a visual mnemonic redolent with notions of aliens, space, and unknown worlds deep in the starlit void.

Timothy Leary, Robert Anton Wilson, and Terence McKenna were fascinated by flying

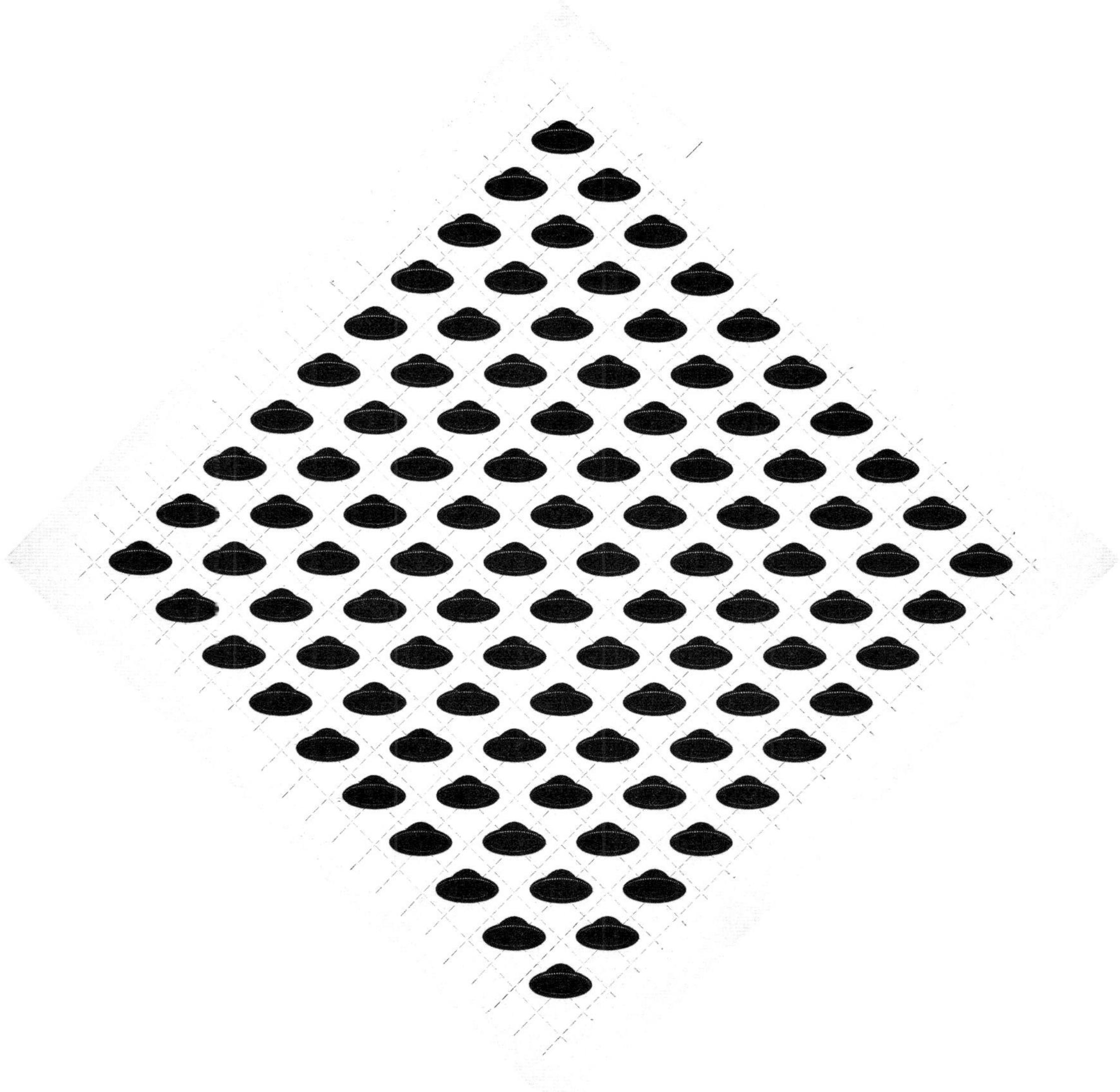

saucers and the message they conveyed. For many, they offered hope and salvation from the stars, as Neil Young sang in "After the Gold Rush." Flying saucers attended Hendrix's Rainbow Bridge concert, Jefferson Airplane queried "Have You Seen the Saucers?" and bands like ELO and Wishbone Ash adorned their album covers with them. Parliament/Funkadelic's acid-drenched fascination with all things extraterrestrial even extended to having a massive flying saucer on stage from which the band emerged.

Those who accepted the strange invitation offered by taking one or more flying saucer blotters would find themselves catapulted through the lysergic portal not to outer space but to inner space, opening up a saucerful of secrets and the chance to commune with perhaps the strangest alien of them all—the human brain!

Andy Roberts

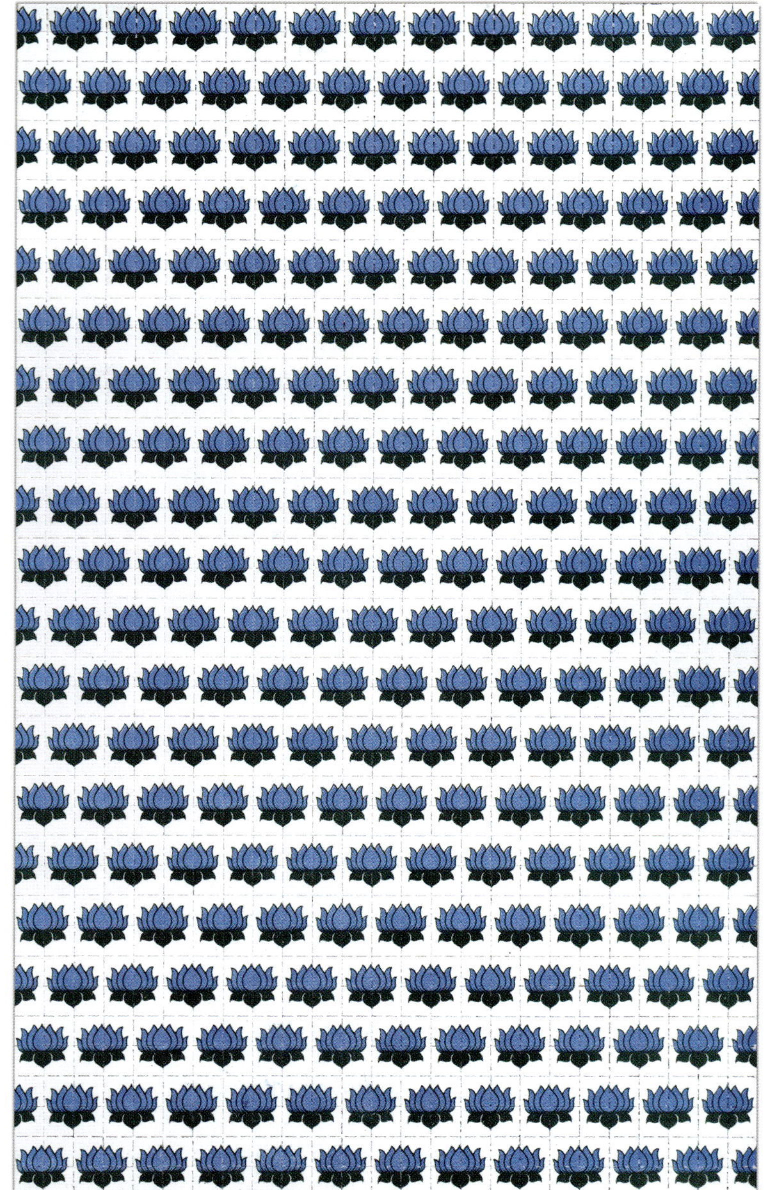

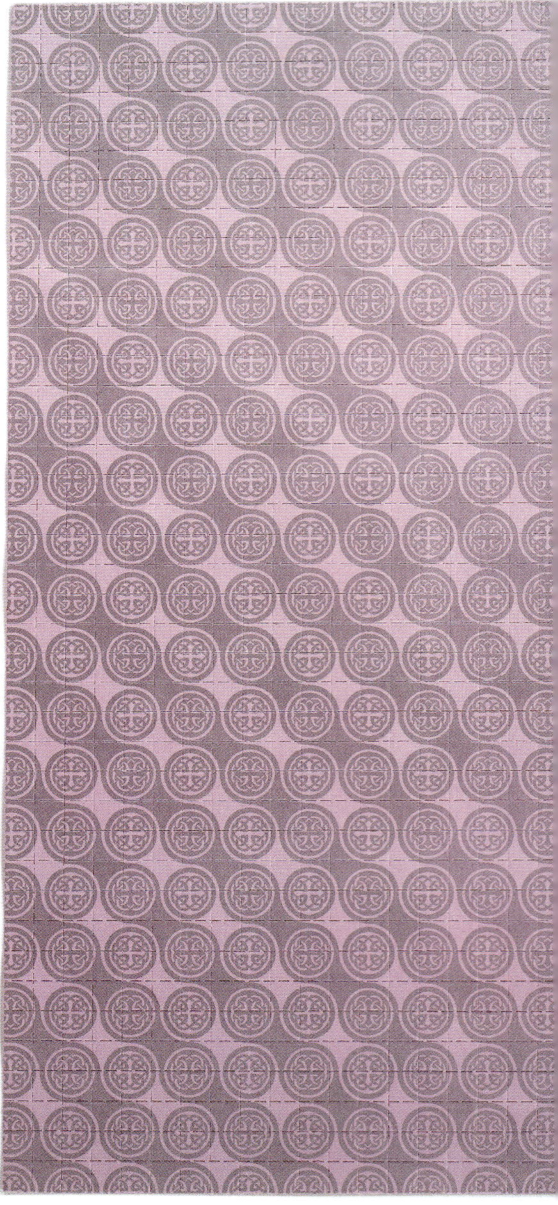

Blue Lotus, Gilfeather, San Francisco, mid-1980s. 6¼ × 10 in.

Celtic Coins, Gilfeather, San Francisco, mid-1980s. 6¼ × 10 in. (left).

Celtic Lotus, Gilfeather, San Francisco, mid-1980s. 6¼ × 10 in. (right).

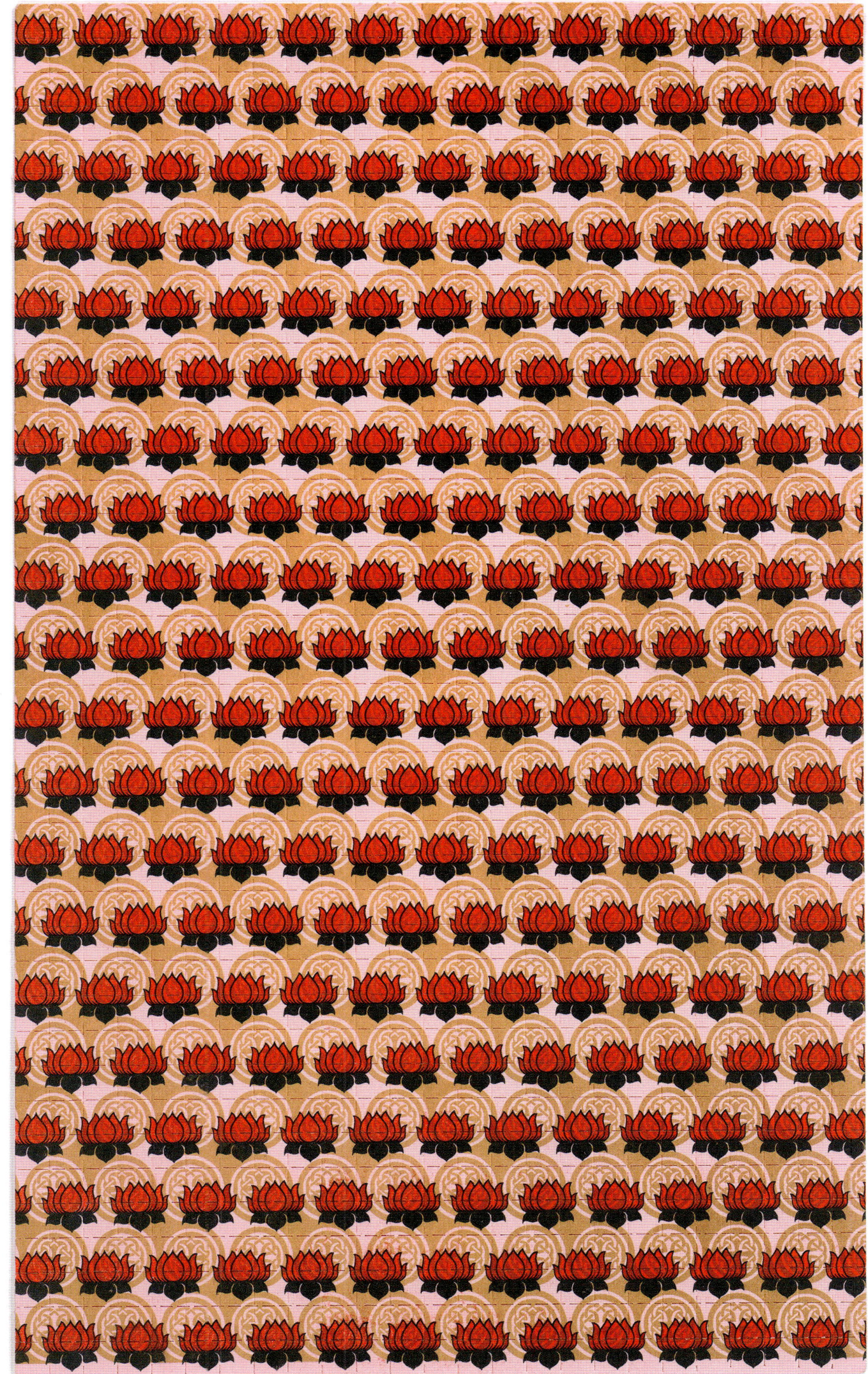

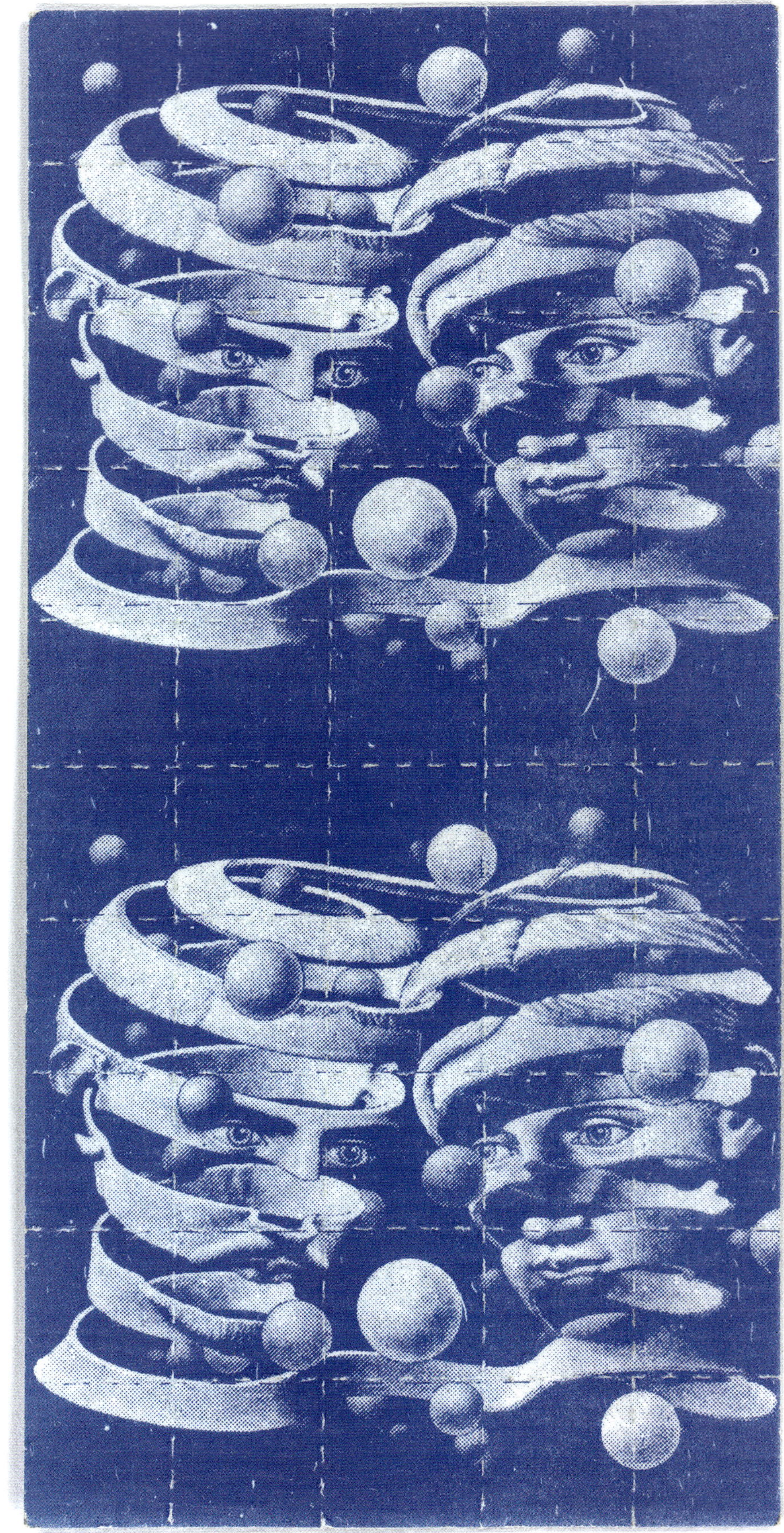

Bond of Union, William Leonard Pickard, San Francisco, 1984. 2 × 4 in. Sourced from M. C. Escher, *Bond of Union* (1956).

At the age of nineteen, while on acid, I experienced what felt like the collapse of spacetime, reframing my own view of reality. Recently, I was speaking to Stephen Hawking's collaborator Thomas Hertog about the holographic principle, the theory that the universe can be understood as a vast and complex hologram, where a two-dimensional version of everything, including us, exists simultaneously elsewhere. We also discussed my own holographic theory of art history, where I hypothesize that all artistic activity from cave painting to the present day may be the result of subconscious attempts to describe the holographic nature of reality. During the conversation, Hertog mentioned the artist Maurits Cornelis Escher (1898–1972), whose work he and Hawking felt described the geometry of the universe in relation to their theory of how it emerged from the Big Bang, uniting gravity and quantum mechanics.

I asked Hertog whether he thought that taking psychoactive drugs might usefully remove the lid on consensus reality in the minds of such physicists and allow them to break through the current theoretical impasse in relation to the Standard Model of particle physics. He thought not; because the mathematical way of thinking is so embedded, they would be unable to transcend their own methodologies. Some he knew had tried and failed. But then, in a sense, these scientists are always already on acid, imagining and theorizing beyond consensus reality, their theories already mirrored in the art on this blotter.

Suzanne Treister

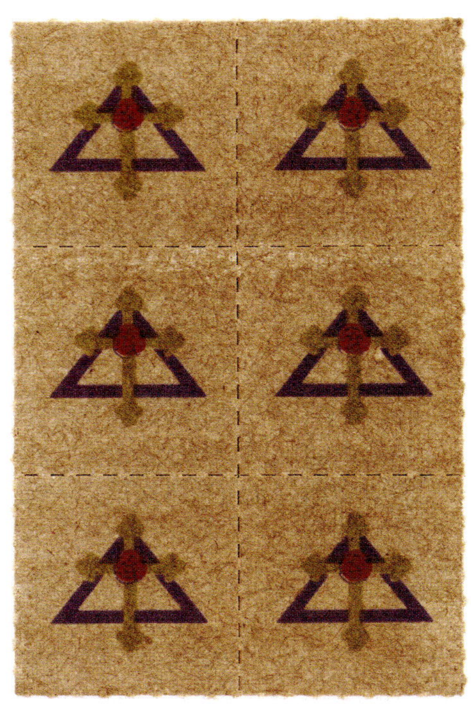

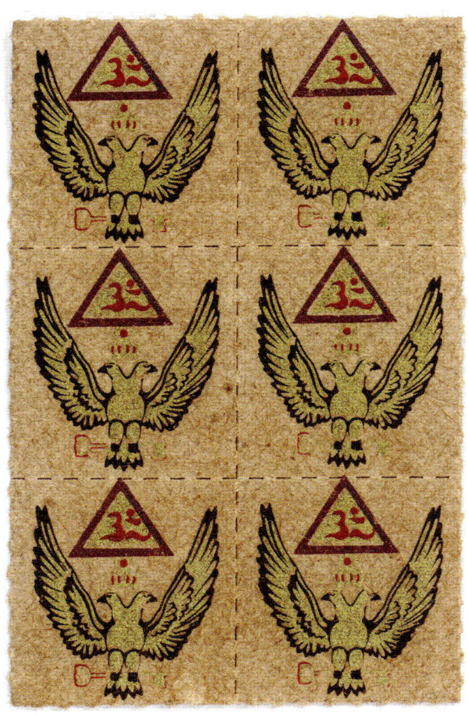

Rosicrucian, Walter Bloch, San Francisco, ca. 1983. 1 × 1½ in.

Masonic, Walter Bloch, San Francisco, ca. 1984. 1 × 1½ in.

Ganesha, San Francisco, late 1980s. Handstamp, 7½ × 7½ in.

Dancing Ganesha, San Francisco, late 1980s. 2 × $3\frac{7}{10}$ in. Based on an image by California artist Phoenix & Arabeth.

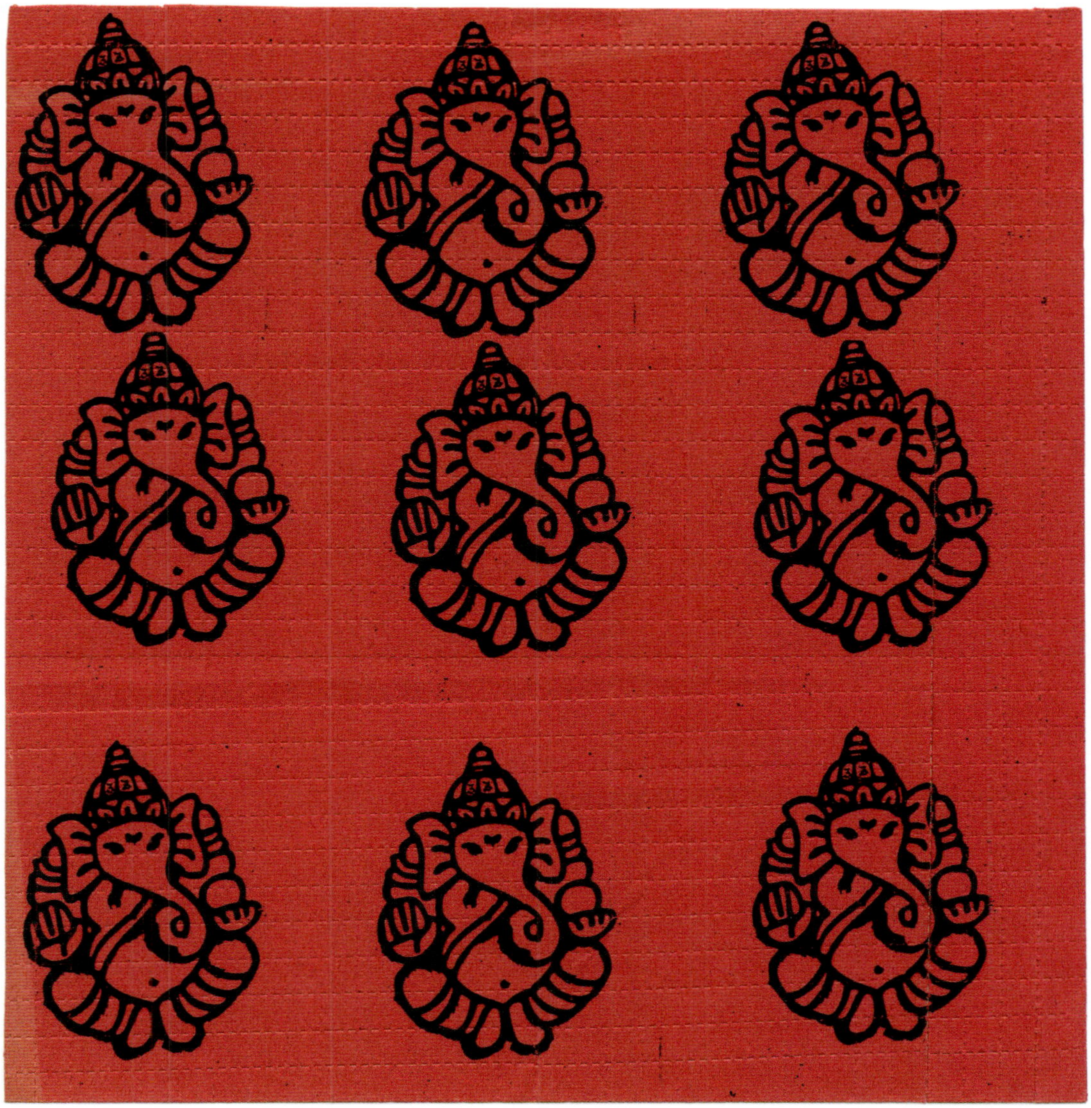

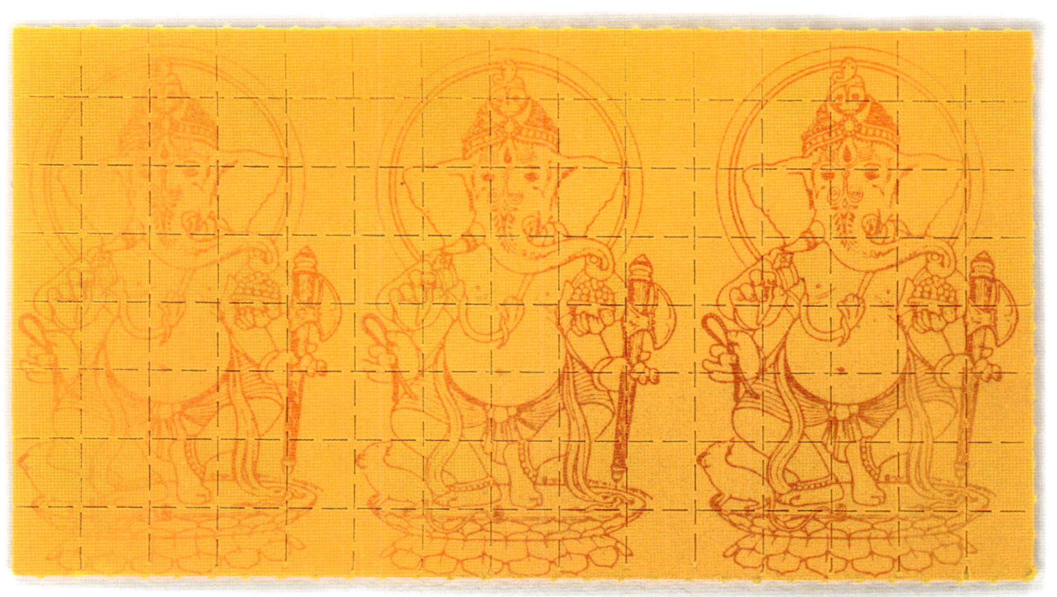

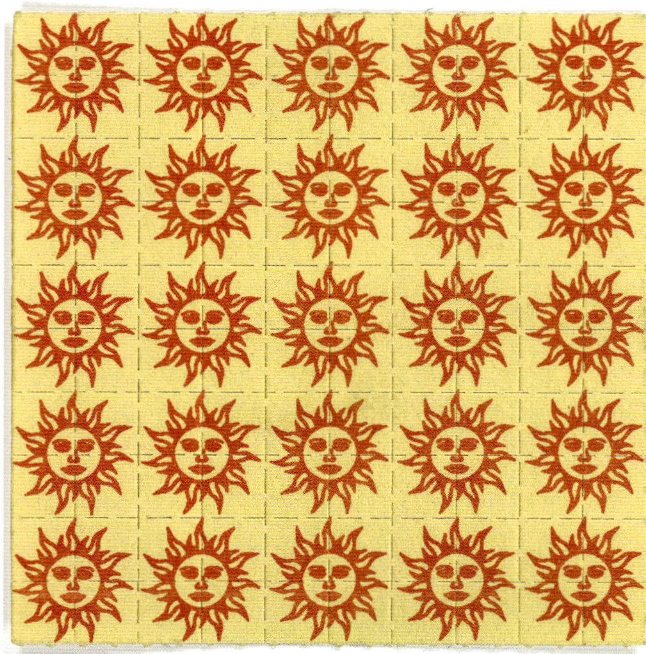

Orange Sunshine, Gilfeather, San Francisco, ca. 1986. 2½ × 2½ in.

It's the late 1970s and I'm a teenager hanging out with my older boyfriend Peter, who lives in a barn outside Philadelphia. Peter reaches up to a beam above our heads and tells me he has something for me that he's been saving for a special occasion. He brings down a glass jar that contains a sheet of plain white LSD blotter. Back in that time and place, much of the available blotter was unmarked to make it more discreet and less visible to authorities. Peter carefully breaks off a square and hands it to me. I was very young and I had never tried LSD. I had a feeling my life was about to change in a significant way, and it did. More than forty years later, Peter and I both still remember that night and the sublime sensuality that LSD sometimes amplifies.

In years that followed, I had many more experiences with blotter. I especially remember the Orange Sunshine blotter that was produced in a four-way hit that was fun to share. It was a clear tip of the hat to the famous Orange Sunshine tableted LSD produced in the 1960s by Nick Sand and Tim Scully in their underground lab in Sonoma County, California. Holding that blotter in my hand felt like I was connected to a lineage of all those who risked their freedom to produce that molecule—and all the intrepid young girls who said yes to their first LSD experience.

Annie Oak

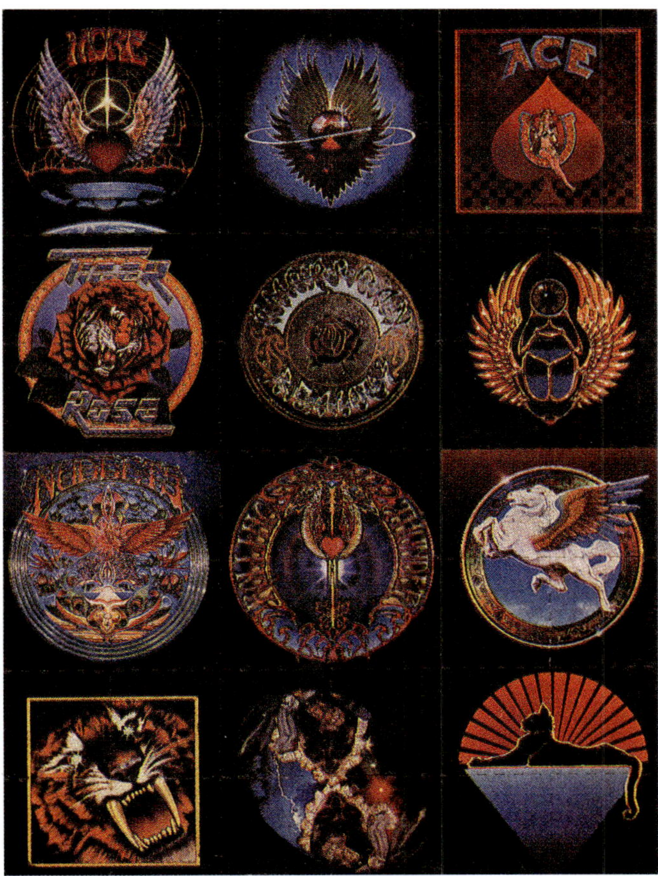

Album Covers, William Leonard Pickard, San Francisco, 1986. 3 × 4 in. Designs sourced from the art catalog *Mouse & Kelley* (1979).

When you see blotters, generally there is a story behind them. This one was done out of love, a deep love for another person. The underground chemist responsible for *Album Covers* had fallen in love with a woman who lived at Project Artaud, a converted artist warehouse in the Mission. She was an impressionist painter, with exotic green eyes and a coke problem. Said chemist was madly in love with her, but the love was unrequited. Most of his production was kilograms of pure crystal, a tiny fraction of which was distributed by the woman and her friends. He thought that, with a profound enough issue, he might please her, free her from the cocaine demon, and win her affections.

There were three issues done in an attempt to win her heart, and this was the last. All these beautiful album covers from Mouse and Kelley were gathered together and ordered in a certain way. There was a link between each row of images, though one might have to hunt for the connection. A devoted printer lovingly prepared them on a black background with black edges. The sheets were packed in a black lacquer shiny box like all the other issues, except it was a larger box to fit the unusually large hits. No effort spared in terms of the art. The woman was from New Mexico, and the boxes were embossed with a silver New Mexico sun so there would be no misunderstanding of where it came from or for whom it was made.

The attempt failed. But you had people all over Northern California, and America, getting this very finely executed issue. They had never seen anything like it. And no one knew the story it secretly contained, that of unrequited love.

William Leonard Pickard

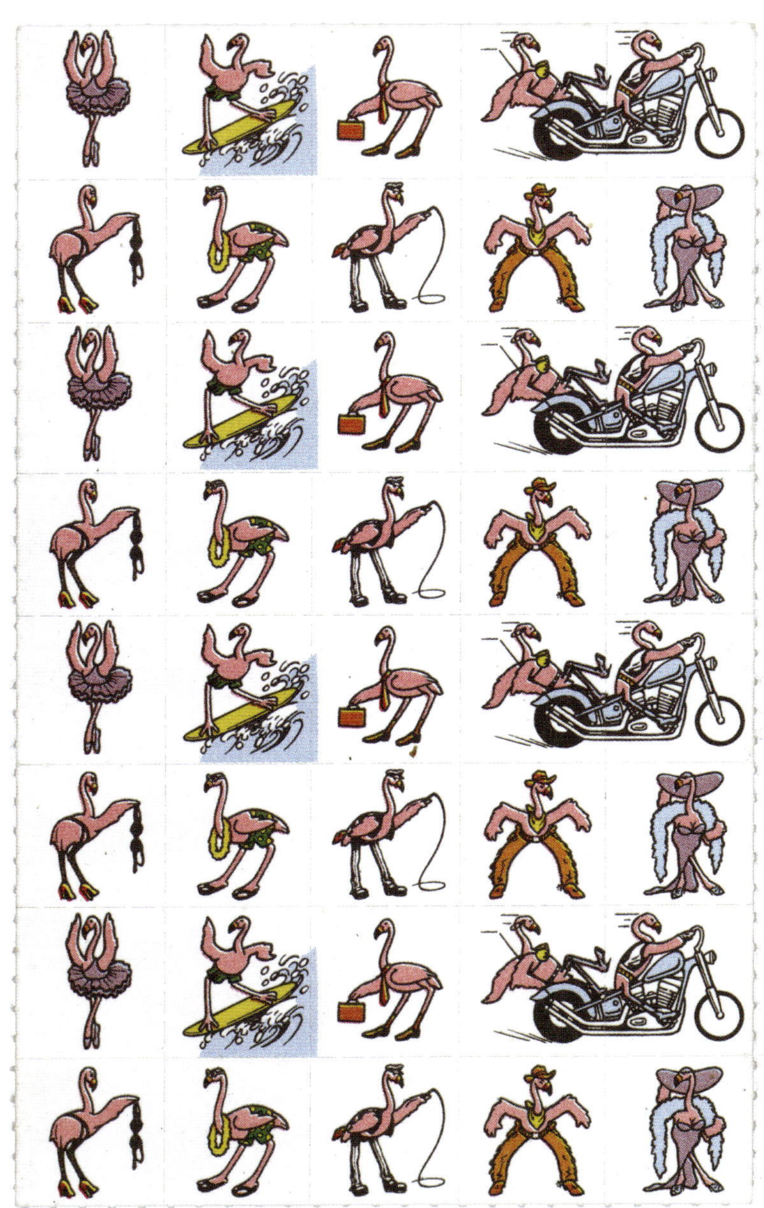

Pink Flamingos, Grandpa, San Francisco, ca. 1988. Large four-ways, 3⅛ × 6¼ in.

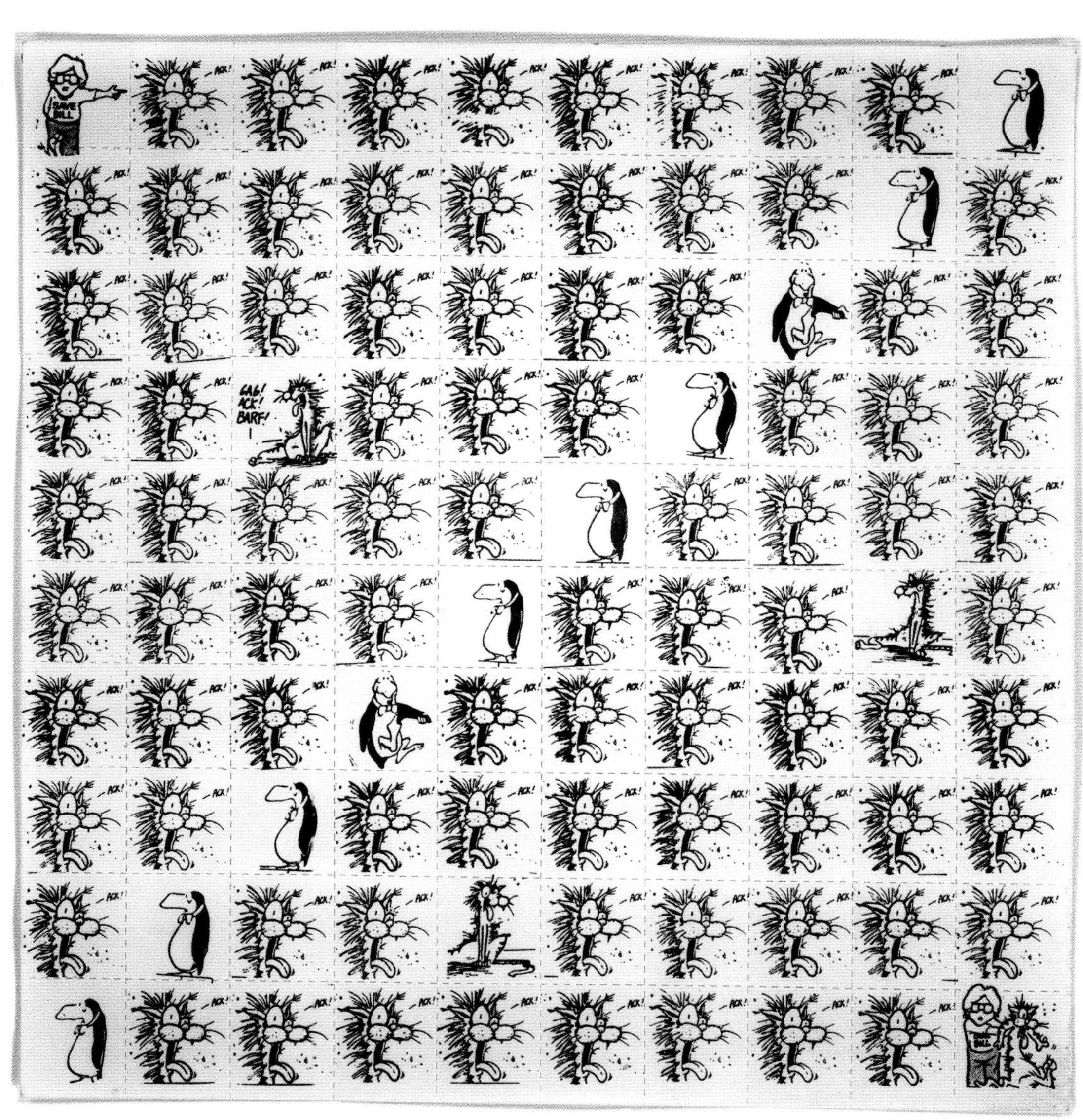

Opus, ca. 1985.
Lifted from Berkeley
Breathed's *Bloom*
County comic strip.
5 × 5 in.

Screen/Mosquito Netting, San Francisco, late 1980s. 6¼ × 10 in.

Wavy Gravy, early 1990s. 6¼ × 10 in.

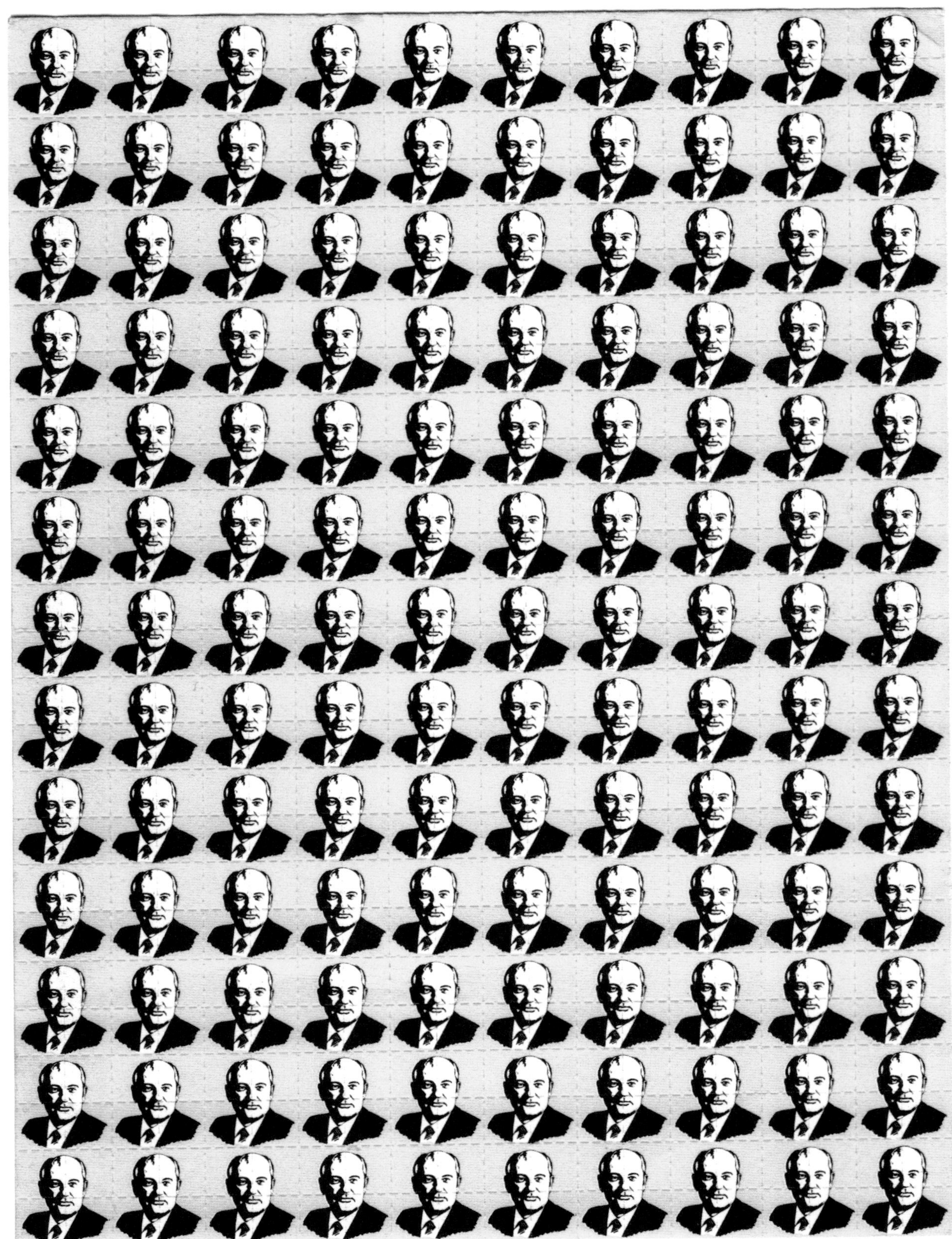

Gorbachev, Acid
Eric and Ed Visser,
Amsterdam, 1988.
$6\frac{2}{7} \times 8\frac{1}{5}$ in.

It wasn't Stalin's tyranny that the Cold War destroyed. What Thatcher, Reagan, NATO, and the western European powers finally beat down was Mikhail Gorbachev's vision of the workers' state democratized and demilitarized, of Soviet society liberalized, of a noncapitalist power bloc moving forward into the twenty-first century. Mark Fisher gave the retrospective name "acid communism" to the radical sense of hope that had animated the counterculture of the late '60s and early '70s, and to the sense of a future—subsequently canceled—that it took with it while receding into history. But on a global scale, it wasn't until the '90s—when Gorbachev's hopes were dashed and the most insane program of neoliberalization in history was imposed on Eastern Europe—that the high priests of capitalism could really rest assured that the old specter had finally been exorcised.

I have no idea who produced this painting, or who decided to put it into circulation in the acid underground; but they must have had a sense of what Gorbachev meant, and of how many hopes were shared by the dreamers of psychedelic utopias and the makers of socialist revolutions. What's incredible is how closely the image foreshadows Shepard Fairey's iconic image of Obama, decades later—another herald of missed historic opportunities. It's almost as if acid follows different temporalities than past-present-future. With acid, the time is always out of joint; and the futures we thought we'd lost might always, in fact, be somewhere just over the horizon.

Jeremy Gilbert

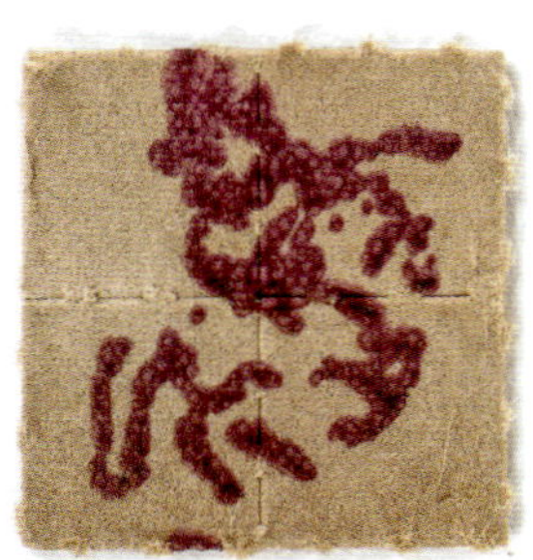

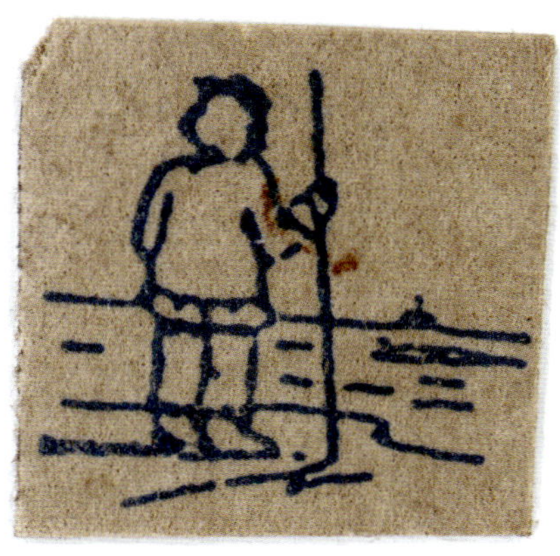

The Mighty Quinn/ Nanook of the North, ca. 1990. One large hit, ⅜ × ⅜ in.

Jouster, ca. 1988. Handstamp, ½ × ½ in. Associated with the Renaissance Faire. Said to be inked with chlorophyll.

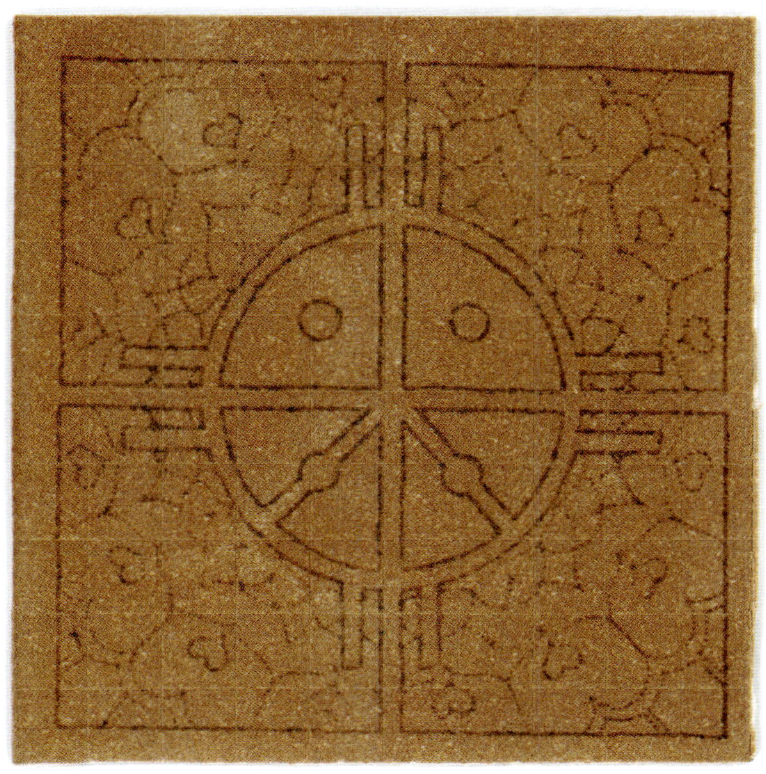

Circuit/Rainbow *Gathering*, late 1980s. Handstamp, 3 × 3 in.

These block-printed, hand-perforated, home-dipped, mind-blowing masterpieces show that LSD was often as much a backyard preparation as a laboratory product. For its imagery, *Circuit* relies on the many 1960s op art–style dot mandalas that were numerous artists' attempts to replicate the patterns seen under the electrifying visual enhancement of LSD. This design conveniently also lets each sheet of one hundred be divided easily into four blocks of twenty-five.

In the ideal, the design would put some of the distinctively colored ink on every one of the individual squares that the design fit, the individual squares circulating to create their own circuit.

The psychedelic hope for conscious awareness to spread throughout humanity is still a possibility. People will find the torch of psychedelia can help guide us out of the gloom of these times and toward a more just, beautiful, and peaceful world. Acid to acid, Dust to dust, Earth to earth, Quest to quest . . .

Garrick Beck

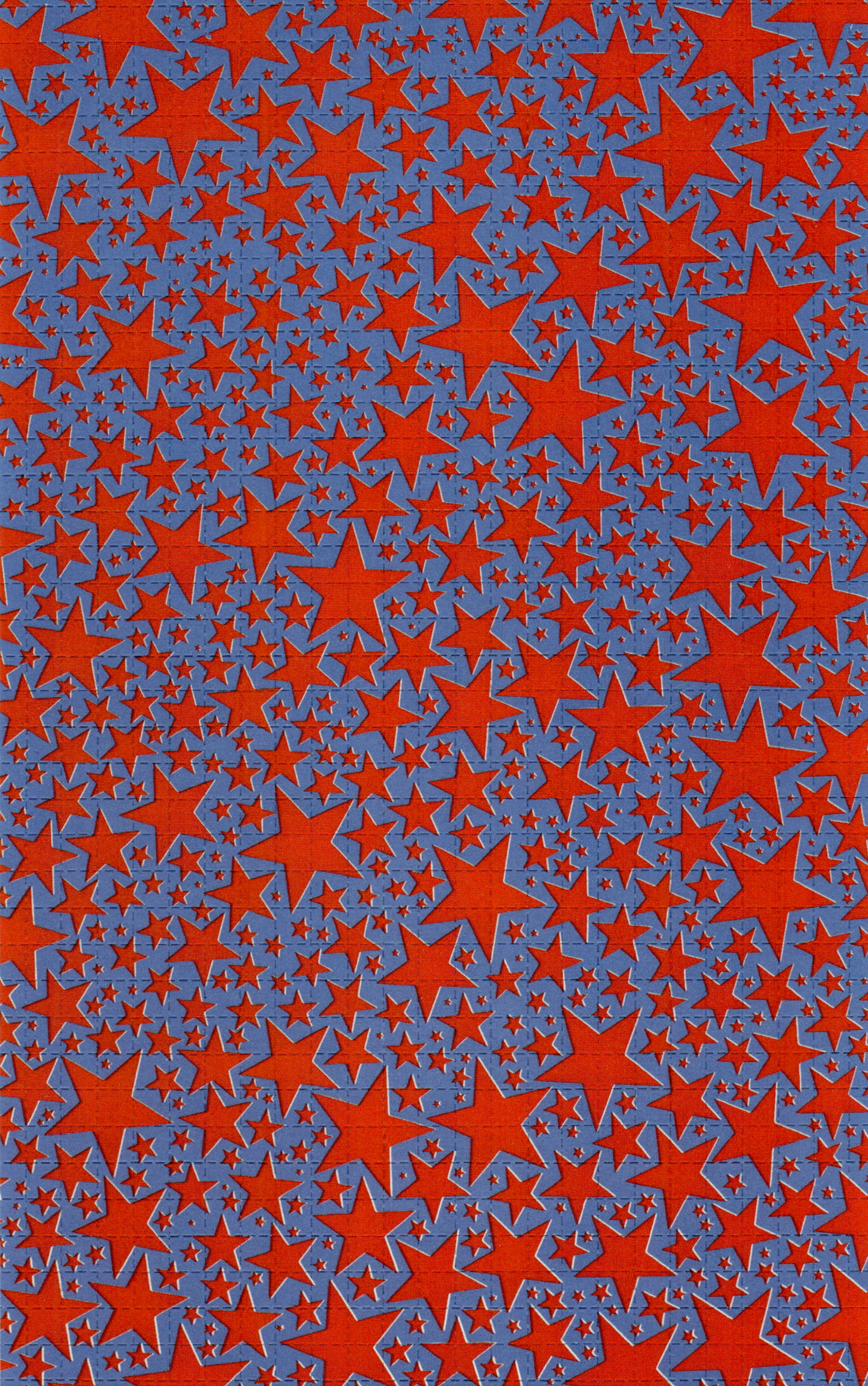

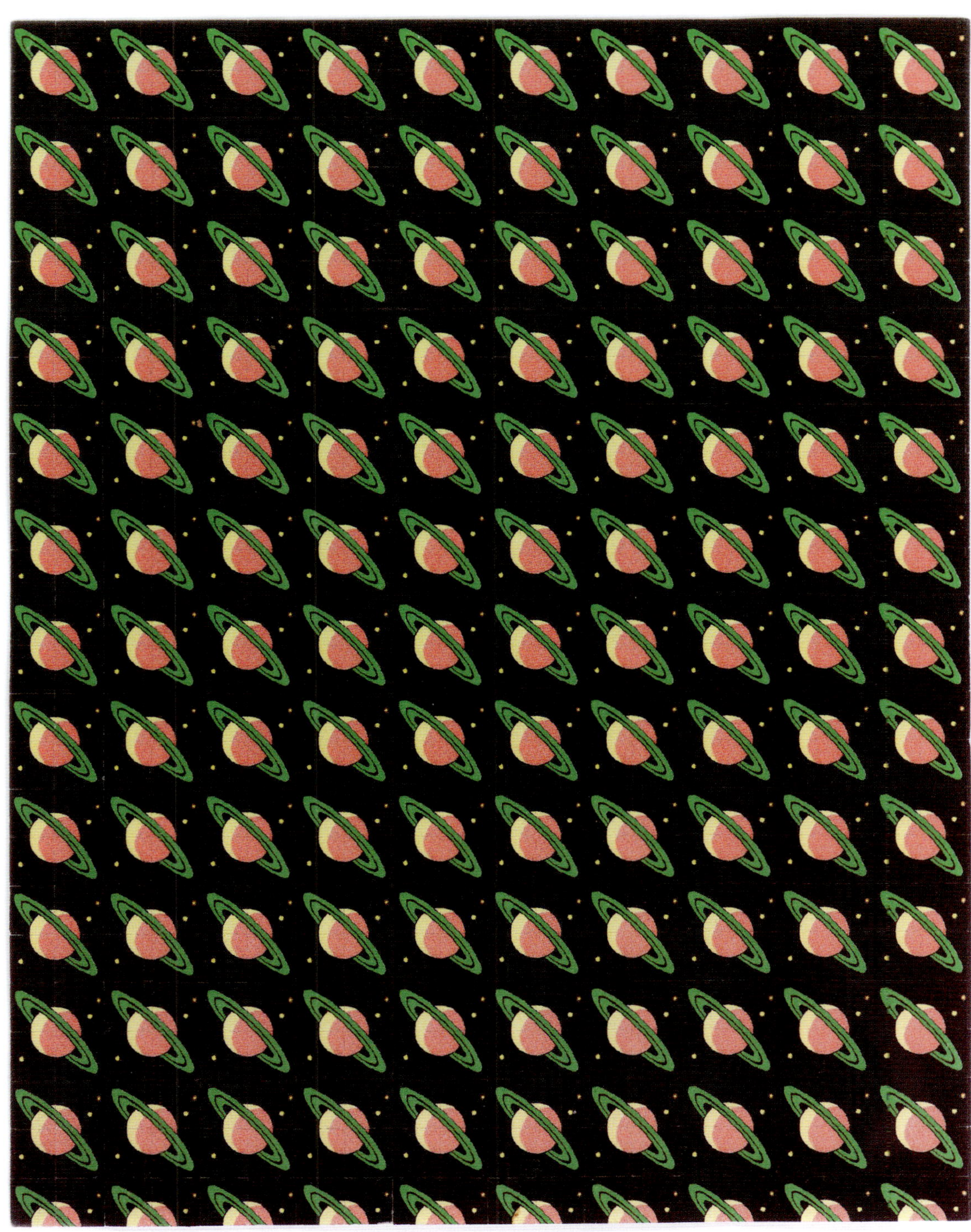

Red Blue Stars, Ed Visser, Amsterdam, late 1980s. 5⅞ × 9½ in.

Black Light Saturns, Amsterdam, early 1990s. Printed with blacklight inks. 6¼ × 7¾ in.

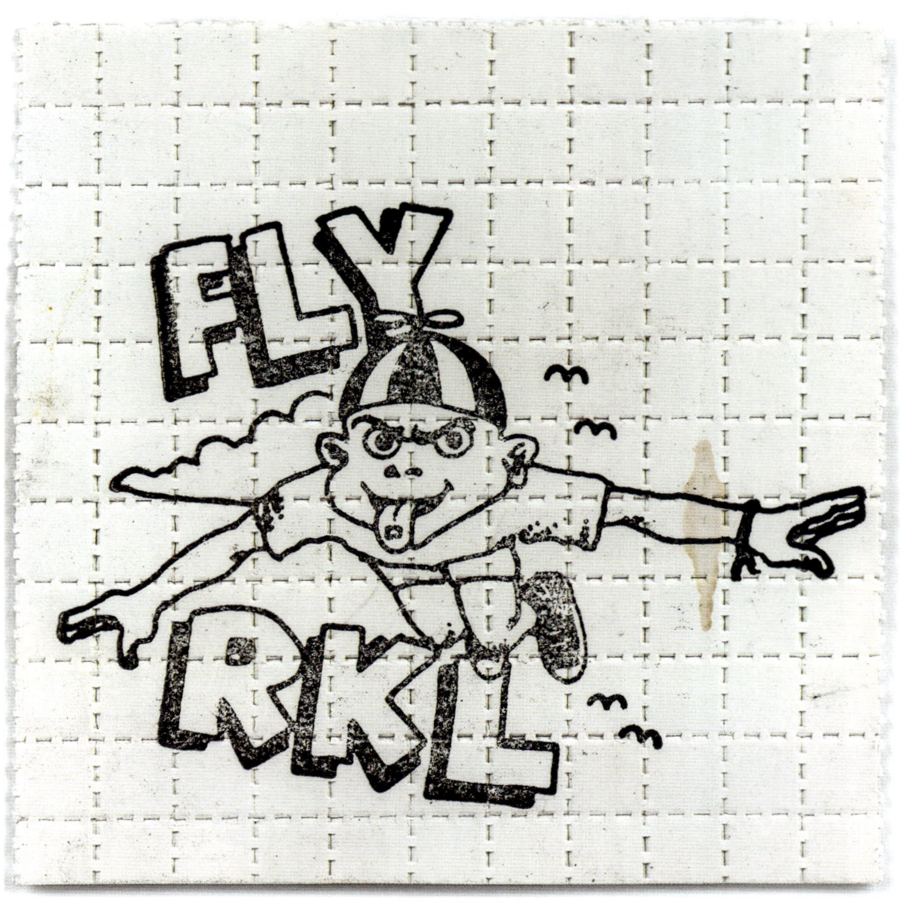

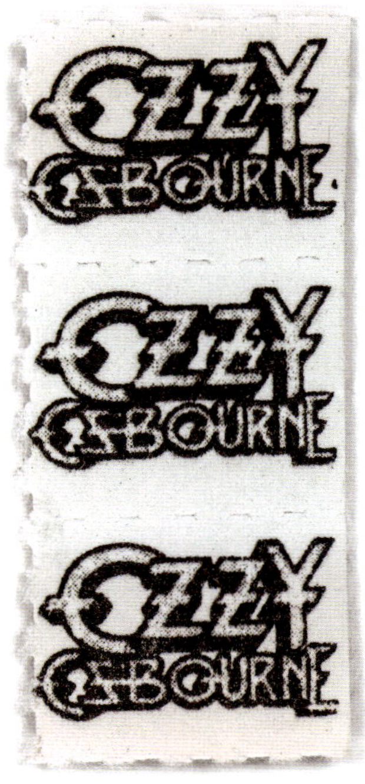

Fly RKL, ca. 1988. Handstamp, 2¾ × 2¾ in. The character is Beanie Boy, the mascot of the California hardcore punk band Rich Kids on LSD (RKL).

Ozzy Osbourne, early 1980s. Three large hits, ½ × 1⅛ in.

Purple Om, Acid Eric, Amsterdam, late 1980s. Single hit, 2/7 × 2/7 in.

I believe Oms made their way to Britain sometime in the mid-to-late '80s. In those days, acid blotters appeared in an information vacuum. Pre-internet, with zero drug culture coverage in the media, there was nothing to contextualize them but unreliable word of mouth and the gnomic symbols printed on them. A printed design offered some assurance of quality control, an edge over the blank, wrinkled, or hand-cut squares that marked amateur or counterfeit product. But it was also a message in a bottle from a faraway continent, the lysergic emanation of an imagined California freak scene. As jaded post-punk hipsters we mocked the Oms' unreconstructed hippie stylings, but there was no denying the gold standard of chemical excellence they represented.

As the designs got more elaborate—I remember the Hofmann anniversary bicycles of 1993 as a step change in technical virtuosity—the frisson of a clandestine communication from the psychedelic underground somehow diminished. Mandelbrot sets and polychrome digital designs added a gloss of consumer sophistication but, as with the crop circle phenomenon that underwent the same evolution at around the same time, never matched the mysterious charge of the original rough-hewn glyphs.

Mike Jay

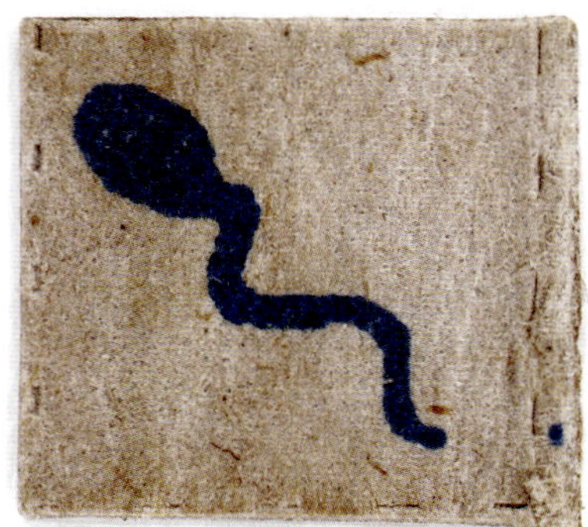

Sperm, ca. 1990.
Single hit, ¼ × ¼ in.

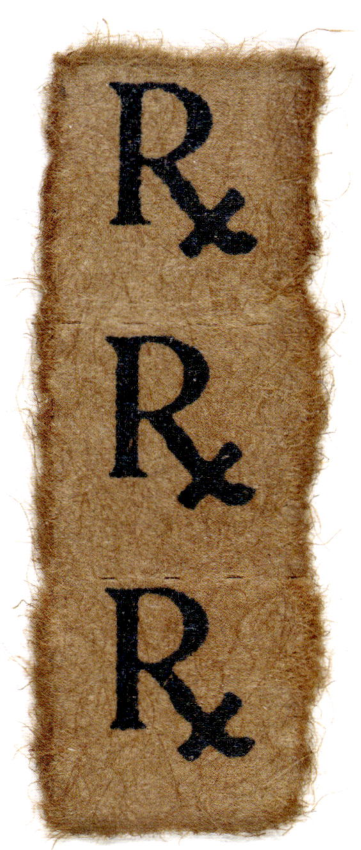

Rx, ca. 1991. ¼ × ¾ in.

Youth Culture Rebellion Blotter Acid, Fred Tomaselli, New York, 1991. 6 × 8¾ in.

Today's blotter acid makes use of full-color, computer-enhanced, high-resolution printing, but my favorite blotter images still have a handmade quality. After I saw the "Cure of Souls" show of blotter acid at Psychedelic Solution in 1988, I thought I'd make my own. So, I drew an image—a sociopolitical take on mandala blotter, a brand that was near and dear to me—on a sheet of paper. I took this drawing to the local copy shop and had them shrink it to the size of a single dose. I went home with multiple copies, which I laboriously trimmed and glued into a grid as a master image for a print. That was life before desktop publishing. I don't know if the original blotter acid makers did the same, but it's likely that more than a few copy shops were once unwittingly involved in this illicit process.

Fred Tomaselli

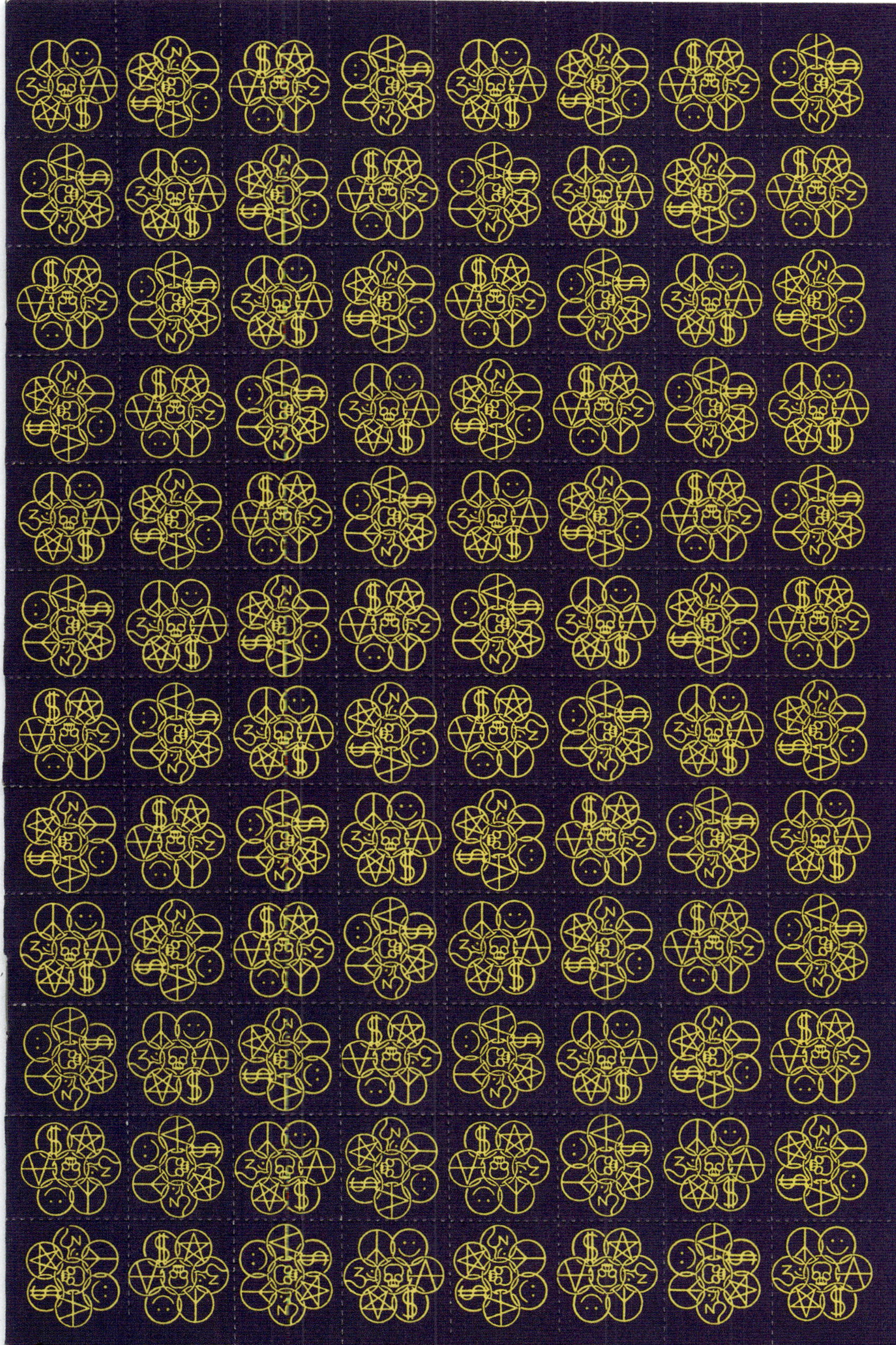

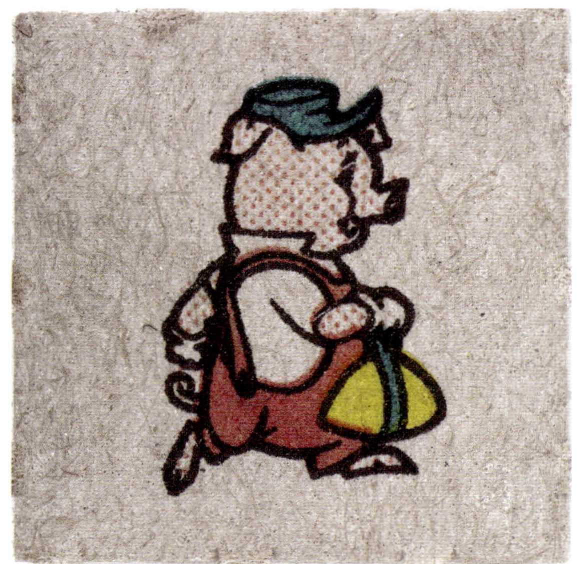

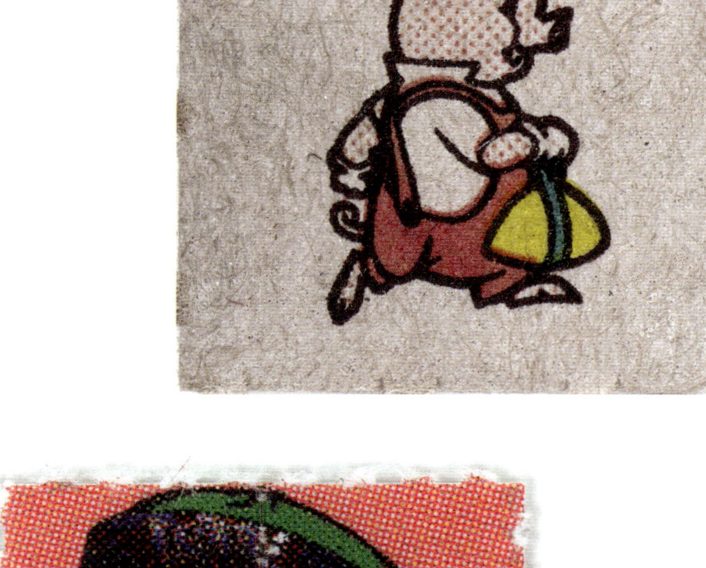

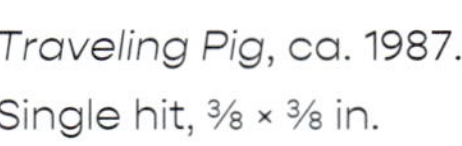

Traveling Pig, ca. 1987. Single hit, ⅜ × ⅜ in.

Monster, Mark McCloud, San Francisco, 1995. ½ × ½ in.

Captain Yin Yang/ Silver Surfer, Amsterdam, ca. 1991. ½ × ¾ in. An eclectic remix of the Marvel Comics hero Silver Surfer.

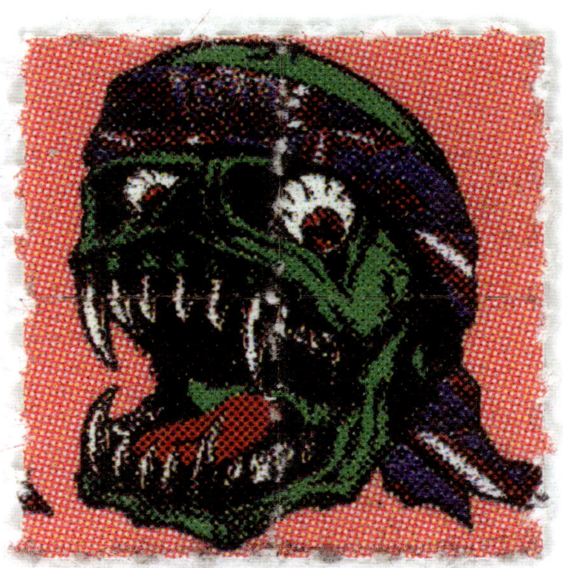

Hermes, the Divine Messenger, is the Greek personification of the lightning stroke that connects sky to earth, linking the airy, insubstantial but influential world of abstract gods to the hard, chemical reality of the material universe. Electric trickster, bringer of language and symbols, this same elaborate complex of ideas about information and meaning shows up in different cultures and systems as Odin, Legba, Ganesh, Ogma and Nabu, Mercury, Nyarlathotep, the Flash, Jack Kirby's Metron and Madonna's "Ray of Light." Could there be a more appropriate embodiment of the category-busting, gender-fluid, speed-of-light illumination of an effective LSD trip than ankle-winged, hat-winged Hermes?

Grant Morrison

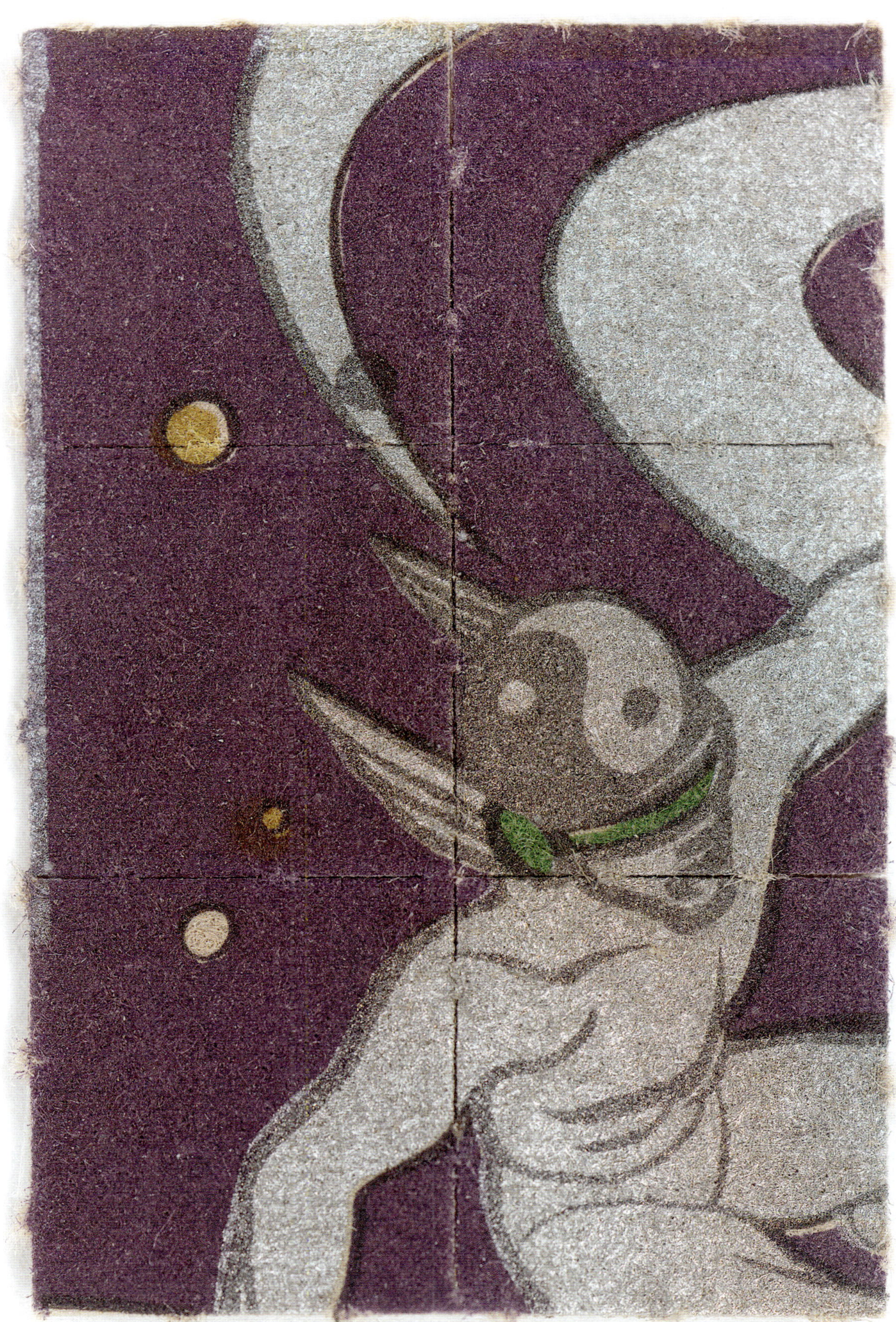

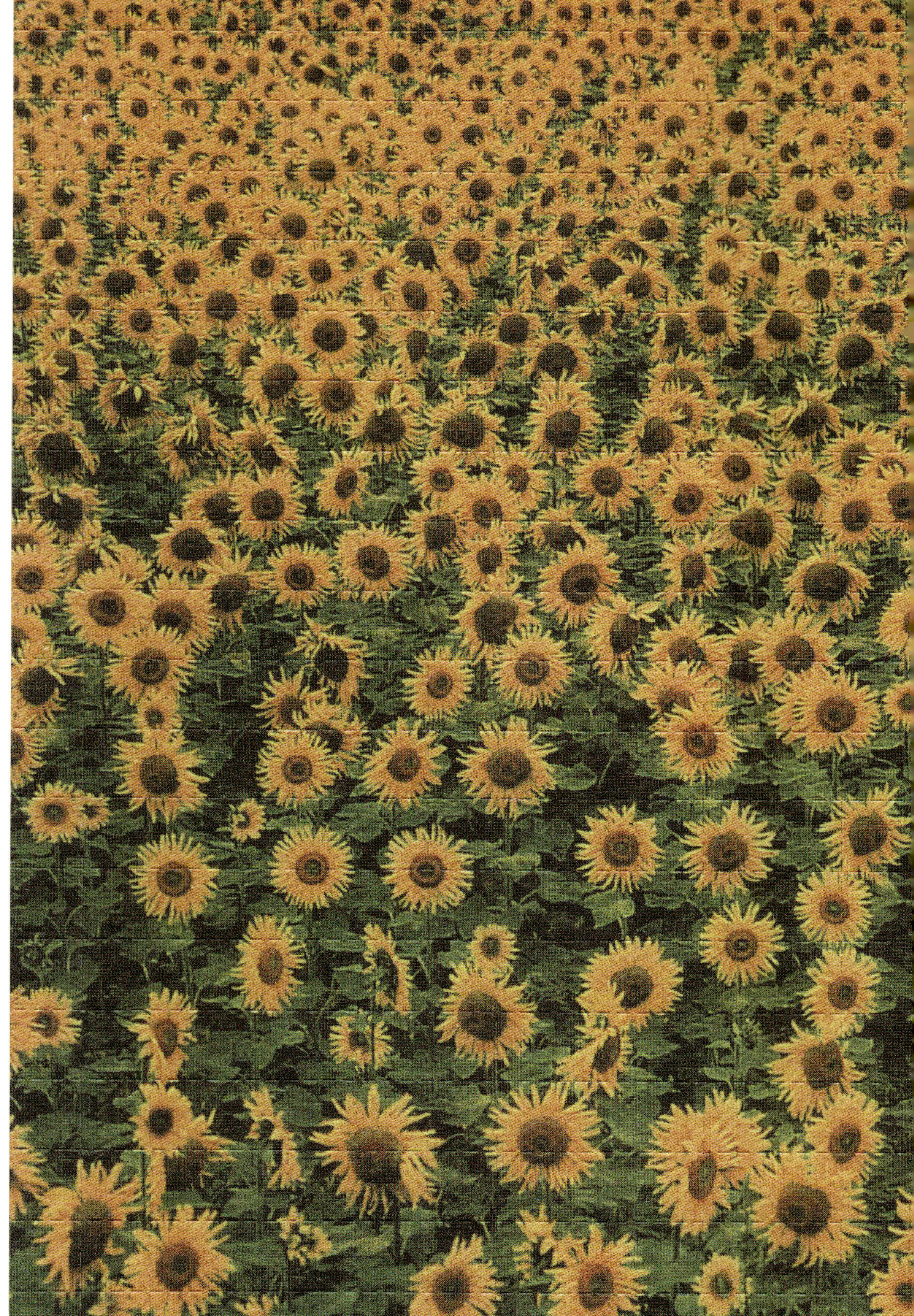

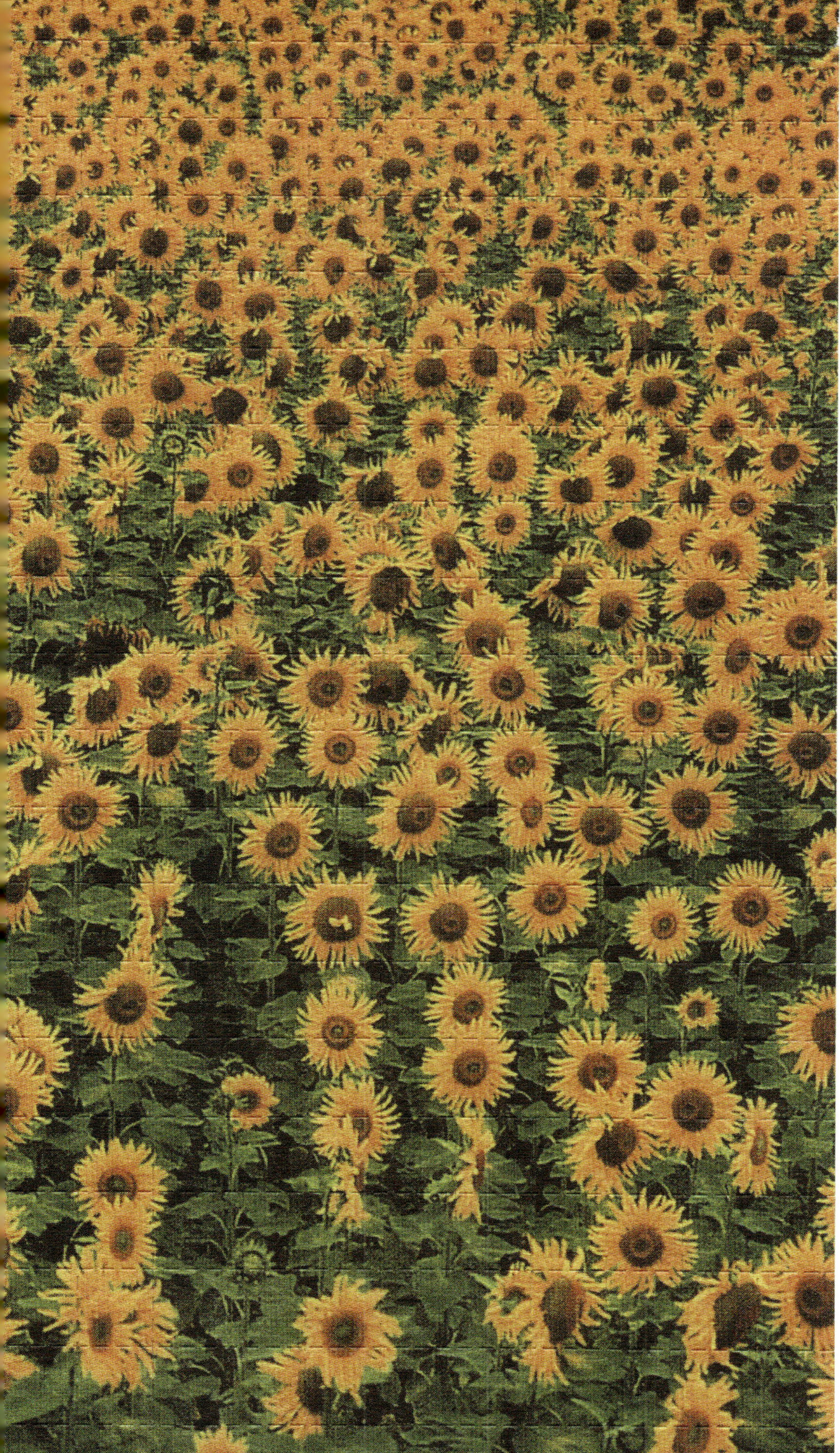

Sunflowers, Ed Visser, Amsterdam, late 1980s. 6¼ × 7⅞ in. Sometimes considered an homage to Vincent van Gogh, the image was lifted by Visser from a postcard found in a magazine store.

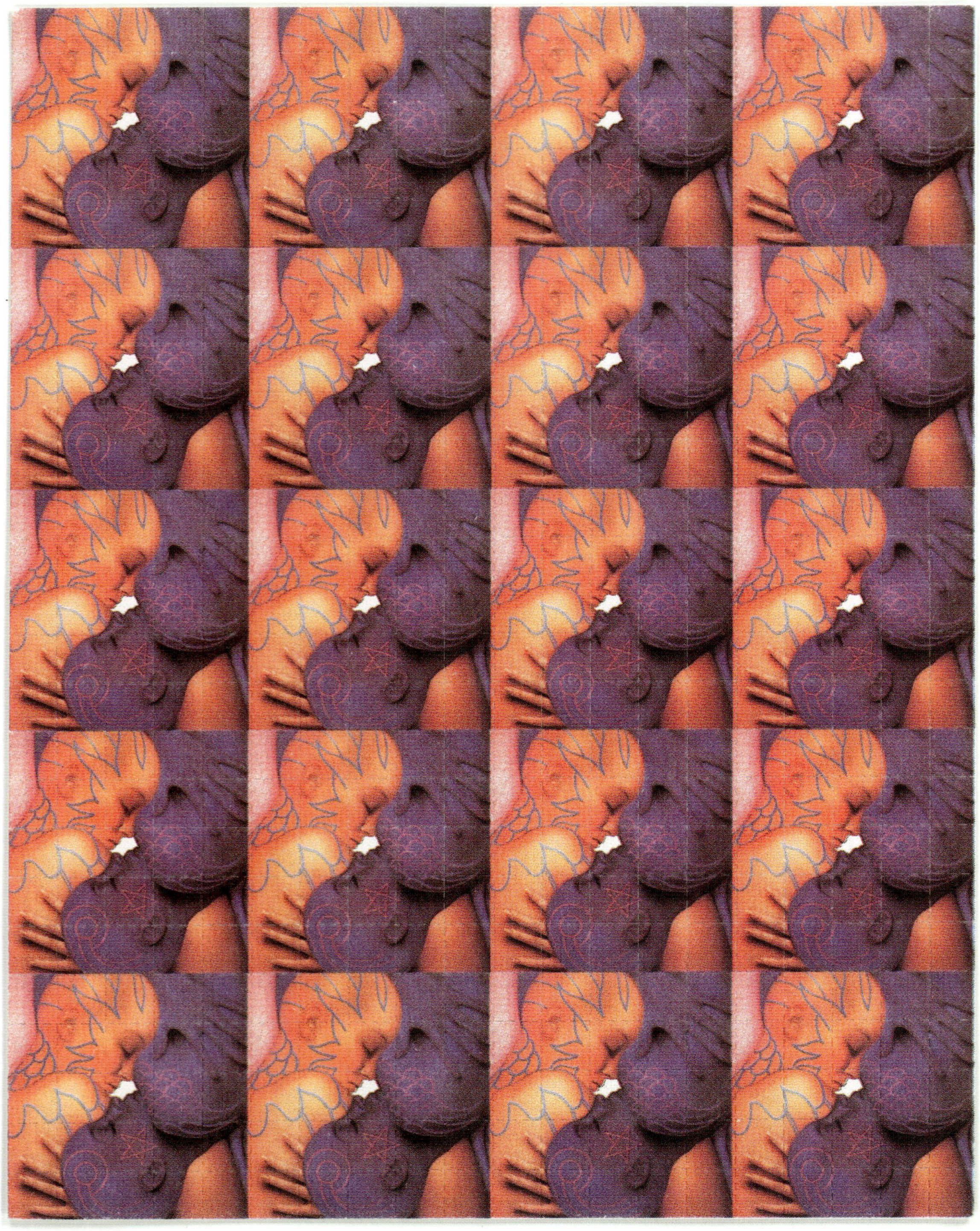

Alien Embrace,
Amsterdam, ca. 1996.
6¼ × 7¾ in.

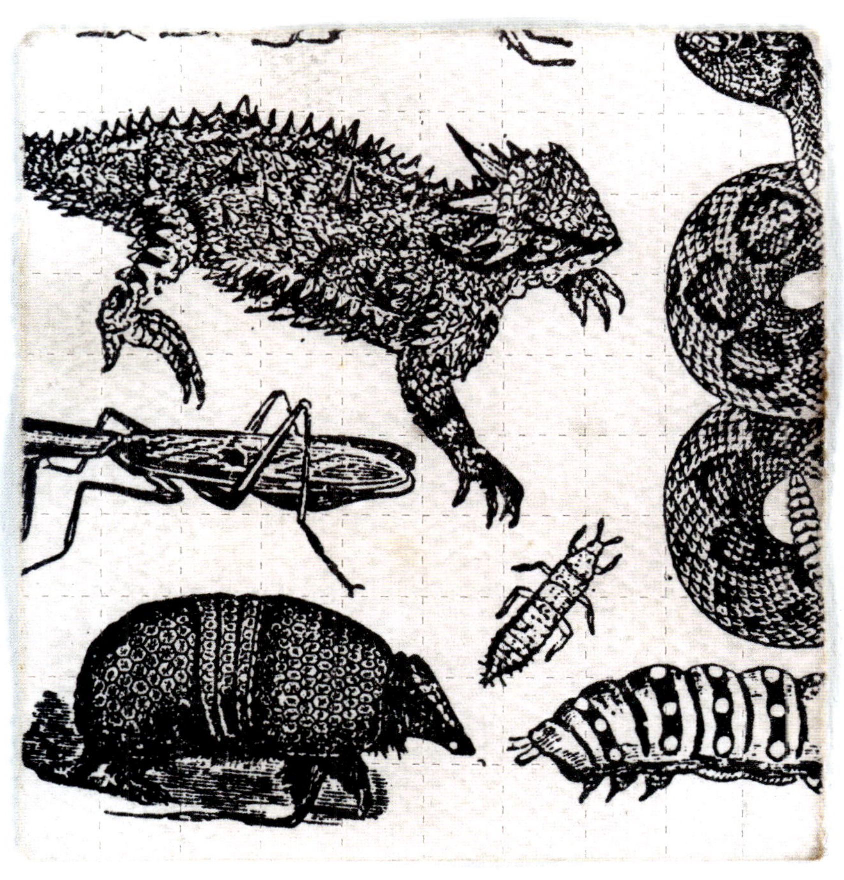

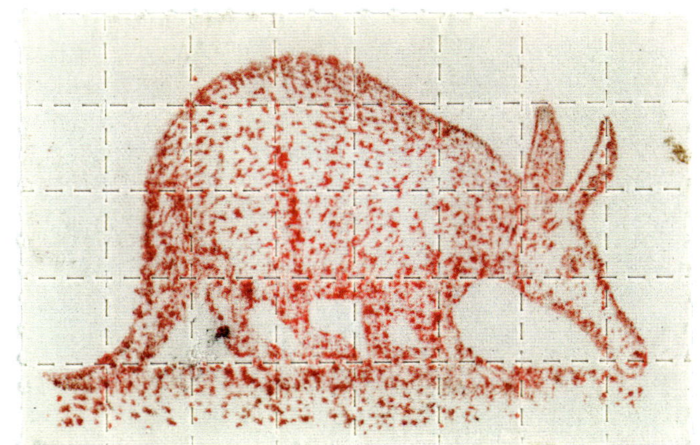

Critters, San Francisco, ca. 1990. 2½ × 2½ in. A portion of a larger "1000 block" print.

Aardvark, San Francisco, late 1980s. Handstamp, 1¼ × 2 in.

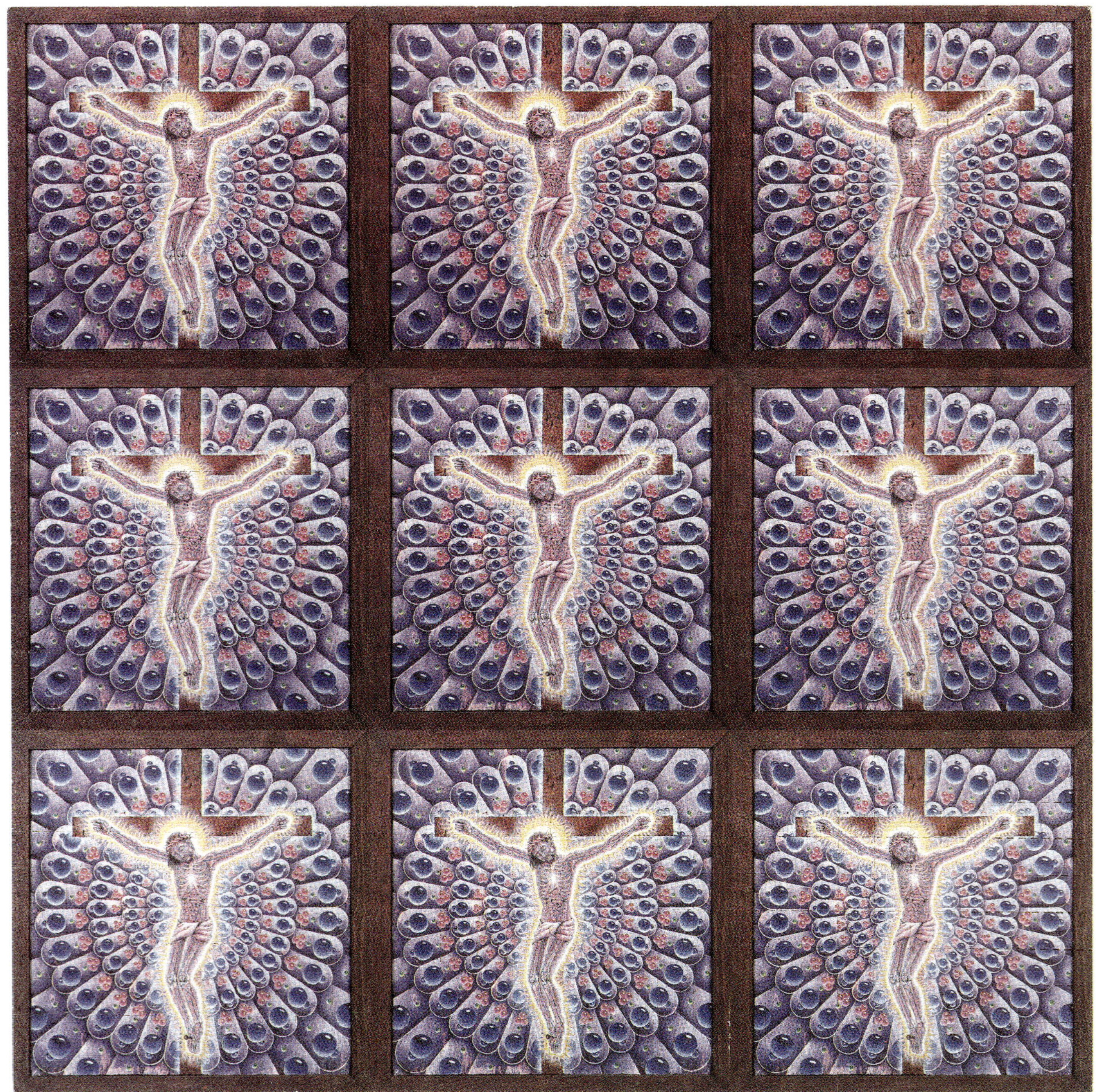

Purple Jesus/Carbon Jesus, Mark McCloud and Alex Grey, San Francisco, 1992. 7½ × 7½ in.

In 1987, I painted *Purple Jesus* for the album cover of a band called Purple Geezus, started by my friend Reverend Mike Osterhout, founder of the Church of the Little Green Man in New York. Later that year, the painting was exhibited in Retrospectacle, an art show in San Francisco curated by art critic Carlo McCormick celebrating the twentieth anniversary of the Summer of Love. The painting was purchased by longtime friend and psychedelic art collector, Mark McCloud.

By the early '90s, and without my knowledge, the painting could be found on perforated blotter prints that became legendary at Grateful Dead concerts. People reportedly wandered through the parking lot scene asking, "Has anyone seen Jesus?" I discovered this use of the art during a lecture in California when someone in the audience asked if I had ever painted a Purple Jesus because it was on some incredible acid and it looked like my work. Hmm.

Our friend Magic Mike paid dearly for selling *Purple Jesus* acid. He spent twenty years in jail. I was asked if I would sign an edition of undosed prints as a fundraiser for his defense. I did. I saw him the day he was released and he had an enormous smile on his face. A true visionary, he told me God had work for him to help suffering people in prison.

It's been an incredible honor having my work intertwined with the psychedelic movement.

Alex Grey

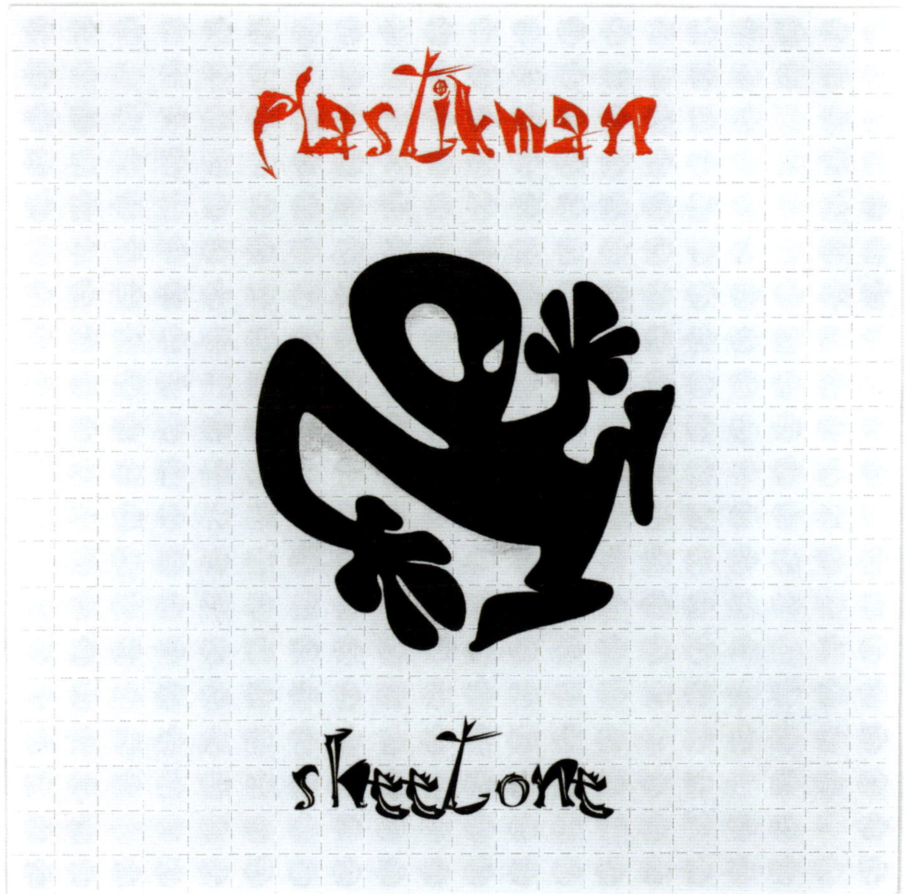

Astrogirl, San Francisco, ca. 1992. Original image created by Claudia Rey and Carlos Soul Slinger for the New York City emporium Liquid Sky. ½ × ½ in. Cotton paper.

Sheet One, Plastikman, 1993. 4¾ × 4¾ in. Cover art for the Novamute CD release from Richie Hawtin.

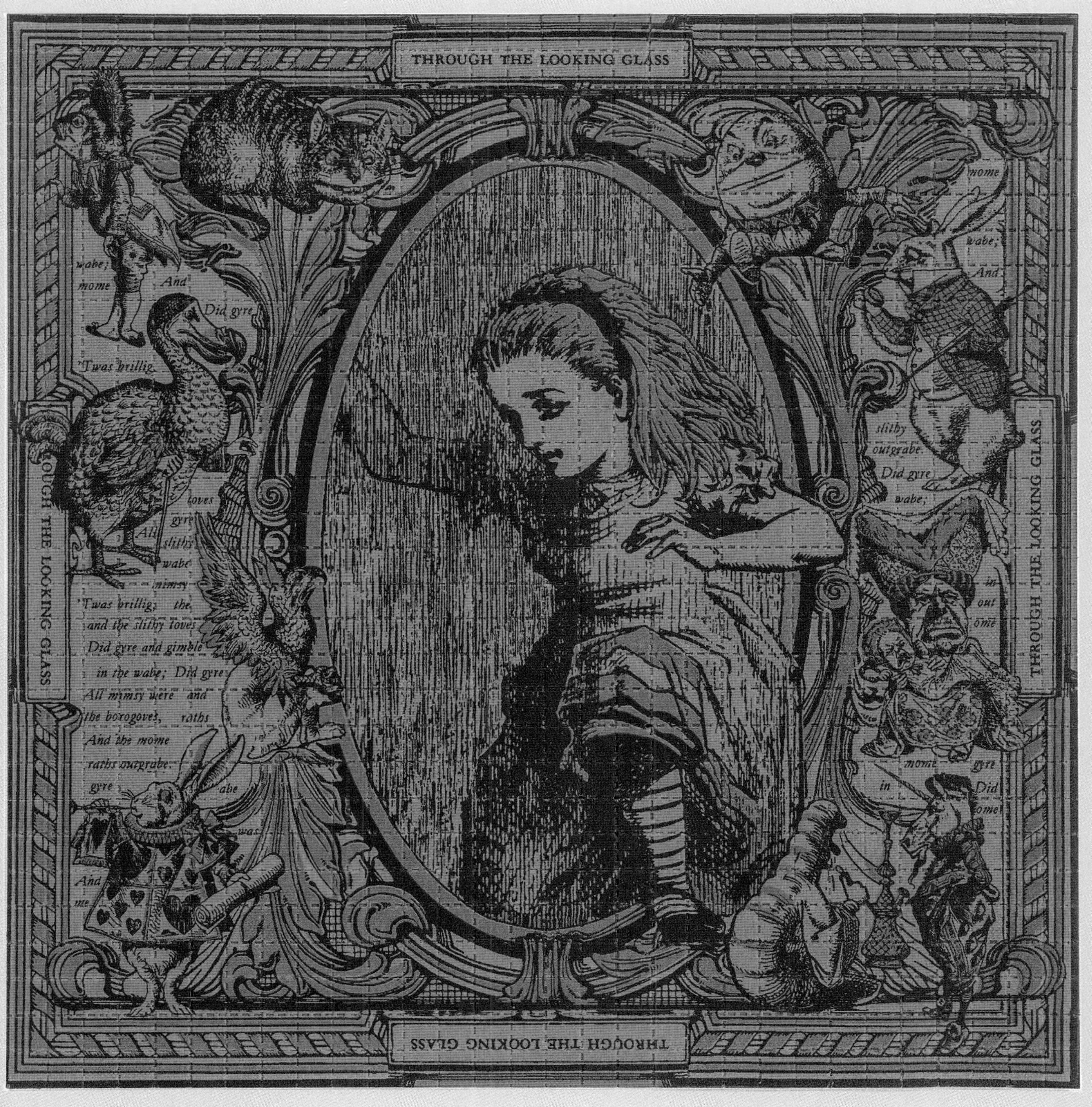

Through the Looking Glass, Mark McCloud, San Francisco, 1995. 7½ × 7½ in.

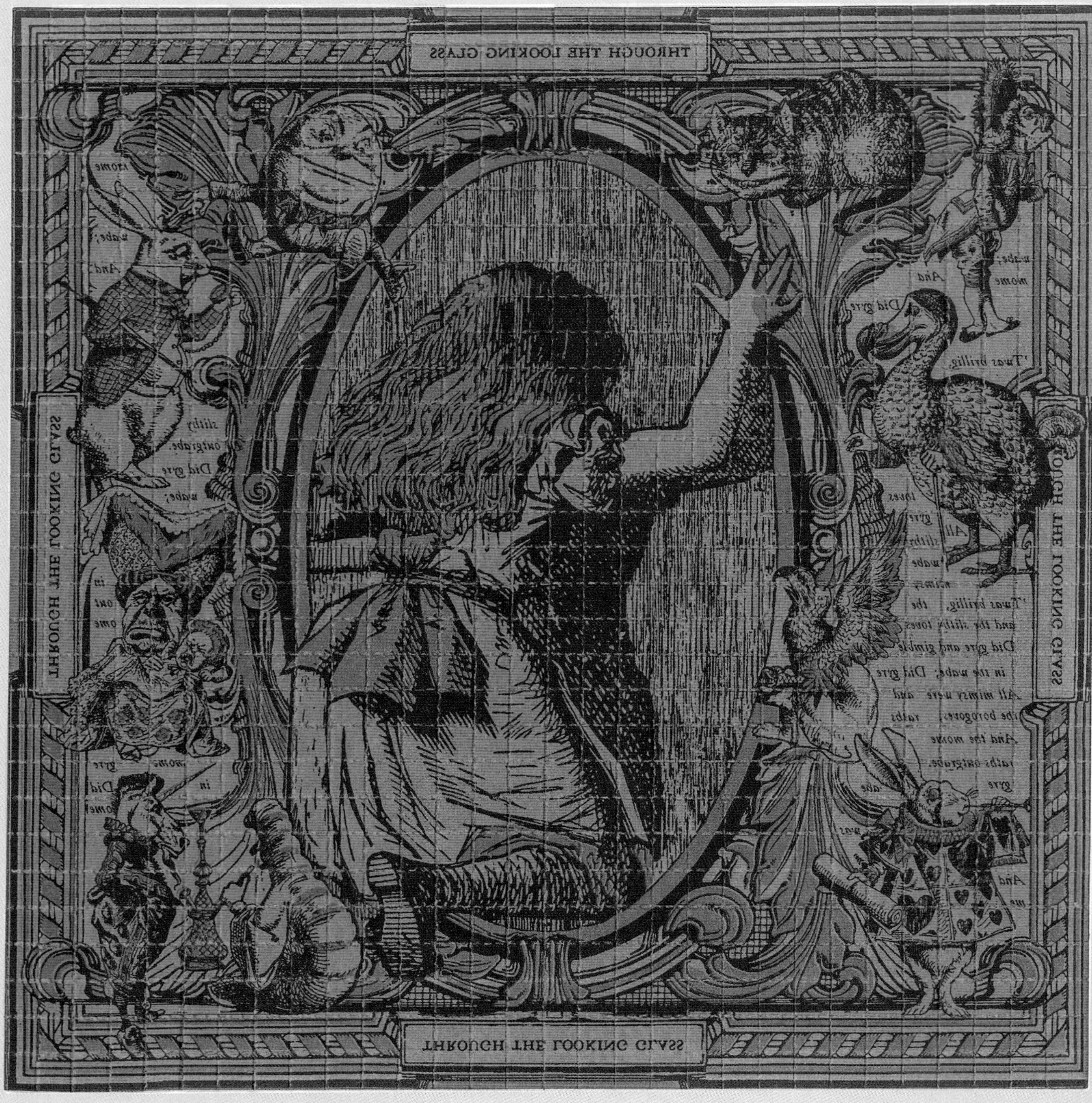

Through the Looking Glass, Mark McCloud, San Francisco, 1995. 7½ × 7½ in.

(reverse)

What a perfectly apt visual incantation for a psychedelic journey—passing through a portal to another world. This blotter incorporates the iconic drawings created by British artist John Tenniel (1820–1914) for Lewis Carroll's *Alice's Adventures in Wonderland* (1865) and *Through the Looking Glass and What Alice Found There* (1871). After first attempting to create illustrations himself, Carroll recruited Tenniel, familiar with his political and satirical cartoons from the British weekly magazine *Punch*. Twelve of Tenniel's pieces are represented here, but all ninety-two of his illustrations for the Alice stories are beautiful, and many would make for wonderful LSD blotter art. But the illustrations forming these back-and-front centerpieces are perhaps the most felicitous, and especially so when employed in this mirror-and-portal like manner. Simply frabjous!

In the opening chapter of *Through the Looking Glass,* Alice positions herself on the fireplace mantle, the Looking Glass before her softens and becomes misty, and she climbs through into another world. Or does she? In that other world, Alice enjoys conversation with flowers and insects, and even with a linguistically clever egg. At one point, she is told about a pudding recipe that begins with blotting paper as an ingredient! And after a variety of adventures and challenges, she connects with her power and potential and becomes a Queen. In the end, was it a dream, or not? Does it matter? The mystics say all of life is a dream, rich with significance, and that the alchemical/yogic/spiritual path is the practice of coming to that realization.

David E. Presti

Alfred E. Pluribus Neuman, Mark McCloud, image commissioned from The Pizz, 1993. 7½ × 7½ in.

Tintin, Ed Visser, Amsterdam, ca. 1994. 5⅞ × 9½ in.

I have no documentation from my visit to Mark McCloud's place some fifteen years ago, but a memory that stretches out in psychedelic durée, the shuttered windows of his cathedral-like house looking like doors as his stories tangled with the framed sheets of blotter art, all intensified by extremely strong grass.

Time bends and spirals in the trip, or it gets sticky and concrete. The word psychedelic itself is a bauble of time with a personal etymology. My favorite childhood cartoon, *The Adventures of Tintin*, gave me a formative premonition of what it meant. A far cry from the looney qualities of the stoner cartoon, Tintin's anthropological settings and dreamy narrative transformations are saturated with post-Surrealist mystique. Tintin is just a cipher: it is the extras who turn things on, such as his alcoholic sidekick Captain Haddock, the opera diva Bianca Castafiore—a sonic monster—and the inept twin police detectives Johnson and Johnson, who grow long, multicolored beards during space travel.

I realized too late that Tintin was the acceptable choice of cartoon for certain kinds of mid-twentieth-century parents in my neck of the woods. Apart from Hergé's obvious craftmanship, being not-American was what in their eyes circumstantially qualified the series as an exception to the pop culture that at the time was perceived as a combative, overseas invention for a defeated Europe. Tintin is as Indo-European as Hieronymus Bosch. Thankfully—as I realized on that Pacific evening with an exhilarating sense of finally receiving something that was promised to me a long time ago—Tintin travels with contraband.

Lars Bang Larsen

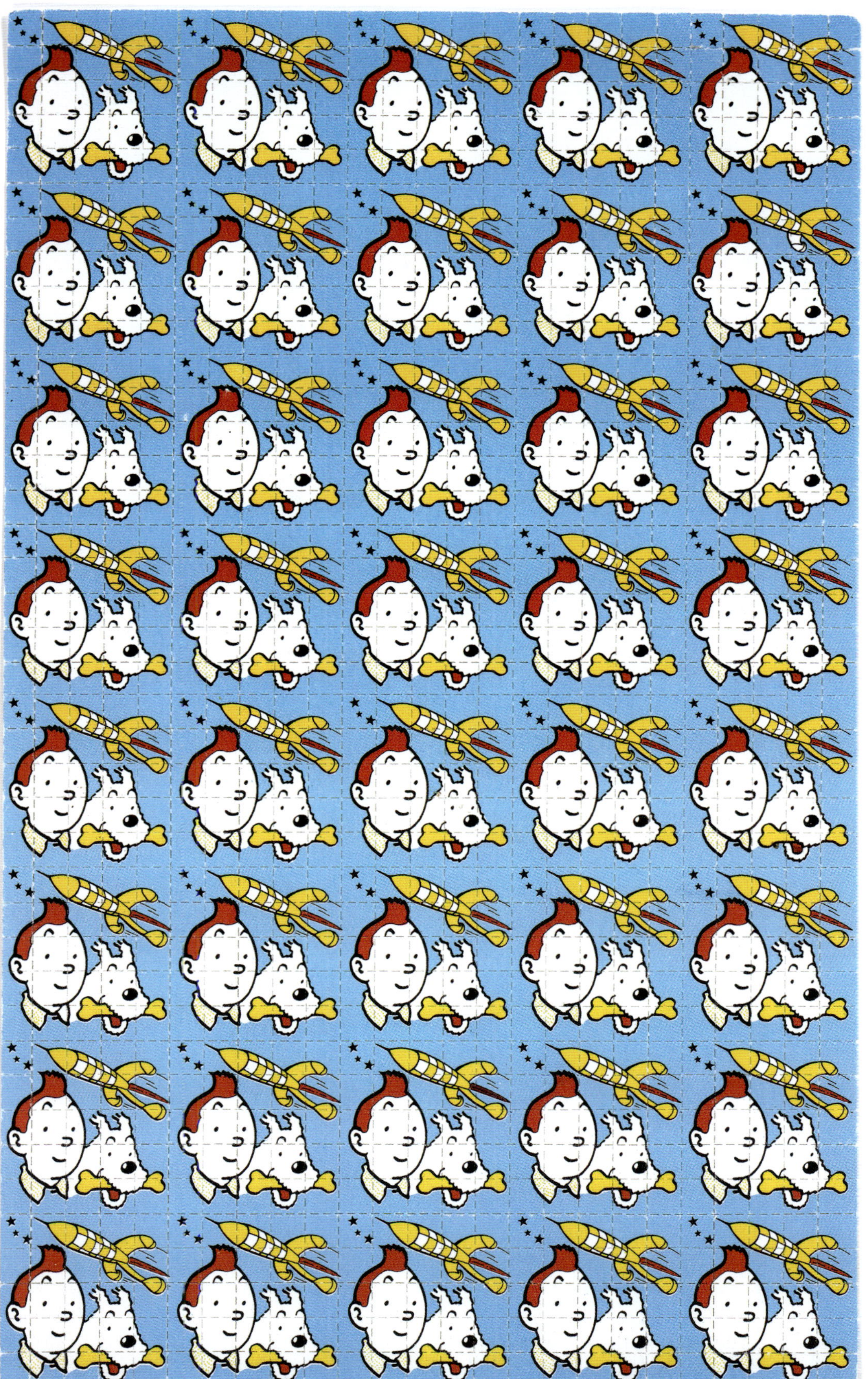

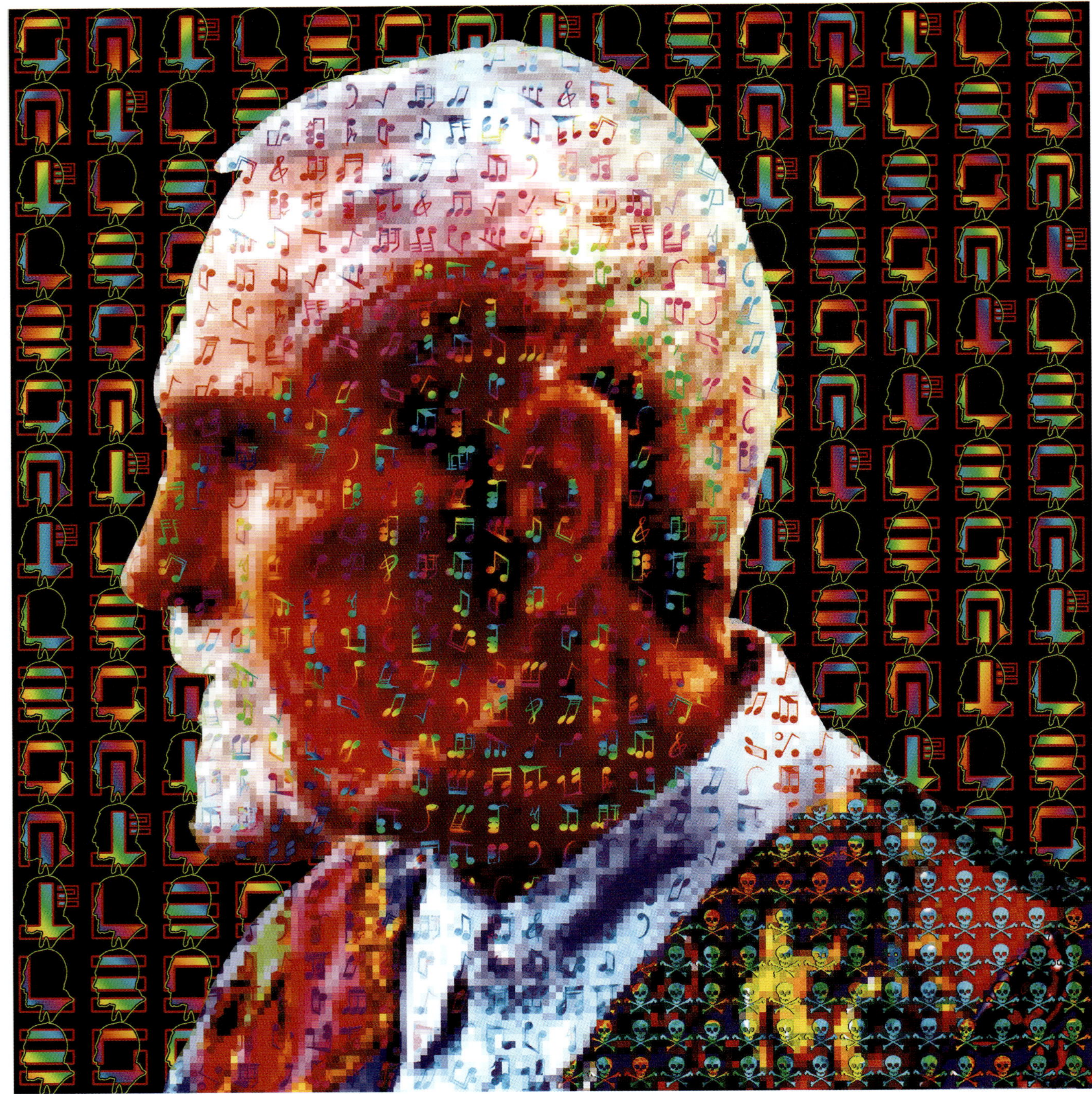

Timothy Leary was still alive when I designed this for Mark McCloud in the early 1990s, but he was dying of cancer. Hence the skulls on his shoulder, along with the angel on his vest. With the swirl of musical notes, I was trying to invoke the legendary rainbow body that is reported to appear when great souls have an enlightened death. In the background, I made reference to my favorite Leary writing, *Neuropolitique*, where he explains and expands the SMI^{2}LE acronym—space migration, intelligence increase, and life extension. This design zeroes in on the background and features each letter of the SMI^{2}LE acronym as a four-way hit.

Dana Smith

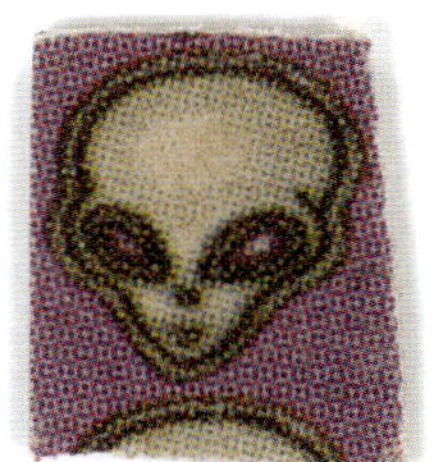

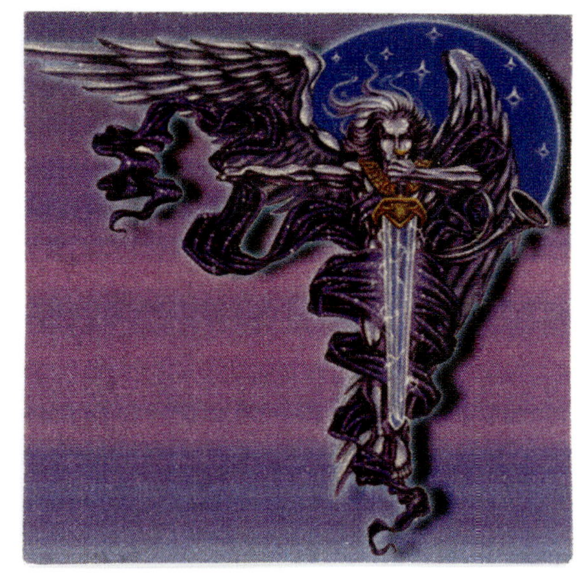

Leary Profile, Mark McCloud and Dana Smith, San Francisco, 1994. 7½ × 7½ in.

Alien, ca. 2010. Cut-along, approx. ½ × ¾ in.

Abraxas, ca. 2004. 2½ × 2½ in. Based on a Ron Spencer illustration of Barachiel the Messenger, a "tome archon" in Forgotten Realms, a Dungeons & Dragons campaign universe. Cut-along grid printed on back.

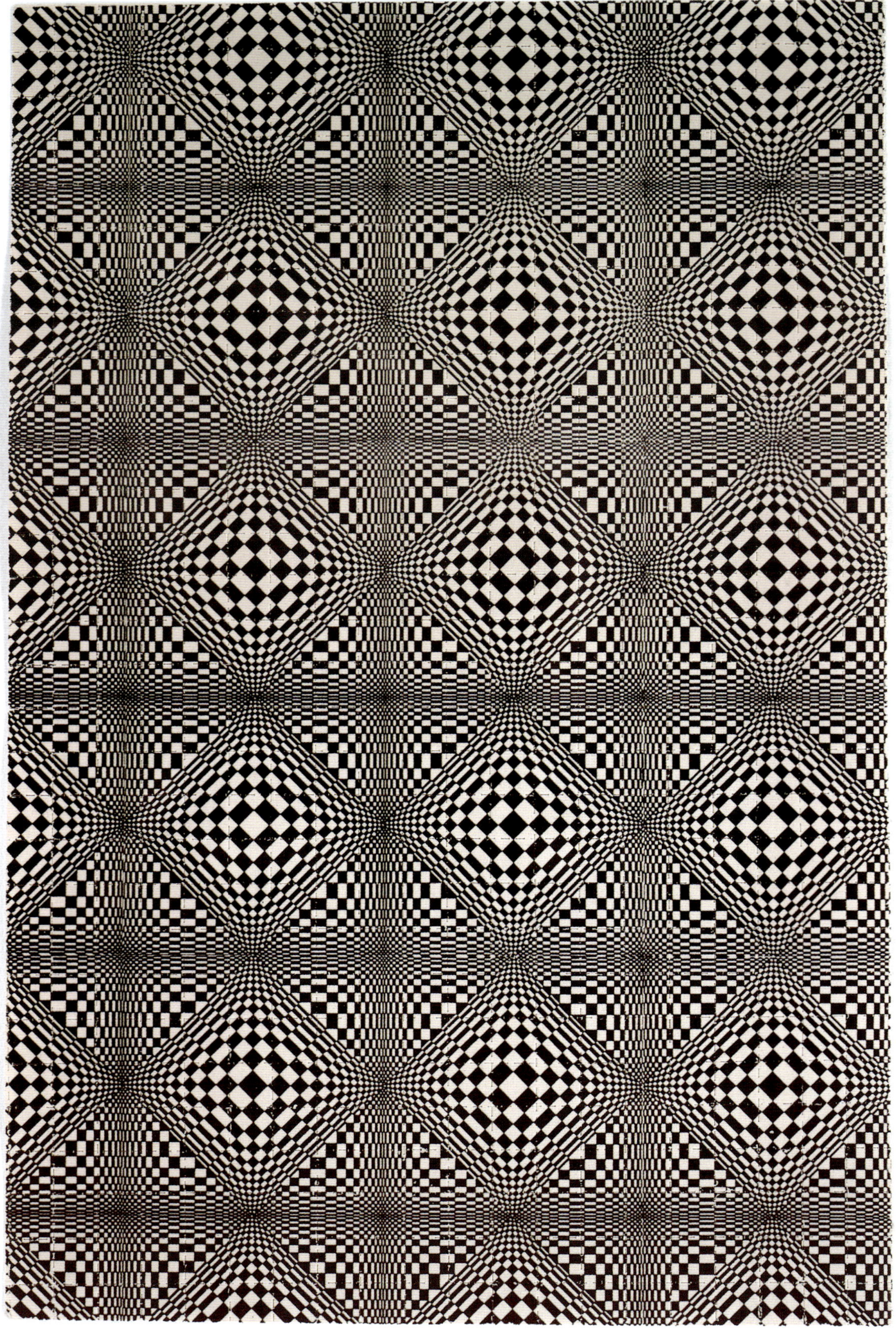

Op Bulge, San Francisco, early 1980s. 5 × 7½ in. Adapted from the French-Hungarian artist Victor Vasarely (1906–1997).

In high school, we dropped "White Blotter" most weekends. Dude who sold it always announced his wares in a tone that conveyed conviction that it was the purest material available. Maybe he was worried about ink poisoning. Maybe he was racist. It was the only paper he sold. A four-strip always delivered, but better branding would've been nice. So on the day dude started in his Bill and Ted announcer voice, "Gentlemen, today's selection is . . ." my buddy James and I were astonished to hear him say, ". . . Trippy Squares!" A pristine sheet: one hundred hits of beautiful black-and-white op art. No more potent, yet somehow more magical. We never saw them again.

Inspired, I vowed to end White Blotter's reign. Commandeering our school photocopier, with its exotic red toner cartridge swappable for the standard black, I created collages mixing op art and Escher drawings. Red-and-black masterpieces, on District cover stock. Using mom's typewriter, sans ribbon, I inserted my art, pounded the hyphen key for ten single-spaced rows, turned the paper 90°, and repeated. Knowing nothing of how the world works, friends drove me to Berkeley to hopefully meet someone needing cool art sheets on which to distribute their product. I got mugged in People's Park. Punched in the face hard. Tooth chipped. Sheets stolen.

Later in life, somewhat wiser, I conceived of the *LSD 60* fundraiser blotter, which Stevee Postman executed and Albert Hofmann autographed. Casey Hardison took the face-punch on that one.

Jon Hanna

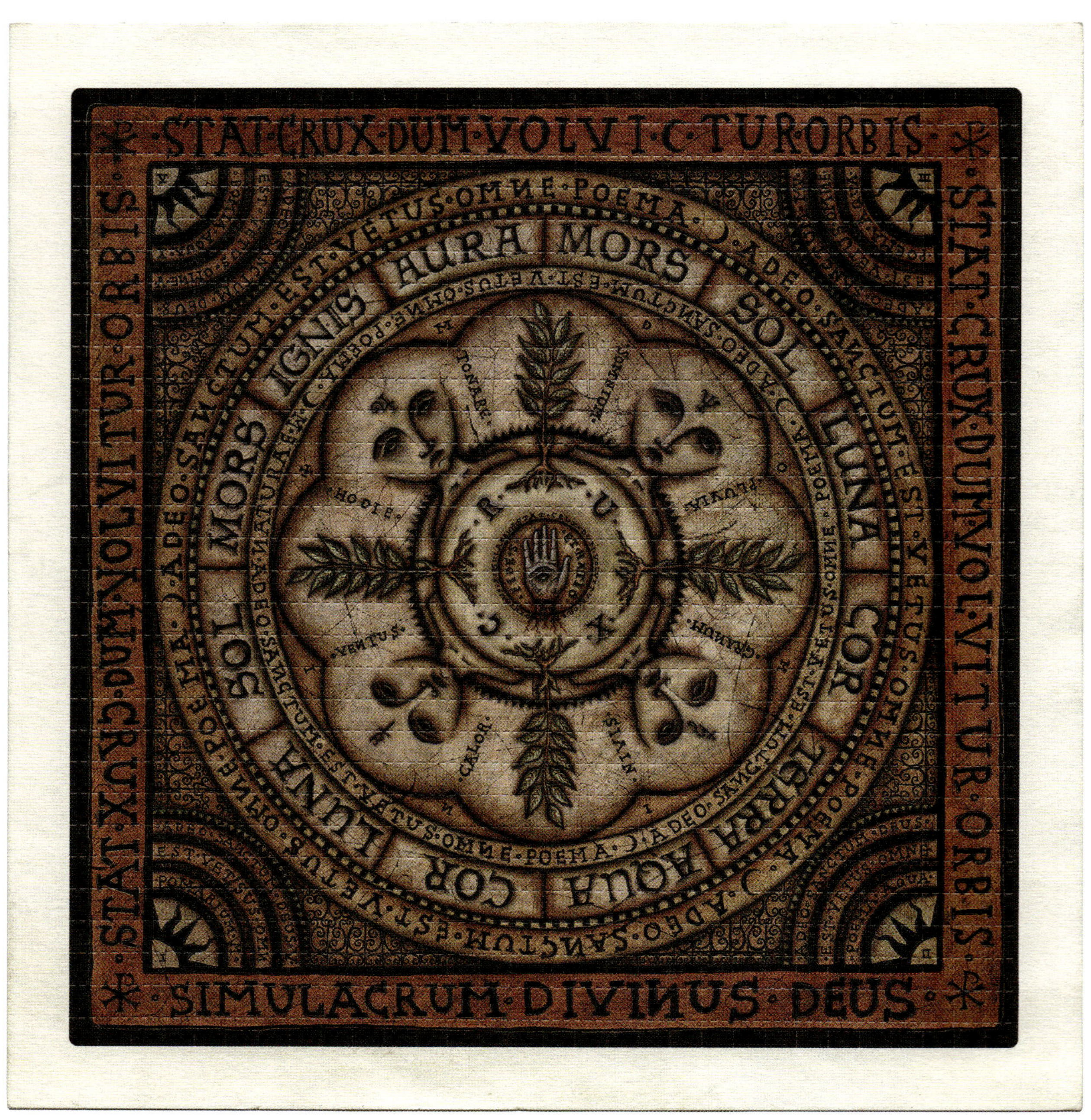

208

Mystery of Faith,
Daniel Martin Diaz,
2003. 7½ × 7½ in.

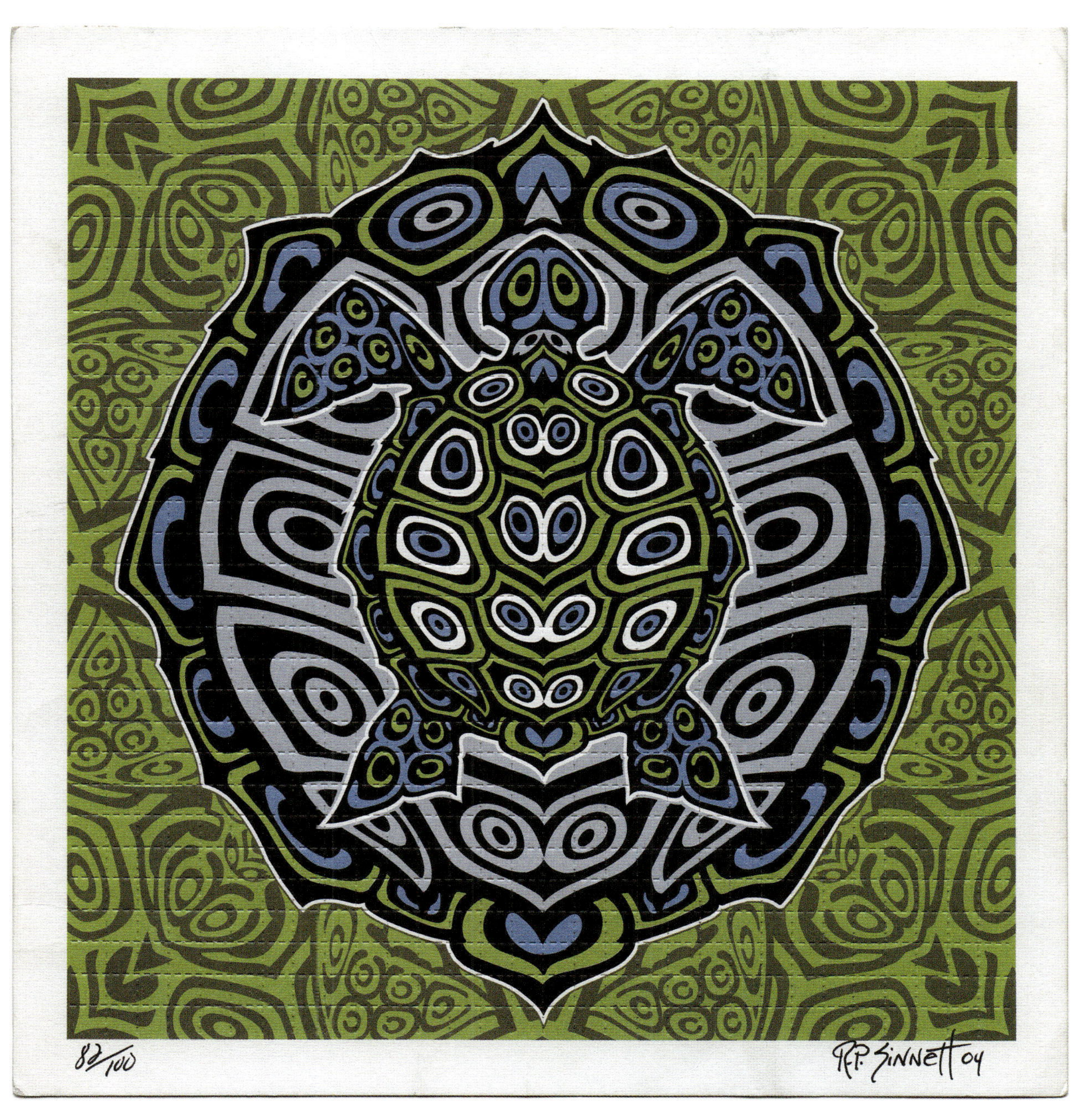

Terrapin, Rick Sinnett,
2004. 7½ × 7½ in. Signed.

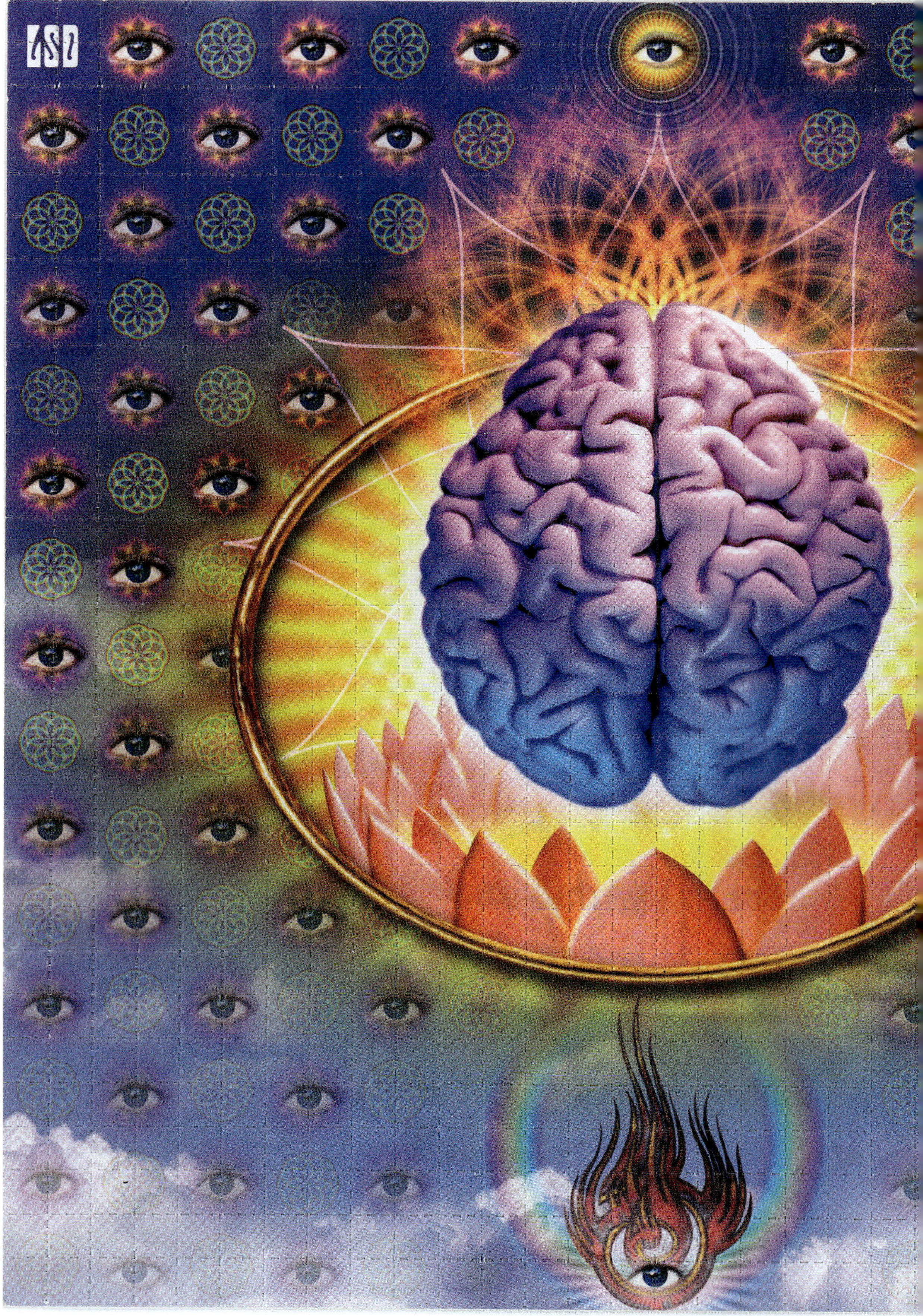
LSD

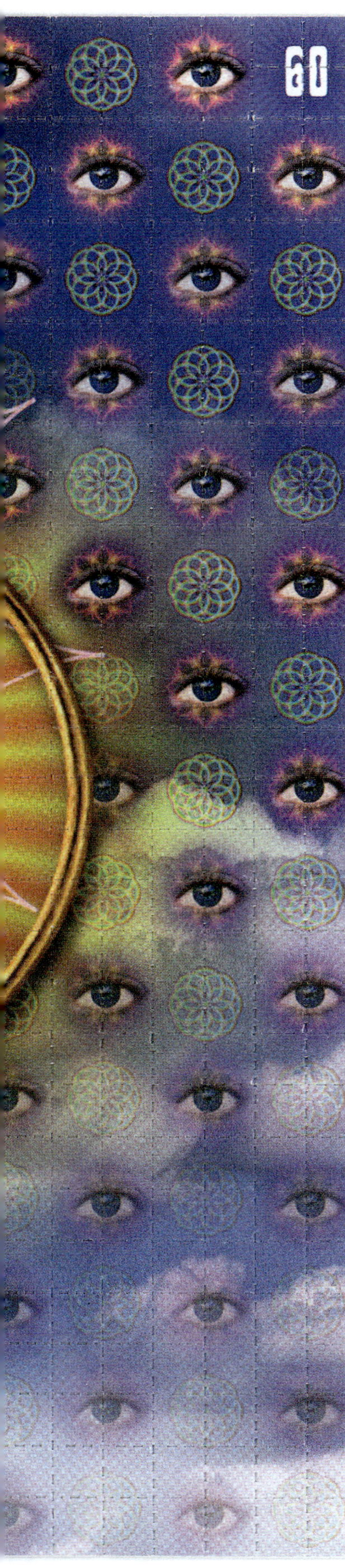

LSD 60, Stevee Postman and Jon Hanna, 2003. 7½ × 7½ in.

As an LSD chemist intentionally birthing a molecule with such lasting and profound effects on the lives of those who choose to imbibe, one could hope to influence the outcome of the experience. And yet, without being at their side whispering in their ear, and desperately desiring to generate mass trance-formation, how does one do it? With liquid, one must trust the words of those handing over the vials; so too with sheets, but a chance to speak again, and again, and again.

This sheet—conceived by Stevee Postman and Jon Hanna, inspired by the sixtieth anniversary of Albert Hofmann's discovery of LSD, and coinciding with the Mind States conference—speaks to all that I could hope for: humanity, alive with freedom, awake in the sacred and profane, where the pairs of opposites cease to have noxious effect.

A winged flying illuminated I, all-seeing, ever-looking. A thousand-petaled unfurling enlightened mind state. A seed flowering an intentional meta-programmed life. A few hundred thousand suspecting victims of Albert's Problem Child touched, elucidated within. If ever there were a sheet to inspire in its imago that which I dreamt, begged, longed for in the communicant, that to which I could attest, this was it—prayer without cessation for the insights generated within and possibly translated into action. The jewel in a Lotus Blossom: our brain, in bare awareness, perceiving beauty in a flower arising from muddy waters eternally reaching for light. *Om mani padme hum.*

Casey William Hardison

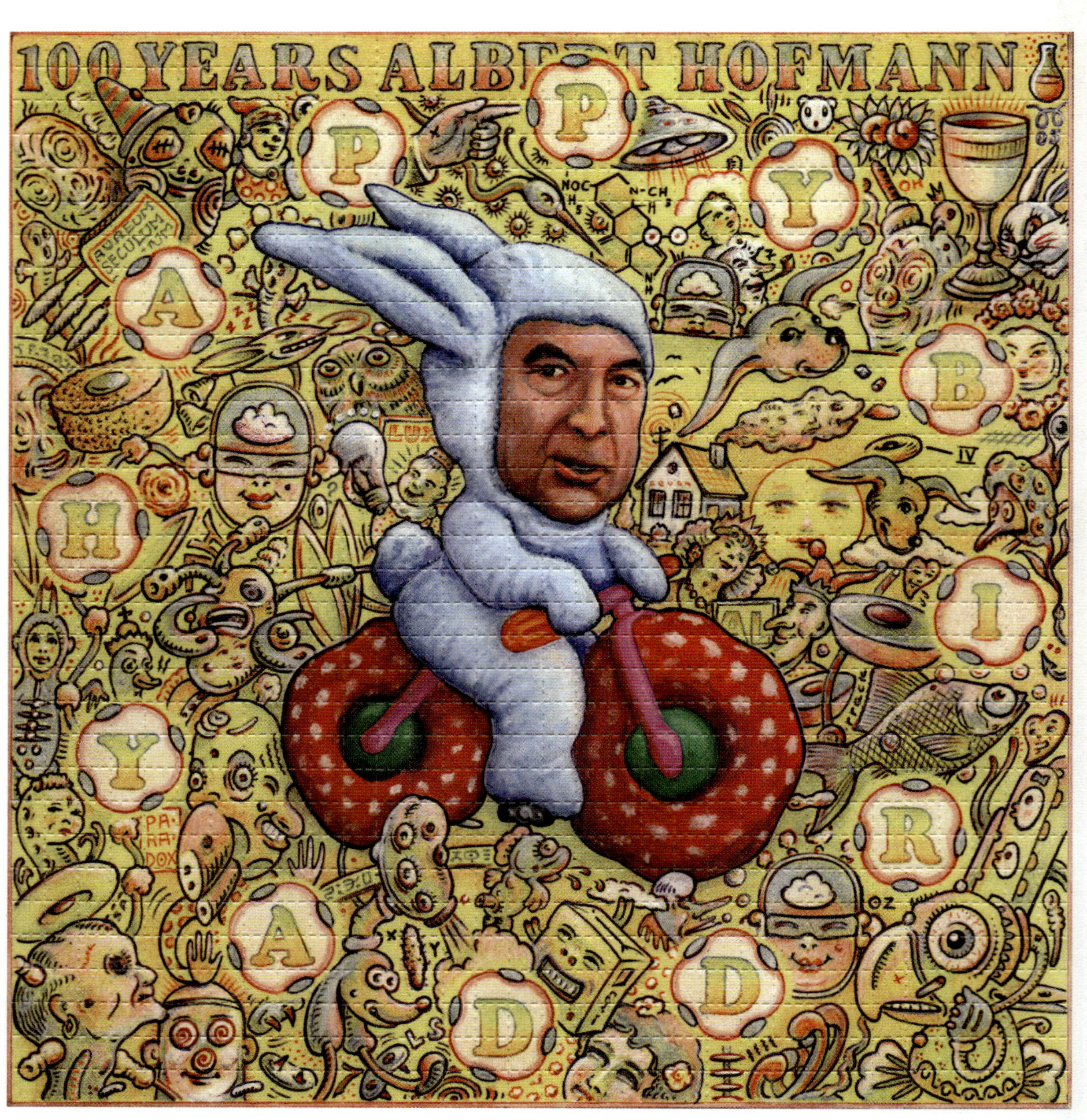
100 YEARS ALB
T HOFMANN
PA-
RA-
DOX

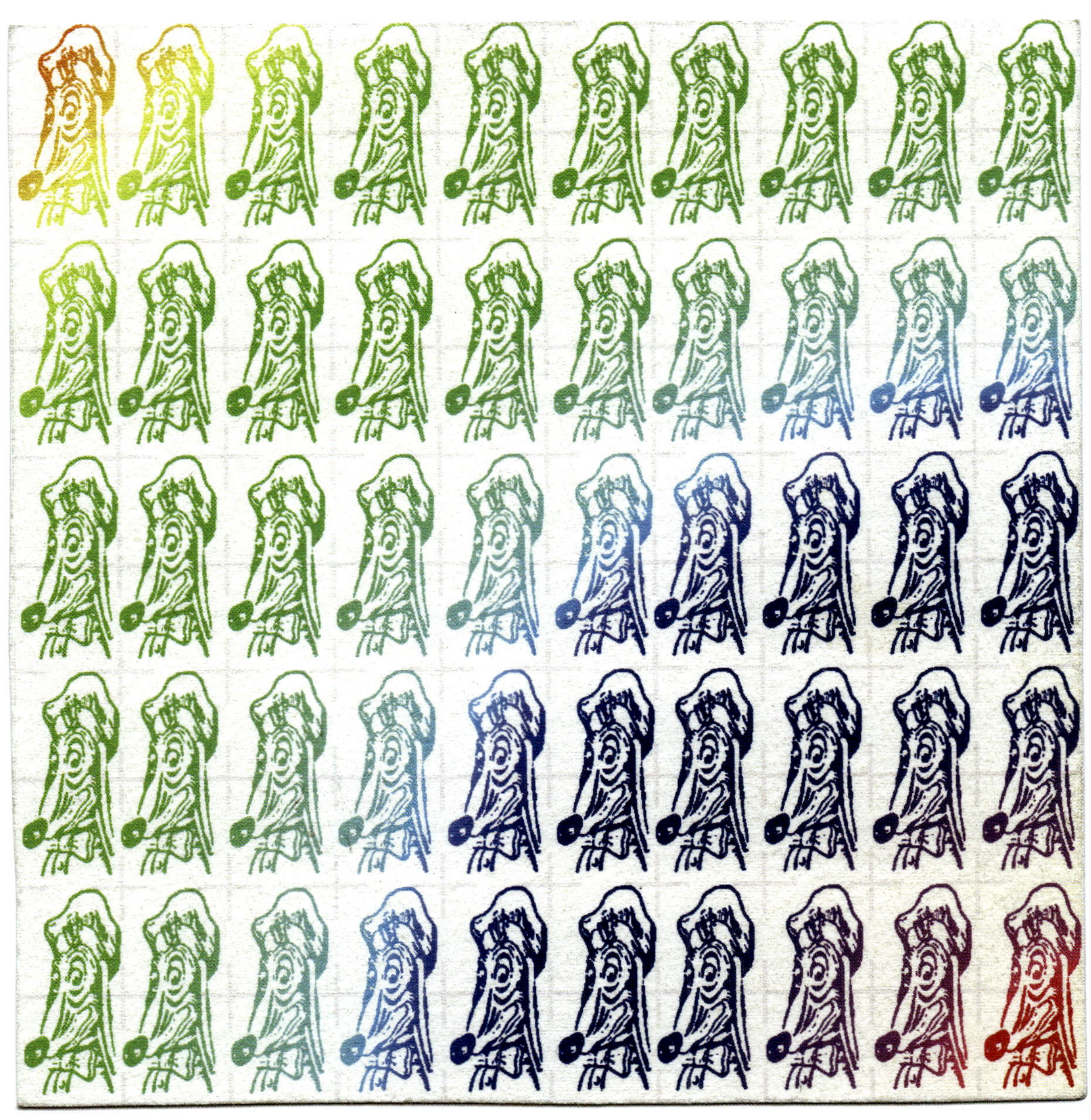

Happy Birdday Albert Hofmann, Dirk Bonsma, Switzerland, 2006. 7½ × 7½ in.

Doggie Diner, San Francisco, ca. 2007. 3⅞ × 3⅞ in. Small edition aimed at the black market, based on the mascot of a defunct local fast-food chain, a popular icon in Burning Man and Cacophony Society culture.

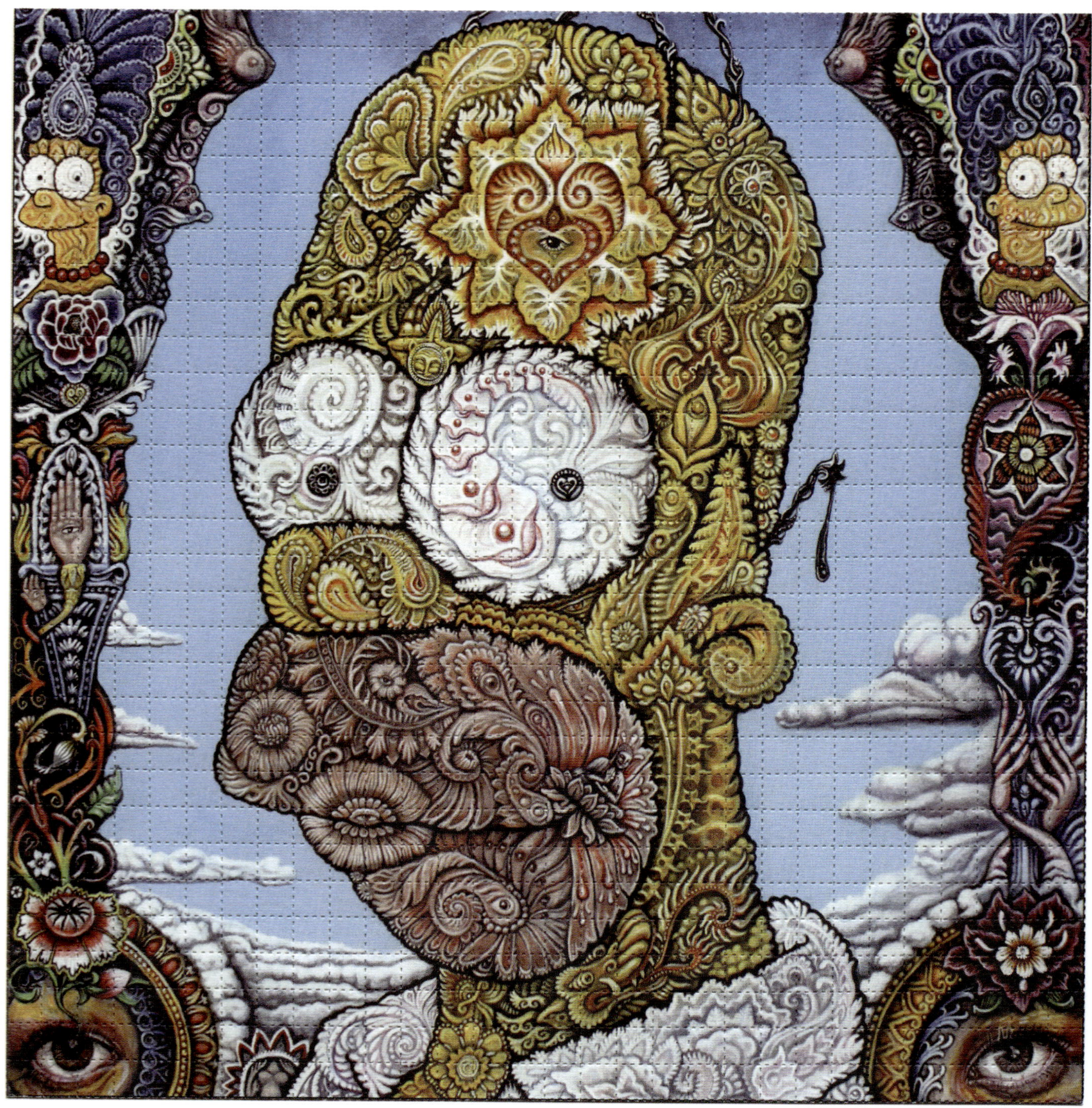

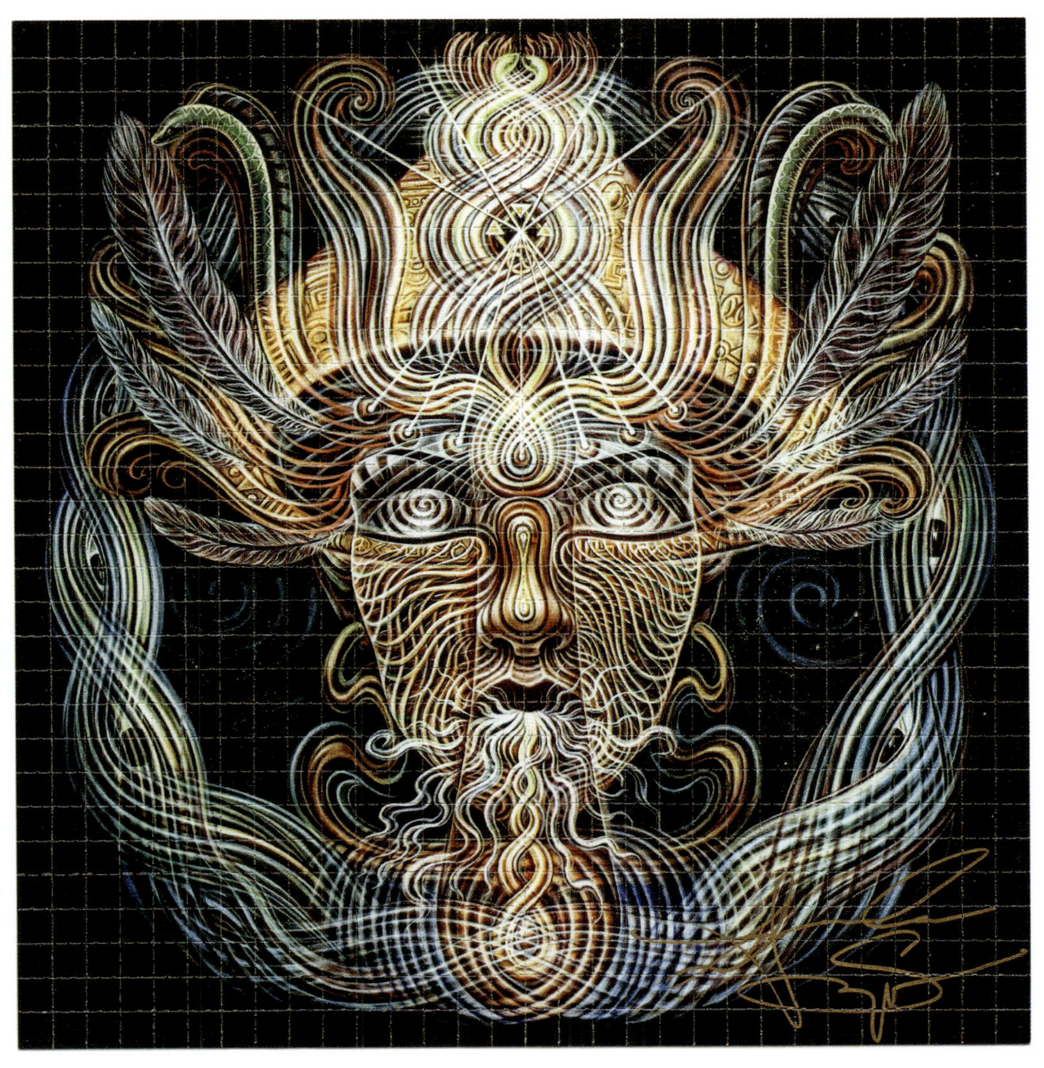

Portrait of Homer, Randal Roberts, 2010. 7½ × 7½ in.

The Shaman, Amanda Sage, 2011. 7½ × 7½ in. Signed.

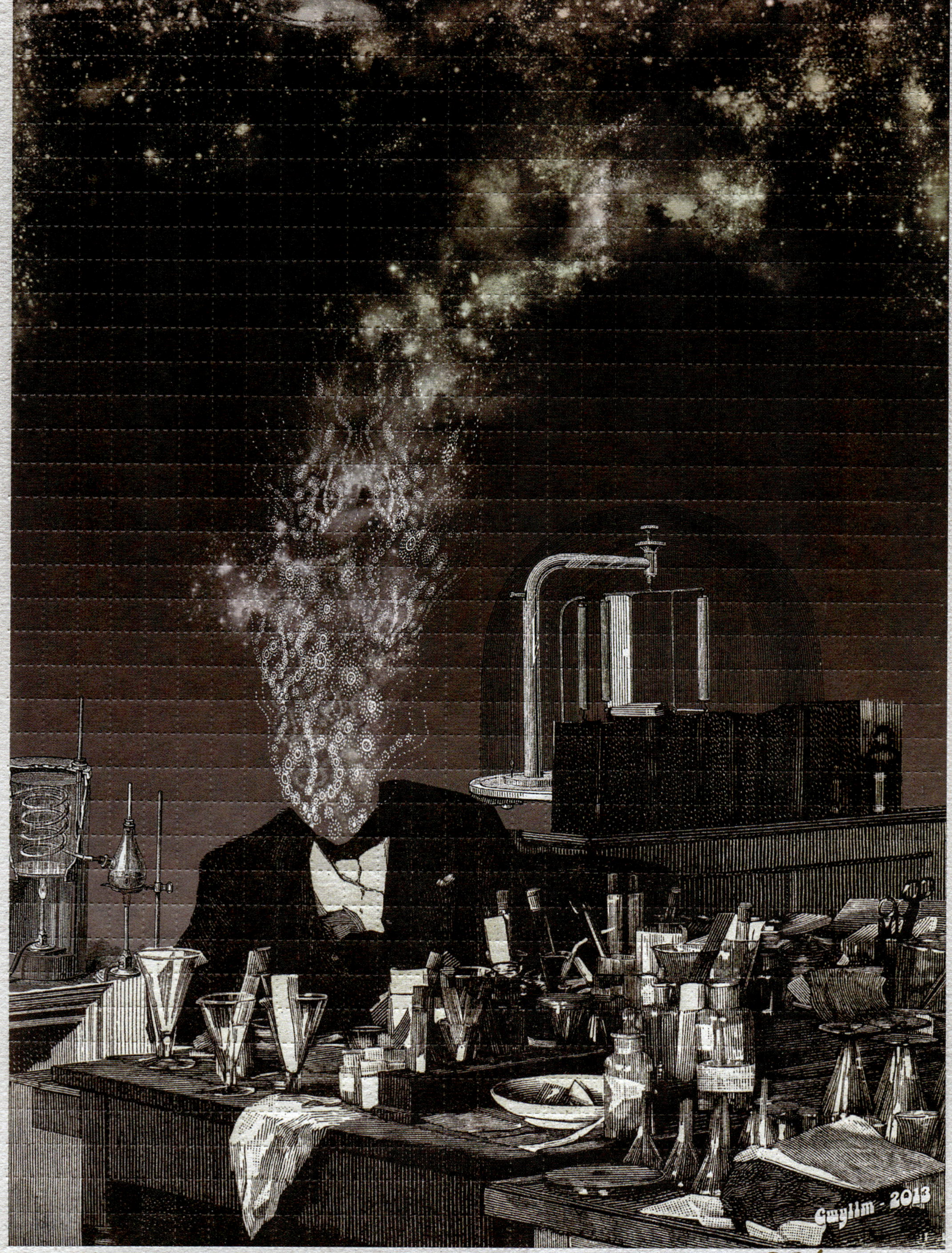
Gwylim - 2013
Gwylim
38/150

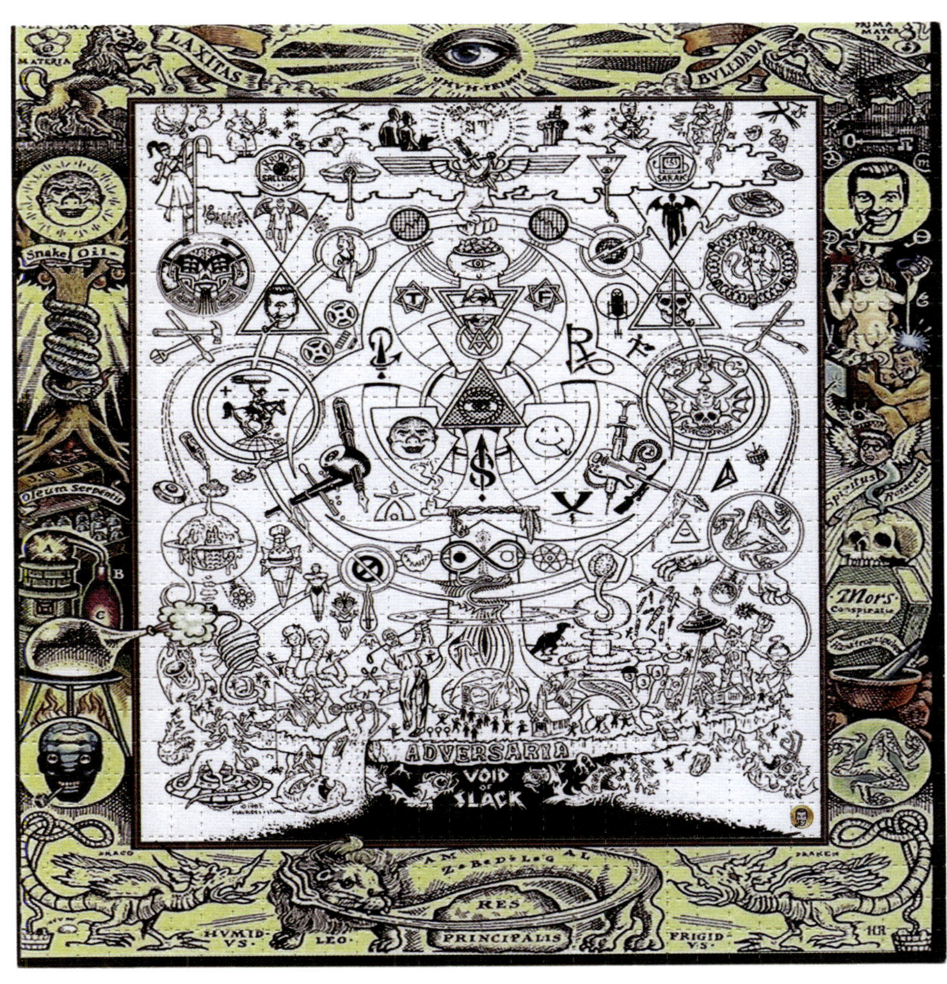

The Chemist, Gwyllm, 2013. 8½ × 11 in. Signed.

The Subgenius Tree of Knowledge, Paul Mavrides, Hal Robbins, and Rev. Ivan Stang, 2016. 7½ × 7½ in. The original image was distorted to fit the square format, to the great chagrin of Reverend Stang.

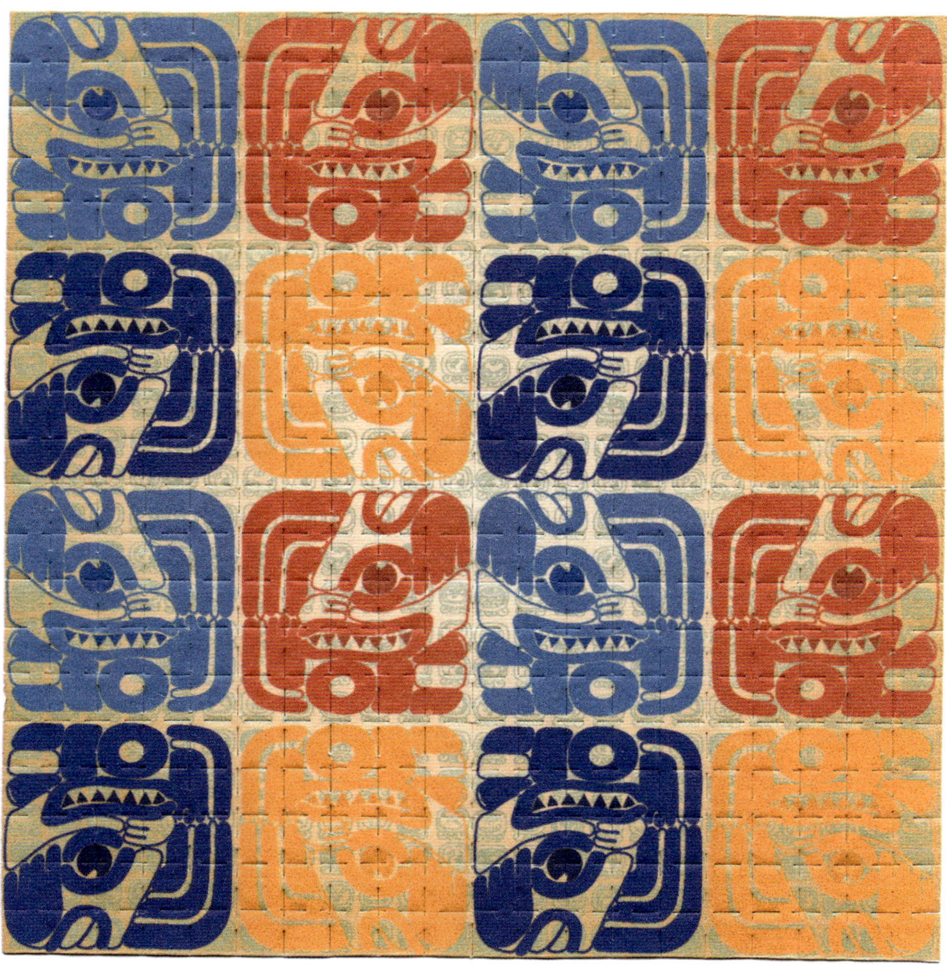

Toltec, Basel, 2018. Two-sided, 5½ × 5½ in. Produced for the black market.

Biker on the Road, Gary Panter, 2019. 7½ × 7½ in.

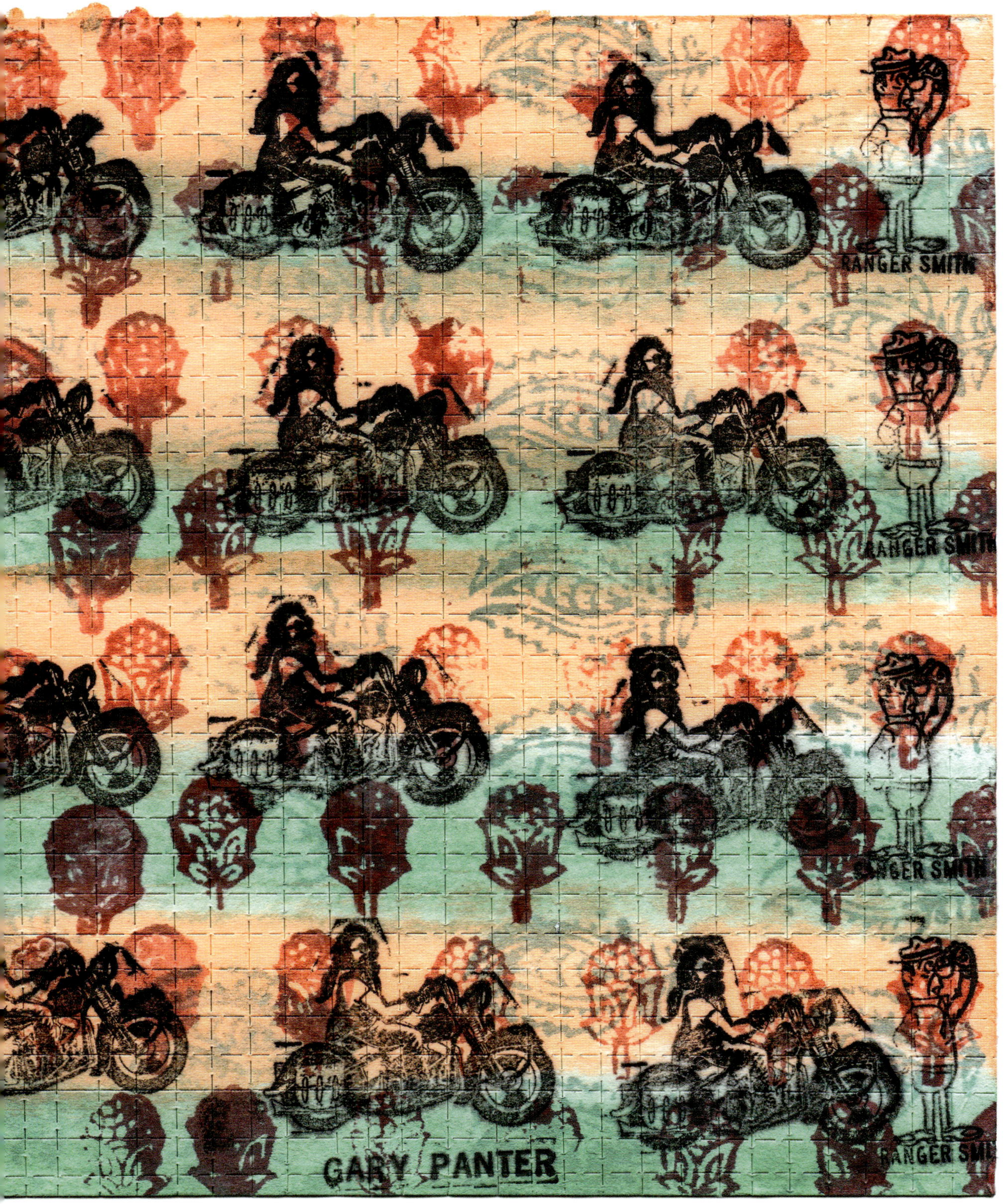
RANGER SMITH
RANGER SMITH
RANGER SMITH
GARY PANTER

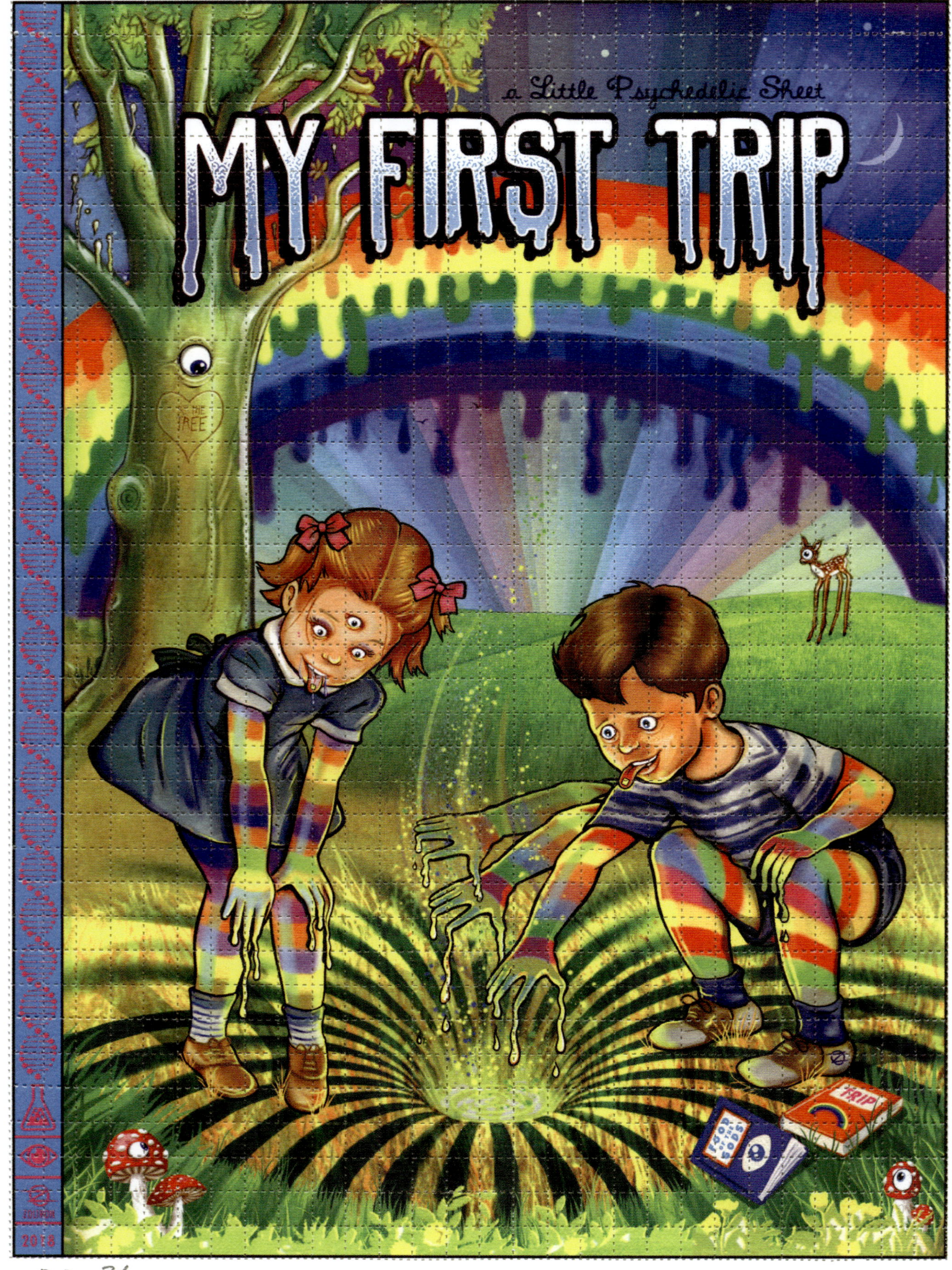

P.P. 3/5

My First Trip, Zoltron, 2018. 9 × 11 in. Signed.

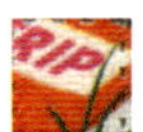

Originally an art print, Zoltron here riffs on the retro aesthetic of the Little Golden Books series for children, a surreal dreamscape that blends the innocence and wonder of psychedelics with their darker and more paranoid experiential facets. The two books strewn on the ground—titled *Trip* and *Food of the Gods*, presumably Terence McKenna's—hint that the "set and setting" of this so-called "first" trip are already laced with the scripts of previous psychedelic journeys. It's perhaps even likely that those books are responsible for piquing the children's psychedelic interests in the first place.

The blotter sheet's dual identity as psychedelic medium—simultaneously a "book" and a potential carrier for actual psychoactive substances—hints at how culture conspires with chemicals to entice the curious into the weird world of psychedelia. The traditional duality between content and artistic form breaks down here, with individual blotter tabs represented visually on the children's tongues—pointing to the very artwork's power to unlock the strange, altered effects represented within it. The image also dissolves the normative distinction between "subject" and "object," as the children's striped and "dripping" bodies reflect both the colors and the texture of the rainbow surrounding them. Sentience is likewise distributed across the landscape, as the trippers' pareidolia animates tree and mushrooms with an uncertain, watchful anticipation.

Neşe Devenot

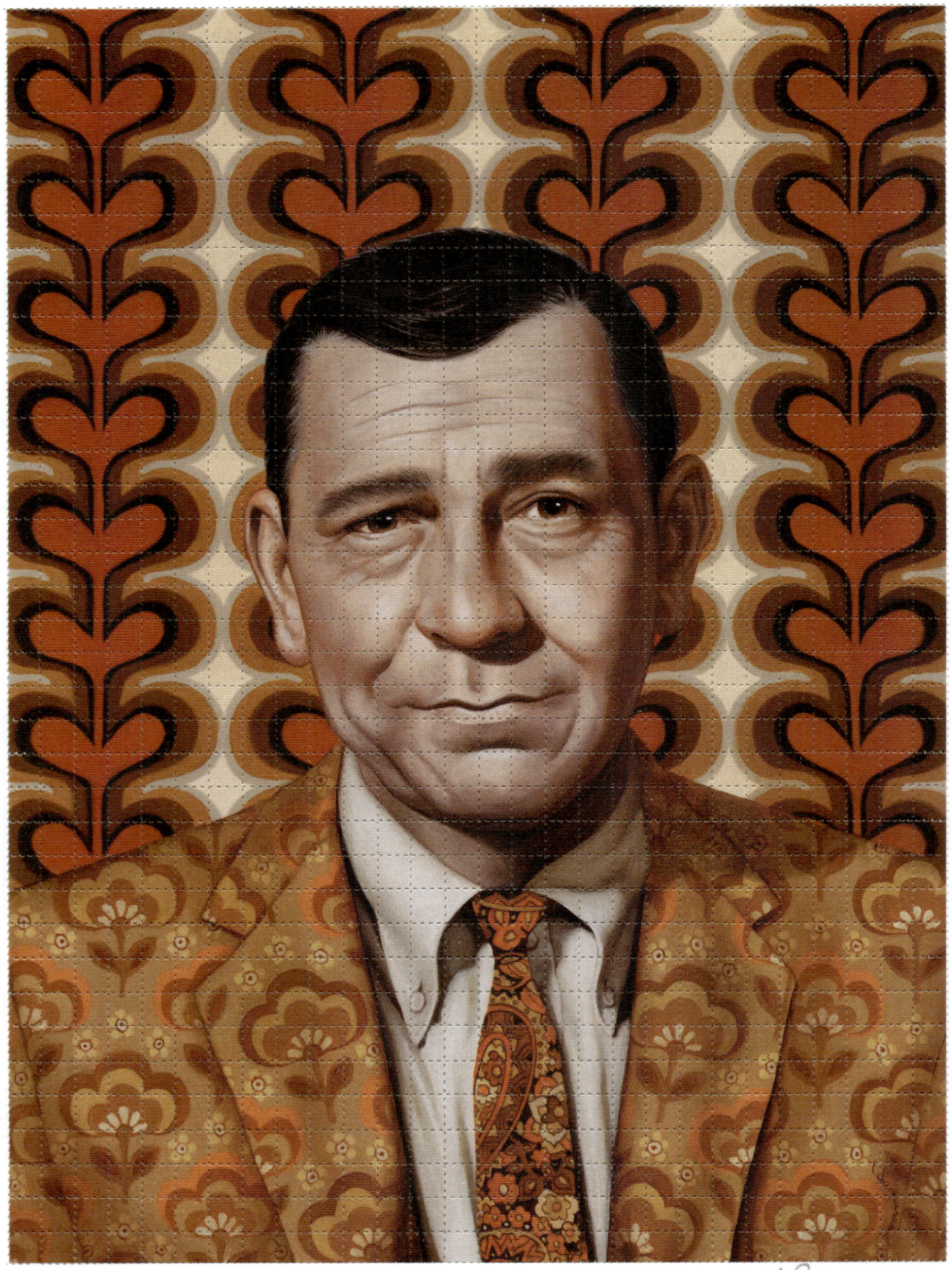
AP 11/18

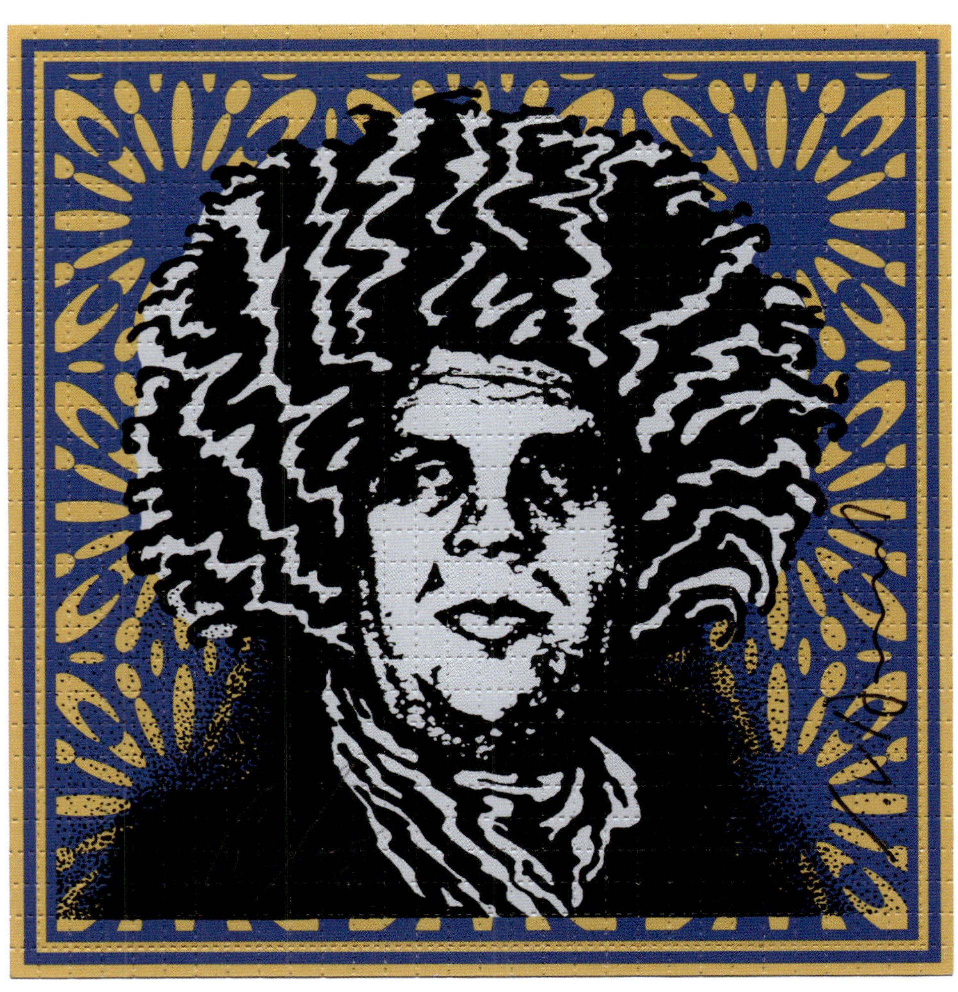

LSD Is the Bomb (The Dirty Deceiver), Isabel Samaras, 2020. 11¼ × 9 in. Signed. Title derives from "The Prophet," a notorious episode of *Dragnet 1968*, starring Jack Webb, pictured here.

Psychedelic Andre, '92 Obey Giant Blotter Variant, Shepard Fairey and John Van Hamersveld, 2020. 7½ × 7½ in. Signed by both artists. As with many vanity blotters, this issue includes multiple variants.

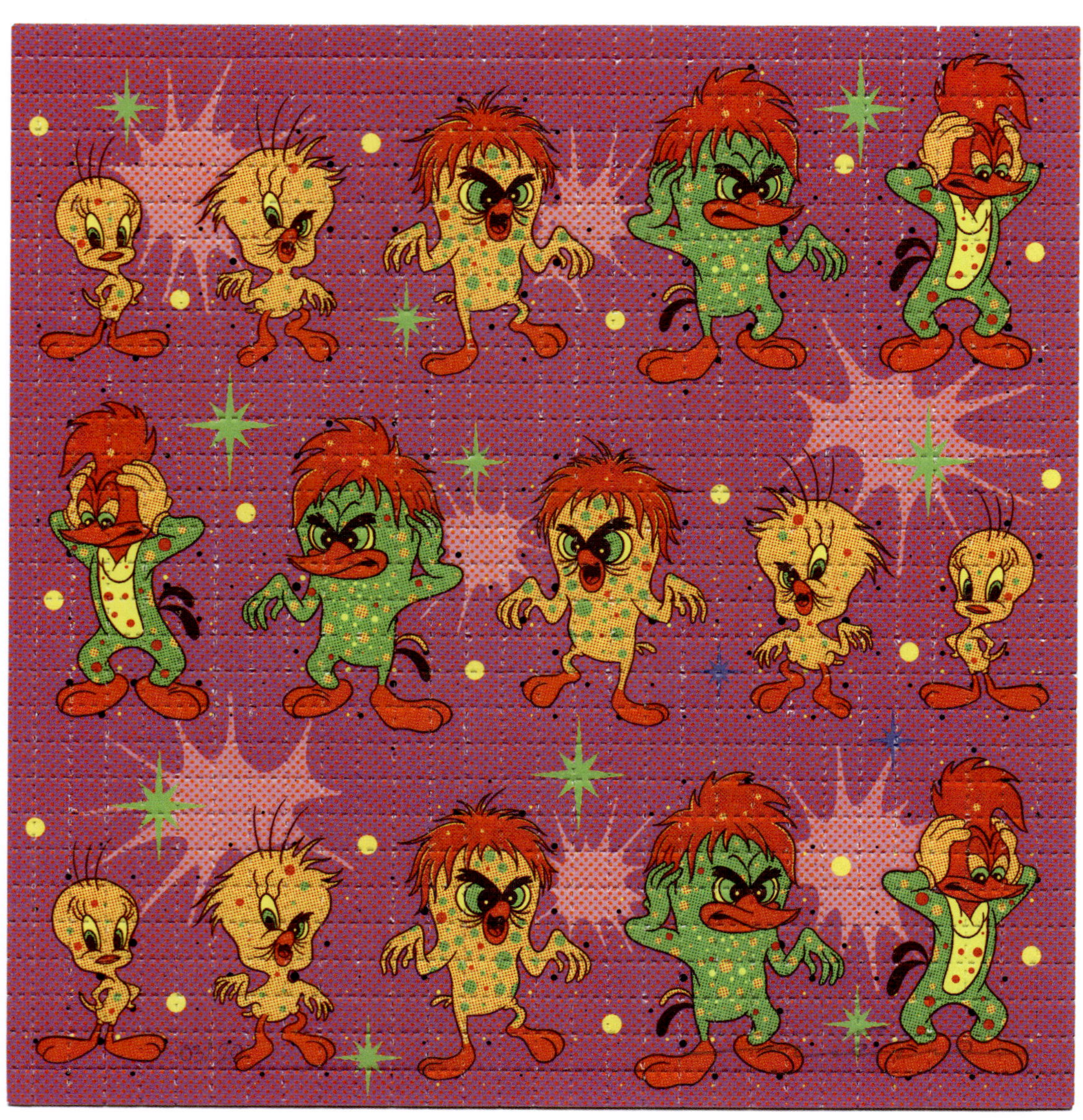

Origin of Species, Ziero Muko, Mexico, 2022. 7½ × 7½ in.

Interdimensional Being, Chris Dyer, 2019. 7½ × 7½ in.

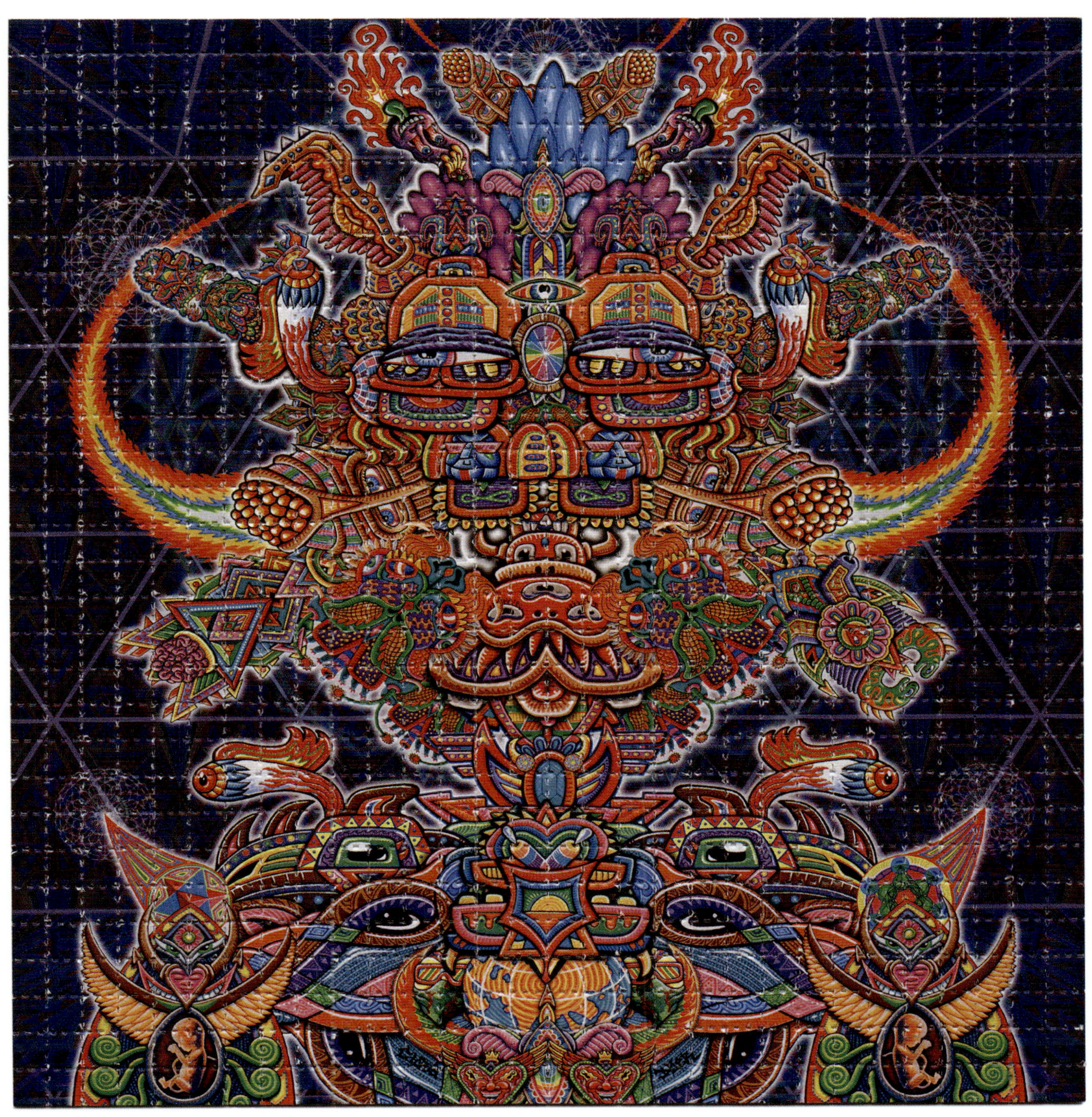

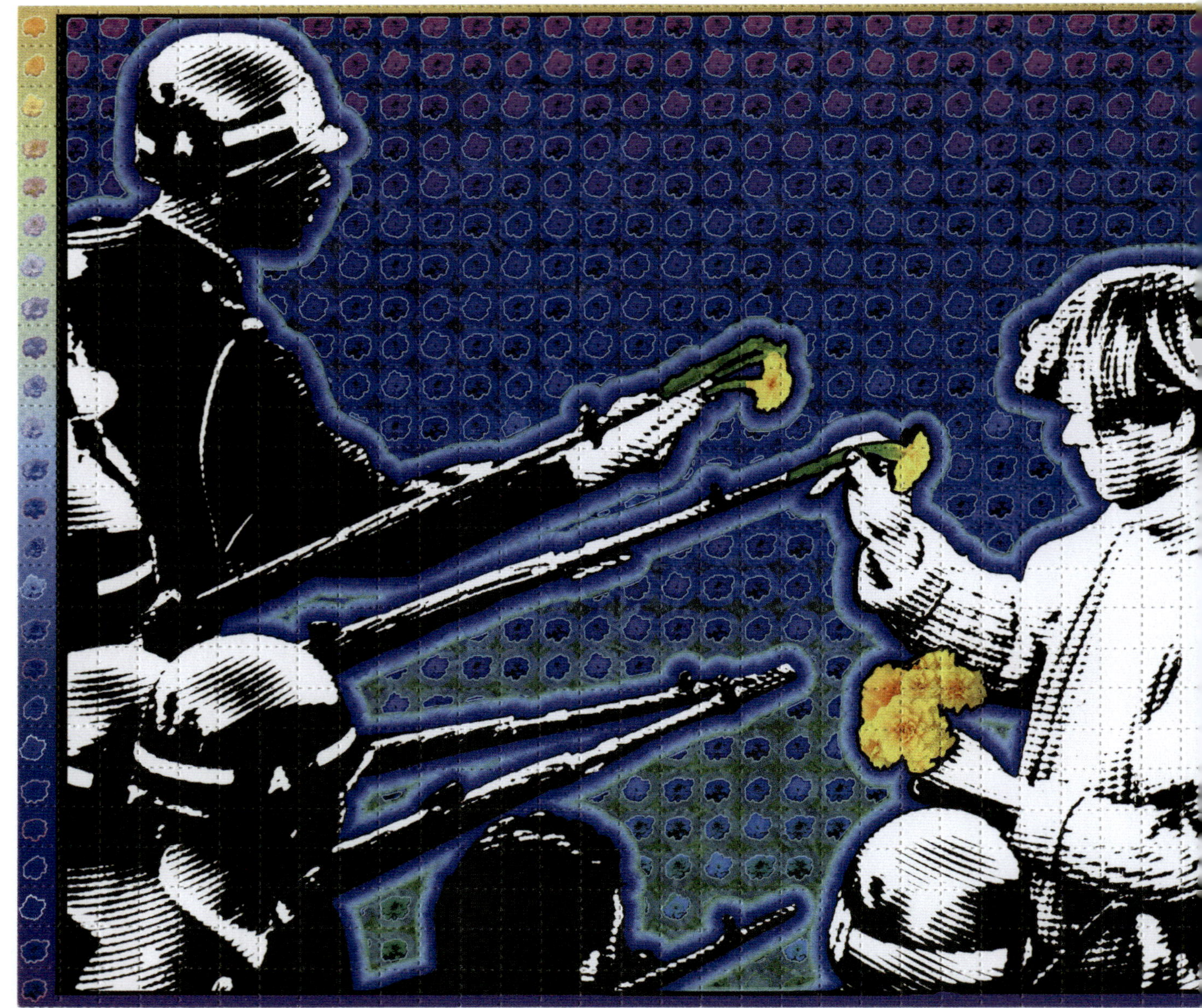

Nominated for a Pulitzer Prize, Bernie Watson took this photograph on October 27, 1967, during the Mobilization Committee to End the War in Vietnam's March on the Pentagon, showing a Vietnam War protestor placing a flower into the barrel of a rifle held by a soldier of the 503rd Military Police Battalion. After years of searching, Boston decided that the demonstrator pictured was George Edgerly Harris III, known as Hibiscus, one of the founders of the Cockettes.

Hibiscus would be a reasonable choice to appear on a blotter, as a person dedicated to breaking down barriers through psychedelic

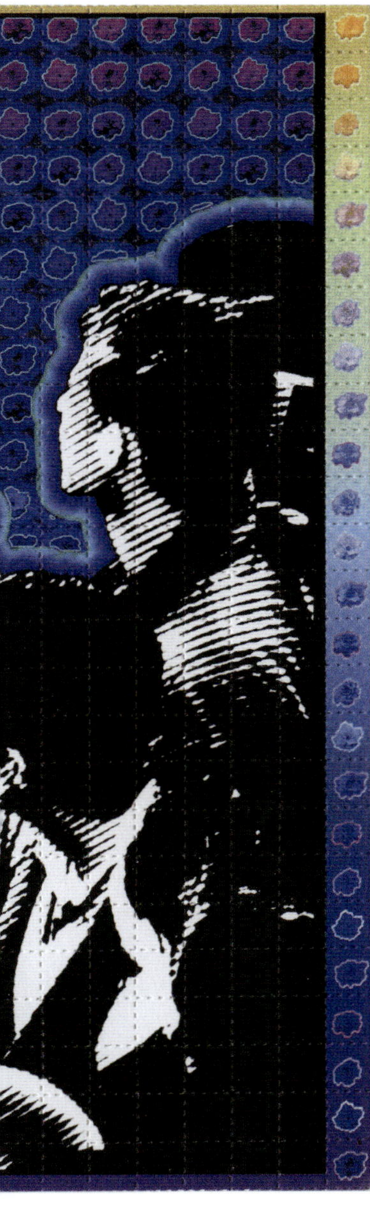

Anonymous Bosch
Flower Power,
Tina Carpenter, 2021.
6¼ × 10 in.

performance art, but it isn't him. Nor is it Berkeley activist "Super Joel" Tornabene, as Paul Krassner of *The Realist* believed.

The fearless young man in the picture is Paul Ennis, known to many as Tall Paul and to others as Vietnam Paul. This picture shows a specific moment when Paul was working to change the world, but he did not stop here. If I had to guess, I'd say his impact went well beyond the thousand hits depicted here, maybe somewhere in the millions.

The title of the photograph, "Flower Power," is not in dispute. Flower power was a guerrilla theater alternative to fear, threat, and anger. Rather than storming the Capitol that day, Ed Sanders delivered an exorcism to levitate the Pentagon and drive out its demons. Peggy Hitchcock bought two hundred pounds of flowers for Michael Bowen to distribute, seen on each square of this blotter.

Mariavittoria Mangini

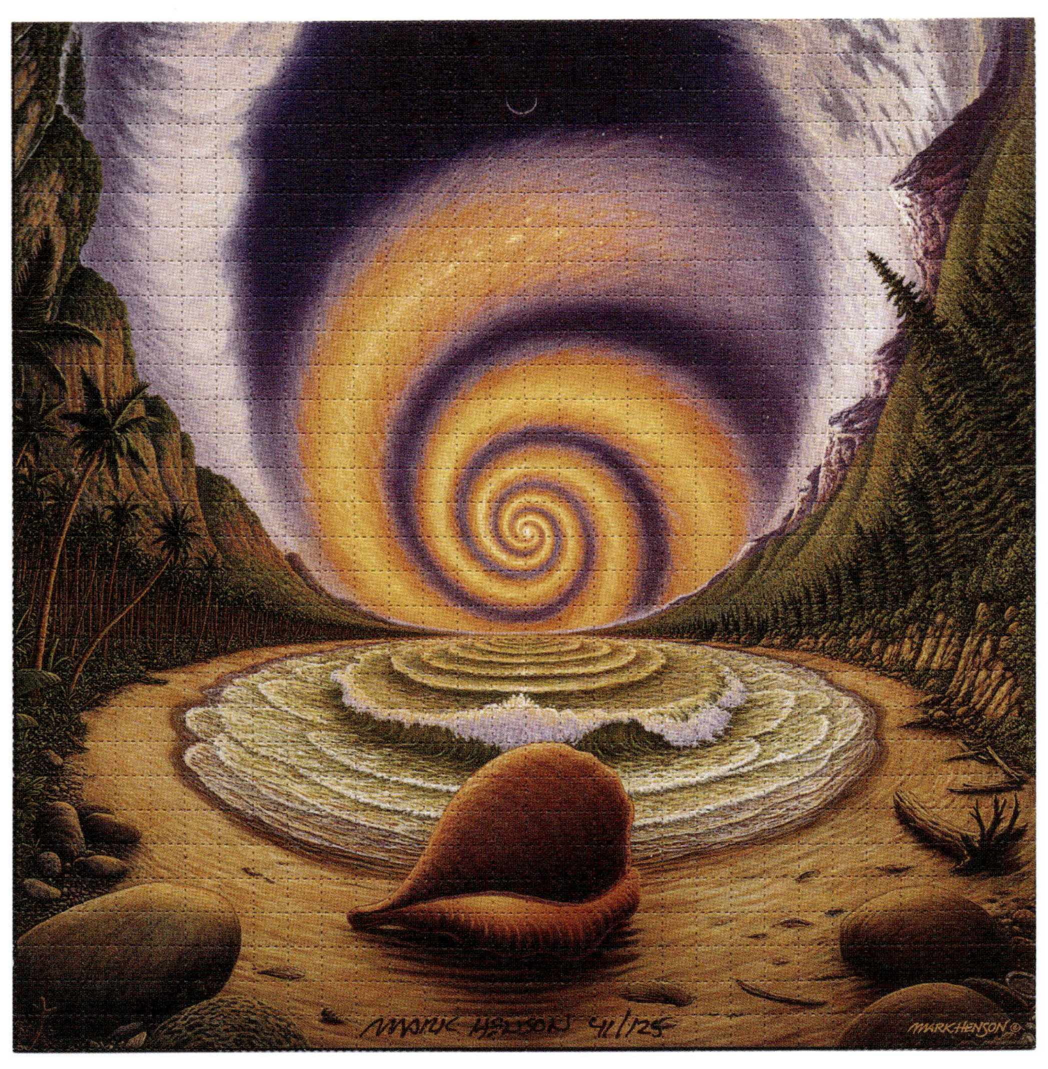

Snail Logic, Mark Henson, 2018. 8 × 8 in. Signed.

Dharma Dragon, Android Jones, 2018. 7 × 9 in. A popular and heavily merchandised image, also reproduced on blank journal diaries, tapestries, yoga mats, and a thousand-piece jigsaw puzzle.

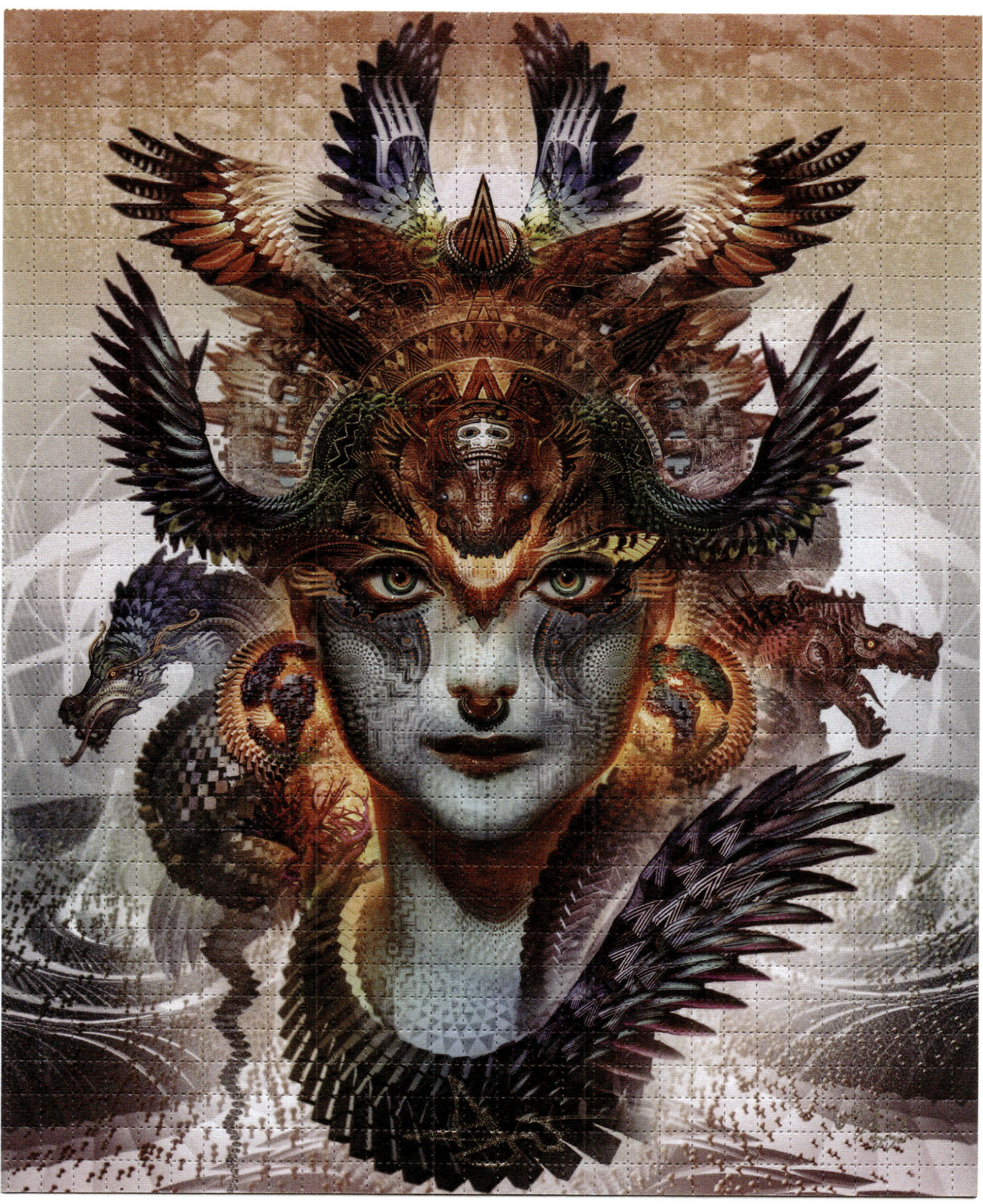

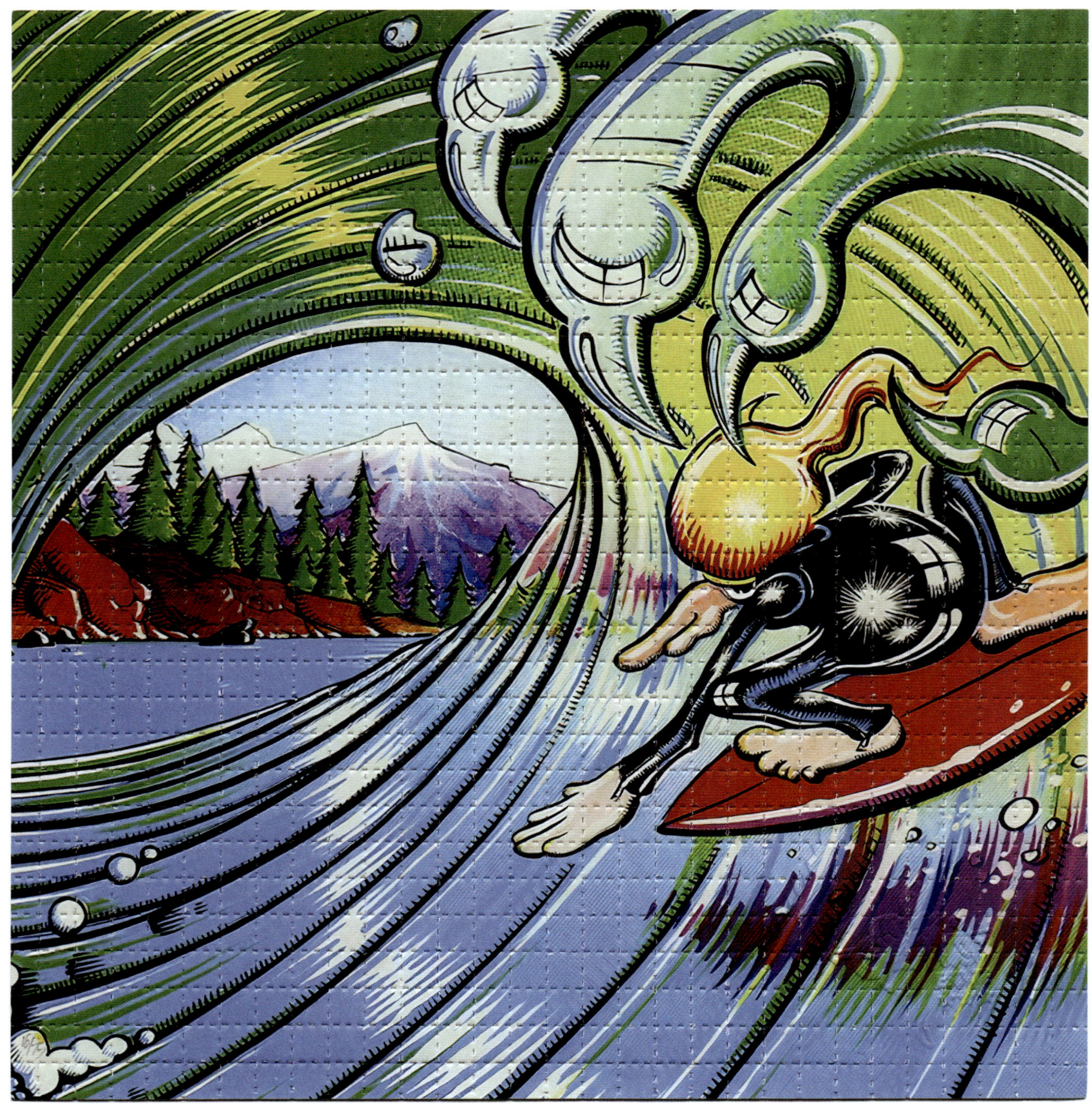

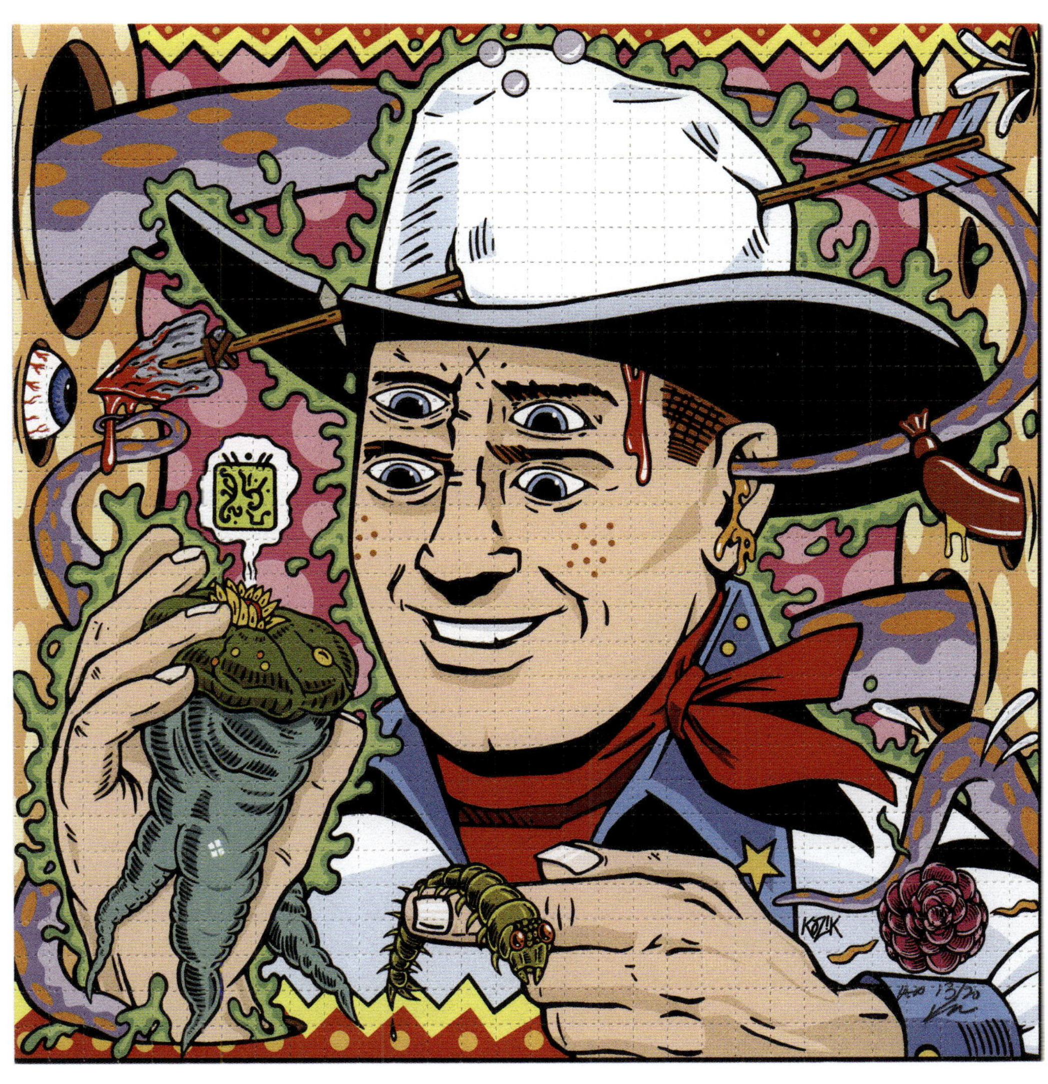

Tales of the Tube, 1XRUN, 2022. 7½ × 7½ in. Licensed reproduction of Rick Griffin's cover art from *Tales of the Tube* (1972).

Peyote Cowboy, Frank Kozik, 2020. 7½ × 7½ in. Signed.

Divine Moments of Trump, Stella SG (Strzyzowska Guillen), 2019. 6¼ × 9 in.

As a visual artist, I am used to receiving inspiration from many different sources. This piece came to me one night during a ceremony. Following a powerful breakthrough, I immediately had a vision of Donald Trump wearing a hippie tribal-type shirt, toking on a pipe. The scene progressed as Trump led "the ignorant ones" through the Amazon on a quest to engage in sacred plant medicine with the indigenous people who lived there. They ended up around a fire with a shaman, purging their darkness after ingesting the brew. They even had a Trump attitude about ingesting the medicine, "BIGGER DOSES, MORE!!!!" The more they threw up, the deeper the connection grew with nature. The Earth was healing as all this was happening and she let me know, "I have all the medicine within me to heal my most toxic parts." There was a deep sense of knowing. Suddenly my organs seemed lined with gold, and an angel from an Alex Grey painting, who resembled Alex himself, appeared over my shoulder, acknowledging my healing.

Eight months later I went to study with Alex and I showed him a sketch of my Trump vision. There wasn't any political aim or strong opinion behind it, since the images just arrived in a pure state of openness. We had a good laugh and he encouraged me to paint it. Later on I shared with him that I had been praying for a powerful vision to change my life and he responded, "Now that you have honored it, they will come back with more."

Stella Strzyzowska

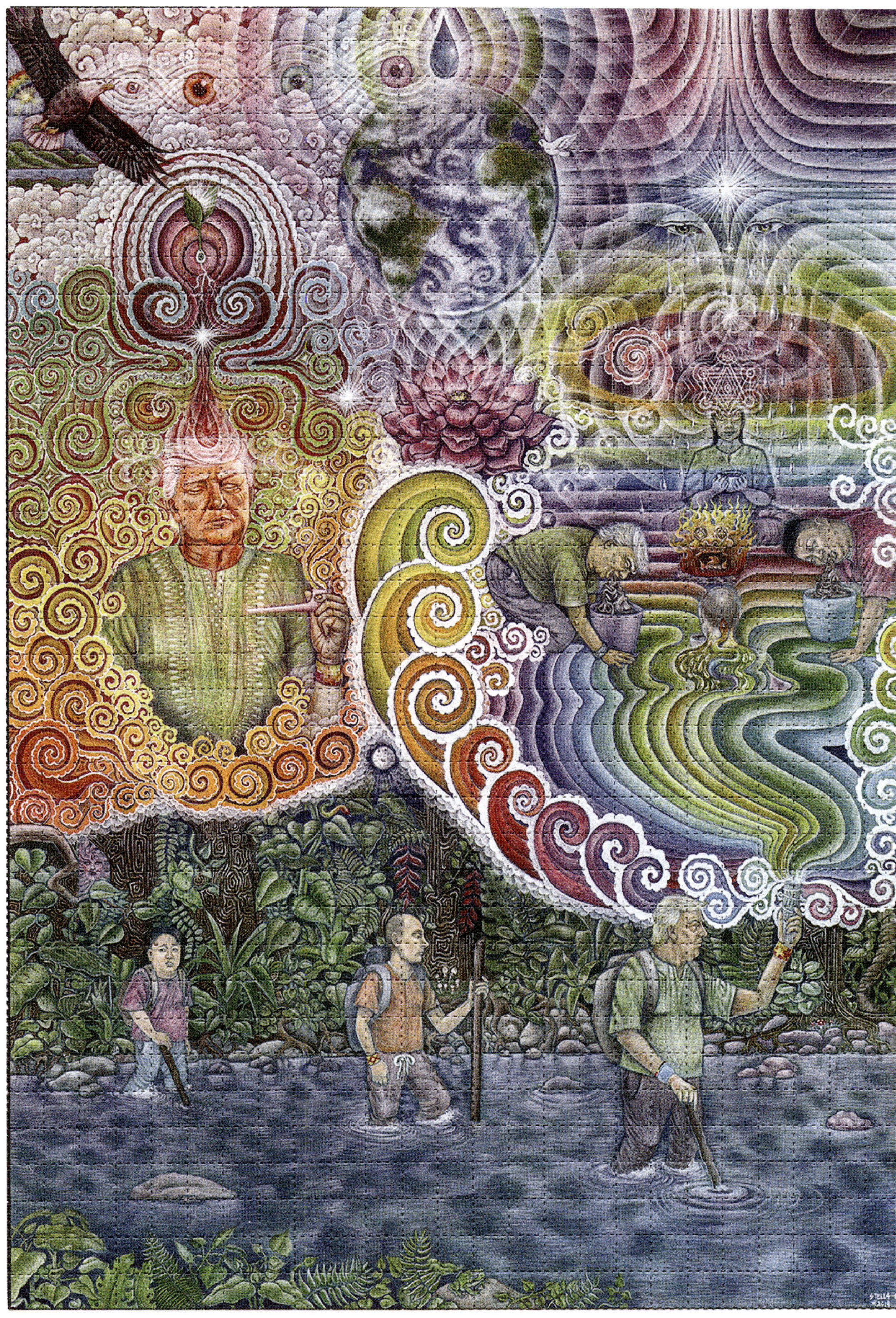

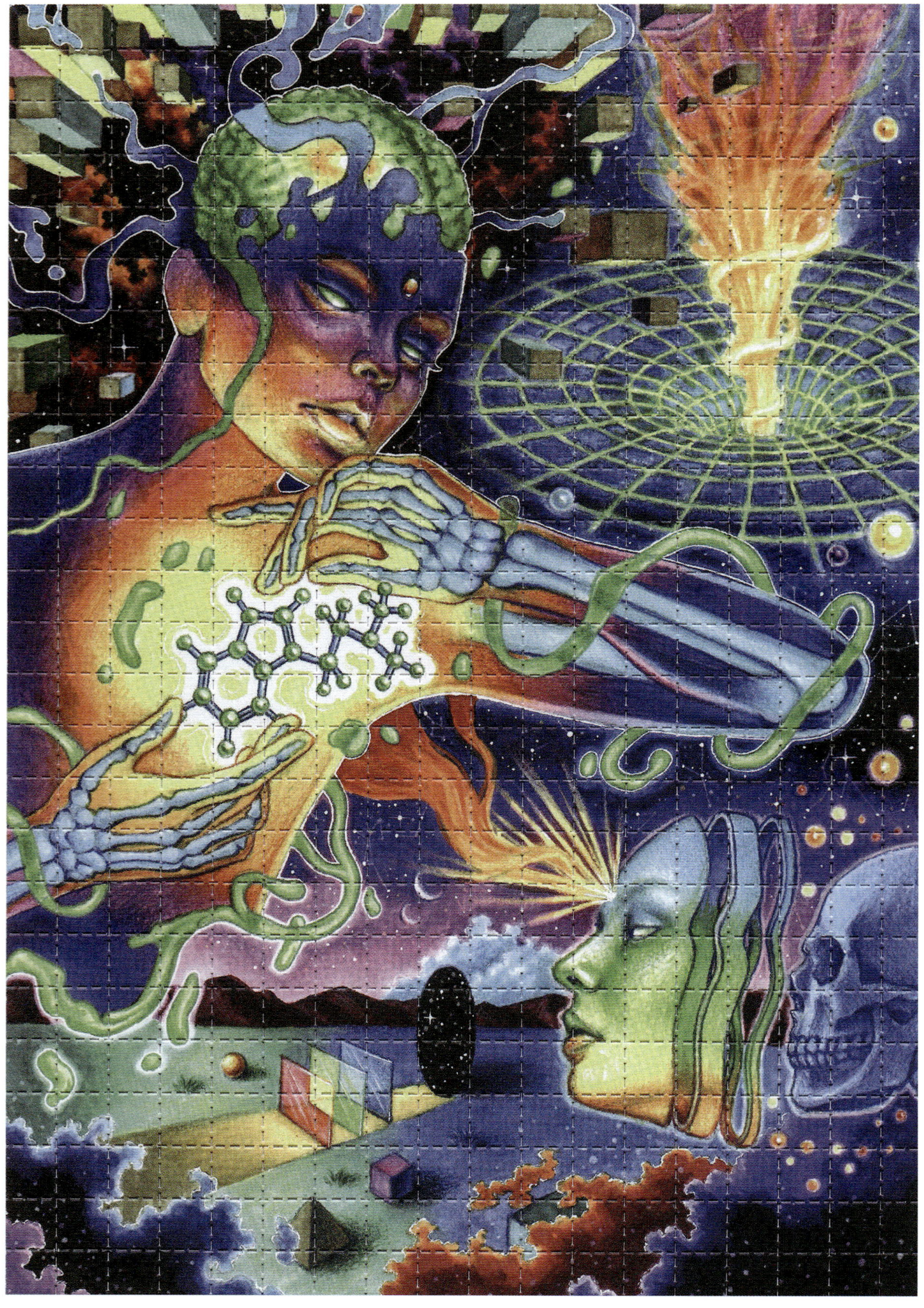

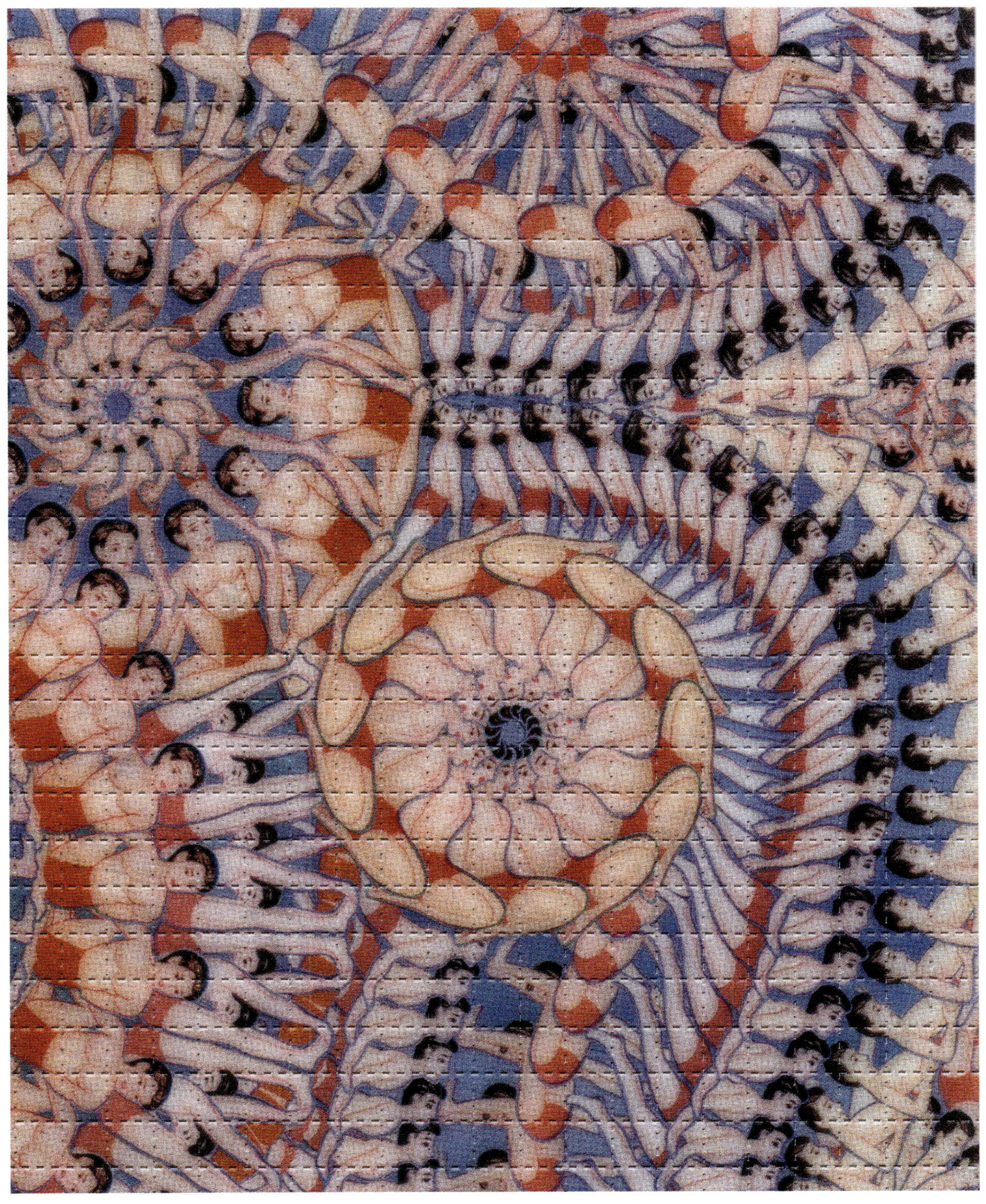

Ascension, Calle Fink, 2017. 6¼ × 9 in.

Reincarnating no. 2, Patrick Turk, 2021. 7½ × 7½ in.

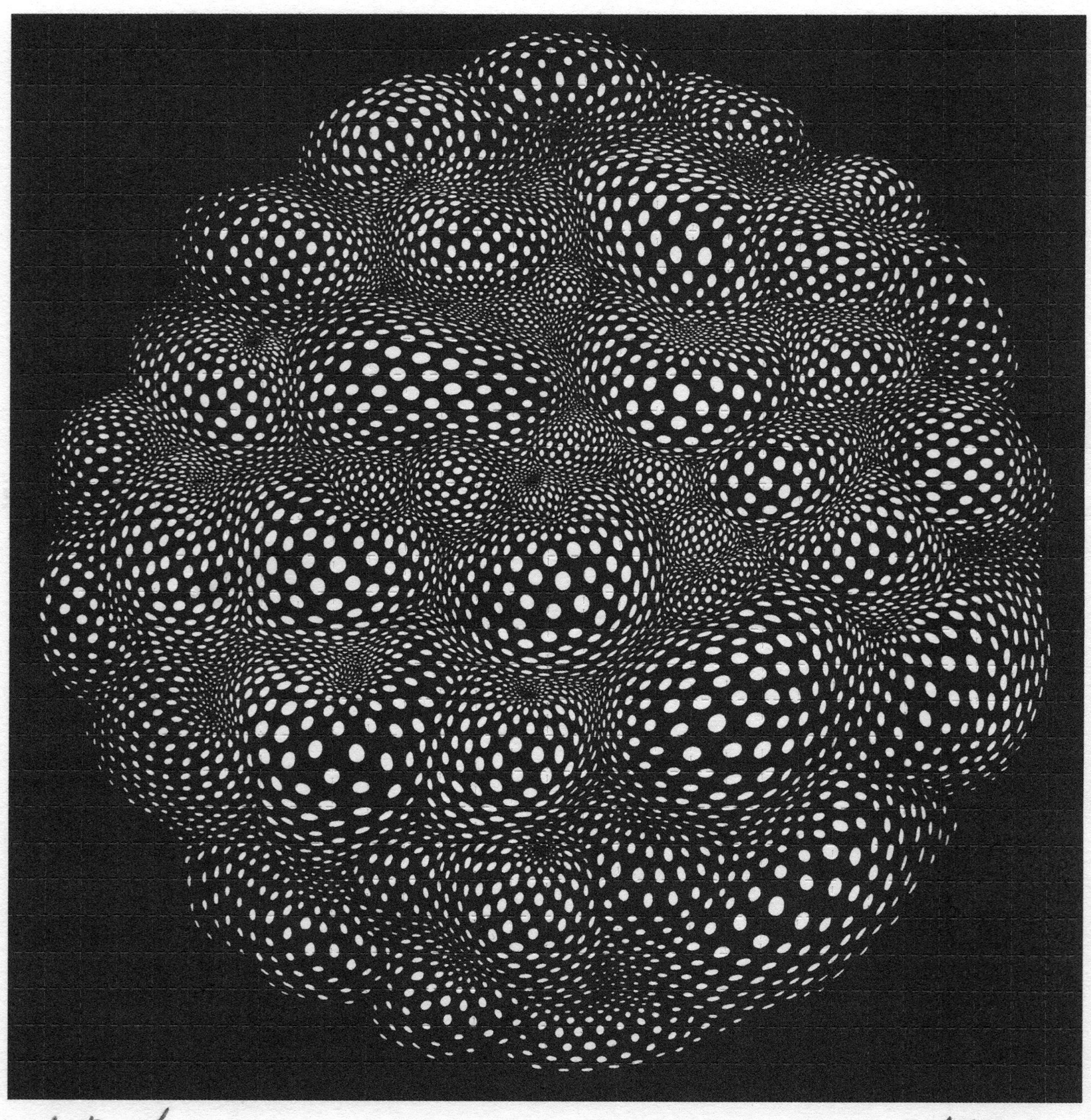

Infinite Tapestry Blotter, Mars-1, a.k.a. Mario Martinez, 2021. 7½ × 7½ in. Signed.

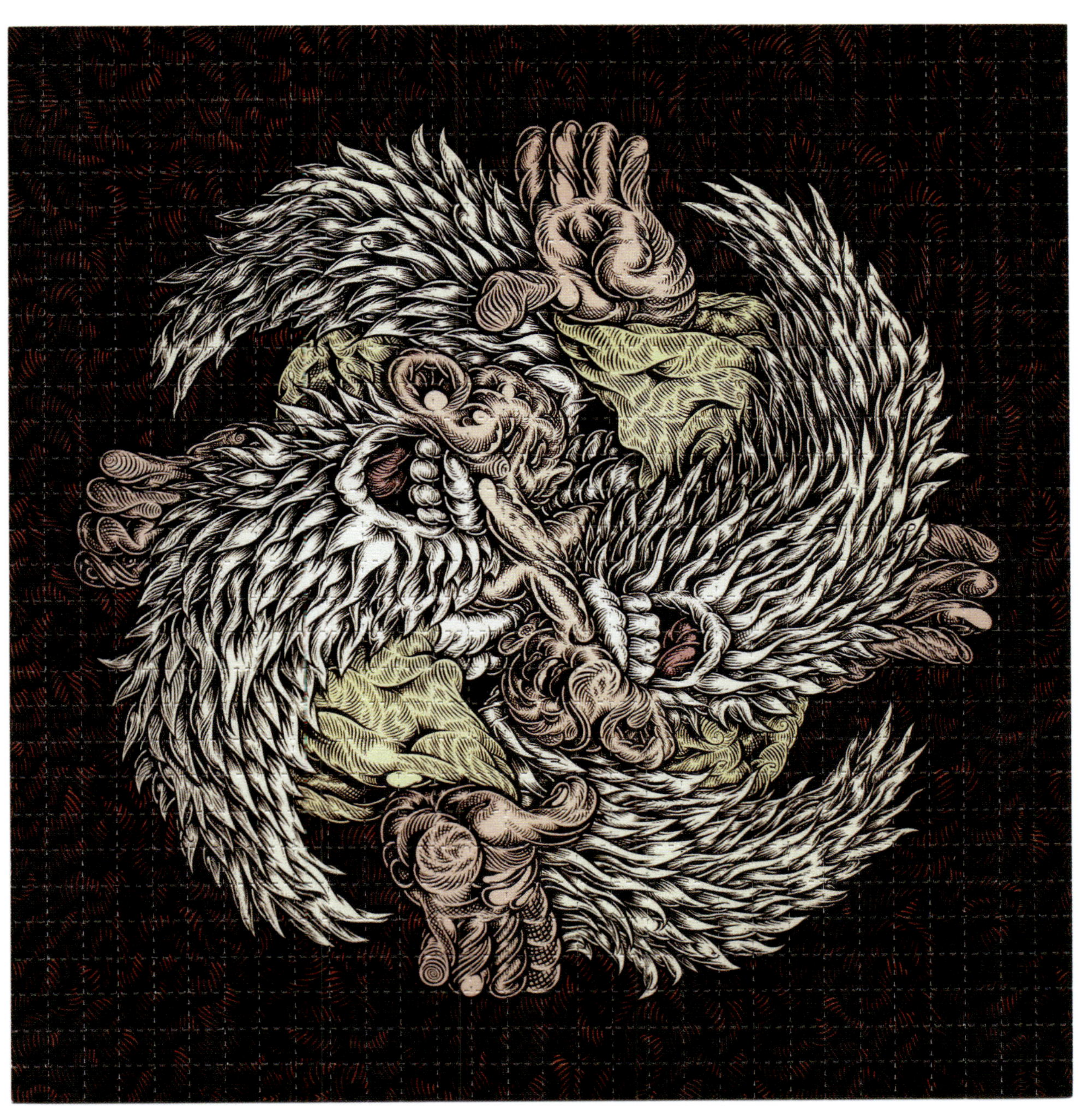

Natch, Mark Dean
Veca, 2020. 7½ × 7½ in.

Strolling through a post–Grateful Dead parking lot bazaar at the Furthur Festival in the late 1990s, we raised the question with a friend of where to buy good LSD. Sure, people walked by every few minutes murmuring "doses," but picking one felt sketchy.

Our friend was sure he'd know the right person when he saw them. So we wandered, browsing the wares of hippie vendors selling grilled cheese sandwiches, pipes and bongs, tie-dye shirts, and cold bottles of beer. Eventually our friend pointed to a relaxed looking young man lounging in a camp chair and suggested, "He looks like he's having a really good time, ask him."

Earth uncomfortably approached the dude and introduced himself, leading to a name-bonding moment when the guy said his name was Plant. Earth asked if he could suggest where to buy a few hits of good acid. Plant smiled, and said he could help us out. He described that he was, in fact, following the "family" all summer to help spread "the word" and "the light." He'd had a profound experience on LSD earlier that year and was on a mission to share it.

Grabbing a small hardbound sketchbook from his backpack, he flipped past drawings to the middle where there was a small loose piece of paper tucked. Taking it in hand, Plant held up scissors and asked, "How much do you want?" The paper was unmarked white watercolor paper, thicker than typing paper, and it was unperforated.

Flummoxed, Earth asked how much we'd get for $40. Plant moved the scissors back and forth, suggesting a narrow strip about ¼ by 3 inches, and Earth said, "okay!" Plant cut the strip so it fell onto Earth's palm. The exchange complete, we thanked him and we wandered away in amused disbelief. Was that a psychedelic grift?

Weeks later we tried the blank paper and it was not only strong, but Plant's white light was some of the highest quality LSD blotter we've ever had.

Earth and Fire Erowid

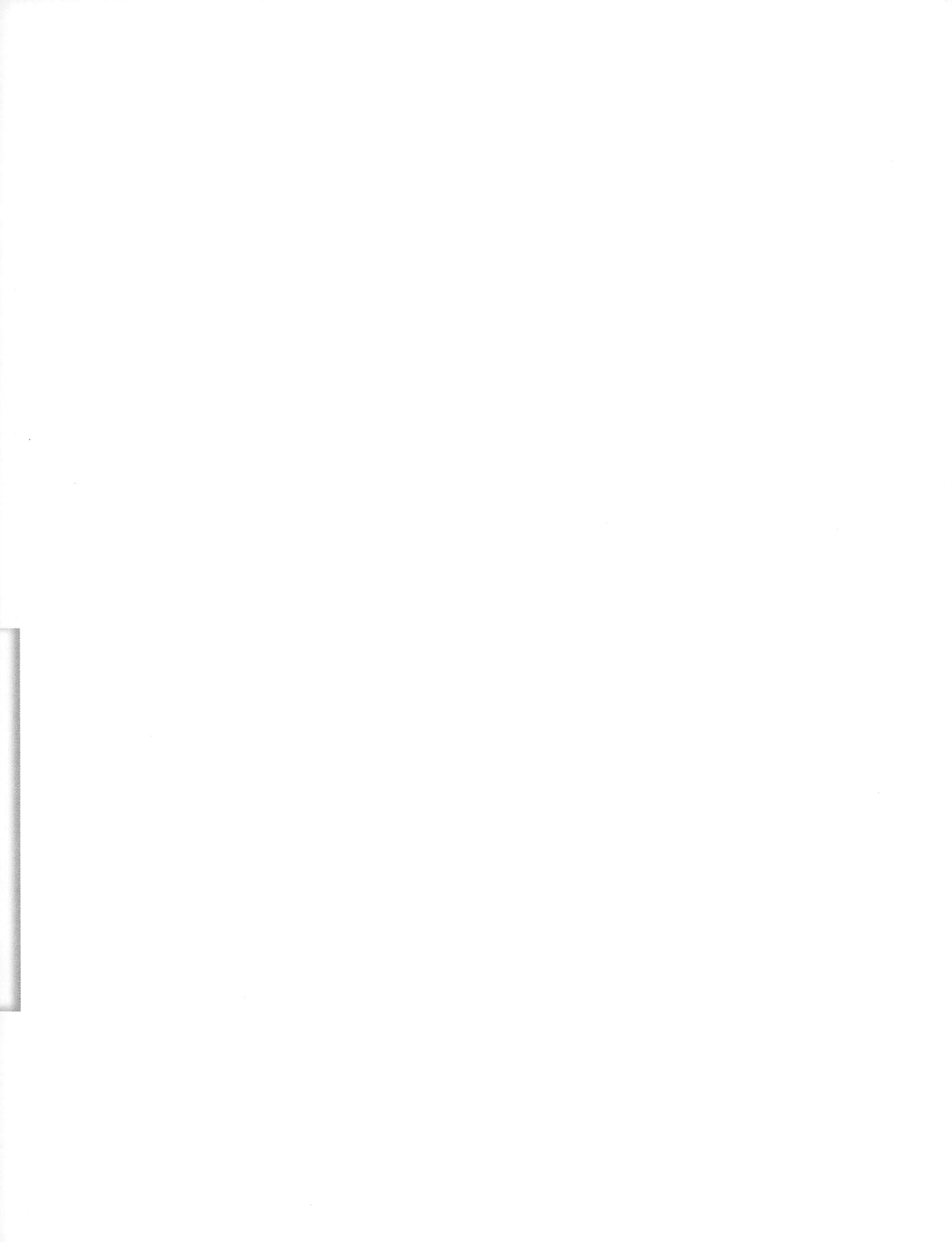

ACKNOWLEDGMENTS

Blotter was my pandemic project, which meant that one of the few places I spent time outside my apartment or Golden Gate Park those long months was the Institute of Illegal Images, hanging out with Mark McCloud. Mark is a gregarious soul, but a cryptic and often mischievously stoned one, as well. So it took a lot of hanging out to get a handle on his vast repertoire of stories, riffs, jokes, and insider references, which often referred to insides that I was not privy too, or not yet anyway. I generally passed on the bombers, and when the smoke cleared, we'd get down to business. I deeply thank Mark for his unwavering generosity, humor, and patience over the months and ultimately years, as well as his forbearance from making demands about the project and its shape. Nonetheless, this book is as much his as mine, and more so in some ways. I am just pleased as Kool-Aid that he trusted me with the telling.

That said, any errors herein are my own responsibility. Writing about the history of a largely criminal enterprise poses special challenges, and I have no doubt that a more extensive and perhaps more accurate book could have been written under different conditions. If I nonetheless feel confident about the book and its story, which I do, it's in large part because of my reliance on an extensive and often personal network of fringe scholars and holders of underground lore, some of whom illuminated hidden corners of the narrative in sometimes surprising ways. These wonderful people include, first and foremost, assistant editor Jesse Jarnow, who helped me find my way through many strange corridors in the project. Other stalwarts included Jon Hanna, Tod Pratum, Kat Harrison, Jeremy Gilbert, Earth and Fire Erowid, Will Tomlinson, Daan Keiman, Jeff Frame, Mike Jay, Mike Power, Corey Dansereau, Tim Scully, and the always reliable Keeper Trout. Matthew Rick was my rabbi for the world of vanity and art blotter, whose largely untold story was also clarified with input from Rick Sinnett, Fred Tomaselli, Zane Kesey, and Lucifero. The loopier conundrums of blotter ontology were clarified by conversations with Carlo McCormick, Claire Fanger, and Christian Greer.

I am also grateful to everyone who shared their thoughts and stories in the brief notes that accompany many of the blotter images in the book. These contributions round out the psychedelic story immeasurably. Extra thanks to Jesse for herding and editing all these psychedelic kittens. I am also thankful for the handful of informants who shared their true-life stories when they didn't have to, especially when those stories were freighted with legal complexities and habits learned through a lifetime of discretion. These include "Neil Benedict," Leonard Pickard, Ed Visser, and Strider Smith, as well as a number of LSD veterans who shall remain forever unnamed, one of whom, though refusing to spill all but a couple beans, nonetheless offered great support to the project by nodding with a smile of satisfaction when I read him the section on the Hayes Street Gang.

Mark and I were both thrilled to be working with the MIT Press, who really understood the unusual twists and turns of the project. My thanks to my editor Matthew Browne, senior designer Molly Seamans, and all the folks at the press for their care and enthusiasm. Back in San Francisco, Dana Smith and Carlos Seligo both helped create and process images with care and alacrity.

Finally, I couldn't have done it without the patience and enthusiastic support of my wife, Jennifer Dumpert. Thanks for weathering it all with humor and aplomb.

CONTRIBUTORS

A traveler and early conceptualizer of the Rainbow Gathering, **Garrick Beck** grew up among the Living Theater, a third-eyewitness of the transformation from Beatnik radicalism to the wild beyond. He is the author of *True Stories: Tales from the Generation of a New World Culture.*

Marcus Boon is a writer, journalist, and Professor of English at York University, Toronto. He is the author of *In Praise of Copying, The Road of Excess: A History of Writers on Drugs,* and other books. He collaborates with his wife and partner Christie Pearson as TheWaves on immersive vibratory environments.

Dana Smith is a multimedia artist practicing photography and digital printing in the context of fine art prints, painting, and artists' books and publications. She launched Dana Dana Dana Limited Editions in 2004, a fine art digital press, to create very small editions of artists' works. Her handmade editions are currently held by libraries and museums worldwide, including the Library of Congress, The Victoria and Albert Museum, and many more.

Neşe Devenot, PhD, is a Senior Lecturer at Johns Hopkins University, an Affiliate Scholar at OSU's Center for Psychedelic Drug Research and Education, and a Research Fellow with Psymposia. Their research examines the function of metaphor and other literary devices in narrative accounts of psychedelic experiences. They were a founder of the Psychedemia conference, a Research Fellow at the NYPL's Timothy Leary Papers, and a Research Fellow with the NYU Psilocybin Cancer Anxiety Study.

After a misspent youth immersed in occulture, **John Eden** found his feet in the cosmic communism of the Association of Autonomous Astronauts in the 1990s. He coedited the reggae and grime fanzine *Woofah* in the noughties and has written for music magazines *Datacide, Wire,* and the anti-fascist website Who Makes the Nazis, as well as his own uncarved.org blog and fanzine *Turbulent Times.* He lives in the London Borough of Hackney.

Earth and Fire Erowid founded Erowid.org in 1995 as a repository for information on psychoactive plants and chemicals. The project grew into the nonprofit educational Erowid Center, which continues to provide accurate information about the usage and history of psychoactive substances.

Jeremy Gilbert is Professor of Cultural and Political Theory at the University of East London. An activist and DJ, he is the author or coauthor of several books, including *Twenty-First Century Socialism, Discographies: Dance Music, Culture, and the Politics of Sound* (with Ewan Pearson) and other titles.

J. Christian Greer is a scholar of Religious Studies with a special focus on psychedelic culture. Currently a lecturer at Stanford University, his forthcoming book, *Angelheaded Hipsters: Psychedelic Militancy in Nineteen Eighties North America,* analyzes the growth, diversification, and expansion of psychedelic culture within fanzine networks in the late Cold War era.

Alex Grey is a visual artist, expressing the psychedelic experience through visionary paintings and other mediums since the mid-1970s. With Allyson Grey, he founded the Chapel of Sacred Mirrors in Wappingers Falls, New York.

Anuj Gupta is a graduate student in the Rhetoric, Composition & the Teaching of English program at the University of Arizona. He works at the intersection of composition studies, applied linguistics, and digital humanities and is interested in researching the relationships between emotions and writing.

Jon Hanna is a longtime psychedelic journalist, creator of the *Psychedelic Resource List,* organizer of the Mind States conferences, and former editor of the *Entheogen Review* and the *MAPS Bulletin.*

Casey William Hardison was imprisoned for making LSD in the United Kingdom from 2005 through 2013, a prisoner in the war on cognitive liberty. He is running for president in 2024.

Mike Jay is the author of *Mescaline: A Global History of the First Psychedelic, High Society: Mind-Altering Drugs in History and Culture,* and other collections, and writes regularly for the *London Review of Books.*

Jacaeber Kastor is an artist, curator, and proprietor of New York's Psychedelic Solution gallery from 1986 to 2004.

Jeffrey J. Kripal is an author and the Associate Dean of the School of Humanities at Rice University, where he chairs the Department of Religion, holds the J. Newton Rayzor Chair in Philosophy and Religious Thought, and helped create the GEM Program, a doctoral concentration in the study of Gnosticism, esotericism, and mysticism. He is the Associate Director of the Center for Theory and Research at the Esalen Institute in Big Sur, California.

Lars Bang Larsen is a writer, curator, and art historian whose work has focused on cybernetics and psychedelia. He is professeur invité at the Haute École d'Art et de Design in Geneva.

Dave Lee is a magician, writer, and educator. He has spent over four decades exploring consciousness and alternate realities, and is the author of *Life-Force: Sensed Energy in Breathwork, Psychedelia, and Chaos Magic* and other books.

Mariavittoria Mangini is a founder of the Women's Visionary Council. A lead clinician at the Haight Ashbury Free Clinic, she has been a Family Nurse Midwife for thirty-five years, and was in primary care practice with Frank Lucido MD, one of the pioneers of the medical cannabis movement, for twenty-five. She is Professor Emerita of Nursing at Holy Names University in Oakland.

Carlo McCormick is an American culture critic and curator living in New York City. He is the author of numerous books, monographs, and catalogs on contemporary art and artists.

Since the 1980s, **Grant Morrison** has been a groundbreaking writer for comic books, creating bestselling works for both Marvel and DC while providing a countercultural bridge to the medium, including his own *The Invisibles* and definitive runs for many iconic characters, including Batman, Superman, X-Men, and more.

Annie Oak is a journalist and public health activist. Cofounder of the Women's Visionary Council, she is the creator of the Full Circle Tea House, and cofounder and managing editor of *Lucid News*.

Piotr Orlov was born in Leningrad and lives in Brooklyn. His writing has appeared in the *Village Voice*, *Arthur*, *Love Injection*, *Stop Smiling*, and other independent publications; corporate ones too.

Alleged to have produced "90% of the world's LSD," **William Leonard Pickard** is a former drug policy fellow at Harvard's Kennedy School of Government, and research associate in neurobiology at Harvard Medical School. Given two life sentences without parole, he served twenty years in maximum security federal prisons, and was released in 2020. His book, *The Rose of Paracelsus: On Secrets & Sacraments*—written in pencil while he was imprisoned—is published by Synergetics Press.

David E. Presti is a teaching professor of neurobiology, psychology, and cognitive science at the University of California, Berkeley. He also teaches neuroscience to Buddhist monks and nuns in India and Bhutan. He is the author of *Foundational Concepts in Neuroscience: A Brain-Mind Odyssey* and other books.

Andy Roberts is the author of *Albion Dreaming: A Social History of LSD in Britain*, *Divine Rascal: On the Trail of LSD's Cosmic Courier, Michael Hollingshead*, and *Acid Drops: Adventures in Psychedelia*.

Douglas Rushkoff is an author and documentarian who studies human autonomy in a digital age. His over twenty books include *Present Shock*, *Program or Be Programmed*, *Life Inc.*, and *Media Virus*.

Starfinder Stanley is a veterinarian and President of the Owsley Stanley Foundation, dedicated to preserving the legacy of his father, the LSD alchemist and sound engineer Owsley Stanley.

Stella Strzyzowska is an artist whose paintings explore female forms, psychedelic experiences, and dense provocative visions. She has exhibited with Mosha Family Arts Collective and been a featured live painter at the Chapel of Sacred Mirrors and elsewhere.

Michael Taft is a meditation teacher, author, and podcaster. He is the author of *The Mindful Geek*, *Nondualism: A Brief History of a Timeless Concept*, and other books.

Fred Tomaselli is an American contemporary artist, mixing painting with collage techniques to create vivid, detailed, and often psychedelic multimedia works.

Suzanne Treister is a British contemporary artist. Initially recognized in the 1980s as a painter, she became a pioneer in the digital/new media/web-based field from the beginning of the 1990s, making work about emerging technologies, and developing fictional worlds and international collaborative organizations.

NOTES

1. R. E. L. Masters and Jean Houston, *The Varieties of Psychedelic Experience* (New York: Holt, Rinehart & Winston, 1966), 27–29.

2. Lars Bang Larsen, "One Proton at a Time: Art's Psychedelic Connections," RavenRow.org, 2013, http://www.ravenrow.org/texts/51/.

3. Peter Coyote, "It's All in the Line," in *Art of the Dead*, ed. Phil Cushway (New York: Soft Skull Press, 2012), 9.

4. From "The Playboy Interview: Marshall McLuhan," *Playboy* (March 1969), 56; Alexander R. Galloway, "Love of the Middle," in Alexander R. Galloway, Eugene Thacker, and McKenzie Wark, *Excommunication: Three Inquiries in Media and Mediation* (Chicago: University of Chicago Press, 2014), 29.

5. Alan Watts, *The Joyous Cosmology: Adventures in the Chemistry of Consciousness* (New York: Vintage Books, 1965), 26. (These comments only appear in the later Vintage editions of the book.)

6. "LSD in the United States," DEA San Francisco Field Division, October 1995, DrugLibrary.net, https://druglibrary.net/schaffer/dea/pubs/lsd/LSD-6.htm.

7. Carlo McCormick, "A Culture in Disguise," 4; xeroxed loose-leaf essay contained in *The Holy Transfers of the Rebel Replevin* (San Francisco: San Francisco Art Institute, 1987). We might also consider blotter as a variety of "street art," a zone of subcultural production that, in the case of graffiti at least, is also enmeshed in illegal practices. As Jesse Jarnow reports in *Heads*, the early graffiti writer LSD-OM (Chad Stickney) directly tied together the acid trade and New York City graffiti culture. See Jesse Jarnow, *Heads: A Biography of Psychedelic America* (New York: De Capo Press, 2016), 104–105.

8. McCormick, "A Culture in Disguise," 3.

9. Roland Barthes, "Towards a Psychosociology of Contemporary Food Consumption," in Carole Counihan and Penny Van Esterik, eds., *Food and Culture: A Reader* (New York: Routledge, 2013), 21.

10. Martin A. Lee and Bruce Shlain, *Acid Dreams: The Complete Social History of LSD: The CIA, the Sixties, and Beyond* (New York: Grove Press, 1985), 99.

11. Brian Barritt, *The Road of Excess: A Psychedelic Autobiography* (London: Psi Publishing, 1998), 9.

12. Lee and Shlain, *Acid Dreams*, 146.

13. Ibid., 146–147.

14. Samuel M. McClure, Jian Li, Damon Tomlin, Kim S. Cypert, Latané M. Montague, and P. Read Montague, "Neural Correlates of Behavioral Preference for Culturally Familiar Drinks," *Neuron* 44, no. 2 (Oct. 14, 2004): 379–387.

15. Karin Meissner and Klaus Linde, "Are Blue Pills Better Than Green? How Treatment Features Modulate Placebo Effects," *International Review of Neurobiology* 139 (2018): 357–378.

16. Ido Hartogsohn, "Constructing Drug Effects: A History of Set and Setting," *Drug Science, Policy and Law* 3 (2017): 3.

17. "Glossary," *Microgram* 3, no. 6, October 1970, 177, https://erowid.org/library/periodicals/microgram/microgram_1970-10_v03n06.pdf.

18. David V. Erdman, ed., *The Complete Poetry & Prose of William Blake* (Berkeley: University of California Press, 1981), 39.

19. Gale later ploughed his profits into the very successful Rainbow Surfboards, one of the first surf shops to sell boards with multicolored fins and airbrushed cosmic designs, including floating buddhas and exploding suns.

20. Lee and Shlain, *Acid Dreams*, 243.

21. Ibid., 197.

22. Silenus, "Family Dogcatcher," *Berkeley Barb* 4, no. 7 (Feb. 17, 1967), 3.

23. Francis Miller, "Eric Ghost: A Religious Biography," n.d., n.p.

24. Vince Pawlak, "Dope Scoreboard," *Los Angeles Free Press* 9, no. 412, June 9–15, 1972, 17.

25. Stuart H. Stock, "Synthetic Drugs: A History of Ups and Downs," *PharmChem Newsletter* 15, no. 4 (1986): 5.

26. "The Dope Scope," *St. Louis Outlaw* 3, no. 10, October 27–November 16, 1972.

27. This book is not a forensic collector's guide. The titles I have assigned to individual blotters, which I have chosen to italicize, are drawn from makers, the street, McCloud, the DEA, and occasionally myself; as such, they should be considered provisional. Little effort has been made to solve a variety of hairy cataloging challenges, including multiple editions and numerous variations of the same print (often from different makers); the variety of prints based on the same figure or character (like the many Mr. Naturals or doves); and the problem of hand-crafted blotter issues that are seemingly too singular or informal to be treated as a proper "edition." When possible, street blotters have been attributed to the "blotter makers"—the designers and printers—rather than the artists responsible for the images themselves, which were often appropriated or produced by nameless craftspeople. Sometimes only geographical origins have been listed. Details about hit size and sheet dimensions, hit number per sheet, paper type, and printing method have largely been left to hardier archivists.

28. Andy Warhol and Pat Hackett, *Popism: The Warhol Sixties* (Boston: Mariner Books, 2006), 28.

29. Lorraine Wilde and David Karman, "Agency and Urgency: The Medium and Its Message," in *Hippie Modernism: The Struggle for Utopia*, ed. Andrew Blauvelt and Ross Elfline (Minneapolis: Walker Art Center, 2015), 46.

30. Wilde and Karman, "Agency and Urgency," 46.

31. Phil Cushway, *Art of the Dead* (New York: Soft Skull Press, 2012), 161.

32. Wilde and Karman, "Agency and Urgency," 48.

33. Edward J. Woodhouse and Gary W. Webb, *The Drug Atlas* (Kansas City, MO: Midwest Research Institute, 1974), 46.

34. "Dope Report," *Windsor Freek Press*, no. 3 (August 1974), 2; https://www.ukrockfestivals.com/freep-day-3-74.html; *Watchfield Freek Press*, no. 2 (August 24, 1974), 2; https://www.ukrockfestivals.com/watchfield-freek-press-2.html.

35. *Microgram* 6, no. 11 (November 1973), 167.

36. There were variations a plenty. The same 20 × 20 grid was often printed onto substantially smaller-sized sheets, while the individual hits were sometimes loaded with 1000 μg, making each hit a four-way (and making five sheets the equivalent of two grams). Clearly the difference between 250 and 1000 μg was the sort of difference that makes a difference; in the case of the *Blue Notes*, the number 1000 was screened diagonally on the sheet as a handy reminder—at least if you procured that part of the sheet.

37. There are no extant examples of the *Disco Hits* package in the III or any other known blotter archive, making it one of the most desirable collectables in the history of the craft.

38. Andy Roberts, *Albion Dreaming: A Popular History of LSD in Britain* (London: Marshall Cavendish, 2008), 247.

39. Following the Anti-Drug Abuse Act, part of a raft of statutes focused on mandatory minimums, sentencing for drug crimes was based not only on the weight of the substance in question but also on the weight of the neutral carrier medium. This means that an ounce of acid distributed across pressed tablets garners a considerably longer sentence than the equivalent amount soaked into blotter; more absurdly, it means that a handful of sheets impregnated with a gram of acid could earn the poor sap holding it more prison time than an ounce of pure LSD crystal. But this demented piece of legislation was not passed until 1986, which means that, while the law did compel blotter makers to immediately start using the thinnest paper possible, blotter itself had already established its dominance as a distribution medium by the time the act passed.

40. Jarnow, *Heads*, 162–165.

41. liquidcrystalvision, "LSD Blotter ART Collector Mark McCloud on Visionary ART," YouTube video, 13:00, January 13, 2022, https://www.youtube.com/watch?v=TkK_TwOjLAs.

42. Stephen Gaskin, *Amazing Dope Tales and Haight Ashbury Flashbacks* (Summertown, TN: Book Publishing Co., 1980), 92.

43. One of the ironies of McCloud's work at the institute is that he deploys the same sort of forensics practiced by the DEA, who have built whole cases on ballistics information provided by characteristic irregularities in perforating machines, paper stock, and other material minutia.

44. Visser made his last blotter, a section from the central panel of Bosch's *The Garden of Earthly Delights*, around 2003. In recent years he cofounded Amsterdam Blotter Company to celebrate and vend his old blotter stock and school collectors on the finer points of blotter and the difference between reproductions and originals.

45. Eric Williams, "LSD 1993: Is the DEA Getting Paranoid?" *High Times* (May 1993), 19–20.

46. Two-sided sheets were generally made for aesthetic reasons, though street interpreters sometimes thought that two-faced hits meant they were double-dipped. Other times, more pragmatic considerations came to the fore. Ed Visser notes that impure crystal sometimes left a gray film on the sheets, which would then be hidden by printing an image on both sides of the paper.

47. Leslie A. King, Kathleen Clarke, and Alison J. Orpet, "LSD Paper Doses: The Situation to 1992," technical note no. 777, October 1992, Drug Intelligence Laboratory, Aldermaston Laboratory, Reading, Berkshire, 15; https://www.researchgate.net/profile/Leslie-King-5/publication/268745589_LSD_Paper_Doses_The_Situation_to_1992/links/5474dccd0cf2778985ac2423/LSD-Paper-Doses-The-Situation-to-1992.pdf.

48. Earth Erowid, interview with the author, California, May 23, 2020.

49. Timothy Leary, "Deal for Real," *East Village Other*, 1968; HighTimes.com, October 23, 2020, https://hightimes.com/culture/high-times-greats-timothy-leary/.

50. According to the chemical analyses regularly included in the *PharmChem Newsletter* in the 1970s, LSD was one of the most reliable street drugs, rarely adulterated and rarely mislabeled ("mescaline," however, frequently proved to be LSD). In 1986, the newsletter reported that, over the previous eleven-year period, LSD's validity rate was 88 percent. Similarly, the newsletter found only a slight increase in street price from 1973 to 1986. See Stock, "Synthetic Drugs," 1–7.

51. King, Clarke, and Orpet, "LSD Paper Doses," 7, 11.

52. Bob Stearne, "LSD 81," *High Times*, August 1981, 38; https://archive.hightimes.com/issue/19810801.

53. King, Clarke, and Orpet, "LSD Paper Doses," 16.

54. Andrew Blauvelt, "Preface," in Blauvelt and Elfline, eds., *Hippie Modernism*, 11.

55. Ibid., 19.

56. Larsen, "One Proton at a Time," http://www.ravenrow.org/texts/51/. Larson could be talking about blotter here: evanescent esoterica that manifests only in order to dissolve.

57. Ken Johnson, *Are You Experienced? How Psychedelic Consciousness Transformed Modern Art* (New York: Prestel, 2011), 21.

58. See Matteo Guarnaccia, "Interview with Adrian Piper," http://www.adrianpiper.com/art/Over_the_Edge/interview.shtml (accessed Dec 30, 2022).

59. Johnson, *Experienced*, 23.

60. Timothy Leary, Richard Alpert, and Ralph Metzner, *The Psychedelic Experience: A Manual Based on the Tibetan Book of the Dead* (New York: University Books, 1964), 25.

61. Johnson, *Experienced*, 17.

62. Rosalind Krauss, "Grids," *October* 9 (Summer 1979), 50, 54.

63. Johnson, *Experienced*, 22.

64. Marcus Boon, *In Praise of Copying* (Cambridge: Harvard University Press, 2013), 74; 45.

65. Carl Nolte, "Huge LSD Ring Broken in the Bay Area," *San Francisco Chronicle*, August 17, 1985.

66. Christian Rätsch, "LSD-Artefakte: Das Unsichtbare sichtbar machen," trans. Corey Dansereau, *Entheogene Blätter* 11, April 2003, 172, 173.

67. As Greer characterizes this development, "The mainstream proved incredibly capable of commodifying the aesthetics, ethos, and social customs of hip psychedelicists, which in turn incited this militant minority to become ever-more rebellious in its rejection of modern society. It is precisely through this on-going process of hip innovation and commercial assimilation that hip culture is constructed dialectically." J. Christian Greer, *Angelheaded Hipsters: Psychedelic Militancy in Nineteen Eighties North America* (Oxford: Oxford University Press, forthcoming).

68. Philip K. Dick, *Valis* (New York: Mariner Books, 2011), 254.

69. Walter Benjamin, "The Work of Art in the Age of its Technological Reproducibility: Second Version," in *The Work of Art in the Age of its Technological Reproducibility, and Other Writings on Media*, ed. Michael W. Jennings, Brigid Doherty, and Thomas Y. Levin (Cambridge, MA: Belknap Press, 2008), 51.

70. Cited in "Media Freak," *The Realist*, no. 115, January–February 1991, 8.

71. Evidence for this possibility is provided by the folklorists Opie and Opie, who collected a folktale that emerged following the introduction of the world's first postage stamp in 1840. They record that when the Penny Black stamp first appeared, rumors circulated that "the glue used was poisonous, that the most vile ingredients were employed in its manufacture, that human material was not excluded, and that those so rash as to lick the Queen's head were in danger of contacting cholera." See Ross Coomber, *Pusher Myths: Re-situating the Drug Dealer* (London: Free Association Books, 2006), 109.

72. Jason S. Sexton, "Jesus on LSD: When California Blotter Acid got Religion," *Boom: A Journal of California* 5, no. 4 (Winter 2015), 80–81.

73. Claire Fanger, email to author, May 15, 2021.

74. Casey Logan, "Adventures in Wonderland," *The Pitch*, April 19, 2001, https://www.thepitchkc.com/adventures-in-wonderland/.

75. Ibid.

76. The quality folks did have one secret weapon. Around 2010, Blackburn discovered the HP Indigo, a "digital offset printer" that debuted in 2005. Using electrostatically charged inks instead of toner, and a heated transfer roller to melt the charged particles before application, the Indigo produced an ultrathin layer of plastic ink that did not mask the underlying surface of the paper the way that standard inkjet or laser printers do. As such, the Indigo could print small runs that had the matte look and feel of offset. Along with the techniques of proper perfing, the Indigo became something of a "trade secret" of modern blotter making.

77. McCloud tells one story from the 1990s, when an associate who disliked ArtRock's Phil Cushway sold the poster king a batch of undipped "vintage blotters" for thousands of dollars. The sheets had actually been photocopied at a Kinko's, and when Cushway attempted to present them at a gallery show, McCloud whipped out a loupe and showed him the toner's globby telltale shine. "It's bunk," McCloud declared. "The minute you put it in the sauce it'll come right off."

78. Here one cannot fail to mention Homer Simpson's Castanedesque encounter with the Space Coyote after eating a chili pepper in *The Simpsons* episode "El Viaje Misterioso de Nuestro Jomer" (season 8, episode 9, January 5, 1997). But only if one also mentions the identity-melting wormhole that swallows up the eponymous heroes of *Rick and Morty*—and sneakily samples visionary artist Alex Grey—in "The Whirly Dirly Conspiracy" (season 3, episode 5, August 20, 2017).

79. Franz Vollenweider's Zurich lab has extensively studied LSD phenomenology and the key role played by the 5-HT2A receptor. See also Robin L. Carhart-Harris, Suresh Muthukumaraswamy, Leor Roseman, and David J. Nutt, "Neural Correlates of the LSD Experience Revealed by Multimodal Neuroimaging," *Proceedings of the National Academy of Sciences* 113, no. 17 (April 11, 2016).